TURIZM

The Russian and East European Tourist under Capitalism and Socialism

EDITED BY

Anne E. Gorsuch
Diane P. Koenker

CORNELL UNIVERSITY PRESS   ITHACA AND LONDON

First published 2006 by Cornell University Press
First printing, Cornell Paperbacks, 2006

Printed in the United States of America

Library of Congress Cataloging-in-Publication Data

Turizm : the Russian and East European tourist under capitalism and socialism / edited by Anne E. Gorsuch and Diane P. Koenker.
p. cm.
Includes bibliographical references and index.
ISBN-13: 978-0-8014-4483-8 (cloth : alk. paper)
ISBN-10: 0-8014-4483-7 (cloth : alk. paper)
ISBN-13: 978-0-8014-7328-9 (pbk. : alk. paper)
ISBN-10: 0-8014-7328-4 (pbk. : alk. paper)
1. Tourists—Russian—History—19th century. 2. Tourists—Soviet Union—History.
3. Tourists—Europe, Eastern, History—19th century. 4. Tourists—Europe, Eastern—
History—20th century. 5. Tourism—Russia—History—19th century. 6. Tourism—
Soviet Union—History. 7. Tourism—Europe, Eastern—History—19 century.
8. Tourism—Europe, Eastern—History—20th century. I. Gorsuch, Anne E. II. Koenker, Diane, 1947– III. Title.

G155.R8T875 2006
338.4'79147—dc22

2006023265

Cornell University Press strives to use environmentally responsible suppliers and materials to the fullest extent possible in the publishing of its books. Such materials include vegetable-based, low-VOC inks and acid-free papers that are recycled, totally chlorine-free, or partly composed of nonwood fibers. For further information, visit our website at www.cornellpress.cornell.edu.

Cloth printing   10 9 8 7 6 5 4 3 2 1
Paperback printing   10 9 8 7 6 5 4 3 2 1

FOR BILL ROSENBERG

CONTENTS

A longer version of Louise McReynolds's essay appeared as chapter 5, "The Russian Tourist at Home and Abroad," in her book, *Russia at Play: Leisure Activities at the End of the Tsarist Era* (Ithaca: Cornell University Press, 2003). It is reprinted here by kind permission of Cornell University Press. We are grateful to the University of Illinois at Urbana-Champaign Campus Research Board for providing a publication subvention.

TURIZM

Introduction

Anne E. Gorsuch and Diane P. Koenker

Consider the group tour as a metaphor for the modern world. The modern age of leisure travel allows hundreds of thousands of ordinary individuals to range widely across borders, pursuing sights and attractions that have been validated by generations of tourists before them, packaged conveniently by tour operators to make the most efficient use of the tourist's limited time and resources. Such mobility is liberating. The group provides safety in numbers, sociability, and efficiency. But it also constrains the individual, whose gaze is regulated by the collective wishes of the group as well as by the iron logic of the tour timetable. Yet even within the group, individuals encounter new sights and cultures, make meaning out of their spatial displacements as individuals, and try on new traveling identities, based on their own cultural makeup, life experiences, expectations, and fantasies. Together and apart, the modern tourist travels with the crowd, but mediates the travel experiences as an individual.

The contradictions implicit in the "group tour" are embedded in scholarly contestation over the meaning of tourism as a human practice. The distinction between the traveler and the tourist, for example, is often cast in terms of high and low culture, of individual versus mass consumption, of authenticity versus superficiality. "The traveler, then," writes Daniel Boorstin in an often-cited passage, "was working at something; the tourist was a pleasure-seeker. The traveler was active; he went strenuously in search of people, of adventure, of experience. The tourist is passive; he expects interesting things to happen to him."[1] "Tourism requires that you see conventional things, and that you see them in a conventional way," writes Paul Fussell.[2] Anthropologists and historians, however, have rejected the model of the "tourist as degraded traveler" and have instead emphasized the emancipatory and democratizing effect of modern tourism. In his foundational text, *The Tourist*, the sociologist Dean MacCannell suggests that "tourism is the cutting edge of the worldwide ex-

1. Daniel Boorstin, "From Traveler to Tourist: The Lost Art of Travel," *The Image: A Guide to Pseudo-Events in America* (New York, 1961), 85.
2. Paul Fussell, ed., *The Norton Book of Travel* (New York, 1987), 651. This opposition is the central theme of James Buzard, *The Beaten Track: European Tourism, Literature, and the Ways to Culture, 1800–1918* (New York, 1993); and Jean-Didier Urbain, *L'Idiot du Voyage: Histoires de Touristes* (Paris, 1991).

pansion of modernity." Tourist attractions, sights to be visited, become "the locus of a human relationship between un-like-minded individuals, the locus of an urgent desire to share—an intimate connection between one stranger and another, or one generation and another."[3] An historical approach to tourism indicates ways in which "tourism and vacations have been constitutive of class, social status, and collective identities," suggest Shelley Baranowski and Ellen Furlough in their recent anthology on western Europe and North America.[4] Tourism can be understood as part of the history of consumption and of the history of leisure, the antidote to work. But its distinctiveness arises from a "consciousness of displacement,"[5] the sense of "being elsewhere." The ways in which individuals seek to make sense of their experiences of voluntary border-crossings provide a powerful tool for understanding the culture of modern life.

What questions arise when we turn east and investigate the history of tourism in what would become the socialist world of the twentieth century? For eastern Europeans inside multinational empires, tourism became one mechanism to help to define self and other, and it contributed to reifying nation-building projects. In the twentieth century, a new kind of internationalism forged by socialism competed with national distinctiveness, but tourism here also became an instrument of developing new national coherences. Socialism would bring access to tourism to the masses, sponsoring both collective tourism experiences and mass access to tourism for individuals. Socialist tourism sought to overcome the inequalities and inefficiencies of the market with rational, centrally planned guidance for individuals' encounters with new territories and new experiences. Socialist tourism was purposeful, and it perfected the socialist citizen by insisting on both the physically and the mentally restorative elements of tourism. Yet socialism too was part of the modern world, and socialist tourism also reflects the ineffable tension generated by traveling in groups, or according to officially arranged itineraries, in order to produce individual meaning.

The very terms *turist* and *turizm* reflect this tension and the multiple meanings potentially generated by actual practice. The Russian word turizm possesses both a broad and a narrow definition: a tourist was anyone who followed a leisure-travel program of visual, cultural, and material consumption, whether the military travelers discussed in Susan Layton's chapter or the Khrushchev-era travelers to socialist eastern Europe explored in Anne Gorsuch's contribution. But Soviet tourism activists in the 1920s and 1930s, as Diane Koenker and Eva Maurer point out, insisted that a turist could be only that traveler who embarked on a purposeful journey, a circuit (tour) using

3. Dean MacCannell, *The Tourist: A New Theory of the Leisure Class* (Berkeley, rev. ed., 1999), 184, 203.

4. Shelley Baranowski and Ellen Furlough, "Introduction," in *Being Elsewhere: Tourism, Consumer Culture, and Identity in Modern Europe and North America*, ed. Baranowski and Furlough (Ann Arbor, 2001), 7.

5. Rudy Koshar, *German Travel Cultures* (Oxford, 2000), 8.

one's own physical locomotion. (As Scott Moranda notes, the German Democratic Republic adopted the same sense in its term *Touristik*.) Travelers in search of pleasure could take excursions; turizm was meant to involve work, the enhancement of one's intellectual and physical capital, not leisure. Travel to a destination to spend a holiday, whether or not it involved excursions, was labeled "rest" (*otdykh*) in Russian: rest could be recuperative, but it did not presume that resters would interact self-consciously with the world to which they had transported themselves. Nascent nationalist tourist societies in Hungary and Latvia, as Alexander Vari and Aldis Purs document, also adopted the purposeful definition of tourism: "Goal-minded tourism trains the body, freshens up the mind, deepens our knowledge, and could bring valuable benefits to numerous branches of science," wrote the Hungarian advocates. By the 1970s, distinctions between rest and tourism began to disappear, as Christian Noack's chapter on unplanned tourism on the Black Sea coast makes clear. In the late Soviet Union, the "tourist hike" (*turistskii pokhod*) was a euphemism for a boy and a girl's weekend getaway, with tent and sleeping bag, for sex.[6] In post-Soviet Russia, what used to be labeled "turizm" is now called "adventure tourism." The changing definition of the term, in the Soviet Union and elsewhere, constitutes one of the elements of the history of socialist tourism.

This volume reveals the innate historicity of tourism by focusing on differences and similarities between tourist practices under capitalism and socialism in nineteenth- and twentieth-century eastern Europe, Russia, and the Soviet Union. Socialist—and other authoritarian—states may have sought to regiment and regulate their citizens' encounters with crossing borders, as many of the chapters in this collection acknowledge. But socialist tourists had their own agendas. By the 1960s and 1970s, for example, they traveled to shop as well as to see. The adaptation of socialist states to consumerist and other demands of tourists helps to conceptualize socialism as a project with a history and provides an important lens through which to examine the interrelations of socialist states and their citizens.

In both the capitalist and the socialist "East," tourism was too important to leave to the private sector alone. The rise of tourism is associated with the expansion of a middle-class consumer market in the nineteenth century in Europe, and as Louise McReynolds shows, Russian commercial tourist agencies followed the model of Thomas Cook in seeking customers among the empire's rising middle classes. But noncommercial tourism societies competed alongside businesses chartered for profit, reflecting a renunciation of market principles that would provide a cultural antecedent for socialist values in the twentieth century. In the late nineteenth century, the Russian Society of Tourists arose from an association of bicycle enthusiasts; as Maurer reports, societies of alpinists emerged in Russia around the same time, an integral part of the turist movement. Further to the west, competing societies in Hungary used tourism

---

6. Personal communication with Viktoriia Tiazhel'nikova, 2 April 2005.

to the Tatra mountains to support a growing nationalist project.[7] Purs shows how in interwar Latvia, tourism became an essential state project, located squarely in the Ministry of Social Affairs. In fascist Italy and Nazi Germany, state-affiliated agencies, the Dopolavoro ("After Work") and Kraft durch Freude ("Strength through Joy"), organized and coordinated an extensive range of leisure activities. Strength through Joy, as Shelley Baranowski details in her recent book, became a mass packager of tourist travel for middle and working-class Germans in the 1930s.[8] In the Soviet Union, too, as Koenker and Maurer describe, quasi-independent tourist organizations, the Russian Society of Tourists and Sovetskii turist, merged in the course of the late 1920s and 1930s into agencies formally subordinated to the state economic apparatus. In short, whether under socialism, capitalism, or some form of corporatism, authoritarian regimes in the twentieth century found it useful to organize the opportunity for their citizens to experience leisure travel.

State ownership of the tourism industry brought its own problems, as several of the articles in this collection reveal. The chronic deficits of the socialist economy are by now well known: tourism agencies never received the resources that they believed necessary to accomplish their goals. The planned economy might be able to pinpoint problems, as Noack and Shawn Salmon reveal, but acquiring resources and using them wisely stymied the Soviet tourist industry throughout its history. Access to tourism in the USSR came primarily through the grant of a travel voucher, the *putevka*, a nonmarket mechanism for the allocation of the scarce resource of a place on a tour or in a tourist destination. As Maurer, Noack, and Gorsuch all discuss, the economic organization of Soviet tourism revolved around the voucher, rather than disposable income, personal savings, or consumer demand. Shawn Salmon's discussion of Inturist's quest to maximize foreign convertible currency paints a vivid picture of the clash between market values and socialist practices: Inturist's desire to "sell socialism" using the unfamiliar techniques of capitalism led to inefficiencies, failures, and recriminations. Nor, as Noack shows, were tourism planners in the Krasnodar region any more successful in managing the flow of "free-market" wild tourists who descended upon the Black Sea beaches every summer without regard to the limits of the infrastructure the state economy could provide.

---

7. Nor were Hungarian nationalists unique in seeking to exploit the Tatras for their national project. Tourism to the Polish Tatras also helped define Polishness within the Austro-Hungarian Empire and during independence. See Patrice Dabrowski, "Discovering the Galician Borderlands: The 'Discovery' of the Eastern Carpathians," *Slavic Review* 64, no. 2 (2005): 380–402; and Daniel Stone, "The Cable Car at Kasprowy Wierch: An Environmental Debate in Interwar Poland," *Slavic Review* 64, no. 3 (2005): 601–24.

8. Shelley Baranowski, *Strength through Joy: Consumerism and Mass Tourism in the Third Reich* (Cambridge, 2004), esp. chap. 4; see also Victoria de Grazia, *The Culture of Consent: Mass Organization of Leisure in Fascist Italy* (Cambridge, 1981).

Authoritarian socialist regimes facilitated state control over the message tourists should receive and replicate. Guidebooks highlighted historical accomplishments and economic achievements. Travel accounts encouraged would-be tourists to imagine themselves sharing in the fraternal friendship of socialist peoples. Travel writing and tourism served to educate socialist citizens about the wider world within a framework that emphasized the superiority of socialism. Nonetheless, as several contributions point out, state agencies could not wholly manage the way in which tourists would receive these messages. Karl Qualls delineates the acts of remembering and forgetting contained in a series of post-1945 guidebooks to the military city of Sevastopol, but there is no way to know which parts of these messages would-be tourists read and internalized. In Eleonory Gilburd's account of Sergei Obraztsov's cultural mediations between his personal travel to Great Britain and the Soviet reader, a disconnect between regime intentions and reader response similarly arises. Even in the 1930s, Koenker argues, proletarian tourism's emphasis on the independence and self-actualization of tourists allowed individuals to chart their own paths and make their own meanings, quite apart from state intentions.

Histories of tourism in the West emphasize the importance of tourism for the formation of an independent and confident middle class.[9] Tourism created citizens, "aesthetic cosmopolitans," in John Urry's words, who believed they had a right to travel anywhere, approached travel with curiosity and openness, who cultivated an ability to locate their own society in terms of broad historical and geographic knowledge.[10] These middle-class travelers distinguished themselves from their aristocratic predecessors on the Grand Tour by emphasizing effort and purpose. Rudy Koshar reminds us that the word "travel" is derived from "travail," meaning suffering or labor. "Tourism finds its meaning through effort."[11] In advocating similarly purposeful tourism in the twentieth century, socialist tourist activists claimed they were creating a new kind of proletarian tourist, in direct contrast to the imagined bourgeoisie. In fact, the tourist practices celebrated as socialist—planned, purposeful, knowledge-producing, rational, and efficient—mirrored those touted for Europe's nineteenth-century middle classes. Whether prescribing to Yugoslav and Soviet tourists how to behave in department stores, as Bracewell and Gorsuch outline, or vicariously to become an aesthetic cosmopolitan through reading

9. Douglas Peter Mackaman, *Leisure Settings: Bourgeois Culture, Medicine, and the Spa in Modern France* (Chicago, 1998); Koshar, *German Travel Cultures*; Cindy S. Aron, *Working at Play: A History of Vacations in the United States* (Oxford, 1999); and Jan Palmowski, "Travels with Baedeker: The Guidebook and the Middle Classes in Victorian and Edwardian England," and Patrick Young, "La Vieille France as Object of Bourgeois Desire: The Touring Club de France and the French Regions, 1890–1918," both in *Histories of Leisure*, ed. Rudy Koshar (Oxford, 2002), 105–30, 169–89.

10. John Urry, *Consuming Places* (London, 1995), 167.

11. Koshar, *German Travel Cultures*, 8.

about Obraztsov's tours to Britain, socialist tourism advice emphasized intelligence, moderation, politeness, self-control. Socialist tourism, like socialism itself, would dissolve class differences, but the new norms would look remarkably similar to bourgeois norms.

Such tourism faced the perpetual dilemma of balancing pleasure and purpose, again nothing new in the annals of capitalist European tourism. Yugoslav teachers and students who visited interwar Czechoslovakia, as Noah Sobe writes, combined educational travel with the emotional uplift of Slavic fraternity. Soviet tourist activists, as Koenker recounts, labeled the pursuit of pleasure as purely bourgeois, but the unabating lure of the mountains and the sea appealed above all to the senses and the emotions: sublime mountains and salt sea air could be enjoyed actively, through rugged alpinism, but also tranquilly and in luxuriant comfort, whether the touring army officer Nikolai Berg, in Layton's article, Stakhanovites aboard a Black Sea steamer (Koenker), or wild tourists staking out their square meter of beach in Anapa (Noack). As Layton and Qualls note, the enduring appeal of Crimea, like the Tatras, derived from its multiple opportunities for accessing historical continuity, national self-identification, imperial pride, and cosmopolitan subjectivity, but the natural beauties of these mountain and seascapes also were sought largely for the pleasure they were said to produce.

Comparing tourist experiences under socialism, capitalism, and authoritarianism reminds us that consumerism and consumption became a part of the modern world in the twentieth century that transcended ideological or economic systems.[12] But socialism perhaps distinguished itself, especially in the early years of socialist regimes, in emphasizing the consumption of experiences rather than things. Working together in small groups, sharing this work as well as dangers and pleasures, learning self-reliance, gaining knowledge about the world—these intangibles constituted the "product" of early socialist tourism. Tourists should observe and record, instructed the Society of Proletarian Tourists to alpinists and others alike, but what they should bring home from their tours would be memories, knowledge, at best a notebook and some photographs.[13] Well into the 1960s, as Gorsuch points out, Soviet tourism authorities remained anxious about combining tourism with shopping, and they paid

---

12. Consumption has its own history. Europeans in the 1920s and 1930s consumed frugally, writes Victoria de Grazia. It took the American model, she argues, to convince Europeans that the good life revolved around consumerism. See Victoria de Grazia, "Changing Consumer Regimes in Europe, 1930–1970: Comparative Perspectives on the Distribution Problem," in *Getting and Spending: European Consumer Societies in the Twentieth Century*, ed. Susan Strasser, Charles McGovern, and Matthias Judt (Cambridge, 1998), 59–83; and de Grazia, *Irresistible Empire: America's Advance through 20th-Century Europe* (Cambridge, Mass., 2005).

13. German travelers to the Soviet Union in the 1920s and 1930s—many of them sympathetic socialists—paid virtually no attention to souvenir commodities in the accounts of their travels. See Matthias Heeke, *Reisen zu den Sowjets: Der ausländische Tourismus in Russland 1921–1941* (Münster, 1999).

special attention to the "dangerous" proclivities of women in particular to elevate their desire for fraternal socialist things over fraternal socialist comradeship. Yet as Bracewell's article makes clear, shopping was about both the acquisition of things and the experience of seeking them out. Shopping required
of the tourist the same kinds of skills as mountaineering or long-distance hiking: know-how and planning in addition to cash resources. And the feat of acquiring a scarce good abroad could generate just as much satisfaction as the
good itself. If the consumption of things became more acceptable in socialist
societies by the 1960s and 1970s, whether in Yugoslavia, Germany or the Soviet Union, tourism planners remained uneasy and often ignorant about how
to respond, in a nonmarket system, to consumer demand. Tourism officials in
Anapa called conferences to discuss the provision of goods and services; Inturist likewise devoted much effort to determining what experienced western
travelers might wish to purchase with their valued hard currency.

One particular arena of consumption remains frustratingly opaque in these
accounts of tourism in eastern Europe and the Soviet Union: sex. Have historians internalized the official prudishness of Soviet socialism? Only recently has
oral history added to anecdotal evidence from memoir literature and fiction to
indicate the extent to which the pursuit of sexual adventure and initiation motivated Soviet tourists to transport themselves elsewhere.[14] The volumes of reports of Soviet group leaders abroad rarely acknowledge sexual activities
among their charges, nor the presence or the pursuit of prostitutes on these
journeys. Prostitution, after all, was a characteristic of capitalist societies;
women did not need to sell themselves under socialism. The problem of
sources is not particular to the history of sex, of course. In general, we know
more about the organization of tourism and its meaning than we do about the
lived experience of the tourist. There are very good reasons for this, including
archival records which emphasize the organizational and an historical (and
historiographical) emphasis on the role of the state in authoritarian regimes.
Additionally, in the socialist Soviet Union and eastern Europe, even travel accounts and memoirs are better as a source of official understanding than of
private meaning and experience. This means that we largely have to "read" the
tourist experience through the eyes of the state, which provides some obvious
limitations. That said, many of these chapters do give us an entry into the
"messiness" of the travel experience: the physicality of travel, the challenge of
harsh conditions, the delight of discovery. Those authors that look at consumption, be it of material items, hotels, or tourist sites, also provide glimpses

14. Anna Rotkirch, "Traveling Maidens and Men with Parallel Lives—Journeys as Private
Space during Late Socialism," in *Beyond the Limits: The Concept of Space in Russian History and
Culture*, ed. Jeremy Smith (Helsinki, 1999), 131–65; Mary M. Leder, *My Life in Stalinist Russia:
An American Woman Looks Back* (Bloomington, Ind., 2001); see also the 1963 film, *Tri plius dva*,
based on Sergei Mikhalkov's 1956 play, *Dikari*, Teatr dlia vzroslykh (Moscow, 1979). For a recent fictional representation of erotic attraction during a summer in Crimea, see Ludmila Ulits-
kaya, *Medea and Her Children*, trans. Arch Tait (New York, 2002).

of the pleasures and preoccupations of tourism. Further work will hopefully tell us more about the intimate spaces of tourism as yet unexplored.

This volume emphasizes the distinctive contribution of tourism to building socialist societies and creating socialist citizens. But tourism also has an important role to play in the construction of states and nations. Our volume makes clearly visible the role of travel in shaping relations of power and privilege among the peoples of imperial Russia, of eastern Europe, and of the USSR. Travel writing and tourism often re-presented ("translated") the periphery back to the center in ways that reinforced official discourses of authority.[15] McReynolds and Layton explore the processes by which travel in tsarist Russia to the spas and seacoasts in the East and the South contributed to a Russian appropriation of non-Slavic territories. In his chapter, Vari describes the civilizing project of middle-class tourists from the central regions of Hungary who were sent to educate and incorporate the Slovak, Romanian, German, and Ruthenian ethnic groups living in Hungary's mountainous regions. Tourism of this sort is an example of what some historians have called "unofficial imperialism," projects of exploration and knowledge gathering which obscured tourism's role in the processes of expansion and domination.[16] Mary Louise Pratt has called the strategies by which European powers in the eighteenth and nineteenth centuries legitimated their imperial interventions, strategies of "anti-conquest" which included "new legitimating ideologies" such as the civilizing mission and "technology based paradigms of progress and development."[17] So too in the land-based empire of multiethnic imperial Russia. "The politics of imperialism mandated that ethnic Russians come not simply to conquer but also to improve the lives of the other people being incorporated into the empire," argues McReynolds.

The Soviet Union was eager to distinguish itself from the empire-making projects of tsarist Russia and bourgeois Europe. Early Soviet indigenization policies promoted local languages, cultures, and elites from the ethnically diverse peoples of the USSR and downplayed Russian language and culture.[18] As Francine Hirsch argues elsewhere in an article on ethnographic exhibits as So-

---

15. On the implications of travel writing as a form of "translation," see James Duncan and Derek Gregory, "Introduction," in *Writes of Passage: Reading Travel Writing*, ed. Duncan and Gregory (London, 1999), 5. This role for travel writing is, of course, not particular to Russia. Inderpal Grewal describes the ways in which through travel books, exhibitions, newspaper reports, and children's literature "the [Indian] empire became a part of the British imaginary." See Inderpal Grewal, *Home and Harem: Nation, Gender, Empire, and the Cultures of Travel* (Durham, N.C., 1996), 87.

16. See the discussion of "unofficial imperialism" in Roy Bridges, "Exploration and Travel Outside Europe (1720–1914)," in *The Cambridge Companion to Travel Writing*, ed. Peter Hulme and Tim Youngs (Cambridge, 2002), 53.

17. Mary Louise Pratt, *Imperial Eyes: Travel Writing and Transculturation* (London, 1992), 7, 74.

18. Terry Martin, *The Affirmative Action Empire: Nations and Nationalism in the Soviet Union, 1923–1939* (Ithaca, N.Y., 2001).

viet "virtual tourism": "the Soviet Union defined itself as a postcolonial multi-national state that was the sum of all its parts" in contrast to imperial Russian and European powers "which defined their metropoles in opposition to their colonized peripheries."[19] We can see this at work in the Soviet guidebooks described by Qualls, in which both tourists and residents were encouraged to celebrate the unique role of Sevastopol in supporting larger Soviet ideals of military prowess, courage, and sacrifice. The socialist transformation of the Soviet Union was not supposed to be imperialist but a process, as described by Hirsch, which integrated the multiethnic populations of the Soviet Union "into the struggle for socialism" through a transformation of consciousness.[20] The transformative and state-building role of tourism in the 1920s and 1930s is explored by Koenker and Maurer. According to Maurer, Soviet mountaineers were expected to proselytize for the virtues of the new Soviet power while climbing in the remote and ethnically non-Russian periphery. And yet, despite the hostility of the Soviet regime to the idea of empire, the history of mountaineering, and of tourism more generally, suggests that the Soviet Union still "ruled imperially."[21] The imperialist function of tourism is particularly evident, but not exclusively so, following World War II, when the rehabilitation of Russians as "the first among equals" facilitated the privileging of Moscow as a focus of Soviet patriotic tourism and deemphasized the unfamiliar or exotic elements of the Soviet periphery.[22]

The Soviet Union's complex legacy toward ethnic difference did distinguish it, however, from countries such as interwar Latvia, whose tourist itineraries deliberately ignored areas with non-Latvian minorities (Jews, Russians, Germans, Poles). According to Purs, the authoritarian regime of Kārlis Ulmanis hoped to use travel to reinforce a national identity built on a Latvian rural purity in opposition to urban cosmopolitanism. In contrast, while travel in interwar Yugoslavia was also an important source of national identity, this identity was defined by deeply held, cross-border, and pan-Slavic emotions of fraternal solidarity which were, Sobe argues, seen as positively cosmopolitan. In both cases, tourism as a means of creating national identity distinguished these projects (and many others) from tourism as a Soviet state-building project in which the periphery was made homogeneously "Soviet" rather than explicitly "national."[23] Still, as Joshua Sanborn has argued persuasively, just because the So-

19. Francine Hirsch, "Getting to Know 'The Peoples of the USSR': Ethnographic Exhibits as Soviet Virtual Tourism, 1923–1934," *Slavic Review* 62, no. 4 (2003): 684. Italics in original.

20. Ibid., 687.

21. See the discussion on imperial rule in Ronald Grigor Suny, "The Empire Strikes Out: Imperial Russia, 'National' Identity, and Theories of Empire," in *A State of Nations: Empire and Nation-Making in the Age of Lenin and Stalin*, ed. Ronald Grigor Suny and Terry Martin (Oxford, 2001), 26.

22. Anne E. Gorsuch, "'There's No Place Like Home': Soviet Tourism in Late Stalinism," *Slavic Review* 62, no. 4 (2003):771–75.

23. On the transformation of Soviet space through tourism and maps, see Evgeny Dobrenko, "The Art of Social Navigation: The Cultural Topography of the Stalin Era," in *The Landscape of*

viet Union did not call itself a nation, did not mean that the effort to create a
Soviet political and civic community was not similar to other nation-building
projects.[24] In the Soviet Union, as in so many other places described in this volume, tourism was supposed to help individuals to internalize the nation; and
through this process the nation, in turn, would become like the human body—
united and functioning as a whole. Thus turn-of-the-century Hungarian
tourist enthusiasts described Budapest as the "heart" of the Hungarian body
"from which the nerves [sic]—under the form of tourism—will carry the necessary blood flow to all of its parts" (Vari). Interwar Czechs were made "'conscious' [through tourism] of their bodily (e.g., 'heart,' 'blood,' and 'nerves')
connections to [homeland]" (Sobe). In the postwar period, Soviet citizens were
told that tourism was a means of integrating the body politic: "Travel in our
country is great and purposeful; it is as beneficial as blood circulation."[25] In
every case, it was youthful bodies—strong enough for hardy turizm and mountaineering, emotionally enthusiastic, and still moldable—that were the major
targets of tourism as a way of remaking self and nation-state.

Many of the essays in this volume demonstrate that tourism did not always
create a greater sense of belonging to an often multiethnic homeland, but that
it contributed to a greater sense of difference, threatening the supposed coherence of the state building and/or imperialist project. Tourist trips from urban
Riga to the Latvian countryside often "strengthened urban-rural divisions"
(Purs). rather than encouraging national unity, for example. One problem for
socialist states was that tourism was a form of recreation older than the regimes themselves and thus contradictorily evoked pre-socialist, and often more
localist notions of national identity. East German participants in the Friends of
Nature participated in a travel culture "remarkably similar to that of many
[prewar] middle-class tourist associations" which included stubborn attachment to their local *Heimat* as opposed to a larger national identity (Moranda).
In the late 1920s, Soviet activists were so anxious about the class physiognomy
of the still-existing prerevolutionary Russian Society of Tourists that they
"claimed the society for their own," flooding the organization with new
working-class members and renaming it the Society of Proletarian Tourists.
But as Koenker shows, even in an authoritarian Soviet Union private pleasures
coexisted and sometimes conflicted with public purpose. Likewise in East Germany, where tourism did not result in the creation of a "stable East German
identity," but instead "tourism, like the countryside itself, became fractured"
with private groups, youth groups, and local groups "never sharing a sense

---

Stalinism: The Art and Ideology of Soviet Space, ed. Evgeny Dobrenko and Eric Naiman, 163–200
(Seattle, 2003).

24. Joshua Sanborn, "Family, Fraternity, and Nation-Building in Russia, 1905–1925," in *A
State of Nations*, ed. Suny and Martin, 93–110.

25. Gorsuch, "'There's No Place Like Home,'" 776.

that they had a common destination" (Moranda). Gorsuch argues similarly about Soviet tourism to eastern Europe in the Khrushchev era. While published travel writing about eastern Europe described a relationship of Soviet superiority, willing subordination, and socialist fraternalism, the experience of travel often challenged these discourses when Soviet tourists discovered that the "colonies" were more developed than the center. This is part of what distinguishes the Soviet experience in eastern Europe from that of western Europe in its colonies. In western Europe, the barbarous processes of colonialization led some to question who was the savage and who the civilized, but the question was a moral, not an economic or technological, one.[26]

If tourism is often about the tourist "seeing" and having feelings about the visited Other, the tourist was also, of course, the object of the local gaze. Research in this volume suggests that tourism often contributed to the assertion of local identity despite efforts by central authorities to use travel to incorporate local spaces and minorities. Vari and Moranda describe conflicts between center and periphery in Hungary and Germany that threatened the agenda of central tourism authorities.[27] Maurer describes the frustration of local mountaineers from Central Asia who could not climb in their own republic but were sent to the Caucasus to climb because of the highly centralized control over the resources and functions of mountaineering. Historians of capitalist tourism elsewhere have documented the ways in which local peoples were able to capitalize on the curiosity of "foreigners," promoting and emphasizing regional cultural differences in order to attract visitors and money.[28] These opportunities were notably more limited in the Soviet Union where so many aspects of tourism were heavily centralized. But further research might tell us more about the ways in which indigenous peoples in the Soviet republics may have also used tourism as a place to push the boundaries of permissible nationalism.[29]

Tourism was also a place of international competition between "East" and "West." In late imperial Russia, the gaining and maintaining of control over the non-Russian southern and eastern periphery, accomplished in part through tourism, was one way of asserting Russia's claim to be the equal of Europe. Crimea was a particular location for the clash of empires. This clash was

---

26. On this point, see the discussion in Helen Carr, "Modernism and Travel (1880–1940)," in *The Cambridge Companion to Travel Writing*, ed. Hulme and Youngs, 73.

27. See also Pieter Judson, "'Every German visitor has a völkish obligation he must fulfill': Nationalist Tourism in the Austrian Empire, 1880–1918," in *Histories of Leisure*, ed. Koshar, 147–68. Also see Pieter Judson and Marsha Rozenblitt, eds., *Constructing Nationalities in East Central Europe* (New York, 2005).

28. Jill Steward, "Tourism in Late Imperial Austria: The Development of Tourist Cultures and Their Associated Images of Place," in *Being Elsewhere*, ed. Baranowski and Furlough, 116.

29. On permitted and not-permitted forms of national expression, see Teresa Rakowska-Harmstone, "The Dialectics of Nationalism in the USSR," *Problems of Communism* 23, no. 3 (1974): 1–22.

sometimes physical (the Crimean War), and sometimes rhetorical.[30] The contest for national superiority was not only between East and West, of course. In the late nineteenth and twentieth centuries, tourism became an internationally acknowledged form of competition among many nations hoping to claim for themselves the best scenery, the most impressive sights of historical significance, the most beautiful beaches. This was true for socialist countries as well as capitalist. Although most aspects of life and politics in a socialist country were said to differ from what occurred elsewhere, socialist countries still generally operated within the larger context of international understandings of "what elements make up a proper nation," and a proper provision for the citizens of that nation.[31] Tourism was understood to be one of these provisions. During the Cold War, the ability to provide a good tourist experience, both for people at home and for international visitors, was one way of competing. As Salmon shows us, the Soviet travel agency Inturist modeled itself after western tourist firms in order to do a better and more profitable job of "selling socialism." In East Germany, tourism was used to bolster the legitimacy of the new regime in the competition with West Germany over material living standards and the provision of consumer pleasures.[32] The East German experience is a good reminder that Europe was not the only pole of reference. The major model for most east European socialist regimes was the Soviet Union not western Europe.

Still, much of the making of a Russian, Soviet, or east European self, be it capitalist or socialist, occurred in relation to "Europe." As McReynolds tells us, the "quintessential Russian traveler," Peter the Great, "journeyed to western Europe to find not only himself but, more to the point, to find a nation he embodied." Nineteenth-century Russian tourists traveled to Europe hoping to accrue "cultural capital" that would give them a "socially convertible complement to their financial resources." For these tourists, and for the east European and even Soviet tourists who followed them, the acquisition of cultural sophistication sometimes meant "consuming" landscapes, sites of antiquity, and the great cities but also material items, including silk blouses and cigarette lighters. As this suggests, the comparison with western Europe was often a disadvantageous one. In late imperial Russia, tourism promoters were eager to keep Russian rubles at home and worked hard to improve facilities to ensure that poor

30. See Kerstin S. Jobst, "Die Taurische Reise von 1787 als Beginn der Mythisierung der Krim. Bemerkungen zum europäischen Krim-Diskurs des 18. und 19. Jahrhunderts," *Archiv für Kulturgeschichte*, no. 83 (2001): 121–44.

31. The quote is from Orvar Löfgren, "Know Your Country: A Comparative Perspective on Tourism and Nation Building in Sweden," in *Being Elsewhere*, ed. Baranowski and Furlough, 138.

32. On other forms of competition over consumption in the Cold War, see Susan E. Reid, "Cold War in the Kitchen: Gender and the De-Stalinization of Consumer Taste in the Soviet Union under Khrushchev," *Slavic Review* 61, no. 2 (2002): 211–52; and the articles in a special edition of *Cultural Studies* on consumption, shopping, and tourism in the socialist countries of eastern Europe (*Cultural Studies* 16, no. 1 [2002]).

local conditions did not encourage Russians to spend their money at western resorts. But the desire to keep tourists at home was also motivated by nationalism. Turn-of-the-century Hungarian tourist enthusiasts hoped that the development of tourism at home would put a stop to "the pilgrimage of Hungarians to foreign sites" and encourage a new appreciation of the "beauty of the Hungarian land" (Vari). Latvian tourist authorities in the interwar period denounced any travel abroad (East or West) as a "shameful stain" on "country and nation" (Purs). Yugoslav pan-Slavism in the 1920s and 1930s, in contrast, encouraged fraternal travel to Czechoslovakia and Poland but not to "Mother Russia," which was now under the control of Soviet communism (Sobe).

In the Soviet Union under Stalin, it was ideological anxieties that kept most Soviet tourists at home and largely limited Soviet travel to western Europe to the cultural and political elite.[33] Europe was Other, if still an ambivalent Other which contradictorily also served as the template for comparison and achievement (or failure). For a de-Stalinizing Soviet Union in the 1950s, and for Tito's Yugoslavia, permitting travel to western Europe was one of the clearest expressions of a new confidence in the capacity of the "East" to compete with the "West." Sergei Obraztsov's travelogue, written on the basis of trips to London just after Stalin's death, sought to overcome this ideologically imposed sense of distance between socialist East and capitalist West. Gilburd shows us how Obraztsov made the foreign appear familiar by basing his travel account around friendly images of England familiar to Soviet audiences from English literature, especially the works of Charles Dickens. Even in the 1950s, however, those Soviet citizens who traveled to the West were still largely members of the cultural elite. It was the safer, "demi-other" of eastern Europe, as Gorsuch describes it, where most Soviet international tourists would travel. Eastern Europe offered some of the attractive aspects of a trip to the "West," including opportunities for consumption, but without the perceived dangers of exposure to too much "difference." In socialist Yugoslavia, in contrast, even the average Yugoslav was able to travel abroad to western Europe from the late 1950s on, and without overt surveillance. Bracewell argues that the right to travel freely to western Europe, and to buy something while there, epitomized the regime's confidence in its separate road to communism. Indeed, "Yugoslav travelers repaid this confidence: they went abroad, [they shopped], and they came straight back home again." For Yugoslav tourists, travel to Poland, Hungary, or the Soviet Union was "travel in the wrong direction."

A history of tourism in Russia, eastern Europe, and the Soviet Union requires consideration of the range of borders the tourist journey could cross: not only geographic and physical borders, or state and national borders, but also conceptual borders made vivid in the journey from the second (socialist) world to the first (capitalist) one, around different sites of socialism, and to

---

33. See, for example, Michael David-Fox, "Stalinist Westernizer? Aleksandr Arosev's Literary and Political Depictions of Europe," *Slavic Review* 62, no. 4 (2003): 733–59.

"Europe." Such movement became an increasing source of self-identity as well as national identity: as the manuals proclaimed, tourism expanded one's horizons. Tourism in socialist and other authoritarian regimes of eastern Europe was a state-sponsored project dedicated to educating and strengthening both the citizen and the nation-state. And yet, as many of our authors argue, there were limits to the capacity of these regimes to control what tourists did and what meanings they took from their travels (something made more difficult by shifting and sometimes contradictory understandings of just what the ideal for tourism was). Authoritarian regimes were able to control tourism on the largest level—by limiting those who could travel abroad, for example—but individuals even in authoritarian systems often appropriated the state tourism project for their own purposes. Yet we must be careful not to assume that the individualistic experience that tourism could provide was necessarily a form of opposition. Tourism may have also reinforced positive relations between regimes and individuals. Some individuals surely accepted the larger lessons they were supposed to learn. Others may have accepted that what tourism promised was possible for a socialist regime as well as a capitalist one, namely, consumer satisfaction and material progress. The history of tourism exposes the particularities of Russian and east European culture and the socialist experience, but also joins this region to discussions of travel and tourism as components of the modern condition everywhere.

PART I

TRAVELS IN CAPITALIST RUSSIA AND EASTERN EUROPE

CHAPTER I

The Prerevolutionary Russian Tourist

Commercialization in the Nineteenth Century

Louise McReynolds

Nikolai Leikin, a journalist from the merchant estate who enjoyed terrific popularity among them for his lampoons of their often confused contacts with modern life, spoofed a group of Russia's nouveaux riches on a tour of the European continent in 1892 in *Where the Oranges Ripen*. Uncomfortable in fashions that did not suit them, served dishes that soured their appetites, fluent only in vocabulary words for "hotel room" and "liquor," and in constant distress over cross-cultural gaffes, Russia's merchant tourists had reason to question why they should imitate the nobility and tour the continent. However, these hapless wayfarers embodied an important cultural as well as social transformation: through them, the educated traveler became the commercial tourist.

In the eighteenth century, Europe's young noblemen, including Russians at the behest of Peter the Great, embarked on de rigueur tours of the continent that were stylized sentimental journeys for purposes of self-discovery.[1] A century later, the merchant-tourists were following the same routes hoping that, through imitation, they could accrue some of the cultural capital that, as Pierre Bourdieu has argued, would provide a socially convertible complement to their financial resources.[2] Discomforts aside, they had very practical reasons for accumulating cultural to match their financial capital.

Caricaturing his tourists as yokels, Leikin was playing upon the irony that they were in fact primary protagonists of modernity. The development of tourism as a commercial industry paralleled that of the emergence of a middle class, and the influence of capitalism on modes of, and motivations for, travel proved paramount. Capitalist principles affected all aspects of tourism, beginning with the transportation revolution that facilitated commercial travel. On the psychological front, tourists welcomed the vacation as an intermission in the work cycle. As James Buzard noted, a vacation promised a "time or imaginary space out of ordinary life for the free realization of (an) otherwise

---

1. Thomas Nugent's *The Grand Tour*, published in 1749, made the trip to the continent, especially to visit sites from classical antiquity, an essential part of the education of young men with ambitions.

2. Pierre Bourdieu, *Distinction: A Social Critique of Judgment*, trans. Richard Nice (Cambridge, 1984), 64–69.

thwarted potential."[3] This freedom, though, would be fixed by time and wages. Time now had to be properly structured so that transportation schedules could be met, and specific amounts of it must be apportioned to be able to follow the recommendations of the commercial guidebook. Those who developed the tourist industry learned from commercial capitalism how to package and sell experience. Financed by advertising, tourist-oriented publications promoted the commodification of adventures into souvenirs to take back home.

Tourism evolved as a means through which the emergent middle classes developed an identity that paradoxically combined cosmopolitanism with conservative nationalism, a relationship that held equally true into the Soviet era. It began with the conversion of the noble "traveler" into the bourgeois "tourist," with all the implications of social change implicit in this movement from elitism to commercialism.[4] Harvey Levenstein has demonstrated how this dichotomy depended upon a falsely fantasized notion of "traveler" at the expense of that "despised word tourist," but it makes a useful social distinction between educational and recreational travel, a distinction that continued to hold true for Soviet tourists as anxious as Leikin's merchants to reap social dividends from cultural contacts.[5] As Diane Koenker and Anne Gorsuch point out in their chapters, the debate about "purpose" became more emphatically articulated as political in the Soviet era, but the central issues predated communism in Russia.

More than just one of many emerging modern industries, tourism, as is evident from this collection of essays, functions as a discursive category in the analysis of modernity, and even postmodernity. Not surprisingly, tourists have always proven themselves active agents on behalf of change. The sociologist Dean MacCannell has argued that "the empirical and ideological expansion of modern society (is) intimately linked in diverse ways to . . . tourism and sightseeing."[6] In Russia's case, because the most attractive spots for tourists were the spas and seacoasts in the non-Slavic territories in the East and the South, and later the mountain ranges in Asiatic Russia, tourism played a uniquely imperialist role throughout its history. The appropriation of geographical names marked a first step in this process, facilitating the creation of what Edward Said termed "imaginative geographies."[7] As Mary Louise Pratt has observed, renaming was one way in which the "discoverer" transformed local knowl-

---

3. James Buzard, *The Beaten Track: European Tourism, Literature, and the Ways to Culture, 1800–1918* (New York, 1993), 102–3.

4. James Clifford has written that "I hang onto 'travel' as a term of cultural comparison, precisely because of its historical taintedness, its associations with gendered, racial bodies, class privilege, specific means of conveyance, etc." ("Traveling Cultures," in *Cultural Studies*, ed. Lawrence Grossberg, Cary Nelson, and Paula Treichler [New York, 1992], 110).

5. The "despised word tourist" is a quote from Henry James. See Harry Levenstein, *Seductive Journey: American Tourists in France from Jefferson to the Jazz Age* (Chicago, 1998), ix–x.

6. Dean MacCannell, *The Tourist: A New Theory of the Leisure Class* (New York, 1976), 2.

7. Quoted in Arturo Escobar, *Encountering Development: The Making and Unmaking of the Third World* (Princeton, N.J., 1995), 9.

edge into that of the conqueror.[8] For example, Catherine the Great's tour of the Crimea in 1787 absorbed the peninsula with an imaginative panache, emphasizing the exotica of the Orient that would become part of Russia's national identity.[9] Catherine Russified by restoring the ancient place names, attempting historical revision by writing out the region's Tatar past, especially its Muslim heritage. Her primary purpose was to connect the peninsula to ancient Greece, which in its later incarnation as the Byzantine Empire had been the source of Russia's Orthodox Christianity.[10] The Tatar Gezlev, for example, reverted to the Greek Evpatoriia, and it became a leading tourist attraction after the Crimean War because a major battle had been fought there. Custom had a way of prevailing, though, and not even Catherine's efforts to restore the peninsula's first historical name, Tavrida, could win out over the Turkish Krym, or Crimea.[11]

Russification through translation extended cultural conquest. In the Caucasus, Piatigorsk acquired the name which translates loosely as "five mountains" from the original Persian word for the area, Besh-Tau.[12] At times the new conquistadors of the Caucasus named places after themselves. At Borzhom, which would earn the reputation as "the Russian Vichy," the commander of the Russian forces there in 1845 named the two mineral springs for himself and his daughter.[13] On the Baltic, when the area around the place where the Narva River flows into the Gulf of Finland began attracting summer tourists in the 1870s, local leaders changed the name Peter the Great had given them, Gungerburg, or "Hungertown," to the more appealing Ust'-Narva, or "Mouth of the Narva."[14]

The geographical sites might be Russified, but the reverse held true when it came to naming the places where tourists would seek respite after a day trekking through culture and history. It seemed that the first hotel to go up in any Russian city was called the European (*Evropeiskaia*), an indication of the superior level of service guests were supposed to be able to anticipate. Other popular names included Russian transliterations of the Bristol, the Grand Hotel, the Belle-vue and even the San Remo. Moscow's Slavic Bazaar, which had grown into one of the second capital's favored hotels, complete with a fine

8. Mary Louise Pratt, *Imperial Eyes: Travel Writing and Transculturation* (New York, 1992), 202.

9. Larry Wolff, *Inventing Eastern Europe: The Map of Civilization on the Mind of the Enlightenment* (Stanford, Calif., 1994), 128. See also Andreas Schönle, "Garden of Empire: Catherine's Appropriation of the Crimea," *Slavic Review* 60, no. 1 (2001): 1023.

10. Grigorii Moskvich, *Putevoditel' po Krymu*, 27th ed. (Petrograd, 1915), 4.

11. On historical aspects of the changing terminology, see K. Kogonashvili, *Kratkii slovar' istorii Kryma* (Simferopol', 1995).

12. Susan Layton, *Russian Literature and Empire: Conquest of the Caucasus from Pushkin to Tolstoy* (Cambridge, 1994), 36.

13. *Borzhom. Spravochnaia knizhka* (Tiflis, 1903), 11–13.

14. In the Soviet era this acquired the Estonian spelling, Narva-Iyesuu. See E. Krivosheev, *Narva-Iyesuu* (Tallin, 1971), 13–14.

restaurant, stood out for marketing its local identity. The extent to which these hotels maintained the standards of the places whose names they bore undoubtedly varied and improved over time. Although western guidebooks hardly used Russian norms for measuring quality, one written in 1912 applauded that "the service and cuisine of the hotels in (Russia's) chief cities cannot be excelled."[15]

The Russian Traveler

The quintessential Russian traveler would be Peter the Great, who journeyed to western Europe to find not only himself but, more to the point, to find the nation he embodied. The requisite trip west for the elite among the nobility then began under him as a form of state service. The diaries of one such noble, Peter Tolstoy, sent to Italy in 1697, show him to be more appreciative of cultural differences than Leikin's merchants, but just as needful of an appropriate terminology.[16] In this as in many other matters of forced westernization, Russians were imitating rather than duplicating experiences. As Andreas Schönle pointed out, Russian writers had to educate their readers about cultures already familiar to most other European readers at the same time that the Russians were also searching for self-identity.[17] Not surprisingly, two of the writers most influential in the creation of a Russian literary language, Nikolai Karamzin and Alexander Pushkin, were also crucial in the development of the genre of travel writing. Through their stylistic and psychological innovations they taught Russians to articulate themselves into their changing surroundings. Karamzin and Pushkin differed in both style and substance, the former a sentimentalist in Europe and the latter, a Romantic along the southern fringes of the empire. But each in his own way made clear how significant travel had become to the development of the evolving sense of self. Karamzin emphasized the experience that others might enjoy vicariously, and then he wrote the history that provided the framework for Russia's geopolitical position. Pushkin provided imagination and the motivation necessary for Russians to visit other parts of *their* empire in images that inflamed Russian feelings of superiority. They created for readers what eighteenth-century American traveler John Ledyard called "philosophic geography," that is, the redrawing of the physical within the predominant philosophical boundaries.[18]

15. Ruth Kedzie Wood, *The Tourist's Russia* (New York, 1912), 3. She also noted that the internal transportation system was both good and the least expensive in Europe.

16. *The Travel Diary of Peter Tolstoi: A Muscovite in Early Modern Europe*, trans. Max Okenfuss (DeKalb, Ill., 1987).

17. Andreas Schönle, *Authenticity and Fiction in the Russian Literary Journey, 1790–1840* (Cambridge, Mass., 2000), 210.

18. Quoted in Wolff, *Inventing Eastern Europe*, 6.

Describing his 1790 journey across the continent, Karamzin traced English-man Thomas Nugent's seminal *The Grand Tour* (1749) and made a Russian contribution to the current style of travel writing popularized by Laurence Sterne's *A Sentimental Journey* (1768). Karamzin's *Letters of a Russian Traveler*, serialized in *Moskovskii zhurnal* (The Moscow Journal) shortly after his return, mixed descriptive reportage with imaginative self-reflection.[19] Writing in the first person and addressing his "dear friends" as though his readers walked alongside him, Karamzin foresaw the birth of the armchair voyager.[20] He wrote, "At this point, would you like to look at the most famous buildings in Paris with me? No. Let us leave that for another time. You are tired, and so am I."[21] His *récits de voyage* told Russians to make themselves, not science, the objective of their travels.

Karamzin was Russia's most prominent proponent of sentimentalism, a genre that encouraged travel because it held that knowledge accumulates through sensory experiences.[22] Highly emotional in his descriptions, Karamzin made internal connections to the external world. Upon his return to Russia, landing at the naval base just beyond Petersburg, he wrote, "I stop everyone I meet, I ask questions only to speak Russian and to hear Russian people. . . . You know it would be difficult to find a more miserable town than Kronstadt, yet it is dear to me!"[23] Moreover, as Karamzin grew increasingly self-confident, he became Russia's first important historian, providing texts for Russians to inscribe themselves into their geography, philosophic as well as physical.[24]

Pushkin, in contrast, never realized his dream of visiting western Europe because for political reasons the autocracy refused him a passport. But having studied French, English, and the classics at his lyceum, he was familiar with the literature. A nominal state servitor in Odessa and Kishinev, he used his poetry to create a literary experience of travel. He took readers to the new imperial frontiers in Piatigorsk in "The Prisoner of the Caucasus" (1821), to the Crimea in "The Fountain of Bakhchisarai" (1822), and to Bessarabia in "The

19. On Karamzin's style, see Iurii Lotman and Boris Uspenskii, *Pis'ma russkogo puteshestvennika* (Moscow, 1984), 535–40.

20. Layton, *Russian Literature and Empire*, 23. See also Michael Butor, "Traveling and Writing," trans. John Powers and K. Lisker, *Mosaic* 8 (Fall 1974): 1–3.

21. Nikolai Karamzin, *Letters of a Russian Traveler, 1789–90; An Account of a Young Russian Gentleman's Tour through Germany, Switzerland, France, and England*, trans. and abrid. Florence Jonas (New York, 1957), 187.

22. Roger B. Anderson, "Karamzin's *Letters of a Russian Traveler*: An Education in Western Sentimentalism," in *Essays on Karamzin, Russian Man of Letters, Political Thinker, Historian*, ed. J. L. Black (The Hague, 1975).

23. Karamzin, *Letters*, 340.

24. As Schönle writes, Karamzin "hoped that his self-fashioning would . . . enable Russia to participate in the advance of world civilization toward enlightenment" (*Authenticity and Fiction*, 210).

Gypsies" (1824). Despite his limited personal experience, having journeyed to the Caucasus for only two months in 1820 and again in 1829, Pushkin's landscapes, like his heroes, were imagined more vividly than reality would have allowed. Critics have explored the influence of England's Romantic idol Lord Byron over Pushkin because of the common theme of the disillusioned hero who has rejected civilization and sought the meaning of society among the peoples outside its borders.[25] Despite his intention of turning his back on society, though, the hero indulges his fantasies of superiority and refuses to be assimilated by the outsider community with whom he seeks refuge.[26] Through their highly idealized contacts with these "Others," to borrow the vocabulary of postcolonialism, Pushkin's heroes inspired travel by presenting exotica as obtainable. Equally telling, his works masked the violence with which the frontier had been conquered by depicting a fierce Other who is at heart eager for assimilation into the superior culture.[27] His poetry provided an immediate psychological connection to place, to the borders of empire.[28]

These Romantic travel writers inspired readers to follow their paths, literally.[29] Ironically, both Byron's and Pushkin's bodies were posthumously transformed into tourist attractions. Byron's untimely death in Greece brought his fellow countrymen there in droves, hoping to recreate the poet's experience. Pushkin, too, died the death of one of his protagonists, and not only did the site of his fatal duel at Chernaia Rechka in St. Petersburg become a shrine, but so did every place he ever lived or worked. An advertising appeal made in 1912 for the profitable tourist industry in the Caucasus used the pitch that Russians "raised on Pushkin have dreamed since childhood of visiting that area."[30] Almost two hundred years after his birth the excursion around Pushkin's old haunts remains a pilgrimage of sorts, a journey intended for the discovery of both the self and Russia, whatever its current political or geographic guise.[31]

---

25. Stephanie Sandler, *Distant Pleasures: Alexander Pushkin and the Writing of Exile* (Stanford, Calif., 1989).

26. Layton, *Russian Literature and Empire*, 104, argues that in Pushkin's "The Gypsies," the author "suggested that a civilized outsider's intrusion into a primitive society merely sows discord and destruction."

27. Layton, ibid., 158–59, discusses a later form of "the myth of regenerative violence."

28. Buzard, *Beaten Track*, 120, discusses how British travelers and tourists carried Byron's poetry to Greece with them. Pushkin had a similar effect. See also Layton, *Russian Literature and Empire*, 24–27.

29. Ruth Kedzie Wood noted that in 1909 "Bakshisari was a favorite wedding journey for Russian young people." See Ruth Kedzie Wood, *Honeymooning in Russia* (New York, 1911), 295.

30. G. G. Evangulov, "Glavnyi komitet pooshchreniia turizma na Kavkaze i ego zadachi" (copy of an official report with no publishing information).

31. Andrei Sinyavsky (Abram Tertz), *Strolls with Pushkin*, trans. Catharine Theimer Nepomnyashchy and Slava I. Yastremski (New Haven, 1993). An intellectual rather than a geographical stroll, Sinyavsky's still captures Pushkin's influence on the Russian imagination.

Less deified by posterity, Karamzin was nonetheless equally influential. His observations that "the individual with the pack on his back and the staff in his hand is not responsible to either officialdom or academics" replayed frequently in epigraphs in subsequent travel writing.[32] State servitors began camouflaging the official objective of their travel in purple prose imitative of Karamzin's. In 1828 State Councilor Gavriil Gerakov published an account of some of his travels through provincial Russia.[33] Gerakov's travel diary is especially valuable because of how he used the narrative of self-discovery to open up the territory he was visiting.[34] In Nizhnii Novgorod he weeps at the grave of "the eternal Minin," the local butcher credited with organizing a national army that drove out the Swedes and Poles during the Time of Troubles in 1612. Gerakov successfully used the emotional experience of being at the site to connect himself to Russia's past, accentuating the need to be an eyewitness in order to authenticate the experience.[35]

Gerakov traveled as far as Simferopol in the Crimea. Sprinkling history onto verbal portraits of the peoples and terrain he encountered, he introduced the Tatars, Georgians, and Cossacks as exotic co-subjects with Russians of a shared geography. The "foreigners" in this travelogue are the western Europeans who came to the Crimea for the mineral waters.[36] Equally innovative, Gerakov emphasized issues fundamental to the activity of traveling: roads, meals, and lodgings.[37] These very basic problems had to be resolved before the singular traveler, out for self-reflection, could be replaced by the horde of tourists, out for holiday. As Pratt has pointed out, the new tourist was an economic pragmatist rather than a romantic, out to overcome logistical rather than military obstacles.[38] In 1837 the first of several editions of a pocket guide appeared, steering readers from Moscow to Petersburg and to houses whose proprietors would feed and lodge paying customers. Not quite hotels, these establishments foretold that the days were numbered when travelers had to presume upon acquaintances or the local peasantry to put them up.[39]

Describing his excursions in *Travel Notes and Impressions of Eastern European Russia* in 1851, Iosif Berlov walked the figurative border between traveling

32. Schönle states that by 1816 Russians had 105 books, including translations, from which to choose with the title *Journey to . . .* (*Authenticity and Fiction*, 6).
33. Gavriil Gerakov, *Putevye zapiski po mnogim rossiiskim guberniiam, 1820* (Petrograd [sic], 1828).
34. Gerakov dedicated his travelogue to "the venerated fair sex," whom he assured that "I am happy and satisfied with only your smile and your approval" (ibid., n.p.).
35. Ibid., 19.
36. Ibid., 98.
37. Pushkin's novella "The Station Master" captured life on the road before the advent of provincial hotels, when travelers stayed at the postal stations.
38. Pratt, *Imperial Eyes*, 148.
39. I. Dmitriev, *Sputnik ot Moskvy do Peterburga* (Moscow, 1841). This is the second, updated edition of the 1837 original.

and touring.[40] His constant allusions to economizing make plain that he was a transitional figure, no member of the idle rich. The sheer variety of his lodgings reflected Russia's changing profile: the nobles in rustic Perm welcome the outsider as a link to Moscow, but on the road he must stay in the squalid huts of his coach drivers. Generally contemptuous of the habits of the non-Orthodox subjects of the Russian tsar, he enjoys a brief interlude with one Tatar family. For longer layovers, Berlov provides useful information about inexpensive furnished rooms in Moscow and Kazan. As tourism became increasingly popular, hence profitable, entrepreneurs around the empire opened *pansiony*, or "pensions," economical lodgings especially well suited for tourists who wanted to stay longer than a few days.

Berlov, though traveling solo, mentions encountering other groups on tour, which included women as anxious as men to expand their identities.[41] Berlov includes the obligatory history lessons, but he also showed a keen eye for ethnic differences in the empire, especially the Tatar population in Kazan. Keeping his distance as a neutral observer, Berlov uses travel as a means of incorporation of peoples from "the Great Wall of China to a French province" into Russia.[42] He looked about with an ethnically specific gaze "that survey(ed) and catalogue(d) other races while remaining unmarked and unseen itself."[43] His distanced mode of observing and use of historical snippets established a Slavic presence atop the political hierarchy of this kaleidoscope of peoples, anticipated a corollary "tourist gaze," a structured way of looking that would allow the viewer to locate him/herself in unfamiliar surroundings.

When Alexander II launched his Great Reforms following the disastrous defeat in the Crimean War in 1856, he gave Russians both reason and opportunity for travel: the expanded meaning of citizenship gave people reasons for wanting to insert themselves into the broader imperial mission, and the ensuing industrialization added the commerce and technology that increased opportunity. Entrepreneurs came from the West: the Englishman John Murray III pioneered in guidebooks marketed for the tourist in the 1840s, and his success was quickly improved upon by the German Karl Baedeker, who ultimately dominated this business because he appreciated the commercial aspects and published travel guides in many languages. Russians, though, had to turn first to the Imperial Geographical Society, founded in 1845, which published books that covered the geographical terrain but without the personal information.

40. Iosif Berlov, *Putevye zametki i vpechatleniia po vostochnoi evropeiskoi Rossii* (Moscow, 1851).

41. Edmund Swinglehurst, *Cook's Tours: The Story of Popular Travel* (Poole, Dorset, UK, 1982), 35, pointed out that "ladies were to be the mainstay of Cook parties throughout the century."

42. Berlov, *Putevye zametki*, 79.

43. This is how Vicente Rafael describes the U.S. colonizers watching Filipinos in "White Love: Surveillance and National Resistance in the United States' Colonization of the Philippines," in *Cultures of United States Imperialism*, ed. Amy Kaplan and Donald Pease (Durham, N.C., 1993), 200.

Later, ethnographers began producing a multivolume series of textbooks on what they referred to as the "homeland" (*otechestvovedenie*) rather than the "empire," another source of information that scripted the new lands into the empire for travelers, now metamorphosing into tourists.[44] Heralding the arrival of the tourist in 1875, a newssheet with information about hotels in both Russian capitals, financed completely by advertisements, appeared in Petersburg and circulated in major European and Russian cities.[45]

Organized Travel and the Development of Tourism

The Englishman Thomas Cook is generally recognized as the founder of commercial tourism in the middle of the nineteenth century because of the effects of his organizational innovations in travel. As the secretary of the Leicester Temperance Society and committed to "leveling upward," Cook began his business by organizing outings for the local working classes in order to divert them from drink; his argument that workers should be encouraged to travel for educational purposes resonated in Soviet Russia, just as his commercial strategies did in the prerevolutionary years. Cook realized that the railroad offered the possibility to rethink many of the fundamentals of travel, just as he saw how practical organization and mass production could streamline efficiency and reduce costs. The tourist's financial investment in the journey was then rationalized on the grounds of self-improvement.[46]

Cook had devised a formula that would translate the ideas behind "vacation" and "disposable income" into what would eventually become the world's largest industry.[47] He brought together people of various backgrounds by removing some of the psychological impediments that had intimidated the less sophisticated. As Edmund Swinglehurst pointed out, tourists who signed on with Cook "felt something of the gloss of their social superiors descended on their shoulders and, as many of them were the teachers, doctors, and clergy who served the upper classes, they reasonably hoped that in the course of time the closing of the cultural gap would lead to the bridging of the social gap as well."[48] Soviet tourists would also use packaged tours not simply to acquire the

44. See, for example, D. Semenov, *Otechestvovedenie. Rossiia po rasskazam puteshestvennikov i uchenym issledovaniia* (Uchebnoe posobie dlia uchashchikhsiia), 4: *Vostok i zapad*, 2nd ed. (Moscow, 1879).

45. *Peterburgskii listok dlia gostinnits. Ezhednevnaia spravochnaia gazeta ob"iavlenii* (St. Petersburg, 1875–1876).

46. Much has been written on Thomas Cook and his agency. See, for example, Swinglehurst, *Cook's Tours*.

47. In 1990 the tourism industry employed over 101 million worldwide, with gross sales surpassing $2 trillion, or 5.5 percent of the world's gross national product. See Donald Hawkins and J. R. Brent Ritchie, eds. in chief; Frank Go and Douglas Frechtling, eds., *World Travel and Tourism Review: Indicators, Trends and Forecasts* 1 (Wallingford, UK, 1991), ix.

48. Swinglehurst, *Cook's Tours*, 34.

patina of sophistication associated with the desirable quality of "being cultured" (*kul'turnost'*), but, to cross perceived cultural gaps between themselves and Westerners.

The organizational model Cook pioneered was easy to duplicate, and Russians founded numerous smaller agencies capitalized by dues-paying members and joint-stock companies that facilitated tourism both within the empire and, less frequently, abroad. The first major such company, the Russian Society of Shipping and Trade (ROPT), recognized that people, too, were commercial objects. Chartered in Odessa in 1857, ROPT benefited from government subsidies in the push to industrialize. The shipping company then joined with the developing network of railroads, carrying passengers as well as freight.[49] By 1897 forty-seven (almost half) of ROPT's fleet accepted passengers, including two cruise ships designed for tourist travel.[50] In most years, barring such natural and social disasters as the famine and cholera epidemic of 1892 and the 1905 revolution, the company showed a healthy profit.[51] Pilgrims to the Holy Land, even though they tended to buy the cheap tickets, traveled in sufficient numbers to provide ROPT with one of its most profitable sidelines.[52] By 1915 it boasted connections to numerous national and international lines and organized discounted excursions for groups of twenty or more. Headquartered in Petersburg, ROPT maintained bureaux in all major cities and in seacoast resort areas.

The enterprise that claimed to be Russia's first tourist agency was founded in Petersburg by Leopol'd Lipson, who began organizing tours of Italy and Spain as early as 1867. Borrowing from Cook's system, Lipson advertised the ease of travel, promising to assume "all the worries about spiritual and physical comfort . . . all the annoyances associated with tickets, baggage, guides, transportation, and tips." What distinguished him from his competitors was that his tours moved slowly, giving customers time to appreciate the people and country so that they could take home "memories to last a lifetime."[53]

Replicating relations in the modern city, members of his tour met as strangers, and Lipson welcomed both sexes. By making proper social behavior a condition for joining one of his groups, Lipson anticipated the relationship between tourism and kul'turnost', the advantageous acquisition of sophistication. Because success depended upon the compatibility of the group, for example, he advised against discussions of religion and politics. To maintain a hierarchy of

49. *Istoricheskii ocherk Piatidesiatiletiia uchrezhdeniia Russkogo obshchestva parokhodstva i torgovli, 1857–1907* (Odessa, 1907).

50. *Putevoditel' po Chernomu moriu* (Moscow, 1897).

51. This is based, in addition to the above-cited history, on the company's annual reports (*otchety*) after 1903, published by E. Arnol'd.

52. *Zamechanie F. K. Fontona na obshchem sobranii aktsionerov 11 iiunia 1913 g.* (St. Petersburg), 2.

53. Leopol'd Lipson, *Pervoe v Rossii predpriiatie dlia obshchestvennykh puteshestvii, 1885–86* (St. Petersburg, 1885).

authority, he insisted that complaints be made directly to the leader, and never in front of the others. In another move that unwittingly anticipated Soviet tourism, he cautioned that anyone caught trying to bring contraband across international borders would embarrass the whole group. Lipson's prices in 1885 ranged from 350 rubles for three weeks in Finland and Sweden to 2,500 rubles for a three-month voyage that included Paris, Italy, and Egypt. These arrangements would have been affordable to newly moneyed Russians, who would require Lipson's skills to compensate for their lack of experience in such matters.[54]

The data on Russia's commercial agencies are hopelessly scattered; the most solid conclusion to which they point is that several existed and enjoyed sufficient success to stay in business for at least a few years. Motivated presumably by similar corporations trying to set up resorts, a group of investors established a joint-stock company in 1903, Turist. The slender sources do not enlighten on the extent of Turist's success or failure, but its charter reflects the issues central to the growing industry. Although Turist solicited members at a cost of three rubles per annum, the primary funding was to come from agents who invested at a rate of 5,000, 3,000, or 1,500 rubles, depending on their degree of responsibility; all would share profits proportionally. The organizers understood the significance of volume to their enterprise and explained that "we do not want to enter into agreements with shops or petty enterprises." They also recognized that the underdeveloped provinces could not always accommodate tourists, so they promised to find adequate housing and eating arrangements. A push to recruit multilingual agents indicated a desire to bring in foreign tourists. Essentially, the founders of Turist had recognized that profits depended upon keeping people and products in circulation. The company negotiated to produce and sell commodities essential for tourism, from soap to postcards, in railroad stations around the country. It may well have failed, though, because it also honored the capitalist principle of exploiting labor: those agents who were saddled with the most work earned the least.[55]

Officially chartered societies competed with these private agencies. Alpine clubs, for example, brought amateur mountain climbers together in the Caucasus and the Crimea from the 1890s. Like other voluntary associations, these societies did not have to turn a profit because they could solicit outside funding from those sympathetic with their objectives. Many were also chartered to sponsor fund-raising events. Moreover, these societies emphasized in their charters a commitment to using tourism as a medium of education, especially about health. Some even published their own journals, which competed with commercial journals such as *Puteshestvennik* (The Traveler), founded in 1905, and *Prekrasnoe daleko* (The Beautiful Faraway), circulating from 1912. Whereas the first tried to mount an educational platform by mixing scientific information with sensational stories, the latter capitalized heavily on contribu-

---

54. Ibid.
55. *Instruktsiia agentam akts.-ogo obshchestva "Turist"* (St. Petersburg, 1903).

tions from readers. The brisk prose and objective eye of the new tourist differed markedly from the traveler's emotionalisms of old.

The Russian Society of Tourists became the largest of these associations. Based in Petersburg, it grew out of the Touring Club of Bicyclists-Tourists, founded in 1895. Bicycling was an appropriate activity from which to begin this agency for two reasons, the most obvious being that cycling was a comparatively inexpensive mode of travel. In addition, regulations relevant to cyclists varied from city to city and the requirements at customs for taking bikes across borders were sufficiently complex to warrant such a centralized organization. The cyclists had begun organizing excursions and coordinating with similar organizations in other cities. Their journal, originally entitled *Velosiped* (The Bicycle), was rechristened *Russkii turist* (The Russian Tourist) in 1898.[56] In 1903 the society boasted 2,153 members.[57]

The new name switched more than the image of the tourist as a cyclist. Although it continued to use *russkii*, which implied ethnic Russian, in the title of its journal, the society adopted the more inclusive *rossiiskii*, which held an insinuation of empire, for its official title. It maintained representatives in major cities, plus agents positioned in towns and villages throughout the empire. By 1910 the society boasted more than a hundred representatives and twenty-five larger committees in major urban areas.[58] A partial list of agents in 1899 denoted their diversity: they included a postmaster, a village doctor, a Lutheran pastor, and a prince.[59]

Russkii turist peddled images of the open road, but for all the reports on trips to Italy or walking tours of China, most excursions were considerably more modest. Primarily, local agents organized day trips to points of interest in their locales, at a cost of ten kopecks. Moreover, these trips helped to activate the concept of "weekend," filling the time away from work with pleasurable projects for self-improvement. A day trip to a Moscow candy factory, captured for memory by a Kodak (the company advertised in the magazine), converted a Saturday into an experience.[60] The Tula branch initiated what would today be called "Tolstoy Tours," arranging for visits to the great man's estate at Iasnaia Poliana.[61] Members in Rostov-on-Don arranged picnics at the estate of N. I. Pastukhov, the former bar owner who had made millions publishing Moscow's most successful tabloid, *Moskovskii listok* (The Moscow Sheet), and who had then retired to his provincial birthplace.[62]

56. *Russkii turist* (Organ obshchestva velosipedistov-turistov russkogo turing-kluba), no. 1 (1899): 2, 4.

57. The charter is published in *Russkii turist*, no. 6 (1903): 188–90. See also *Russkii turist*, no. 3 (1904): 85.

58. *Russkii turist*, no. 1 (1910): 1.

59. *Russkii turist*, no. 1 (1899): 12.

60. *Russkii turist*, no. 4 (1904): 104–6. A photo accompanying the article showed the approximately thirty tourists hoisting their flag in front of the factory.

61. *Russkii turist*, no. 1 (1899): 11.

62. *Predstavitel'stvo rossiiskogo obshchestva turistov. Spravochnik i programma ekskursii* (Rostov-on-Don, 1910).

The Tourist Society gave lessons in sophistication, underscoring the notion that one reason to be a tourist was to acquire cultural skills that could bridge social divisions. For example, it explained how to use automatic ticket machines being installed in train stations around the turn of the century.[63] The advertisements in its journal indicated the extensive commercialization of the industry. Just as the society could arrange for group passage across borders, so could it negotiate discounts for hotels or tourist-related paraphernalia, such as cameras. Merchants would arrange with the society's local representatives to offer bargains for members on tour. Thus the official badge awarded for the initiation price of two rubles had a negotiable cash value. In addition, the society offered members a quasi-political outlet, as when it mobilized groups to complain to authorities about the inadequate maintenance of Russian roads.[64]

The Moscow branch of the Russian Tourist Society declared its independence in 1910 in order to expand its agenda.[65] Echoing Cook's original creed of "leveling upwards," it arranged educational tours for those in public service on the lower socioeconomic rungs, such as schoolteachers, students, and subordinate medical personnel. Significantly, tourism was being recognized not only as something everyone might *want* to do, but something that they *should* do. The *Vestnik znaniia* (Herald of Knowledge) group of self-styled "people's intelligentsia" joined the fray in 1910, publishing their own guidebook and hoping to organize tours for the journal's subscribers.[66] Snobbish about commercialism, they refused to bore readers with train schedules, focusing instead on philosophical issues. But by incorporating the slogan "learn your native land" into their motto "learn and teach,"[67] they reflected shifting attitudes toward tourism, which would prove crucial to the inclusion of access to tourism on the list of worker demands, and government favors, after 1917.[68]

The Tourist's "Gaze": New Ways of Seeing the Self on Tour

Buzard emphasized the function of tourism as a medium that "fundamentally engages and tests cultural *representations*,"[69] and the nature of this engagement becomes visible in how the tourists "see." Locating this view in the nineteenth century, John Urry discussed how various institutions, technologies,

63. *Russkii turist*, no. 7 (1903): 213.

64. *Russkii turist*, no. 12 (1899): 323–25. The road problem became all the more acute after the zemstvos were freed from mandatory upkeep in 1891.

65. Moskovskoe otdelenie rossiiskogo obshchestva turistov, *Otchet kompanii za 1911* (Moscow, 1912), 3.

66. On this group's cultural ambitions, see Jeffrey Brooks, "Popular Philistinism and the Course of Russian Modernism," in *Literature and History: Theoretical Problems and Russian Case Studies*, ed. Gary Saul Morson (Stanford, Calif., 1986), 90–110.

67. V. V. Bitner, *Sputnik ekskursanta* (St. Petersburg, 1910).

68. Dr. D. M. Gorodinskii, *Chto nuzhno znat' pri poezdkakh na kurorty Kryma i Kavkaza* (Leningrad, 1926).

69. Buzard, *Beaten Track*, 13.

1.1. The guidebook, or *Sputnik*, published by *Vestnik znaniia*. Louise McReynolds, *Russia at Play: Leisure Activities at the End of the Tsarist Era* (Cornell University Press, 2002), 170.

and ideologies constructed a "tourist gaze," a specific way of incorporating new contacts into a previously held worldview.[70] The travel literature, guidebooks, and periodicals that promoted various forms of travel provided the starting point for structuring the tourist's way of looking, or gaze, in such a way that they prompted the reader to see him/herself fitting into unfamiliar surroundings. This literature normalized differences between the seer and the seen, making it appear that what the tourist was observing fell quite naturally into place and was not the result of haphazard incidents or controlled government policies.[71] Bourdieu has argued persuasively that tourists misrecognize social reality in such a way as to "(maintain), by naturalizing, (their) advantages."[72] These *méconnaissances*, or willful misrecognitions, helped tourists to adapt by recreating the familiar in a strange environment. Postulating that "other regions give back what (the visitor's) culture has excluded from its discourse," Michel de Certeau has suggested that tourists also go to look for something denied them at home.[73] This might help to explain why people strike out to "discover" new worlds, but it glosses over the extent to which tourists demand to have enough of the familiar recreated to anchor them. A Russian guidebook to Palestine published in 1890, for example, provided a detailed tour of sites around the Holy Land, but it managed to script both Catholicism and Judaism out of the geography.[74] This example underscores a key point of commercial tourism: politics is in the eye of the beholder.

Tourists abetted the political mission of imperialism by the way in which they appropriated the peoples in the borderlands areas they visited. The politics of imperialism mandated that ethnic Russians come not simply to conquer, but also to improve the lives of the other peoples being incorporated into the empire. As Pratt has argued, "It is the task of the advance scouts for capitalist 'improvement' to encode what they encounter as 'unimproved' . . . available for improvement."[75] Travel literature charted Russia's civilizing influence, highlighting integration, as opposed to conquest. Living like a Tatar in 1873 meant sleeping on an uncomfortable floor, as in a stable. A visiting doctor to the "underdeveloped" Crimea worried that healthy people would get sick here rather than vice versa. He observed that "one can eat shashlik, but you need the stomach of a Tatar to digest it."[76] Less than a decade later, an 1881 guidebook noted that Tatars clean by burning, which can result in foul air, but it

70. John Urry, *The Tourist Gaze: Leisure and Travel in Contemporary Societies* (London, 1990).

71. Ibid., 11.

72. Quoted in Buzard, *Beaten Track*, 83.

73. Michel de Certeau, *The Practice of Everyday Life*, trans. Steven Rendall (Berkeley, Calif., 1984), 50.

74. *Putevoditel' v Palestinu po Ierusalimu, sviatoi zemle i drugim sviatyniam vostoka* (Odessa, 1890).

75. Pratt, *Imperial Eyes*, 61.

76. *Morskie kupal'ni Chernogo moria. Iz putevykh zametok vracha I. N. Lagogy* (Chernigov, 1873), 25–27.

was generally possible to rent rooms in their homes, which could be preferable to a hotel because they were often good cooks.[77] After 1900, perhaps the clearest impression of cultural imperialism can be found in the numerous restaurants throughout the empire advertising that they served the ethnic cuisines from around the empire.

The guidebooks record just as readily Russian detachment from local customs. A 1913 guidebook to Borzhom commented on the difficulty of finding good female help, without any recognition that this might be a reflection of local gender relations. Fortunately for Russian tourists, though, male servants were reasonably competent. The closest village, Rebiatishki, was described as "rather clean for a poor Georgian village. Their dwellings are rather like peasant huts, indigent and unpleasant on the inside."[78] The march of modernity can be traced through the attempted domestication of the empire's ethnic minorities as they appear in the travel literature: from Pushkin's erotic Circassians, to Berlov's unhygienic Tatars, to the Bashkirs who are particularly poor at building roads because "they do not like physical labor in general or compulsory work in particular."[79] The guidebook thus helped to establish standards for both difference and hierarchy, and it provided the basic text in which the discourse of nationalism was conflated with that of imperialism.

Healthy Body, Healthy Empire, Healthy Nation

It would be impossible to calculate whether tourists thought first about fortifying their bodies or their souls, but by the twentieth century the physical and mental were not so clearly distinguished that tourists would be making a conscious choice. People treating a specific illness differed from those who had adopted the notion that they needed a break from work to restore lost energy and to re-create themselves. Mineral waters, with their restorative powers, had been fashionable destinations since antiquity, and the spas built around them offered recuperation to those under stress or in otherwise poor health.[80] The tourist industry transformed the spa into a vacation resort, catering to the middle-class family and offering a variety of entertainments to complement the mineral and mud baths.[81] To be sure, even before, this spa culture had involved much more than simply taking the cure. It offered possibilities for ro-

77. Dr. V. I. Guchin, *O klimatolechebnykh mestakh iuzhnogo berega Kryma*, no. 1 (Khar'kov, 1881), 2, 21.

78. *Borzhom*, 139, 246.

79. *Russkii turist*, no. 12 (1899): 325.

80. Layton, *Russian Literature and Empire*, 54–56, describes the popularity of Russia's first spas in the 1820s.

81. As Swinglehurst, *Cook's Tours*, 183, points out about British tourists of the era, "visitors to these watering places disguised their true motives for being there by a pretended concern for their health."

mance with mysterious strangers and with the even more mysterious peoples who lived along the borderlands, where the most popular spas were located.

Spas appeared frequently in pre-tourism travel literature. Russian theater audiences attending Prince A. A. Shakhovskoi's enormously popular 1815 comedy *The Lipetsk Spa* knew that these mineral springs in Tambov Province provided an ideal setting for the play, which developed around its subtitle, *A Lesson to Coquettes*. The dominant male characters were, appropriately, officers recovering from the Napoleonic wars, but the main character was a scheming young widow. The spa provided a serviceable backdrop because it brought transient characters together for short periods of time. The most famous work of Russian literature set at a spa, though, would be Mikhail Lermontov's *A Hero of Our Time* (1841).[82] Lermontov, whose checkered military career had seen him banished twice to outposts in the Caucasus, also found himself dispatched for reasons of health to a spa in Piatigorsk in 1841.[83]

The romantic Caucasus, where Pushkin and Lermontov stimulated wanderlust with tales of passion and dark eyes, were sprinkled with mineral waters. The other regions in the empire so blessed by nature included the Crimea, especially along the Black Sea littoral, and the Baltic coast. Thus spa culture developed as an offshoot of imperialism, tourists following the troops, so to speak (see also Susan Layton's chapter in this collection). Because of the custom of sending officers off to recuperate, the tsarist government inadvertently accelerated the development of this branch of tourism.[84] Establishing mineral-bath resorts in the Caucasus represented a rearguard action of cultural appropriation in the long and costly conquest of the mountainous region.[85] Piatigorsk was the first to be officially recognized in 1803, although serious construction did not begin for another twenty years. Essentuki, with its twenty springs, had begun as a military outpost but became a resort in 1839. Borzhom, its ultimate rival in popularity, began receiving soldiers in the 1820s.

Borzhom's history encapsulates that of the area's development. Buildings and baths began going up in the 1830s. When General Golovin brought his daughter down to partake of the cure in 1845, he expedited the official transfer of the waters from the military to civil authorities. Located approximately

82. Simon Karlinsky, *Russian Drama from Its Beginnings to the Age of Pushkin* (Berkeley, Calif., 1985), 232.

83. Tat'iana Aleksandrovna Ivanova, *Lermontov na Kavkaze* (Moscow, 1968).

84. On the systematic creation of *faux* national borders, see Benedict Anderson's seminal *Imagined Communities: Reflections on the Origins and Spread of Nationalism*, rev. ed. (London, 1991). On some ways in which frontiers were artificially created in Russia, see Ronald Grigor Suny, *The Revenge of the Past: Nationalism, Revolution, and the Collapse of the Soviet Union* (Stanford, Calif., 1993).

85. V. Perevalenko, *Abastumanskie i Urabel'skie mineral'nye vody* (Tiflis, 1851), for example, discusses the relationship of the military to the development of some Georgian spas.

130 miles from Tiflis, Borzhom could grow only as quickly as transportation to the area would permit. The 1859 capture of Shamil, the Islamic tribal leader who had kept Russian forces at bay in the northern Caucasus for over forty years, facilitated development of the entire region. Royal family members established estates there, which upped its desirability. Nicholas II's sickly younger brother Georgii lived and died here. In 1901 the number of ethnic Russian inhabitants (2,031) outstripped the native Georgians (1,424) for the first time—an indicator of development, if not necessarily of progress.

Tourism would also have been encouraged by the Society for the Restoration of Christianity in the Caucasus, founded in 1860 with the objective of erasing cultural differences in ways that would make the Russian tourist more at home in the region.[86] The mineral waters were now being bottled for export, and Borzhom shed its hospital image of quartering invalids for a new reputation as "the kingdom of the hearty appetite." Climbing and horseback riding competed with bathing, and orchestras and touring stage companies played during the summer season. By 1903 advance reservations quickly filled the available hotels, dachas, and rental apartments.[87] Russians, no less than the western Europeans Buzard described, did not so much "wish to cast off the familiar and experience the native, but rather have the familiar recreated in a new environment."[88] The tourist boom in the region paralleled the proliferation of images of the Caucasus in popular urban culture, which suggests that the two reinforced each other.[89]

Combining health with recreation, Russia's seacoasts could accommodate thousands more tourists than the spas. The Crimea, with its beautiful beaches, mountains, and temperate climate, would form the nucleus of Russian tourist development.[90] When the railroad finally connected the peninsula to the two capitals in the 1870s, possibilities for economic development turned into probabilities. The spark came when S. P. Botkin, physician to Tsar Alexander III, "sent his august patient to Livadia," a settlement close to the port city of Yalta where the Romanov dynasty had maintained an estate since 1834.[91] Regular visits from the Romanovs turned nearby Yalta into the first genuine resort area on the Black Sea: "it grew not by days but by hours."[92] The first luxury hotel, the Rossiia, came with the railroad, and its construction illustrated as-

---

86. Austin Jersild, "Faith, Custom, and Ritual in the Borderlands," *Russian Review* 59, no. 4 (2000), 520. Jersild does not discuss tourism, but the connections are likely because of their coincidence in both time and purpose.

87. *Borzhom*.

88. Buzard, *Beaten Track*, 8.

89. Thomas Barrett, "Southern Living (in Captivity): The Caucasus in Russian Popular Culture," *Journal of Popular Culture* 31, no. 4 (1988): 85–88.

90. At the time of the Russian annexation in 1783, however, the air was described as "unwholesome, the waters poisonous." Wolff, *Inventing Eastern Europe*, 124.

91. Dr. V. N. Dmitriev, *Ialta. 25 let tomu nazad* (St. Petersburg, 1892), 1. Dmitriev was an active member of the local climbing society and organized numerous excursions over the years.

92. Ibid.

1.2. Yalta's first luxury hotel, the Rossiia. Louise McReynolds, *Russia at Play: Leisure Activities at the End of the Tsarist Era* (Cornell University Press, 2002), 175.

pects of tourism's modernizing impact. First, the hotel required plumbing, which entailed revamping the water supply system. The local Tatar population could not furnish the requisite construction workers, so Russian peasants were brought in from surrounding provinces, and many of them remained. Bazaars with Tatar, Jewish, and Greek sellers gave way to permanent shops.[93] The tourist boom had begun.

Odessa, site of some of the first sanatoria, was long the only spot on the seacoast accessible by train.[94] A physician who prescribed bathing in the Black Sea noted in the guidebook he wrote in 1873 that the ill effects of urbanization had nearly doubled the population since the Crimean War, and the dirty air of the city and the torturous climb down the famous steps to the beach diminished the health benefits.[95] Costs ran high because many locals inflated prices, exploiting those who came to recover. ROPT, however, was making its move into tourism with scheduled trips to the spots that would become famous vacation areas: Evpatoriia, Sevastopol, Alupka, Feodosiia, and the jewel in the royal resort crown, Yalta. The good doctor's recommendations for life after one has restored one's health (which happened "not by the day but by the hour") included counsel to dance to the strains of the orchestras that played in public garden rotundas, usually on Sundays and Thursdays.[96]

93. Ibid., 7–10. Demands for lodging ran faster than the building could keep up with them, allowing the locals to gouge visitors for a spot on a balcony or in a basement when the Romanovs were in town.

94. *50 let sushchestvovaniia gidropaticheskogo zavedeniia vracha L. Shorshtein* (Odessa, 1898). See also P. K. A-in, *Mineral'nye vody voobshche i tselitel'nost' vody i griazei Odesskikh limanov* (St. Petersburg, 1880).

95. In 1858, the population was 104,493; in 1873, it was 193,513. See Frederick W. Skinner, "Odessa and the Problem of Urban Modernization," in *The City in Late Imperial Russia*, ed. Michael Hamm (Bloomington, Ind., 1986), 212.

96. *Morskie kupal'ni Chernogo moria.*

Another doctor describing the Black Sea littoral in 1881 rued the intrusion of entertainments because they attracted tourists out for a good time, whose boisterous behavior could upset his patients. He described another phenomenon, the conversion of private estates into resorts built for paying customers. The princely Golytsin family, whose estate in the region predated Peter the Great, anticipated Anton Chekhov's drama *The Cherry Orchard* by subdividing and selling off lots.[97] Prince Vorontsov, who owned Alupka, kept growth slow by forbidding restaurants or orchestras on the resort he built. Count Shuvalov's Miskhor offered complete quiet, but without a cook on site, was less desirable. General Mal'tsev had built a miniature crystal palace as an attraction at his Simeis, and fountains in front of the rental cottages, but the rooms smelled bad. The doctor did manage to find "the only comfortable place on the whole south shore of the Crimea," Limany, a pansion styled on the Swiss model, with comfortable rooms, good food, and a ballroom with a grand piano for socializing. The proprietor's "desire to make his pensioners happy" had produced such success that he built a second wing.[98] At least two joint-stock companies formed, one in 1899 and the other in 1901, to solicit private investment for development of resorts along the coast of the Black Sea.[99]

Within a few decades, this intense development had victimized Yalta. Enlarging the port facilities had filled the coastline with debris and eroded the shore so severely that ships docked almost at the entrance to the once chic Rossiia hotel. The city's indeterminate population reflected the uncontrolled growth.[100] What upset the sanitation inspectorate, though, delighted promoters of the tourist industry. Chekhov, a native of southern Russia and a virtuoso at depicting social change, set his short story "The Lady with the Lapdog" (1899) at a Yalta spa, an environment with which he was especially familiar from his sojourns there to treat his tuberculosis and which he characterized as "a mixture of something European that reminds one of views of Nice, with something cheap and shoddy."[101] Twelve hotels and numerous pansiony welcomed guests year round, including Europeans come to explore the battle-grounds of the Crimean War.[102] An American tourist in 1912 described it as

97. Dmitriev, *Ialta*, 11.

98. Guchin, *O klimatolechebnykh mestakh*.

99. *Ob "iasnitel'naia zapiska po delu osnovaniia obraztsovogo kurorta v Chernomorskoi gubernii* (1899). This company sold six thousand shares at 250 rubles per share. See also *Ustav aktsionernogo obshchestva Chernomorskikh kurortov* (St. Petersburg, 1901). This company raised 4 million rubles at 250 rubles per share.

100. P. Rozanov, "Dvizhenie sanitarnogo i kurortnogo blagotvoritel'stva g. Ialty za poslednye 5 let," *Russkii vrach*, no. 49 (1903): 6–8.

101. Quoted in Janet Malcolm, "Travels with Chekhov," *New Yorker*, 21 and 28 February 2000, 239.

102. John Murray's popular guidebook devoted its longest section to the Crimean War. *Handbook for Travelers in Russia, Poland, and Finland, including the Crimea, Caucasus, Siberia, and Central Asia*, 4th ed., thoroughly revised with maps and plans (London, 1888).

"the gayest, the most exclusive, and the most expensive Russian resort . . . the social capital of the Crimea."[103]

Tourism to the Crimea continued its steady growth. In 1901 Prince Alexander Ol'denburg began turning much of Gagry, his family's large estate on the eastern shore of the Black Sea, into a luxury resort that also included discounted accommodations for some patients who could ill afford steep prices. Gagry offered the private family zoo, donkey rides for children, two hotels with telephones even in the least expensive rooms (rates ranged from 1 to 13 rubles), restaurants "better than the first-class (ones) in the two capitals," a grand piano for guests, an orchestra, and even a stage for amateur and summer stock companies. On weekends Ol'denburg opened the grounds to picnickers who rode the train down from Novorossiisk. The beach was segregated for male and female swimming, as were the other public beaches.[104] Gagry could remain open year-round because the other side of the estate was rife with game for hunters. It was sufficiently popular that the ROPT kept an agency on site.[105]

The improved lines of transportation (which like all else in the industry grew "not by days but by hours")[106] permitted the conversion of a small fort on the coast into Sochi, the first resort specifically constructed on the beach and projected to vie with the French Riviera for foreign tourists. New docking facilities and paved roads made it accessible. Public parks, an esplanade, hotels and pansiony for a variety of budgets, and warm weather year round turned Sochi into the largest resort in the Soviet era. By 1913 one could travel quickly from the two capitals on the Black Sea Express, or purchase rail passes that saved the time of having to buy a specific ticket for each leg of a journey, which made possible spontaneous tours around the area.[107]

At the northern end of European Russia, the Baltic coast provided a quite different site of intensive tourist development, its popularity intimately connected with Petersburg. Even the casual visitor to the imperial capital in any season quickly appreciates the toll that the marshy climate takes on the human organism, and the pressures of urbanization were adding approximately fifty

---

103. Wood, *Tourist's Russia*, 212–13. When first visiting Yalta in 1909, she appreciated the absence of foreign tourists, noting that it "is a resort of the Russians, for the Russians" (*Honeymooning in Russia*, 303).

104. Dr. A. S. Kraevskii, *Morskie kupan'ia v Batume* (Batum, 1886). This 40-kopeck brochure explained some of the new bathing etiquette. Apparently men were still permitted to swim naked, but women, never.

105. *Gagry. Klimaticheskaia stantsiia na Chernomorskom poberezh'i* (St. Petersburg, 1905).

106. Vasilii Sidorov, *Volga. Putevye zametki i vpechatleniia ot Valdaiia do Kaspiia* (St. Petersburg, 1894), III. See also Dr. P. N. Andreev, *Illiustrirovannyi putevoditel' po iugo-zapadnym kazen. zh. dorogam* (Kiev, 1898), which includes a history of the growth of the southwest railroad.

107. *Zheleznodorozhnyi sputnik po kurortam . . . Po Peterburgskomu vremeni* (Rostov-on-Don, 1913).

thousand new residents a year from 1890 on.[108] Once the Baltic became a day's ride away and the economy in the capital could support thousands of residents with discretionary income, a summer rental on the seashore became preferable for some to a dacha in the city's suburbs.

Tourism here repeated the familiar formula: it followed the royals, who came to bathe in the 1860s, and then the railroad.[109] A guidebook for the coastal area in 1892 evidenced the ironical chauvinism of Russia's imperial presence on the windowsill of the West.[110] Beginning with the admonition that it is not necessary to vacation abroad, the author appeared pleased that foreigners, especially Germans, would come to Russia. He considered Riga "one of Russia's prettiest cities,"[111] and had much to say about the local language problem. First he tried to amuse the reader with the locals' poor translations into Russian, but then his frustration became apparent in criticisms of signs that appeared in German and local languages. He also noted with disgust that Russian tourists "become quickly Germanized" by falling into the obnoxious, noisy behavior habits of these foreigners.[112] He estimated that summer bathers in the Gulf of Riga, inexpensive when compared to places closer to Petersburg, numbered up to sixty thousand.[113]

The two major resorts built on the Baltic seacoast were Ust'-Narva and Druskeniki, both of which remain active today. Ust'-Narva, in present-day Estonia, became "the pearl of the region by the end of the nineteenth century."[114] In the 1870s a local entrepreneur, A. F. Gan, persuaded other local industrialists to finance the construction of a summer retreat. Gan also solicited support from the city council, which gave money for a road, essential for bringing people to the dachas, hotels, and pansiony. Connected by both shipping and rail lines, Ust'-Narva was welcoming fourteen thousand summer tourists by 1914. Moreover, it served the artistic elite from the imperial capital much as Palm Springs developed from the Hollywood crowd seeking respite from Los Angeles. The common vacationers might thus hope to associate with the famous, sharing the same resort area. And who knew who might be spotted out on a promenade?

Where Ust'-Narva was the result of a specific entrepreneurial vision, Druskeniki boasted the finest natural springs in the area. Located in present-day Lithuania and inland from the Baltic, when the railroad finally connected the resort to the major lines in 1908, the number of those coming for the wa-

108. James H. Bater, "Between Old and New: St. Petersburg in the Late Imperial Era," in *City in Late Imperial Russia*, ed. Hamm, 51.

109. Dr. O. F. Veber, *Pribaltiiskii morskoi kurort "Libava"* (Libava, 1911), 3–4.

110. *Putevoditel' po kurortam i morskim kupan'iam Baltiiskogo poberezh'ia* (St. Petersburg, 1892).

111. Ibid., 47.

112. Ibid., 49.

113. Ibid., 56.

114. Krivosheev, *Narva-Iyesuu*, 15.

ters immediately doubled from eight thousand to sixteen thousand.[115] A joint-stock development company showed profits of almost 20,000 rubles in 1909.[116]

Memoirs of an excursion by Evgeniia Lovitskaia during the summer of 1912 reveal how accessible tourism had become.[117] A single woman traveling alone, she registered no qualms about her solitary position. Looking to get out of Petersburg, Lovitskaia settled on Druskeniki over the objections of her doctor and friends, who thought she should seek out one of the more fashionable German spas. Their fears, though, betrayed ignorance of this region, whose natural beauty was matched by the peace and quiet it afforded, and she described happily how much the local environment had been adapted to accommodate customers such as herself. Like most who came for the entire season, Lovitskaia planned to stay in a hotel only until she could find less expensive lodgings. Not thinking to make advance reservations, she had problems upon arrival, but eventually found a suitable room.

Exploring the town, she discovered the need to purchase tickets for everything from the baths to entrance to the park if she wanted to listen to the orchestra. The system of ticketing was designed more as a medium for maintaining order than to gouge the tourist's ruble because it was intended to keep potential predators away from tourist prey. At the train station, for example, Lovitskaia had met a young man who complained about how much more fun Druskeniki had been before all the new regulations. Lovitskaia's problem with the tickets was that they represented the exact precision with which everything operated. In the old days she could have lingered in the baths, but now someone else had a ticket and could take her cabin at the top of the hour. Staying on until the season ended in September, she departed with the thought that, although it might not compare to the famous European resorts, here one can find "all the peace, loveliness, therapy, and at an affordable price!"[118]

Other indicators of the growth of the tourist industry illustrate how pervasive the idea of a vacation was becoming. Russia's network of rivers, for example, began to offer more than routes connecting travel destinations.[119] An 1894 guidebook attempted to turn the attention away from the Crimea to Russia's other natural wonders, in this instance, the Volga.[120] In 1900 a Saratov publishing firm began publishing an annual *Guidebook of the Volga and*

115. Dr. S. Konverskii, *Otchet o deiatel'nosti Druskeninskogo kurorta za 1907–1911* (Vil'na, 1911), 10.

116. *Otchet aktsionernogo obshchestva Druskeninskikh mineral'nykh vod za 1909* (Vil'na, 1910), 27.

117. Evgeniia Lovitskaia, *Na dache-kurorte (v Druskenikakh)* (St. Petersburg, 1913).

118. Ibid., 39.

119. The ROPT advertised its tours especially along the Volga. *Putevoditel' po Volge*, 5th ed. (Nizhnii Novgorod, 1889).

120. Sidorov, *Volga*. Wood, *Tourist's Russia*, 154–82, describes tours of the Volga for potential western tourists.

1.3. Partaking of the mud baths in Druskeniki. Louise McReynolds, *Russia at Play: Leisure Activities at the End of the Tsarist Era* (Cornell University Press, 2002), 180.

Its Tributaries, so filled with advertisements for cruise ships, hotels, and restaurants along the rivers as to indicate a tremendous appetite for this sort of tour. The building of the Trans-Siberian Railroad eased transportation for those living in Russia's Far Eastern provinces and contributed to the commercialization of the Anninskie mineral waters after 1900. A boat from Harbin ferried tourists more cheaply than the train.[121] In fact, the resorts going up distant from the metropolitan areas advertised their economical rates and served a more localized population than the Black Sea resorts. Where once the Caucasus mountain range had substituted for the Alps,[122] with the completion of the railroad Russia now found its Switzerland in Siberia.[123]

By the 1880s industry promoters were asking why Russians crossed the borders of their empire to visit "foreign," meaning "European" in this case, spas, such as the ultra-fashionable resorts at Carlsbad and Baden-Baden. Better accommodations, which included medical attention as well as lodging and entertainment, seemed the best answer.[124] As one doctor pointed out, however,

121. *Kurort Anninskie mineral'nye vody arend. Dr. V. M. Porvatova i Ko.* (Vladikavkaz, 1912).

122. Layton, *Russian Literature and Empire,* 39–46, discusses the Caucasus as the Russian Alps in the literary imagination.

123. V. P. Aleksandrov, *Illiustr. putevoditel' po Borovomu* (Tomsk, 1913).

124. See, for example, *Krymskie mineral'nye griazi v derevne Saki, i morskie kupan'ia v gorode Evpatorii. Iz vospominanii priznatel'nogo patsienta A. N. N-na* (St. Petersburg, 1883); and

1.4. Enjoying the new fad of roller skating, a popular pastime at resorts. Louise McReynolds, *Russia at Play: Leisure Activities at the End of the Tsarist Era* (Cornell University Press, 2002), 181.

inadequate local arrangements forced many Russians to go to western spas when they would have preferred to remain home, at ease with the culture and language. This observer also noted Russia's national inferiority complex vis-à-vis the West, but without demonstrating any awareness of the irony that Russia's premier tourist areas differed significantly in language and culture from the ethnic Slavic tourists.[125]

The drive to ensure that Russian tourists would spend their rubles at home was greatly abetted by the outbreak of World War I. *Pace* Lenin's theory that imperialism had pushed capitalism to the next stage, international business interests seemed to have rendered national borders quite porous. But war proved good for some elements in the economy and good for nationalism; with the routes to Baden-Baden closed, Russians who would have otherwise headed west had to look east. The privately operated Russian Society for Tourism and Study of the Native Land opened its doors in 1916 to tap the flow of tourist rubles no longer flooding west. The founders appealed on the grounds that "our spacious fatherland includes in its territory many places that, in terms of natural beauty and historical, cultural, and economic importance not only do not stand second to western Europe's, but often surpass them."[126]

In the last years of the imperial era, Russia's tourists represented progress, modernity, and a multicultural nationalism driven by a capitalist engine that dared itself not be stalled by traditional prejudices. Annually by the tens of thousands, they sought cosmopolitan and adventurous identities through the multiple opportunities for contrast offered by travel.[127] Gender barriers were also toppling, exemplified by advice in 1913 to women joining hiking or riding excursions that they should "dress in the masculine spirit."[128] The accumulation of cultural capital through tourism offered the possibility of canceling social divisions of the past, while creating a new sense of self derived from issues of nationalism and imperialism. When Russians found themselves transformed into Soviet citizens following the Bolshevik Revolution, many again turned to tourism as a source of self-fashioning. Despite the socialist politics that now underlay the industry, consumption of material and metaphorical goods remained key to possibilities for self-transformation through "the tour."

O. A. Khaletskii, *Kavkazskie mineral'nye vody, v meditsinskom otnoshenii* (St. Petersburg, 1883).

125. Guchin, *O klimatolechebnykh mestakh*, 33.

126. *Russkoe obshchestvo turizma i otchiznovedeniia* (Petrograd, 1916), 1.

127. In 1903 almost seventy-five thousand Russians visited mud and mineral baths. Those numbers rose yearly, to over a hundred thousand by 1913. *Kratkie statisticheskie dannye o russkikh lechebnykh mestnostiakh i ikh posetitelei. Doklad Dr. S. A. Novosel'skii* (St. Petersburg, 1913), 3–5.

128. Aleksandrov, *Illiustr. putevoditel'*, 30.

CHAPTER 2

Russian Military Tourism

The Crisis of the Crimean War Period

Susan Layton

The military has remained surprisingly marginal in the booming field of research into travel and travel writing. The British observer Sir Thomas Palmer included soldiers in the typology of travelers he compiled in 1606.[1] But today's scholars have barely begun considering the relationships among military service, leisure travel, and the travelogue components of military memoirs.[2] We may define "military tourism" as a typically leisure-travel program of visual, cultural, and material consumption pursued during service away from home.[3] Military tourists relish sightseeing, transnational encounters, and patronizing markets, shops, taverns, restaurants, theaters, and so forth. Like a civilian obliged to travel in the line of work, the military tourist has a preset "itinerary." Yet within those constraints, the military campaigner may find opportunities to profit personally from "travel valued for its own sake."[4] The individual's financial resources, position in the military hierarchy, preferences, and expectations resulting from education will determine the aims and scope of the tourist agenda.[5]

A combination of economic and political factors appears to have made military tourism particularly significant in imperial Russia. During the eighteenth century, only a tiny number of the Russian elite could afford pleasure trips abroad. Some Russian nobles of the time reaped tourist benefits from service in the diplomatic

---

1. William H. Sherman, "Stirrings and Searchings (1500–1720)," in *The Cambridge Companion to Travel Writing*, ed. Peter Hulme and Tim Youngs (Cambridge, 2002), 22.

2. Studies mentioning soldiers include Paul Fussell, *Abroad: British Literary Traveling between the Wars* (Oxford, 1980), 6; and Anne E. Gorsuch, " 'There's No Place Like Home': Soviet Tourism in Late Stalinism," *Slavic Review* 62, no. 4 (2003): 771. On travel pieces by the officers Konstantin Batiushkov and Alexander Bestuzhev-Marlinskii, consult Andreas Schönle, *Authenticity and Fiction in the Russian Literary Journey, 1790–1840* (Cambridge, Mass., 2000), 122–44.

3. On "visual consumption," see John Urry, *Consuming Places* (London, 1995; repr. 1997), 1, 187–92; and Urry, *The Tourist Gaze: Leisure and Travel in Contemporary Societies* (London, 1990), especially 11, 135–36.

4. Quote from analysis of work-related travel in Judith Adler, "Travel as Performed Art," *American Journal of Sociology* 94, no. 6 (1989): 1370.

5. On "wide differentials" in Russian officers' pay, see John Keep, *Soldiers of the Tsar: Army and Society in Russia, 1462–1874* (Oxford, 1985), 237–39, 250.

corps or terms of study in western Europe.[6] But all those individuals belonged to the privileged few. Barring exceptional luck, the average eighteenth-century noble-man could get outside Russia only by participating in military operations (most notably the Seven Years' War).[7] Military service retained its appeal as a travel op-portunity in the nineteenth century. By the 1840s, when Thomas Cook's tours opened the Continent to the British bourgeoisie, there were still relatively few Rus-sians with the financial means to undertake leisure trips abroad. Russia's bour-geois tourists—merchants, for example, keen to acquire cultural capital in the West—did not arrive en masse until the late nineteenth century.[8] Yet, during the campaigns into western Europe in 1813–1815, tens of thousands of Russian army men saw Paris and other major sites of Grand Tourism.

After Nicholas I ascended the throne, new political obstacles conspired with traditional economic constraints to continue enhancing military service as an opportunity for stimulating travel. Under first the impact of the Decembrist re-volt and then the revolution in Paris in 1830, Nicholas I erratically restricted Russian pleasure trips to the West. Best known is his refusal to allow Alexan-der Pushkin to go abroad. But Prince Peter Viazemskii also never managed to obtain official permission to visit Paris (he went anyway, in "semilegal" fash-ion in 1838, after Nicholas let him go to Germany for medical treatment).[9] Having hitherto blocked leisure travel to the West on a case-by-case basis, Nicholas banned it entirely during the Crimean War, a time when many Rus-sians would have liked to go to the international exposition in Paris.[10] These economic and political barriers to Russian travel abroad favored the develop-ment of an alternative: an imperial "pleasure periphery" in the North Cauca-sus and the Crimea, two areas that military as well as civilian tourists en-joyed.[11] In addition, the same barriers whetted the reading public's appetite for military tourism as vicarious experience.

A vast topic, Russian military tourism might be studied from many angles. Following the lead of James Buzard's *Beaten Track*, the present chapter ap-

6. Wladimir Berelowitch, "La France dans le 'Grand Tour' des nobles russes au cours de la second moitié du XVIIIe siècle," *Cahiers du monde russe et soviétique* 34, no. 1–2 (1993): 193–210. See also Sara Dickinson, "The Russian Tour of Europe before Fonvizin: Travel Writing as Literary Endeavor in Eighteenth-Century Russia," *Slavic and East European Journal* 45, no. 1 (2001): 1–29.

7. Marc Raeff, *Origins of the Russian Intelligentsia: The Eighteenth-Century Nobility* (New York, 1966), 70–72.

8. On the rise of the bourgeois tourist, see McReynolds in this volume; and Christopher Ely, "The Origins of Russian Scenery: Volga River Tourism and Russian Landscape Aesthetics," *Slavic Review* 62, no. 4 (2003): 670–82.

9. V. Nechaeva and S. Durylin, "P. A. Viazemskii i Frantsiia," *Literaturnoe nasledstvo* 31/32 (1937): 113–17.

10. On the exposition's appeal to *turisty*, see *Sovremennik* 50 (1855), 4: part 5: 73–75.

11. Quoted phrase from Louis Turner and John Ash, *The Golden Hordes: International Tourism and the Pleasure Periphery* (New York, 1976).

proaches the imperial Russian military tourist as a public identity constituted in print, beginning in the Napoleonic era.[12] Our main sources of knowledge about the public face of military tourism were officers' memoirs, their literary works (especially those of Mikhail Lermontov and Leo Tolstoy), and responses to those writings in the periodical press. Dealing with a selection of prominent publications, my investigation concentrates on the Crimean War, a time of particular interest. It was then that Russian officers' pursuit of leisure-travel agendas first created discernible tensions in the army as well as society. By looking into this critical juncture in the history of Russian military tourism, we gain insight into a broader, neglected problem: when did Russians begin referring to themselves and others as *turisty*, and what meanings did they attribute to that term?

Antecedents of the Crimean War

Writing Russian officers first began styling themselves "travelers" (*puteshestvenniki*) in the Napoleonic era, when Nikolai Karamzin's *Letters of a Russian Traveler* remained the preeminent account of Grand Tourism, Russian style. The pioneer was Fedor Glinka (1786–1880), a versatile author whose *Letters of a Russian Officer* covered his military service from 1805 through 1814.[13] Glinka's memoirs, which made him a prominent literary figure of the time, struck his contemporaries as a transposition of Karamzin into a military key.[14] In recollecting the campaigns in western Europe, Glinka expressed concerns that allow us to read him as a Decembrist sympathizer in the making.[15] His *Letters* about Prussia, for example, related the local peasants' community spirit and prosperity to "benevolent government."[16] But striking as such observations may be, they coexist with the more prominent theme of the personal excitement of encountering the West.

A provincial noble who served as an adjutant of General Mikhail Miloradovich, Lieutenant Glinka lent the campaigns abroad the aura of a poor

---

12. On approaching tourism "mainly from the direction of literary analysis," see James Buzard, *The Beaten Track: European Tourism, Literature, and the Ways to Culture, 1800–1918* (Oxford, 1991), 13.

13. F. N. Glinka, *Pis'ma russkago ofitsera o Pol'she, avstriiskikh vladeniiakh, Prussii i Frantsii s podrobnym opisaniem pokhoda Rossiian protivu Frantsuzov v 1805 i 1806, takzhe otechestvennoi i zagranichnoi voiny s 1812 po 1815 god*, 8 vols. (Moscow, 1815–16; first edition, 1806; 3d ed., 1870).

14. Commentary in *Kliatva vernosti sderzhali. 1812 godu v russkoi literature*, ed. S. R. Serkov (Moscow, 1987), 339–40. See also Schönle, *Authenticity and Fiction*, 7.

15. Glinka joined the Union of Salvation in 1816 and aided the Decembrist Northern Society. After the Decembrist revolt, he was removed from service and banished to Petrozavodsk.

16. Glinka, *Pis'ma*, 5: 8–13. See also Keep, *Soldiers of the Tsar*, 254.

man's Grand Tour.[17] He remembered enjoying active leisure (horseback explorations of Saxon hill country; excursions to battlefields of the Seven Years' War). He also recalled the hospitality, especially the breakfasts, he had savored as an officer quartered in the homes of prosperous middle-class people in Germany. But Glinka expressed greatest gusto for cultural consumption in cities. Recollecting museums and monuments in Dresden and Paris, he featured himself raptly contemplating famous artworks, including Raphael's *Sistine Madonna*, the Belvedere Apollo, the Medici Venus, and the horses of Venice's St. Marco basilica (war trophies Napoleon had installed on the Arc du Carrousel in the Tuileries). Glinka's *Letters* concluded with *A Description of Paris*, an illustrated volume that imitated the style of a guidebook ("That is the Champs-Elysées!—a name known to anybody who has read something about Paris. Let us go took at it!"). Glinka likened the French capital to "Sodom and Gomorrah" but confessed succumbing to temptations. On their first day in Paris, he and his comrades had purchased fashionable clothing to wear instead of their uniforms. They stayed in a posh hotel near the Palais Royale. Even if disapprovingly, Glinka looked at luxury goods on sale in the adjacent shopping arcade. He frequented the highbrow theater and tried a fancy restaurant, where "poetic" terms on the menu had disguised plain, overpriced food.[18] As an adjutant, Glinka sampled Grand Tourism way beyond the means of his social estate, and he expressed gratitude to the army for having given him that opportunity.

Enfolding traditions of the European travelogue into the military memoir, Glinka's *Letters* launched a hybrid genre that flourished in Russia well into the 1830s. Presenting themselves as "travelers," these officers of the Napoleonic wars had varied social backgrounds and projected individualized authorial personalities.[19] But uniting them all were assumptions about tourism as the military hero's reward. Glinka's representative memoirs presented the army as a collective of all ranks united in their performance of "sacred duty" to the fatherland, the tsar, and the Orthodox faith. Suffering and death might befall both the lord and the peasant, as Glinka stressed by recounting battles in gruesome detail. But if war was a series of "labors" (*trudy*), offsetting the work came "leisure" (*dosug*). Warriors needed a "breather" now and then, to stay

17. For Glinka's self-image as a "poor lieutenant," see *Pis'ma*, 4: 103–4. On job hunting as a "poor man's Grand Tour," see Judith Adler, "Youth on the Road: Reflections on the History of Tramping," *Annals of Tourism Research* 12, no. 3 (1985): 335–54.

18. Glinka, *Pis'ma*, 5: 15–25, 29–34, 49–56, 61, 146–47; 7: 26–36; 8: 9–16, 22–23, 51–64, 80–128.

19. Examples are I. Lazhechnikov, *Pokhodnye zapiski russkago ofitsera* (St. Petersburg, 1820); I. R. [Il'ia Radozhitskii], *Pokhodnye zapiski artillerista s 1812 po 1816 god*, 4 vols. (Moscow, 1835); and A. Mikhailovskii-Danilevskii, *Zapiski 1814 i 1815 godov*, 2d ed. (St. Petersburg, 1832). Excerpts from the latter two appeared in periodicals between 1816 and the early 1820s.

2.1. Cossack occupiers of Paris sample the beverages of tradeswomen. Drawing by G. E. Opitsa,
1814. V. M. Glinka and A. V. Pomarnatskii, *Otechestvennaia voina 1812 goda v
khudozhestvennykh i istoricheskikh pamiatnikakh iz sobranii Ermitazha* (Leningrad, 1963), 42.

fit to fulfill whatever new agendas Holy Russia would set.[20] This style of thought conformed to Russia's age-old service ethic.[21] Only now, the work-leisure model served to legitimate the socially humble officer's breakthrough into elitist Grand Tourism, at a time when the vast majority of Russian readers could only dream of visiting western Europe.

Russia's writing officer-travelers of the Napoleonic wars won the ever-lasting esteem of civilian readers who revered their military achievements while desiring to replicate their tourist experiences. Just as Karamzin had served as a pathbreaker for Glinka and other Russian military travelers, so did the military memoirs, in turn, feed back into civilian leisure-travel agendas. The poet Vasilii Zhukovskii went abroad in 1821, serving as Russian teacher to the Grand Duchess Alexandra Fedorovna (wife of the future Nicholas I). A friend of Glinka's and an admirer of his *Letters*, Zhukovskii produced a travelogue casting his journey as a cultural rite of passage.[22] This accent on acculturation paralleled Glinka's narrative. Furthermore, Zhukovskii's sightseeing program overlapped Glinka's, the outstanding coincidence being the *Sistine Madonna*. Raphael's painting had long been the object of pilgrimages on the part of leisure travelers, including Karamzin. But this artwork's reputation as something every cultivated Russian should see was newly strengthened through Glinka's self-presentation as a sensitive soul profiting from military service to acquire cultural capital in the West.

In parallel to the experience of the Napoleonic era, identical interests and activities also united Russian military and civilian tourists in the Caucasus, a theater of colonial war from the late 1810s into the 1860s. Under the impact of Pushkin's romantic poem *The Prisoner of the Caucasus* (1822), the scenic North Caucasus borderland became a site Russian officers and civilian travelers alike sought to see. Early harbingers of military tourism in the region were the *récits de voyage* of Il'ia Radozhitskii, a veteran of the Napoleonic wars who would also take part in the Russo-Turkish War of 1828–1829. Beginning in 1823, he modeled himself as an exalted consumer of the Caucasus's spectacular scenery.[23] But as his extensive citation of Pushkin's poetry foretold, literary masters rather than run-of-the-mill memoirists were the men destined to give Caucasian military tourism an extraordinarily high public profile. During the 1830s the travelogues and stories of the military exile Alexander

20. Glinka, *Pis'ma*, 4: 101, 112–15; 5: 150–52. See also 1: 92–94, 97–98, 103–5; 4: 34–40, 66–73; 5: 112–13, 120–24, 133–34.

21. For stimulating remarks on the service ethic, see Elise Kimerling Wirtschafter, "Military Service and Social Hierarchy: The View from Eighteenth-Century Russian Theater," in *The Military and Society in Russia, 1450–1917*, ed. Eric Lohr and Marshall Poe (Boston, 2002), 227–40.

22. On Glinka and Zhukovskii, see F. N. Glinka, "Preduvedomlenie," in *Pis'ma russkogo ofitsera* (Moscow, 1985), 119–20; and O. B. Lebedeva and A. S. Ianushkevich, eds., *V. A. Zhukovskii v vospominaniiakh sovremennikov* (Moscow, 1999), 575. On Zhukovskii's journey as cultural initiation, see Schönle, *Authenticity and Fiction*, 84–88, 98–110.

23. An example is Il'ia Radozhitskii, "Doroga ot reki Dona do Georgievska na prostranstve 500 verst," *Otechestvennye zapiski* (1823), part 15, no. 41: 343–75.

Bestuzhev-Marlinskii represented Caucasian landscape in ecstatic terms that prompted adventure-hungry young Russians to enlist in the army in hopes of seeing those places for themselves. Much of Lermontov's poetry and his novel *A Hero of Our Time* (1840) had the same impact.[24]

By Lermontov's era and as immortalized in his novel, the spas of the North Caucasus borderland had become fashionable tourist centers where civilian travelers and officers intermingled, taking cures or simply enjoying rest and recreation.[25] Lermontov knew this imperial pleasure periphery first hand. Entailing no combat, his first military exile in the Caucasus (1837–1838) had turned out to be "a long holiday" spent mainly in Piatigorsk, where he was sent to take the waters for rheumatism and influenza.[26] If we can believe Lermontov's testimony, one of the first things he did at the spa was go shopping. He bought six pairs of *souliers circassiennes* (Circassian slippers) to send to ladies in Petersburg.[27] Although cast primarily as an aficionado of mountain scenery, Lermontov's high-society dandy Ensign Grigorii Pechorin of *A Hero of Our Time* also engages in material consumption in Piatigorsk. He keeps a supply of champagne in his rented accommodations and acquires a little booty of empire at a local shop—a Persian rug for which he outbids the Russian vacationer Princess Mary.[28] Russian officers had been in the habit of making such purchases at least since General Alexei Ermolov's time as commander in chief of the Caucasian army (1816–1827). In addition to rugs, other prized commodities were shawls, daggers, swords, *burkas* (felt cloaks), and "Circassian" tunics with sewn-in cartridge pockets.[29] According to a story by the novelist and critic Alexander Druzhinin, dealing with the spas in the 1850s, other souvenirs available from shops were chibouks, pieces of silk, entire outfits of "Circassian" garb, or simply a "stick inscribed 'Caucasus, such and such a year.' "[30] Along with active leisure, mineral water cures, and gazing at moun-

24. Susan Layton, *Russian Literature and Empire: Conquest of the Caucasus from Pushkin to Tolstoy* (Cambridge, 1994), 54, 127–29; and Lewis Bagby, *Alexander Bestuzhev-Marlinskii and Russian Byronism* (University Park, Penn., 1995), 7.

25. Laurence Kelly, *Lermontov: Tragedy in the Caucasus* (London, 1977), 67–69; V. A. Manuilov, ed., *Lermontovskaia entsiklopediia* (Moscow, 1981), 459; Layton, *Russian Literature and Empire*, 54–55; and McReynolds.

26. Lewis Bagby, "Introduction," in *Lermontov's* A Hero of Our Time: *A Critical Companion*, ed. Bagby (Evanston, Ill., 2002), 10.

27. M. Iu. Lermontov, letter to M. A. Lopukhina, 31 May 1837, in his *Sobranie sochinenii v chetyrekh tomakh*, 4 vols. (Moscow, 1983–1984), 4: 427.

28. On "booty brought home from empire" as stimulus to tourism, see Turner and Ash, *Golden Hordes*, 19.

29. A. P. Ermolov. *Materialy dlia ego biografii*, ed. M. N. Pogodin (Moscow, 1863), part 4: 293–94; A. A. Bestuzhev-Marlinskii, "Razskaz russkogo ofitsera, byvshego v plenu u gortsev," in his *Polnoe sobranie sochinenii*, 12 vols., 3d ed. (St. Petersburg, 1838–1839), 10: 20; and Lermontov, "Kavkazets," in *Sobranie sochinenii*, 4: 143–45.

30. A. Druzhinin, "Russkii cherkes," in his *Sobranie sochinenii*, 8 vols. (St. Petersburg, 1865–67), 2: 206–16. For more on the turisty theme, see my "Colonial Mimicry and Disenchantment in

2.2. Lermontov's wounded cadet
Grushnitskii with the *turistka*
Princess Mary at the Piatigorsk
spa. Drawing by M. A. Vrubel'. S.
Durylin, *Geroi nashego vremeni
M. Iu. Lermontova* (Ann Arbor,
Mich., 1986), 151.

tain scenery, the hunt for souvenirs characterized both military and civilian
tourism in the North Caucasus.

Tourism as the Pleasure of Looking

The writings my chapter has surveyed so far featured officers engaging in behavior we consider typically touristy. All the same, none of those sources labeled a military man a *turist*. Not yet current in Russian in Lermontov's era,
the word turist was glossed as a "traveler, primarily a travel-lover" in an early
twentieth-century enlargement of Vladimir Dal's dictionary.[31] In conformity to

Alexander Druzhinin's 'A Russian Circassian' and Other Stories," *Russian Review* 60, no. 1
(2001): 57–58, 63–66.
    31. Vladimir Dal', *Tolkovyi slovar' zhivogo velikorusskogo iazyka*, ed. I. A. Beaudoin de
Courtenay, 4 vols. (St. Petersburg, 1903–1909), 4: 871.

that neutral definition, Viazemskii, in Paris for the first time in 1838, saw nothing remarkable in the title of Stendhal's recently published *Mémoires d'un touriste*. Viazemskii's letters about visiting Paris described other sightseers as cretins, relying on guidebooks to tell them what to look at.[32] Nonetheless, Viazemskii apparently believed he too was a tourist, only in the intelligent manner of his new acquaintance Stendhal. As used in Pavel Annenkov's 1841 account of visiting Venice, turist was similarly neutral.[33] By the late 1840s, however, some Russian authors were stereotyping the turist as a leisure traveler unable or just unwilling to derive serious knowledge from a trip.[34] In 1847, for instance, Fedor Dostoevsky sarcastically declared that an "ultrafamous tourist" from abroad had published slander about Russia after a blinkered visit of Petersburg.[35] The foreigner targeted there was most likely the notorious Russophobe the Marquis de Custine.[36] Arising from offended nationalism, Dostoevsky's remark cast the turist as an alien other.

But while vacationing in western Europe in 1848, one of Dostoevsky's obscure compatriots, named Gersevanov, was pleased to designate himself "just a tourist" (*prostoi turist*), as opposed to a "cultivated traveler" (*obrazovannyi puteshestvennik*). Gersevanov explained that the latter type might stay in a place for months at a time. Our turist, however, was just passing through and knew it.[37] His itinerary was France, Switzerland, and northern Italy, and he was seeking "pleasure every step of the way." Gersevanov craved for beauty (perceived especially in the Alps and artworks). But in Geneva, he tried to visit prisons as well because he thought a turist should emulate the urban *flâneur*, keen to observe everything in his vicinity (alas, the prisons were all closed to sightseers that day).[38] If not so extreme, Gersevanov's desire to see the incarcerated was similar to the curiosity that drove tourists to the Paris morgue to look at unidentified corpses on public display.[39] Both programs invite classification as "negative sightseeing."[40] Expecting to find the sight somehow disagreeable, the tourist goes anyway, believing that the sight's very availability

32. Nechaeva and Durylin, "Viazemskii i Frantsiia," 122, 128.

33. P. V. Annenkov, *Parizhskie pis'ma*, ed. I. N. Konobeevskaia (Moscow, 1983), 19.

34. On tourism as a practice "incapable of producing serious knowledge," see James Clifford, *Routes: Travel and Translation in the Late Twentieth Century* (Cambridge, Mass., 1997), 65.

35. F. M. Dostoevskii, "Peterburgskii letopis'" (1847), in his *Polnoe sobranie sochinenii v tridtsati tomakh* (Leningrad, 1972–88), 18: 24.

36. Joseph Frank, *Dostoevsky: The Seeds of Revolt, 1821–1849* (Princeton, N.J., 1976), 228; and commentary in Dostoevskii, *Polnoe sobranie sochinenii*, 18: 220–21.

37. For "just passing through" as the tourist's conscious program, see Dean MacCannell, *The Tourist: A New Theory of the Leisure Class* (New York, 1976), 51.

38. Gersevanov [sic], "Iz putevykh vpechatlenii turista. Pereezd cherez Simplon," *Otechestvennye zapiski* 57 (March 1848), part 8: 5, 10. Descending Mt. Blanc on a mule, Gersevanov found "pathetic" the "exhausted, sweaty" British turisty hiking up the slope.

39. Viazemskii viewed corpses in the Paris morgue: Nechaeva and Durylin, "Viazemskii i Frantsiia," 126.

40. MacCannell, *Tourist*, 39–40. MacCannell includes slums and garbage heaps in the category of "negative sightseeing" but considers the Paris morgue a "work display" (71–73).

makes it something that *should* be seen, as a component of the "whole" local milieu.

Although strictly concerned with the pleasing, Druzhinin also embraced turist as a self-descriptive synonym of the flâneur. This occurred in his "Observations of a Petersburg Tourist," a newspaper feuilleton he began publishing during the Crimean War. The first installment defined every creative writer as a "consummate tourist" (*turist iz turistov*), a "traveling observer," moving about in search of inspiration, at home or abroad, in the city or country. The authorial persona's sophisticated friends told him he had to go to Paris to practice *flânerie* because there was just not enough to see in Russia, not even in the capital. Setting out to prove those skeptics wrong, the self-styled turist found plenty to ogle in Petersburg, especially on Nevskii Prospekt. The feuilleton likened flânerie to attending an "opera," whose chorus was no less captivating to watch than the "diva." The "Petersburg tourist" thus fashioned himself as a delighted consumer of picturesque spectacles that featured the city's whole social spectrum.[41]

While Druzhinin relished playing turist on the printed page, spectators were feasting their eyes on war in the Crimea. Among the British and French military elite there were officers who took in combat as a spectator sport and enjoyed the "operatic" effects of the bombardments of Sevastopol. Beginning in the spring of 1855, British and French leisure travelers also sailed to the Crimea to watch military operations. They came "to see the fun," as a British gentleman of the period put it; and they included society ladies, featured in a London newspaper illustration that April.[42] Russia's leisured travel-lovers probably would have behaved much the same, had their country been winning the war. Indeed as it was, some wives of Russian statesmen and officers (including Countess Kankrin and Countess Osten-Saken) apparently took the war as an excuse for a trip to balmy climes. We hear of them amassed in Kishinev and Skuliany in February 1855. The ladies received guests there in Petersburg's high-society style, "zealously frequented the theater, and went out dancing in the evening."[43] The official French historian, the Baron de Bazancourt, claimed to have seen women from Sevastopol perched on wagons to watch the battle of Alma (September 1854).[44] Prince Viktor Bariatinskii and Captain Robert Chodasiewicz wrote that they, too, saw Russian women at

41. Druzhinin, "Zametki peterburgskago turista" (1855), in his *Sobranie sochinenii*, 8: 111–17, 644–45. On Russia's emergent "culture of spectacle," see Katia Dianina, "Passage to Europe: Dostoevskii in the St. Petersburg Arcade," *Slavic Review* 62, no. 2 (2003): 239–44.

42. Ulrich Keller, *The Ultimate Spectacle: A Visual History of the Crimean War* (Singapore, 2001), 4–13; and Robert B. Edgerton, *Death or Glory: The Legacy of the Crimean War* (Boulder, Colo., 1999), 228–33.

43. "Zapiski N. G. Zalesov," *Russkaia starina* 114 (June 1903): 537; and "Zapiski Vladimira Ivanovicha Dena [Dehn]," *Russkaia starina* 65 (February 1890): 571–72.

44. Albert Seaton, *The Crimean War: A Russian Chronicle* (London, 1977), 101.

Alma.[45] But the oft-told anecdote about Russian ladies watching the battle from makeshift bleachers appears to be a product of Russophobic imagination.[46]

Although Colonel Porfirii Glebov's diary never referred to civilian spectators of the Crimean War, it seems plausible that an awareness of their presence might have prompted him to seize upon the word turist as a derogatory description of Second Lieutenant Leo Tolstoy. Writing a few days after the fall of Sevastopol, Glebov vented his anger at officers he felt had roamed around too much during the siege. In recent weeks, for instance, those men had been frequenting Bakhchisarai (a place Pushkin's romantic poem *The Fountain of Bakhchisarai* helped to make a tourist Mecca from the 1820s onward).[47] Calling his targets "parasites" and "Bashi-Bazouks," Glebov singled out "Count Tolstoy" for special abuse:

> Tolstoy makes an effort to smell gunpowder, but only on the run like a partisan, distancing himself from the difficulties and deprivations war entails. He travels around from place to place like a tourist, but at the sound of a shot, he appears on the battlefield; once the engagement ends, he leaves again at his own sweet will, following his eyes wherever they lead him. Not everybody manages to conduct war in such an agreeable fashion.[48]

Tolstoy's combat record was in fact more impressive than Glebov allowed. That spring, Tolstoy served at Sevastopol's most exposed bastion (number four). He took part in the Chernaia River battle (4/16 August) and in March 1856 was promoted to lieutenant for "outstanding bravery and courage" at Sevastopol.[49] Glebov's value judgment nonetheless retains historical interest. In the privacy of his diary, Glebov had chosen a relatively new word, turist, to express the professional Russian soldier's traditional resentment toward footloose aristocrats whose military service was clearly transitory.

Had Glebov known Tolstoy was the author of "Sevastopol in December" (first published under the initials L. N. T.), he might have realized the injustice

---

45. Seaton, *Crimean War*, 101; and Captain R. Hodasevich [Chodasiewicz], *A Voice from within the Walls of Sevastopol* (London, 1856), 151. Chodasiewicz fled on horseback to the British in March 1855.

46. The bleacher story apparently stemmed from the Baron de Bazancourt and the following skirmisher who based his tale on hearsay: Henry Tyrrell, *The History of the War with Russia*, 2 vols. (London, 1858), 1: 227. Among those citing Tyrrell is Keller, *Ultimate Spectacle*, 12.

47. On Pushkin and the Crimea's rise as a "tourist attraction," see Simon Karlinsky, "The Amber Beads of Crimea," *California Slavic Studies* 2 (1963): 108–9.

48. P. N. Glebov, diary entry for 13/25 September 1855, "Zapiski," *Russkaia starina* 121 (March 1905): 528–29.

49. Donna Tussing Orwin, "Chronology," in *The Cambridge Companion to Tolstoy*, ed. Orwin (Cambridge, 2002), 5.

of calling him a turist.[50] An artful piece of war correspondence, "Sevastopol in December" stigmatized tourism as a voyeuristic practice.[51] Tolstoy placed his reader in the position of a visitor taking a tour of Sevastopol and witnessing a valiant war effort on the part of the Russian military and the local population. Imitating the style of a guidebook, the author shows "you" (the reader) various sights and urges you to *look* at them.[52] The excursion starts at sunrise on Sapun Hill, where you have a lovely view of Sevastopol and the bay. You then go to the harbor and see an animated marketplace. Next stop: the military hospital, where the author-guide ushers the strong-nerved into the amputation room. Whoever goes in there, he asserts, will see "war in its real guise—blood, suffering, and death." At the end of the tour, you also see a Russian fighter fatally wounded at a bastion. In Gary Saul Morson's formulation, Tolstoy turns "you" into a "tourist of death," with the apparent aim of making every reader realize that sightseeing is "singularly inappropriate" in a military arena.[53]

Tolstoy's other two Sevastopol stories would sustain this anti-tourist theme of the clash between visual seductions and the ghastly reality of war. Gazing through the window of an elegant apartment in the city during the siege, the elite Russian officers of "Sevastopol in May" find distant bombs *un joli coup d'oeil* (beautiful sight).[54] But the narrative then challenges the aesthetic response by showing readers victims of bombs (heaps of wounded Russian soldiers on the bloody floor of the military hospital; and the simple folk of Sevastopol, losing their houses). "Sevastopol in August" highlights the beauty of the Crimea itself, as perceived by the newly arrived officer of the line, Volodia Kozel'tsov. But by the end of the story, both Kozel'tsov and his older brother have died in the fall of Sevastopol. In Tolstoy's representation, the Crimea's tourist allure stands in tragic contrast to the outcome of the war.

At least one Russian reader of the 1850s caught the anti-tourist drift of Tolstoy's Sevastopol narratives. That was Druzhinin, an eloquent witness, in light of his "Petersburg tourist" feuilletons. Discussing Tolstoy's Sevastopol stories in 1856, Druzhinin characterized the author as an active officer who knew both the necessity and tragedy of war. The antithesis, in Druzhinin's view, was the writing turist who merely watched war and then represented it as a colorful "spectacle" to please the "theatergoing reading public."[55] Druzhinin's ill-

50. The story first appeared in June 1855 in *Sovremennik* and the army organ *Russkii invalid* (The Russian Veteran). Tolstoy revealed his name to the reading public in January 1856, when *Sovremennik* ran "Sevastopol in August."

51. Gary Saul Morson, "The Reader as Voyeur: Tolstoi and the Poetics of Didactic Fiction," *Canadian-American Slavic Studies* 12, no. 4 (1978): 465–80.

52. Tolstoy was evidently reacting to an *Odessa Herald* article (April 1854) by an officer named Komarnitskii, who recounted a strictly picturesque visit of Sevastopol: see Iu. V. Lebedev, "L. N. Tolstoi na puti k 'Voine i miru' (Sevastopol' i 'Sevastopol'skie rasskazy')," *Russkaia literatura*, no. 4 (1976): 70–72.

53. Morson, "Reader as Voyeur," 470.

54. "Sevastopol in May" first appeared in Tolstoy's *Voennye razskazy* (St. Petersburg, 1856).

55. Druzhinin, *Sobranie sochinenii*, 6: 170–72, 246–47.

chosen examples of war tourists were "British journalists" (whose dispatches exposing British blunders and inefficiency in the Crimea had in fact caused a public outcry at home). The dichotomy between Tolstoy and the British was shaky. But the important thing here was Druzhinin's new conception of the turist as a voyeur in the military arena. Although Druzhinin would keep publishing his "Petersburg tourist" feuilletons, he had come to proscribe war as an object of the passive gaze and clearly did so under Tolstoy's influence.

War Artist at Work and Play: The Memoirs of Nikolai Berg

The most famous Russian writings that emerged from the Crimean conflict, Tolstoy's Sevastopol stories expressed the powerful moral imagination of a religious thinker in the bud. It should come as no surprise, however, that Tolstoy's resistance to the siege as spectacle was evidently aberrant.[56] One of Evgenii Tarle's archival discoveries was I. M. Debu's recollection of gazing through a telescope at soldiers being shot in the trench zone surrounding Sevastopol in October 1854.[57] In recalling his first day fighting at a Sevastopol bastion that winter, the socially middling artillery officer Andrei Ershov compared himself to an "inexperienced tourist, stunned by a fantastic spectacle." Ershov similarly remembered observing combat from the roof of Fort Nikolai along with "other spectators," including "ladies and maidens" from Sevastopol. This gunner even regretted that he had not been able to spend more time *watching* engagements in which he took part.[58] Ershov and other memoirists also suggest it was common for Russian officers, Sevastopol residents, and even Russian medical personnel to perceive the bombardments as eye-riveting light shows, "dreadful" but "beautiful."[59] In the recollection of the eminent military surgeon Dr. Nikolai Pirogov, the bombs produced "marvelous fireworks" night after night.[60]

---

56. As a staff officer at the siege of Silestria in the spring of 1854, Tolstoy had passively watched combat. "*Le spectacle était vraiment beau*" (The spectacle was truly beautiful), he wrote to T. A. Ergol'skaia, letter from 5 July 1854, in his *Polnoe sobranie sochinenii*, 90 vols. (Moscow, 1928–1958), 59: 270.

57. E. V. Tarle, *Krymskaia voina*, 2d ed. (Moscow, 1950), 138. Debu became one of Dostoevsky's co-conspirators in the Petrashevskii circle.

58. E. R. Sh-ov [A. I. Ershov], *Sevastopol'skiia vospominaniia artilleriiskago ofitsera* (St. Petersburg, 1858), 33–34, 97–99, 132, 147, 166, 168, 206–9. First published in *Biblioteka dlia chteniia* (1857), Ershov's memoirs covered less than Nikolai Berg's, discussed below.

59. "Vospominaniia o Sevastopole (Iz pisem polkovnika S. P. Mezentsova, ubitago na 3 bastione 27 avgusta, 1855 g.)," *Russkaia starina* 138 (June 1909): 532; Glebov, "Zapiski," 524; N. Berg, *Zapiski ob osade Sevastopolia*, 2 vols. (Moscow, 1858), 1: 103–4, 107–8, 149; Ershov, *Sevastopol'skiia vospominaniia*, 5, 45–46, 57; and Ekaterina Bakunina, "Vospominaniia sestry miliserdiia krestovozdvizhenskoi obshchiny, 1854–1860 gg.," *Vestnik Evropy* 133 (March 1898): 147, 156, 158–59, 176.

60. N. I. Pirogov, *Sevastopol'skie pis'ma i vospominaniia* (Moscow, 1950), 165.

Among the writing Russian officers receptive to war as spectacle, the one who enacted the most money-conscious tourist scenario was Nikolai Berg (1823–1884), a man of letters active in Moscow literary circles in the 1840s. To escape his boring job there in the State Bank of Commerce, he used his connections to obtain a position as an artist and translator on the staff of General Prince Mikhail Gorchakov, commander in chief of the Crimean army as of February 1855. Berg soon began publishing his war journal, excerpts from which appeared in *Sovremennik* (The Contemporary), *Biblioteka dlia chteniia* (The Library for Reading), and other periodicals over the next two years. Then in 1858, he brought out his *Sevastopol Album* (a collection of drawings) and *Memoirs of the Siege of Sevastopol*, the first major subjective Russian recollection of the war.[61] His authorial personality had a certain complexity. He identified himself as an officer and made much of his combat-readiness at the Chernaia River battle. His account nonetheless made clear that he had been a passive observer of war. He expressed patriotic sentiments, yet accented self-fulfillment (the siege of Sevastopol, he declared, was the "best time" of his life).[62] With respect to tourism he was a borderline figure. He exhibited the gentleman traveler's traditional interest in scenery and local culture (Bakhchisarai and the ancient city of Kherson). He relished transnational contacts as well. But his travel priorities had shifted to the quest for value in hotels, restaurants, and shops.

Although Berg never designated himself a *turist*, the opening section of his *Memoirs of the Siege of Sevastopol* announced his commercialized orientation to travel. Instead of explaining why and how he came to serve in the Crimean War, he started in a travelogue mode: "I cannot refrain from describing the journey itself from Kishinev to Sevastopol." The trip in question was Berg's first brief mission to Sevastopol in February 1855. He had traveled by post with a hussar, and the highlight of their journey was Odessa. First, they made the rounds of the shops. Then they dined at their hotel, the "Europe," an establishment with "excellent cuisine" and "every imaginable comfort." Evolving as a road story, the rest of Berg's narrative about going to Sevastopol accumulated details about accommodations and meals. In Simferopol, for instance, the travelers had barely managed to get some ham at the Golden Anchor hotel. But at least the scenery was becoming "better and better."[63]

The consumer theme of seeking good deals in food and lodging coexisted with Berg's self-presentation as a voyeur of suffering and death in Sevastopol.

---

61. *Sevastopol'skii al'bom* (Moscow, 1858). Berg joined Garibaldi's fight in Italy in the late 1850s. As a Russian newspaper correspondent, Berg next traveled in the Middle East and then went to Poland to cover the revolt of 1863. He spent the rest of his life there. See his "Posmertnye zapiski," *Russkaia starina* 69 (February 1891): 235–76; (March 1891): 594–99; 73 (March 1892): 637–52.

62. Berg, *Zapiski*, 1: 138. See also P. Alabin, *Chetyre voiny. Pokhodnye zapiski v 1849, 1853, 1854–56 i 1877–78 godakh*, 4 vols. (Moscow, 1892), 3: 166.

63. Berg, *Zapiski*, 1: 6–8, 11–12.

Upon reaching the city, he and the hussar first had tea at the hotel Odessa and then returned to the harbor to collect their belongings, left in the care of soldiers. There on the quay they saw the corpses of Russian and French soldiers ready for burial. Berg counted the bodies, scrutinized the handsome Zouaves among them, and remarked their stylish clothing. One Zouave was actually still stirring, but Berg watched until that man, too, was dead. To shake off the "painful" impressions, Berg and the hussar then did some conventional sightseeing (the marketplace, "beautiful houses," the cathedral, and other buildings). A few days later Berg expanded his sightseeing program to take in amputations at the military hospital (one of his acquaintances, a Prince Dolgorukii, was a doctor). Berg found the first operation difficult to watch, but then got used to them. Like adjutant Kalugin in Tolstoy's "Sevastopol in May," Berg and his comrades also got used to the stellar beauty of the bombs.[64] This artist appeared ready to gaze upon everything with equanimity because it was there, a part of the Sevastopol scene.

In recalling his life in Sevastopol from April 1855 until the fall of the city (27 August/8 September), Berg conjured a resort atmosphere, especially in the springtime, before heavy bombardments began in June. He remembered officers living in fine apartments or hotels, and dining in Sevastopol's restaurants.[65] Unable to find a vacant hotel room, Berg landed a delightful "nest" on a frigate anchored in the harbor near Prince Bariatinskii's yacht. On board the ship, Berg and his comrades enjoyed the services of an excellent cook and managed to sustain that style of life until the day before Sevastopol fell (when a bomb set the boat afire).[66] Like vacationers, Berg and others went swimming in the sea during the war.[67] Russian military personnel also took the opportunity to make excursions to Bakhchisarai.[68] On the path well beaten by leisure travelers, they went looking for "the palace," "the fountain," and so forth—the sights Pushkin's *Fountain of Bakhchisarai* had marked as musts for the visitor to see.[69]

The most original, engaging section of Berg's memoirs was his account of touring with elite French officers in the spring of 1856, shortly after the war officially ended. Early in April, the Russian high command threw a garden

---

64. Ibid., 1: 17, 25–33.

65. Ibid., 1: 101; and Hodasevich, *Voice from Sevastopol*, 160–61. During his break from heavy combat in the spring and summer of 1855, Tolstoy occupied *"un logement très élégant"* (a very elegant apartment) in Sevastopol: see his letter to Ergol'skaia, 7 May 1855, in *Polnoe sobranie sochinenii*, 59: 312.

66. Berg, *Zapiski*, 1: 1, 27, 33, 57, 63, 83, 85–88, 92; 2: 17, 173.

67. Ibid., 1: 139; Hodasevich, *Voice from Sevastopol*, 18; and Tolstoy, letter to Ergol'skaia, 7 May 1855, *Polnoe sobranie sochinenii*, 59: 312.

68. Berg, *Zapiski*, 1: 57–58, 64–74; Hodasevich, *Voice from Sevastopol*, 6; Pirogov, *Sevastopol'skie pis'ma*, 33; and "Pokhodnyia zametki N. A. Obninskago," *Russkii arkhiv* (1891): 11, book 3: 377.

69. On representations as "markers" of sights, see MacCannell, *Tourist*, 41–42; and Schönle, *Authenticity and Fiction*, 57–60.

party for French and British officers in Bakhchisarai (where Gorchakov and his staff had been living for several months). Berg and Colonel Bodin took a mutual liking to one another at the party and then spent a little over a week together touring the Crimea on horseback. A fluent speaker of Tatar, Berg played host, taking Bodin to Simferopol, Karasabazar, and Feodosiia. They had some trouble finding accommodations, since so many other Russian, British, and French officers were roaming about. But in the end, our author and his French guest found agreeable lodgings and good food everywhere. Berg logged the costs—a "handsome bill" here, a "piddling sum" there. He and the colonel always checked out the shops and went sightseeing, most memorably in Karasabazar. A local prince there showed them the ancient fortress, old mosques, more shops, and a panoramic view of the town. Our military tourists roughed it a bit, too, to satisfy Bodin's desire to return to Bakhchisarai through the scenic hinterland. But even in a remote mountain village, they kept their touring on a paying basis. With the help of a Tatar guide, they found lodging in a pleasant house, where the hostess and her beautiful twelve-year-old daughter prepared them "very tasty pancakes, a sort of omelet, bread, honey, and finally coffee with sugar served in little cups from Constantinople." Dressed in "picturesque clothing," local people crammed into the house to talk to the visitors. Presenting himself as the mediator in this transnational encounter, Berg fashioned the Tatars as "exotic co-subjects" of a shared geography.[70] The "jolly" evening passed as a folkloric imperial Russian spectacle, and in the morning the Frenchman lavishly paid their hosts and the guide.[71]

After the two officers returned to Bakhchisarai, they reversed their host-guest roles, as Berg pursued his tourist agenda in a simulacrum of France on Crimean soil. With official Russian permission, Bodin now took Berg to the French and British military zones. After passing through "paradisaical" foothills Berg had never seen before, Bodin announced: "We are now in France!" At dinner in the colonel's living quarters that night, Berg elatedly felt that he was, in fact, "in France"—speaking French with charming French officers, eating French dishes, and drinking French wines. The next morning, one of Berg's hosts gave him a tour of the British area. There they browsed in shops, observed other shoppers (including Russian peasant soldiers), and popped into the billiard parlor at the Queen Victoria hotel. The next day Berg asked the French to take him to Sevastopol, which he had not seen since the city fell. His remembrance of eating establishments continued even here. Finding the city "unrecognizable," he first sought out sites of national significance (the ruined houses of Admiral Pavel Nakhimov and other commanders). Berg entered the devastated cathedral and library as well. He then went looking for his own little Sevastopol lost: his favorite hotel-restaurant; his favorite pretzel

70. Quoted phrase from McReynolds, 23.
71. Berg, *Zapiski*, 2: 79–97.

(*krendel'*) bakery; and Thomas's Confectionary, where he had often eaten "ice cream in July." With his usual impassivity, Berg also noticed that the French had put their tourist stamp on Sevastopol. French graffiti abounded in the devastated city, and both the municipal theater and the house where Catherine the Great once lived were now French cafés. Berg's last stop in Sevastopol was the fourth bastion, where he gathered some bullets as souvenirs. He then returned to the French camp for dinner.[72]

With no effort to sum up his feelings about Sevastopol, Berg rushed on to the grand finale of his tourist's story: his overnight visit of Kamesh in the company of a French officer. Constructed by the French for their amusement and comfort during the war, Kamesh consisted of shops, cafés, restaurants, and a theater, where Parisian actors and actresses performed. Kamesh had hotels as well, and Berg chose one that catered to "foreigners." He marveled at the international variety of currencies and sightseers circulating in Kamesh. Among them were an "English dandy on a marvelous steed," European women, British officers, Turks, and some "Russian gray coats." Before going to the theater, Berg and the Frenchman had dined in a packed restaurant. Our memoirist found the turbot a revelation but preserved for posterity a copy of the entire bill, itemizing everything he and the Frenchman had consumed.[73]

Berg and Battlefield Tourism

Berg's memoirs met a mixed reception in Russia. On the favorable side, they enjoyed some success as armchair traveling and may have even helped initiate Crimean battlefield tourism in the immediate postwar period.[74] In 1856 *Sovremennik*, the leading periodical of the time, featured Berg's account of touring the Crimea with Colonel Bodin, the penetration of the French and British military zones, the return to Sevastopol, and the excursion to Kamesh.[75] Perhaps reflecting positive reader reactions to Berg, the journal's editor in chief, Nikolai Chernyshevskii, soon expressed his conviction that the travelogue remained the Russian readership's favorite prose genre.[76] *Sovremennik* also realized that Russian leisure travelers might now want to visit Sevastopol themselves. In 1857 the journal ran A. Afanas'ev's account of just such a trip, narrated in much the same spirit as Berg's memoirs. Afanas'ev went to Sevastopol to see the "celebrated ruins not yet cleansed of fresh blood." But he had gone in style,

72. Ibid., 2: 101–51.

73. Ibid., 2: 162–68.

74. On the general phenomenon, consult David W. Lloyd, *Battlefield Tourism: Pilgrimage and the Commemoration of the Great War in Britain, Australia, and Canada, 1919–1939* (Oxford, 1998), 13–48.

75. N. Berg, "Iz krymskikh zametok," *Sovremennik* 58 (1856), 4: part 1: 131–202.

76. N. G. Chernyshevskii, review of V. P. Botkin, *Pis'ma ob Ispanii*, in his *Polnoe sobranie sochinenii*, 16 vols. (Moscow, 1939–54), 4: 222.

2.3. The Café Belair and other establishments in the French military zone in the Crimea. Nikolai Berg, *Sevastopol'skii al'bom* (Moscow, 1858).

on a steamboat whose cabins were "very comfortable, even luxurious." Appearing in Afanas'ev's opening paragraph, those quotes revealed battlefield tourism's tendency to attract the idly curious vacationer, along with the pilgrim who seeks to honor the war dead. While not mentioning Berg, Afanas'ev sought out many sites that the latter's memoirs had designated worthy of attention (including Sevastopol's bastions and Balaklava). Afanas'ev reported, however, that wartime Kamesh no longer existed. People engaged in the reconstruction of Sevastopol had dismantled the French enclave and were using those materials to build shelter for the most deprived members of the ruined city's population.[77]

The same year, another Afanas'ev (perhaps a relative?) issued a tourist's *Guide to Sevastopol, Its Bastions and Environs, Published with the Aim of Contributing to Reconstruction.*[78] Directly addressing his readers, the author

77. A. Afanas'ev, "Sevastopol' i ego okrestnosti v nastoiashchee vremia," *Sovremennik* 62 (1857), 3: part 1: 134–46. The likely author was the belletrist and ethnographer Aleksandr Stepanovich Afanas'ev: see I. F. Masanov, *Slovar' psevdonimov,* 4 vols. (Moscow, 1956–60), 1: 113.

78. D. Afanas'ev, *Putevoditel' po Sevastopoliu, ego bastionam i okrestnostiam, izdannyi s tsel'iu blagotvoreniia ego razvalinakh* (Nikolaev, 1857), 1, 3–4, 14–15, 26. See also Qualls in the present volume.

stressed that in buying the booklet, "you" will be augmenting the "fund for the poor of Sevastopol." This assurance legitimated "your" participation in battlefield tourism, while assuming that "you" deserved to have an enjoyable, comfortable trip. The *Guide* advised tourists to make the journey on a steamship running from Odessa. "With all the conveniences of the ship at his disposal, the traveler has no need to stay in the city [Sevastopol] and suffer all the discomforts of accommodations in some hotel hastily constructed amidst the ruins." Making his way through the rubble, the tourist should first go to Sevastopol's Officer hotel and rent a horse, with or without guide. The city sightseeing tour included the ruins of the houses of Admiral Nakhimov and other military leaders; the cathedral, the library, and the bastions (all marked by Berg).[79] With a stab at macabre humor, Afanas'ev sought to approximate combat at the fourth bastion:

> Did you see that bomb explode nearby? An 80-kilogram metal sphere falls before you and sinks deep into the ground. Suddenly there comes a crash: whistling shrapnel and rocks fly in all directions. A huge column of flame, smoke, and dust covers you and everything else in the area. A moment later, you look around and finally notice that one of your legs has run off somewhere in fright, and you learn the inconvenience of trying to scamper away on one foot.[80]

The military arena had thus become a place where "you" were to experience the "strong sensations" of combat, before returning to the comfort of your hotel or steamship cabin. In parallel to Berg's style of military tourism, Afanas'ev's guidebook pursued a sightseeing agenda that distanced the "real guise" of war as Tolstoy's "Sevastopol in December" named it: "blood, suffering, and death." We can only speculate, of course, about the effect Afanas'ev's *Guide* may have had on Russian readers of the time.

As for the pathbreaking battlefield tourist Berg himself, he provoked at least a little Russian soul-searching, specifically by contrast to Tolstoy. In 1857, under Druzhinin's editorship, *Biblioteka dlia chteniia* published Berg's account of his wartime excursion in search of Pushkin's Bakhchisarai (an adventure incorporated into the author's *Memoirs of the Siege of Sevastopol*). But the following year, Druzhinin's journal ran an anonymous review labeling Berg's book "tawdry" (*poshlyi*)—that Russian adjective connoting self-satisfied vulgarity. Concentrating on Berg's treatment of the siege, the reviewer deplored his egocentricity. Having enjoyed "every possible comfort" in Sevastopol, Berg had viewed the war through a "prism of narrow personal feeling," lending everything a "rainbow" aura. In this reviewer's opinion, Berg's book had vivacity and factual value but failed to fulfill the "moral obligation" of addressing the tragic, national import of the siege, as Tolstoy's Sevastopol stories had

79. Afanas'ev, *Putevoditel'*, 1, 3–4, 14–15, 26.
80. Ibid., 30.

done.[81] If not written by Druzhinin himself, the review conformed to his previous public presentation of Tolstoy as a fighter, not to be confused with a turist.

My chapter has homed in on Crimean military tourism as a phenomenon that newly divided Russians. From the standpoint of the Russian state and Russian society alike, the heroic puteshestvenniki of the Napoleonic wars had earned their tourists' pleasures in western Europe. When the Crimean War ended, the empire's defeat of Imam Shamil appeared near, and that victory would legitimate Russian military tourism in a new arena, the Caucasus. The same was probably true of other previous conflicts, including the Russian army's suppression of the Polish revolt in 1830–1831. But in the case of the Crimean War, the officers who derived "vacation" benefits from service did so without paying for them through triumphant military "work." They had gotten their tourist's fun despite the war's unhappy outcome. This situation proved divisive both in society and in the army. In the main, the civilian readership seems to have taken a morally neutral interest in Russian military travels of the Crimean War. But Druzhinin's journal expressed some indignation, to question the ethics of officers' touristy behavior. Within the army, as opposed to society, the concept of the tourist in uniform appears to have created a deeper rift between a sense of self and views of the other. Colonel Glebov made turist an abusive word, connoting a lack of professionalism he believed had undermined the army's performance at Sevastopol. On the contrary, the artillery officer Ershov used turist as self-description, with the accent on the thrills of watching combat. At least one prestigious Russian staff officer, Lieutenant-General Vladimir Dehn, also emerged from the Crimean War content to label himself a turist. Aide-de-camp of Nicholas I as of December 1853, Dehn undertook several missions during the war, including a visit to Sevastopol in October 1854. To help to pass the time there, he and another turist (a diplomat) had ridden along with a reconnaissance squad, in order to see more of the splendid Crimean coast.[82]

How did such tensions between military purpose and military pleasures subsequently evolve? One may wonder, for instance, whether the Crimean experience might have had an impact on army recruitment. In the immediate postwar period, articles addressing the need for military and social reforms dominated Voennyi sbornik (the Military Compendium), the journal established in 1858 at the initiative of the reformist minister of war, Dmitrii Miliutin. But the journal's "unofficial" section also featured colorful accounts of military travels during the Crimean War, the continuing conquest of the Caucasus, service in Poland in 1831, and the Russo-Turkish War of 1828–1829.[83]

81. *Biblioteka dlia chteniia* (May 1858), part 5: 1, 7–9, 18–26.
82. "Zapiski Dena [Dehn]," *Russkaia starina* 65 (March 1890): 664–65 (written in the late 1860s and early 1870s).
83. P. Kroniv, "Desiat' mesiatsev na Dunae," *Voennyi sbornik* 4 (1858), part 2: 498–502; A. Rozellion-Soshal'skii, "Zapiski russkago ofitsera, byvshago v plenu u turok v 1828 i 1829 godu," ibid. 3 (1858), 208–9, 219–20, 365–66; Dmitrii Stramilov, "Iz zapisok ubitago ofitsera, 1831–

One piece sweepingly imagined imperial Russian military history as the service record of one metonymic traveler: "The Swiss mountains, the Caucasus's cliffs, the Crimean plains, luxuriant Italy, the Kvarken glaciers, Turkey's arid lands, placid Germany, and even Paris all know the Russian soldier!"[84] Hear ye, soldier, the world is waiting to meet you! By sponsoring such a message, was the Russian state perhaps attempting to exploit the wanderlust that had found spontaneous expression in Russian officers' writings concerning service in western Europe, the Caucasus, and most recently the Crimea? The appeal would have been strongest for people lacking the money to undertake much travel on their own. Perhaps some broken dreams of grand military journeys even contributed to the sullen resentment, drunkenness, violence, and peculation rampant among Russian officers posted in the bleak backwaters of the empire during the reign of Alexander III.[85] What is certain is that the material for such dreams abounded in imperial Russian military history and its subjective representations.

1838," ibid., 12 (1859), part 2: 473–75; and A. M-v, "Otryvok iz pokhodnykh zapisok o voine v Pol'she v 1831 godu," ibid., 12 (1860), part 2: 12–14, 20.

84. Bez"imiannyi [sic], "Zapiski kavalerista. Pokhod," *Voennyi sbornik* 5 (1859), part 2: 577–78.

85. On this demoralized group, see John Bushnell, "The Tsarist Officer Corps, 1881–1914: Customs, Duties, Inefficiency," *American Historical Review* 86, no. 2 (1981): 753–80.

CHAPTER 3

From Friends of Nature to Tourist-Soldiers

Nation Building and Tourism in Hungary, 1873–1914

Alexander Vari

On 20 April 1889, Dr. Gusztáv Oláh suggested to the presidium of the Budapest section of the Magyarországi Kárpát-Egylet (the Carpathian [tourist] Association of Hungary) that they should take an active part in the organization of a photographic exhibition.[1] Taking their cue from this proposal, the Budapest section soon urged every member of the association—from the capital to the most remote corners of the countryside—to send their amateur photographs to the exhibit's organizers.[2] Belief in photography's ability to portray reality accurately grew rapidly in the late nineteenth century. According to activists of the Budapest section, the images harvested in different parts of the country had to be reassembled in the capital to show the composite face of the homeland to an increasingly visually oriented national audience.[3]

The exhibition opened on 30 April 1890 in the capital's Műcsarnok (Arts Hall), located at that time on Andrássy Avenue.[4] As the catalogue of the exhibit documents, sixty-three amateur photographers from Hungary had several hundred photographs presented on this occasion. A good half of the photographs portrayed natural scenes, mountains, and groups of tourists roaming the countryside.[5] As a member of the association wrote enthusiastically: "The amateur photographic exhibition in the Műcsarnok shows that our desire [to have the homeland photographed] was fulfilled as if with a magic wand. There already exists a whole team of photographers in our country who are turning [its] beauty into a public treasure for the pleasure [of larger audiences]. We can see [in the exhibit] landscapes from every part of our homeland, famous buildings, ruins, folkloric dresses, and faces. This is the real Hungarian land in im-

1. Dr. Ferencz Kemény, "Fotográfiai mozgalmak a Magyar Turista-Egyesületben," in *A Magyar Turista-Egyesület 25 éves multja, 1888–1913*, ed. József Déry and Gusztáv Thirring (Budapest, 1914), 167.
2. See Vincze Wartha's opening speech to the exhibit, in "Az amateur-fotográfiai kiállítás megnyitása," *Turisták Lapja*, 2, no. 5 (May 1890): 155–57.
3. J. Mihalik, "Fotográfiák a Vág völgyéből," *Turisták Lapja*, 2, no. 4 (April 1890): 129.
4. Ibid., 168.
5. *Tárgymutató a Magyarországi Kárpát-Egyesület Budapesti osztályának az Országos Képzőművészeti Társulat Műcsarnokában 1890-ben rendezett műkedvelő-fotográfiai kiállításához* (Budapest, 1890).

64

ages, since photography is not cheating when it is good."[6] The emphasis the association put on the fact that "every tourist is a born photographer"—who should not just travel to the remote areas of the country but share his visual impressions of them—was symptomatic of a new way of approaching the process of Magyar nation building in Hungary.[7] By the turn of the century, leaders of the newborn tourist movement were eager to enrich the nation's linguistic imagining (shaped by an earlier reform era) by adding a visually (and technologically) mitigated spatial dimension.

Recent studies suggest that nineteenth-century nation building—in east-central Europe as well as elsewhere—was related to important spatial developments that included a new emphasis upon concepts of place and space.[8] The rise of tourism made it possible to add a geographic and spatial component to the modern conception of the nation.[9] As part of this process, mountains, lakes, ruins, and a wide array of other natural sights were nationalized, being "incorporated into the fabric of national identity."[10] At the same time, however, tourism allowed for more than just the nationalization of natural landscapes. In multiethnic empires, members of the ruling majority often used tourism as a convenient device meant to further their imperialist aims of spreading elements of the dominant culture to members of the ethnic minorities living in these countries. The purpose of this chapter is to discuss the links between tourism conceived as an imperialist project in the service of nation building and its effects upon youth's preparation for war in the Hungarian lands of turn-of-the-century Austria-Hungary. From a project that initially was consumption-oriented, tourism in Hungary (as conceived by Budapest-

6. Sándor Schmidt, "Néhány szó a fotografáló turistáknak," *Turisták Lapja*, 2, no. 5 (1890): 139.

7. Ibid.

8. Pieter Judson, "Frontiers, Islands, Forests, Stones: Mapping the Geography of a German Identity in the Habsburg Monarchy, 1848–1900," in *The Geography of Identity*, ed. Patricia Yaeger, 382–406 (Ann Arbor, 1996); Rudy Koshar, *German Travel Cultures* (Oxford, 2000); Pieter Judson, " 'Every German visitor has a volkish obligation he must fulfill': Nationalist Tourism in the Austrian Empire, 1880–1918," in *Histories of Leisure*, ed. Rudy Koshar (Oxford, 2002), 147–68; Jill Steward, "Tourism in Late Imperial Austria: The Development of Tourist Cultures and Their Associated Images of Place," in *Being Elsewhere: Tourism, Consumer Culture, and Identity in Modern Europe and North America*, ed. Shelley Baranowski and Ellen Furlough (Ann Arbor, 2001), 108–34; and Pieter Judson, "The Bohemian Oberammergau: Nationalist Tourism in the Austrian Empire," in *Constructing Nationalities in Eastern Europe*, ed. Pieter Judson and Marsha Rozenblitt (New York, 2005), 89–106.

9. See Christopher Ely, *This Meager Nature: Landscape and National Identity in Imperial Russia* (DeKalb, Ill., 2002); Anne-Marie Thiesse, *Ils apprenaient la France: l'exaltation des régions dans le discours patriotique* (Paris, 1997); R. J. B. Bosworth, "The Touring Club Italiano and the Nationalization of the Italian Bourgeoisie," *European History Quarterly* 27, no. 3 (1997): 371–410; and Orvar Löfgren, "Know Your Country: A Comparative Perspective on Tourism and Nation Building in Sweden," in *Being Elsewhere*, ed. Baranowski and Furlough, 137–54.

10. Oliver Zimmer, "In Search of Natural Identity: Alpine Landscape and the Reconstruction of the Swiss Nation," *Comparative Studies in Society and History* 40, no. 4 (1998): 644.

centered tourist associations) turned increasingly into an imperialist and bellicose activity. During the four decades preceding World War I, the alliance between the leaders of the associational tourism movement and school teachers
in Transleithania progressively turned tourism from a model that emphasized
the spreading of knowledge about regional flora, fauna, and beautiful natural
scapes into one in which nature was increasingly equated to a military field
map. By the 1900s and the early 1910s, a new generation of tourists was expected to learn and master nature in order to be better prepared for duties the
outbreak of a war might call upon them.

The Beginnings

Associational tourism made its appearance relatively late in the Transleithan-
ian part of Austria-Hungary. Whereas in England, Italy, Switzerland, Germany, and Austria, tourist associations began their activity as early as the
1850s and 1860s, in Transleithania the first association of this type was the already mentioned Carpathian Association of Hungary.[11] Called to life in 1873
in Tátrafüred (today Smokovec in Slovakia) by a number of local aristocrats
and middle-class notables, the association soon established its permanent
headquarters in the town of Késmárk (Kežmarok, Slovakia).

The Carpathian was a tourist association whose main goal was to focus on
the exploration of the Tatra Mountains, the opening and maintenance of public access to the mountains, and the organization of excursions in their surroundings. In the summoning call for its constitution, the leadership of the
Carpathian clearly emphasized the importance of opening up the region for
economic and leisurely activities.[12] In this spirit, the document listed the main
attractions of the Tatras: the Lomnicz peak, the Kolbach and the Felka valleys,
and the numerous lakes and tarns to be found in its mountain caldrons. Given
the public utility goals formulated in its founding statute, during its first
decade of existence (from 1873 to 1883), the Carpathian focused on such activities as describing and collecting mountain flora and fauna, repairing mountain roads, building and maintaining mountain refuges, marking forest and
subalpine paths, exploring caves and contributing to a better and more accurate mapping of the region.[13]

11. For a discussion of the specific circumstances that led to the creation of the British Alpine
Club, see Claire Eliane Engel, *Mountaineering in the Alps: An Historical Survey* (London, 1971),
111–36; and Peter H. Hansen, "Albert Smith, the Alpine Club, and the Invention of Mountaineering in Mid-Victorian Britain," *The Journal of British Studies* 34, no. 3 (1995): 300–324.
Mór Déchy, "Adatok az alpesi egyletek történetéhez," *Magyarországi Kárpátegylet Évkönyve*, 3,
1876.

12. See "Felhívás a 'Magyarországi Kárpát-Egylet'-beli belépésre" reproduced in Tivadar
Posewitz, *A Magyarországi Kárpátegyesület története, 1873–1898* (Igló, 1898), 9–10.

13. Ferencz Dénes, *A Magyarországi Kárpátegyesület alapítása, fejlődése és működése. Em-
lékirat a magyarországi kárpátegyesület tíz évi fennállásának ünnepére* (Lőcse, 1883), 21–31, 41–
43, 44–50.

Concomitant with its focus on the opening up of the Tatras for tourist consumption, the Carpathian emphasized the need to swell the membership of the
association. During the 1870s and the early 1880s, leaders of the Carpathian
made progress in recruiting members in the neighboring Selmec, Turóc,
Gömör, Liptó, and Árva counties, and organizing distinct sections of the association in some more distant towns such as Budapest (1877) and Breslau
(1887). It is significant that, faithful to its focus on the Carpathians and specifically to the Tatras as a natural whole, the association encouraged the constitution of multiethnically configured sections on each side of the mountains, including—besides the Hungarian—the Galician and Silesian slopes.[14] As this
geographic dispersion shows, the membership of the Carpathian represented a
mixture of Germans, Hungarians, Slovaks, and Poles, who joined the association as a result of a shared interest in the natural beauties of the Tatras. Despite the geographical enlargement of its structure and membership, however,
the Carpathian remained largely a regional association which continued to de-
pend mainly on the functioning of its central headquarters in Késmárk. Moreover, with the rise of national sentiment among its constituent ethnicities, by
the early 1880s interest in the association's activities started to languish. The
Budapest section created in 1877 stopped its activity in 1881, while the Rozs-
nyó and Igló sections—called to life in 1881 and 1882—had to announce their
dissolution only two years after their creation due to a sharp decrease in membership.[15]

Interest in tourism and the Tatras, however, was reborn in Hungary during
the late 1880s. This time the initiative came from Budapest, where in 1888 a
new and, as it soon proved, much more dynamic section was formed by a
number of intrepid intellectuals within the already existing framework of the
languishing Carpathian.[16] Activists of the newly launched section emphasized
the importance of Budapest as a structural base for the development of
tourism in Hungary and called into doubt the legitimacy of the association's
Késmárk leadership. Using the call made by one of its members for the convo-
cation of a countrywide tourist congress as a veiled preparation for the envisaged takeover, the Budapest section launched a public forum of discussion in
which the creation of a national tourist association with its headquarters in
Hungary's capital city turned into a hotly debated topic. A reason invoked in
Budapest's favor, and endorsed indirectly by the new self-proclaimed leadership, was the fact that the capital was the place where one found the *haute
crème* of society, politics, and science—all important factors which could contribute to the elevation of tourism into a national business. In the argument of
one proponent of the congress, the country was described as a human body,
with Budapest represented as "its heart wherefrom the nerves (sic)—under the

14. Ibid., 6.
15. Posewitz, *A Magyarországi Kárpátegyesület története*, 112–52.
16. "Alakuló közgyülés (28 December 1888)," *Turisták Lapja* 1, no. 1 (1889): 20–22.
Gusztáv Thirring, "A Magyar Turista-Egyesület 25 éves multja," in Déry and Thirring, *A Magyar
Turista*, 9.

form of tourism—will carry the necessary blood flow to all its parts."[17] In line with this, Budapest's role as a center of the Hungarian tourist movement was envisaged to extend beyond the cultivation of its immediate hinterland, all the way to the faraway Carpathians that served as Hungary's northern and eastern borders.

To better support the idea of centralism and signal its claim for independence within the structures of the Carpathian, the Budapest section started a new publication, the *Turisták Lapja* (The Tourists' Paper), which appeared bimonthly from 1889 to 1944. During its early years of existence the Budapest section led by Ödön Téry and Gusztáv Thirring (who were also editors of the *Turisták Lapja*) focused intensely on both a definition of tourism and the figure of the tourist. In the appeal to the public written by Téry and Thirring that appeared in the first issue of the journal, tourism was envisaged as an activity that had to be educative and nationwide in scope. Regarding its immediate goals, the new journal pledged to advocate organized tourism, to publish descriptions and photographs of various Hungarian regions in order to acquaint their readership with them, and to engage critically the developing issue of tourist housing and services in the countryside. Given the relative cheapness of such services and the editor's belief in the "beauty of the Hungarian land," there was hope that regular descriptive activity of regional attractions and reporting about local conditions would have an effect on the public's choice of tourist destinations, halting the pilgrimage of Hungarians to foreign sites.[18]

As it appears from this "program," the set of activities envisaged by the Budapest section largely superseded the former pursuits of the Késmárk-based association. Indeed, in 1891 the Budapest section engineered a move from the regional to the national scale, a shift also reflected by the changing of the section's name to that of Magyar Turista-Egyesület (Magyar Tourist Association—hereafter MTA) and its attempts to encompass, in addition to the Tatra Mountains and the northern area of the country, all the other regions of Hungary. Although the Carpathian survived the crisis and continued its activities until 1914, the MTA's creation was a de jure confirmation of its status as a separate association from the Carpathian.

From the early 1890s on, the MTA took an active lead in the promotion and regulation of a nationally conceived project to turn Magyars into tourists, a self-assumed hegemonic position which consistently downplayed the significance of other tourist organizations. In fact, a move in this direction was on its way even before the MTA gained its long-awaited independence. Beginning in 1889, Thirring and Téry criticized the yearbook published by the Carpathian for being too academic in its content and too slow (due to its yearbook form) to record the immediate experiences of the association's membership. They presented their publication, the *Turisták Lapja* (published twice a month) as

17. Dr. Ignácz Künsztler, "Országos turista-kongresszus," *Turisták Lapja*, 1, no. 3 (1889): 79.
18. A szerkesztők, "Tisztelt Olvasóinkhoz," *Turisták Lapja* 1, no. 1 (1889): 1–3.

better suited to the immediate needs of Hungarian tourism, which they described as a rapidly developing activity. The need for shorter articles written in a more readable prose, the use of better rhetorical skills for a more intense popularization of tourism's benefits, and a more accurate recording of associational life were all emphasized. Therefore, during the first ten years of its existence, the journal opened its pages to a large number of contributors who, besides reporting about their experience with natural sites, debated a number of theoretical and analytical issues. These conceptual questions promoted the construction of a national understanding of tourism.

The Nationalization of Tourism

In a June 1889 article published in the *Turisták Lapja*, Ödön Téry defined tourism equally as an individual and a collective sport.[19] "Goal-minded tourism trains the body, freshens up the mind, deepens our knowledge, and could bring valuable benefits to numerous branches of science," wrote Téry.[20] Tourism was further described by Téry as an activity available to both rich and poor. While stressing the democratic features of tourism, he emphasized free will as the governing force behind each individual's decision concerning which particular route to take, which schedule to adopt, and which time of the day to travel. "The tourist is a free man, earning his independence through his own means," claimed the author of the article.[21] This general premise, however, had to be broken down to its specifics. Although Téry admitted that not all aspects of travel were energetic (although one has to travel by foot to climb a peak, one can travel by train and other means of locomotion to and through the mountains), he condemned pleasure seekers who chose to admire the landscape only from a train window, a boat deck, or the comfortable bench of a carriage. He also emphasized that, as the etymology of the word tourist proves (a tourist is someone who does a *tour*, i.e., a circle), real tourists never adopt the same itinerary but strive to always advance on new roads. Téry regarded mountaineers as an important tourist subspecies, with the proviso that while alpinists should be assigned to the vanguard of real tourism, those who climb the mountains in response merely to passing fads or out of vanity must be called bad tourists.

According to him, if done properly, with dedication and skill, alpinism would further the cause of tourism at home. Other commentators heartily agreed: "Alpinism represents a culmination of tourism . . . [since it is an activity] that not only strengthens the heart's muscles and widens the lungs, but raises manly self-consciousness, develops circumspection, a cool head, and

19. Ödön Téry, "Turistaság," *Turisták Lapja* 1, no. 3 (1889): 73–78.
20. Ibid., 74.
21. Ibid.

courage to a degree that no other activity does."[22] Alpinism was seen as turning the practitioner not only into a manly person and a friend of nature but a poet as well.[23] The mountain climber's antithesis was the pleasure seeker. Pleasure seekers were constantly ridiculed through the depiction of their various types and guises: the gluttonous rentier who, while entering the Danube Gorges on a boat, stuffs himself, forgetting to take a look at the surrounding landscape; the German traveler from Pozsony (Bratislava) who looks for beer and drinking spots everywhere he goes; the Hungarian excursionist to Tátrafüred who cannot wake up early enough to join the morning mountain climbing expedition and prefers to hang around the coffeehouse; the railway tourist, the so-called *homo ferrosus vulgaris*, who travels from one station restaurant to the next; the *homo rapidex cursor* who races about on his bicycle, forgetting about nature and his pedestrian peers; and the "Tourist-Hamlet" who spends all day musing on his favorite question—"to go or not to go?"[24] Téry scorned tourists oriented toward pleasure and vanity as contributors to tourism's "bastardization."[25]

Like other commentators, however, Téry not only praised alpinists and condemned pleasure seekers but also emphasized the importance of a new type of tourist. He singled out the importance for Hungarians to learn more about the natural surroundings of the towns and villages they lived in. He encouraged them to roam the countryside and plan vacations in the mountains. Once they would plant the seed of these activities, others would follow. These apostles of local tourism would spread knowledge about the homeland's natural beauties among the larger public at home and abroad.[26] This new type of tourist, another commentator explained, would contribute to the "marriage between the Alföld [Hungary's main plainland] and the Felföld [the mountainous northern area of the country, which culminated in the Tatras]."[27] The Felföld, as represented by the multiethnic Carpathian association, was vehemently criticized for not wanting any such union. Twenty-five years after its creation, the Carpathian was accused of having distorted tourism's goals, as its 1873 statutes had emphasized bringing foreign tourists to Hungary (i.e., to the Tatras), and not on creating Hungarian tourists. The Carpathian's previ-

22. Jenő Rodniczky, "A turistaságról," *Turisták Lapja* 2, no. 3 (1890): 67–68; Miklós Szontagh, "A turistaságról," *Turisták Lapja* 5, no. 3–4 (1890): 33–43; Pál Brózsik, "Az én megtérésem," *Turista Közlöny* 3, no. 4 (1896): 78–79.

23. For discussions about mountaineering at the turn of the century within a different national context, see Peter H. Hansen, "Modern Mountains: The Performative Consciousness of Modernity in Britain, 1870–1940," in *Meanings of Modernity: Britain from the Late-Victorian Era to World War II*, ed. Martin Daunton and Bernhard Rieger (Oxford, 2001), 185–202.

24. Ibid., 68–69.

25. Téry, "Turistaság," 76.

26. Dr. Ede Környei, "Elnöki megnyitó a M. T. E. 1897. évi junius hó 6-án Kőszegen tartott rendes közgyülésen," *Turisták Lapja* 9, no. 6–8 (1897): 129–30.

27. Rodniczky, "A turistaságról," 71.

ous leading role had caused the country—as the vice-president of the MTA dramatically portrayed it in 1896—to have "tourist associations but no tourists." The Budapest association, therefore, considered as one of its most urgent tasks to "educate tourists and get [more] supporters of tourism" among Hungarians: "Because we do not know our mountains and gaze at the solitary foreign tourist [we encounter there] as on an idiot, foreigners cannot feel at ease in our country. I can tell from my own experience that my spirited compatriots whom I encountered on trains, in restaurants, and so on often played jokes on me, not being able to suppose that a hobnail-booted tourist could be a Hungarian."[28]

As the author of the above quote further suggested, locals themselves had to be turned into tourists in order to dissolve the "foreignness" that tourism represented for them. Once they embraced their new identity, the locals (especially local intellectuals) were expected to make the effort to travel around their region. They were commanded to visit the mountains and write new guidebooks and journal articles about them based on personal experience—not on library knowledge, as many of the authors of the studies published in the Carpathian's yearbook were said to have done in the past.

Mountain dwellers—who in most of Hungary's mountainous regions were Slovaks, Romanians, Germans (Zipser), and Ruthenians—were depicted in MTA discourses as having their views limited by the mountains themselves. Since they were living in narrow valleys circumscribed by forested slopes, they were prevented—as MTA commentators argued—from acquiring the larger, more open views of the inhabitants of the Alföld. Middle-class tourists from the plains were charged thus with a civilizing role: to bring the benefits of the plains culture to those living in the mountains.[29] Tourists were charged with becoming cultural missionaries. As part of the nationalist discourse developed on the occasion of the 1896 Millennium celebrations, Magyar tourists were called to metaphorically descend from the horses of their ancestors in order to adopt and help to spread the pedestrian mode among their offspring. They were supposed to walk to the mountains as the "infantry of the[ir] nation," proving that they could give up being a nation of riders to become a nation of tourists. As Baron Loránd Eötvös, the president of the MTA, argued in this context, Hungarians "should make excellent tourists," who would criss-cross the mountains in order to conquer the non-Magyar ethnic groups living there with their "likable behavior, so that in the places where [they] have already been [they] will be seen as guests for whose return at the dawn of every spring [the locals] will joyfully yearn."[30]

28. Lajos Petrik, "Tisztázzuk az eszméket," *Turisták Lapja* 8, no. 3–4 (1896): 50–56.

29. Gyula Csizik, "A tájkép szépségéről (I–II)," *Turisták Lapja* 5, no. 5–6 (1893), 96–97, and no. 7–8 (1893): 148–50.

30. Loránd Eötvös, "Elnöki megnyító a M. T. E. 1896. évi május hó 24 Selmeczbányán tartott rendes közgyülésén," *Turisták Lapja* 8, no. 5–6 (1896): 101–2.

Tourism and the School

Another way to turn Magyars into tourists was to propagate the MTA's goals among the youngest members of the population. In terms of recognizing the importance of schools in furthering the cause of Hungarian tourism, 1892 was a watershed. As one MTA member put it in one of the first full-length articles published in *Turisták Lapja* dealing with this topic: "It is my firm belief that tourism will be rooted in our country only if we educate our youth for it. [Tourism] should become part of school life, and [as a result] the future generation will not only support it but would go to [every] area of our country out of an inner need, finding pleasure and delight in nature's varied beauties."[31]

The Budapest high-school teachers section, under the direction of the MTA, was founded in 1892 by 101 high-school teachers, mostly from Budapest.[32] Membership was limited to elementary, middle, and high-school teachers, excluding thus the more varied professional and middle-class groups represented in several recently founded sections of the mother organization in the countryside. The section's difference and specificity within the larger structure soon led to demands for independence, a claim achieved de jure on 22 December 1896 when the section pronounced itself a distinct association: the Magyar Tanítók Turista Egyesülete (Magyar School Teachers Tourist Association—hereafter MSTTA).[33]

The new association immediately adopted an active agenda in the name of Magyar nation building. While encouraging the increase in the association's membership, its vice-president, Géza Moussong, emphasized as early as 1893 the links among tourism, the education of younger generations, and nation building. In his words: "the cultivation of tourism . . . has incalculable advantages for teachers of elementary, middle, and high schools. Our country's future rests in their hands! As the sapling is trained, so grows the tree!"[34]

Moussong's "directive" led to an extended debate about other specific benefits of encouraging tourism in schools. Inspired by the founding of the MSTTA, which allowed associational tourism to reach a new high point in Hungary, one participant in the debate appreciated that the time was ripe "to address not only the *teacher*, and explain to him why, when, and how to become a *tourist*, but to summon the *tourist* to become the *teacher*, and the true *educator* [in the name of idealism] of a society degenerating in a realistic [i.e., materialistic] direction."[35] Others deemed school excursions necessary to ac-

31. Dr. Hugó Szterényi, "Az iskolai kirándulások kérdéséhez," *Turisták Lapja* 4, no. 5–6 (1892): 146.
32. "Tiz év a magyar tanítók turista egyesülete életéből, 1892–1902," *Turista Közlöny* 9 (1902): 1–76; and Géza Moussong, "Visszapillantás," *Turista Közlöny* 3, no. 12 (1896): 181–84.
33. See "A Magyar Tanítók Turista-Egyesületének alapszabály-tervezete," *Turista Közlöny* 3, no. 12 (1896): 185–90.
34. Géza Moussong, "Turistaság és tanügy," *Turisták Lapja* 5, no. 3–4 (1893): 45.
35. Sándor Romhányi, "Turistaság a népnevelés szolgálatában," *Turista Közlöny* 4, no. 2 (1897): 21.

quaint pupils with nature and physical exercise, to enable them to improve their sense of orientation (the use of inner and external senses said to lead to better self-monitoring), and to help them better to assimilate the geographical, biological, historical, and ethnographical ideas studied in school.[36] Many argued that school excursions would help pupils to acquire a sense of patriotism based on knowledge of Hungary's natural beauties, while others presented them as excellent occasions to reacquaint urban children with nature, provide them with spiritual food, cultivate their aesthetic sense and encourage their ludic impulses, thus compensating for the overprotective education provided them by their parents.[37]

As an illustration of the MSTTA's clever lobbying practices—including a careful cultivation of alliances with such grassroots organizations as the Magyar Tanítók Kaszinója (Magyar Teachers Casino) and Népnevelők Budapesti Egyesülete (Budapest Association for People's Education)—the voicing of these concerns led to a number of practical outcomes.[38] In July 1900 the municipality of the Hungarian capital (in conformity with an earlier ministerial ordinance on this matter) decided to recommend the school excursions' guidelines proposed by the MSTTA as a matter to be discussed in all Budapest schools.[39] As an effect of the municipality's recommendation, in the 1900/1901 academic year over fifty high schools from Budapest and all over Hungary were reported to have included in their curricula school excursions to natural settings located in their vicinity.[40] Concomitantly, the MSTTA tried to persuade primary schools also to take part in these new types of activities. To push the matter even further, the MSTTA called high-school teachers to participate in several

36. Aladár Vágó, "Az iskolai kirándulások," *Turista Közlöny* 4, no. 3 (1897): 47–50; Ábrahám Léderer, "Iskolai kirándulások," *Turista Közlöny* 4, no. 5 (1897): 89–94; and István Drajkó and G. Adolf Ulrich, "Vélemények az iskolai kirándulásokról," *Turista Közlöny* 8, no. 12 (1901): 275–78.

37. See Gyula Deák, "Iskolai kirándulások," *Turista Közlöny* 4, no. 9 (1897): 141–43; Rezső Altai, "A tanuló-ifjúság kirándulásai," *Turista Közlöny* 7, no. 3 (1900): 63–65; Dezső Drégely, "Az iskolai kirándulásokról," *Turista Közlöny* 7, no. 3 (1900): 65–70; János Almásy, Dezső Oláh, "Az iskolai kirándulások kérdeséhez," *Turista Közlöny* 8, no. 2 (February 1901): 26–28; Irén Kintzler (née Soltész), "Fejlesszük az iskolai kirándulások alkalmával a gyermekek szép iránti érzékét is!" *Turista Közlöny* 9, no. 6 (1902): 113–17; Irma Cserháti, "Az iskolai kirándulások kérdeséhez," *Turista Közlöny* 8, no. 4 (1901): 88–90; and László Madarász, "Az iskolai kirándulásokról," *Turista Közlöny* 5, no. 4 (1898): 63–66.

38. See Antal Döller, "Magyarország a prädestinált turistahon," *Turista Közlöny* 3, no. 9 (1896): 135–38; Géza Moussong, "Az iskolai kirándulásokról," *Turista Közlöny* 6, no. 4 (1899): 83–88, and no. 5 (May 1899): 113–17; and Moussong's editorial: "Visszapillantás," *Turista Közlöny* 7, no. 12 (1900): 293–94.

39. See Ministry of Religion and Education, ordinance number 10.098 (12 May 1894), in *Tiz év a Magyar Tanítók Turista Egyesülete életéből*, ed. Géza Moussong, Lajos Hittig, and Aladár Vágó, 58–60, appendix to *Turista Közlöny* 9, no. 5 (1902), and "Budapest hatósága és az ifjusági kirándulások," *Turista Közlöny* 7, no. 5 (1900): 121–22 and 143–44; Géza Moussong, "A szekesfővárosi iskolák kirándulásairól," *Turista Közlöny* 8, no. 3 (1901): 55–66; and Aladár Leviczki, "Az iskolai kirándulásokról," *Turista Közlöny* 11, no. 11 (1904): 232–36.

40. Aladár Vágó, "Adatok az iskolai kirándulások elterjedéséhez," *Turista Közlöny* 9, no. 5 (1902): 86–89.

essay competitions on the subject of the relationship between tourism and the school, awarding substantial prizes to the winning authors.[41]

During the 1900s, as part of the general effort to familiarize schoolchildren of all ages with different natural settings, primary, middle, and high-school students from various Budapest schools were taken by their teachers on day trips to the Gellért, Castle, and Buda hills (located in the immediate hinterland of the Hungarian capital) and to Visegrád and the bend of the Danube.[42] Many excursions targeted much more distant places. The editors of *Turista Közlöny* (Tourist's Courier—the printed mouthpiece of the MSTTA) made reports of such trips a regular feature of their journal. For example, in 1903 a long account was given of a four-day trip that the faculty of Budapest's Eighth District High School organized for 319 boys aged between ten and sixteen to three provincial centers of Transylvania and eastern Hungary.[43] Accounts such as these were often used to familiarize the journal's readership with the topography and specific attractions of other provincial towns, which were also claiming their share of the budding market in school excursions.[44]

Not only did schools take students into the countryside, but they also brought nature exhibits into the schools. Although the idea of familiarizing children with distant nature sites through the medium of film and photography was not new, the MSTTA's attempt to bring and display fragments of the natural world in the classroom can be seen as innovative.[45] Notwithstanding the differences between these approaches, they had a similar impact on large audiences of pupils who became acquainted with a visualized "Magyar" natural setting while visiting Uránia, Budapest's major documentary film theater and slide projection venue, or just simply sitting in the classroom.[46]

As further proof of the importance of tourism in the process of nation building, in 1905 the Hungarian Ministry of Religion and Public Education

41. See Károly Véredy, "Iskolásgyermekek turistasága," *Turista Közlöny* 10, no. 1 (1903): 2–3; Sándor Witkowszky, "Mily módon alkalmazhatók és hasznosíthatók a turisztikai ismeretek és tapasztalatok az iskolában," *Turista Közlöny* 12, no. 5 (1905): 122–34; and Elek Csáky, "Mily módon alkalmazhatók és hasznosíthatók a turisztikai ismeretek és tapasztalatok az iskolában" *Turista Közlöny* 12, no. 6 (1905): 142–49; no. 7–8 (1905): 183–90, and no. 9 (1905): 199–205.

42. János Horváth, "Referádák," *Turista Közlöny* 8, no. 6 (1901): 141–43; János Nyárasdy, "Iskolai kirándulások: A Gellérthegyen és Várhegyen," *Turista Közlöny* 11, no. 12 (1904): 133–37.

43. Lajos Hittig, "Egy tanulmányi kirándulás," *Turista Közlöny* 10, no. 5 (1903): 128–32.

44. Sándor Romhányi, "Útravaló jegyzetek. Kalauzul: Komárom, Győr és Pozsony városokba," *Turista Közlony* 13, no. 3 (1906); 46–57, and no. 4 (1906): 68–72.

45. Ev. János Horváth, "Hogyan rendezzük az iskolai kirándulásokat," *Turista Közlöny* 9, no. 5 (1902): 158–63; and Lajos Perényi, "A turistaság az ismeretterjesztés szolgálatában," *Turista Közlöny* 12, no. 2 (1905): 21–23.

46. "Uránia," *Turista Közlöny* 8, no. 9 (1901): 193–95; "Tizenegyezer tanuló az Urániában," *Turista Közlöny* 9, no. 11 (1902): 185–88; Lajos Lohr, "Inditvány diapositiv képekről," *Turista Közlöny* 10, no. 3 (1903): 60–62; Lohr, "Vetitőgép az iskolában," *Turista Közlöny* 11, no. 3 (1904): 59–63; and Gyula József Wehner, "Jelentés az Uránia elöadásairól," *Turista Közlöny* 11, no. 9 (1904): 181–82.

officially endorsed the goals of the MSTTA. The ministry's regular support for the MSTTA, however, initiated a new, conservative shift in its policies. Although the ministry encouraged centripetal tourism in all its forms, centrifugal tourism had to stop at Hungary's borders. As an ordinance of the ministry issued in December 1905 pontificated: "Since the most important goal of the school excursions—by wrenching students out of their local environment—is to elevate them to the nation (*nemzet*) and homeland (*haza*), and to develop, besides curricular matters, national feelings and a patriotic spirit, *their [destination] should be limited to our homeland (hazai föld)*. . . . The places that can be selected [as destinations] for these school excursions are those about whose national (*nemzeti*) and countrywide (*országos*) importance there is no doubt."[47]

The ministry's suggestions were not lost on the MSTTA leadership. The first issue of *Turista Közlöny*, published in January 1906, presented the "whole Carpathian basin" (in an article meant to reach and mobilize a continuously expanding readership in the service of tourism and the nation) as an "open book of the [Magyar] people's history in which the chapters are constituted by a ruin or a battlefield."[48] As the author of this programmatic article further detailed:

> In our country tourism is not just a sport but a national duty and a mark of patriotism. Our ancestors settled the plains, ceding the mountains to various [other] ethnic groups. . . . The conquest of these ethnic groups is [a task] awaiting the tourists. . . . [Today] every mountain slope, valley, and gorge constitutes a road for the tourist to penetrate [the ethnic areas], making it possible for the [non-Magyar] ethnic groups to become slowly acquainted with Magyar culture. . . . [O]nce they start experiencing its blessings, ethnic conflict will disappear, and the [ethnic groups] will start to give their esteem to the nation which has shared with them its homeland, constitution, and everything without any ulterior motives. But for this [to happen] we need many tourists.[49]

Although the nationalistic tone of this article was related in part to the threat voiced during the mid-1900s by members of the Hungarian political class to secede from the Austro-Hungarian Empire, the symbolic takeover of Hungary's distant border areas by Magyar tourists was encouraged even before the constitutional crisis of 1905–1906.[50] In 1894, for instance, members of the MTA proposed that, in the guise of a welcoming gesture for the millen-

---

47. A[ladár]. V[ágó]. "Az iskolai kirándulások szabályozása," *Turista Közlöny* 12, no. 12 (1905): 260. Emphasis in original.

48. Aladár Vágó, "A turistaság és a magyarság," *Turista Közlöny* 13, no. 1 (1906): 2.

49. Ibid., 3–4.

50. See Peter F. Sugar, "An Underrated Event: The Hungarian Constitutional Crisis 1905–06," *East European Quarterly*, 15, no. 3 (1981): 281–306.

nial celebrations scheduled to take place in Budapest in 1896, a cross should be erected on the Gerlachfalvi (Gerlachstein) mountain peak in the Tatras, Hungary's highest point, and the peak itself should be renamed after Hungary's first Christian king—Szent (Saint) István.[51]

In a similar vein, the association welcomed the 1896 decision of the Hungarian government to build a number of symbolic monuments at Hungary's border to commemorate the passing of one millennium since the arrival of the seven Magyar tribes in the Carpathian basin. Soon after these monuments were erected, one member of the MTA emphatically urged his fellow tourists to visit the monuments every year, in order to turn them into "shrines of patriotism where national pride and enthusiasm would find inspiration from the struggles [awaiting tourists] in the future."[52] Such visits turned into occasions for MTA and MSTTA tourists to demonstrate the symbolic melding of Hungarian tourism's goals and a spectacularly evoked national spirit, since the singing of patriotic songs and of the national anthem, the recitation of poems, and other oratory devices were often included in their program.[53]

The Militarization of Hungarian Youth Tourism Prior to World War I

Knowledge of the country's natural sites was, at the same time, envisaged as serving not only a patriotic purpose but a military goal as well. "The more one knows the configuration of the homeland, the better one will fight for it," wrote an MSTTA author in 1901.[54] The connection between tourism and military exercise was something to which early commentators on tourism's development in Hungary often referred.[55] Moreover, by the early 1900s, public exploration of this connection was encouraged by a number of essay competitions on the topic, which the MSTTA organized specially for its members.[56] From the first tentative probing of the topic in the 1890s and 1900s, the idea of tourism as a military activity had become by the early 1910s one of the main self-legitimating strategies of the MSTTA and other like-minded tourist associations. Decisive in this regard was a generational shift among the MSTTA leadership as younger and more radical members of the association,

51. Dr. Béla Mihálovics, "Millenium," *Turisták Lapja* 6, no. 3–5 (1894): 34–36.

52. See Dr. Lajos Lázár, "Zarándokoljunk ezredévi emlékeinkhez," *Turisták Lapja* 10, no. 3–4 (1898): 43.

53. Mihály Benkő, "A dévényi és zobori kirándulás," *Turisták Lapja* 10, no. 5–7 (1898): 116–20.

54. Imre Barcza, "Turisztikai töredékek," *Turista Közlöny* 8, no. 12 (1901): 263.

55. See, for instance, Dr. Imre Marinovich, "A turistaság jelentősége az állam életében," *Turisták Lapja* (1893): 85–95.

56. One of the MSTTA's 1902 essay contests, for instance, had the telling title "Tourism in the Service of Military and Physical Exercise." "Gondolatok, javaslatok," *Turista Közlöny* 9, no. 2 (1902): 39.

such as Dr. Károly Horváth and József Tas, took over tasks from retiring members, thus making possible a reconfiguration of the association's priorities as early as 1911–1912.[57]

The new leaders emphasized a combination of tourism, schoolchildren, and advancements in the country's capacity to mobilize in its own defense. The two main sources of inspiration for the achievement of these goals were the British-inspired boy scouts and the German *Pfadfinder* and *Wandervogel* movements.[58] On 30 May 1912 the MSTTA created a special committee charged with the task of popularizing their organizing principles in Hungary.[59] The first act of the new committee was to send out a flyer to the leadership of all the schools in the country, trying to attract interested teachers willing to promote these volunteer movements at home.[60] As a follow-up to the responses, 56 experimental excursions—mobilizing a total of 30 teachers and 1,090 schoolchildren—were organized during the summer of 1912 under the aegis of Vándordiák (Wandering Schoolboy), a new section created specially for this purpose within the existing structures of the MSTTA.[61]

To rally even more pupils, at the end of that month the MSTTA set up the Magyar Őrszem (Hungarian Guard), a new informal structure open to all members.[62] Its hybrid philosophy—as developed by Dr. Károly Horváth—incorporated military practices, concepts of patriotic duty, and the honor code of the boy scout and Pfadfinder movements.[63] The Hungarian Guard's goals as advocated by the MSTTA brought the tourist association a welcome ally: a

57. Géza Moussong, "Búcsúzóm," *Turista Közlöny* 19, no. 12 (1912): 177–78; and József Tas, "Beköszöntő," *Turista Közlöny* 20, no. 1–2 (1913): 1–2.

58. Dr. Károly Horváth, "A diákvándorlások szervezéséhez," *Turista Közlöny* 18, no. 11 (1911): 173–77; Horváth, "Turista-kirándulás, tanulmányút és diákvándorlás," *Turista Közlöny* 19, no. 2 (1912): 23–32; Horváth, "Turistaság az iskola szolgálatában," *Turista Közlöny* 19, no. 4 (1912): 62–65; József Tas, "Scouts-boy," *Turista Közlöny* 19, no. 9 (1912): 125–27; "A magyar tanítók turista egyesülete Berlinben," *Turista Közlöny* 20, no. 1–2 (1913): 14–15; and "Jung Deutschland," *Katonás nevelés* 27, no. 1 (1912): 8. For a discussion of the British boy scouts and German Pfadfinder and Wandervogel movements in the international context of the time, see Michael Rosenthal, *The Character Factory: Baden-Powell and the Origins of the Boy Scout Movement* (New York, 1986), Robert H. MacDonald, *Sons of the Empire: the Frontier and the Boy Scout Movement, 1890–1918* (Toronto, 1993), Walter Laqueur, *Young Germany: A History of the German Youth Movement* (New York, 1962), Peter D. Stachura, *The German Youth Movement: An Interpretative and Documentary History, 1900–1945* (New York, 1981) and George L. Mosse, *The Nationalization of the Masses: Political Symbolism and Mass Movements in Germany from the Napoleonic Wars through the Third Reich* (Ithaca, N.Y., 1991).

59. "Diákvándorlás," *Turista Közlöny* 19, no. 6 (1912): 93–94.

60. Dr. Ferenc Déri, "Körlevél a főreáliskolák, felső kereskedelmi iskolák, polgári és elemi fiuiskolák és az iparostanonciskolák vezetőihez," *Turista Közlöny* 19, no. 6 (1912): 94.

61. Antal Háros, "Beszámoló a diák-vándorlásról," *Turista Közlöny* 19, no. 9 (1912): 128–32, and "Magyar Őrszem," *Turista Közlöny* 20, no. 1–2 (1913): 2–5; Miksa Bokor, "Egy diákvándor út," *Turista Közlöny* 21, no. 5–6 (1914): 59–62.

62. "Egyesületi élet. Titkári jelentés az 1912-ik évről. Irta és felolvasta Tas József titkár, a XXII-ik évi rendes közgyülésen," *Turista Közlöny* 20, no. 1–2 (1913): 9–12.

63. Dr. Károly Horváth, "Magyar Őrszem," *Turista Közlöny* 20, no. 4 (1913):25–28.

vocal group of army officers who since the 1880s had been interested in promoting military education and spartan rules of conduct among Hungarian youth through a monthly publication with the significant title of *Katonás Nevelés* (Military Education) (which, it must be said, was up to then a relatively marginal mouthpiece in the larger landscape of the Hungarian media).[64] A boy scout oath adapted to Hungarian realities was also elaborated by MSTTA's ordinary members Gyula Papp and Ede Bing.[65] Concomitant with the elaboration of the MSTTA's guiding principles and by-laws, the leadership took over the task of popularizing the ideas behind the Hungarian Guard movement among other tourist and affiliated associations, such as the Mecsek Tourist Association based in Pécs and the Temesvár (today Timişoara, Romania) and Budapest sections of the National Middle-School Teachers Association.

In the second half of 1913, the MSTTA—acting on behalf of the Hungarian Guard—entered into negotiations with the Hungarian Scouts Federation. These talks ultimately led to the establishment of the National Scout-Guards Federation, an organizational structure incorporating the two competing associations with their almost twelve hundred scout-guards.[66] The creation of this federative association led many to hope that its militarized tourism would turn its young members into "able self-defenders and defenders of their home and nation."[67] It was a joyful moment for the MSTTA. As József Tas, the editor of *Turista Közlöny*, put it at the beginning of 1914: "The institutionalization of the Scout-Guards is the creation of the MSTTA, since we were the first to try to transplant the Boy Scout movement to Hungary. . . . Today the idea is being realized, and we should get satisfaction from having fulfilled our duty when we strongly urged the formation of this association."[68]

The outbreak of World War I maximized the importance of these developments. By then Hungarian tourism and tourists had become accustomed to functioning under the sign of Mars. As an MSTTA editorial published in *Turista Közlöny* in the autumn of 1914 explicitly stated: "The tourist-teacher cannot hide the conviction growing in his soul—that this war, and especially that taking place on the southern front, represents the culmination of all the touristic ideas [we] propagated."[69] What tourists had learned during their excursions

---

64. Captain Lajos Sároi Szabó, "Iskola és hadsereg," *Katonás nevelés* 23, no. 5 (1908): 1–5; Aladár Töttösy, "Az ifjuság, katonás nevelésének célja, jelentősége és haszna. A honvédelmi minister ur által közlésre ajánlott—átdolgozott-mű," *Katonás nevelés* 28, no. 6 (1913): 4–5.

65. "A 'Magyar Őrszem'," *Katonás nevelés* 28, no. 4 (1913): 3–5; and "Előadás a cserkészmozgalomról," *Katonás nevelés* 28, no. 6 (1913): 2–3.

66. "Egyesületi élet. Titkári jelentés 1913. évről. Irta és felolvasta Tas József," *Turista Közlöny* 21, no. 2 (1914): 23–25; and "Országos Cserkész-Őrszem szövetség," *Katonás nevelés* 28, no. 7–8 (1913): 9.

67. Ede Galambos, "A cserkész mozgalom," *Katonás nevelés* 29, no. 2 (1914): 2–3.

68. "Egyesületi élet. Titkári jelentés 1913," 25.

69. "Turistaság és háboru," *Turista Közlöny* 21, no. 7–10 (1914): 81.

and field trips was finally confirmed as necessary for their transformation into well-prepared soldiers and able defenders of their homeland. "It is now that the tourist-teacher is truly convinced that, when he is going up to a mountain or finds himself in the middle of a plain, the signs written by the sun, the wind, and the water on the face of the earth come all to life in front of him, telling truth to his eye: things that he passed complacently before but now are of utmost interest to him since they can help him track his enemy."[70]

In less than half a century, therefore, the ideological construction of tourism in Hungary turned from support of a consumption-centered and multiethnic organizational model focused on admiration of nature and of beauty into one in which nature was assigned the role of a military map contributing to the achievement of nation building and related goals of territorial preservation. This move from tourists defining themselves as idealistic "friends of nature" and "nature lovers" to disciplined "tourist-soldiers" can be ascribed, undoubtedly, to the strong alliance between tourism and the schools that the MTA called for during the early 1890s and the MSTTA was able to forge during the two decades preceding World War I. The MTA's centralizing drive not only turned Hungarian tourism into a Budapest-controlled activity but destroyed a transnational model of its management as embodied by the early functioning of the Carpathian. Once the ethnicity of tourists was turned into the main criterion defining their relationship to Hungary's natural landscape, the chances of admiring and consuming "nature for nature's sake" (and thus eluding the attachment of national signifiers to it) were seriously reduced. Although individual tourists might have been able to continue to support the consumption view and practice an "apolitical" encounter with nature, group tourism as managed by the MTA and the MSTTA turned admiration of (and work toward the creation of) an imaginary "mountain-loving Magyar nation" into a precondition of association members' access to the country's natural sites.

It is worth comparing the specifics of this transition in Hungarian tourism to the evolution of associational tourism in other contexts. Turn-of-the-century "nationalist tourism in Austria," as Pieter Judson has recently emphasized—be that envisaged by German, Czech, Slovene, Italian or Polish associations—"reinforced particularistic loyalties and undermined official attempts to create an inter-regional, unified public culture around dynastic patriotism."[71] In contrast, in Hungary nationalist tourism as envisaged by the MTA and the MSTTA turned into a centralizing enterprise supported by Hungarian state officials. It became an attempt of the center (Budapest) to create a "unified public culture" around a nationalistically framed notion of state patriotism. As a secondary effect of this, state-sponsored and centralizing associational tourism

70. Ibid.
71. Judson, " 'Every German visitor,' " 149.

in Transleithania succeeded in opposing and eventually marginalizing the nature-centered and transnationally structured activity of the Késmárk-based Carpathian.

If we compare this outcome with a late nineteenth-century western perspective on national tourism—that of the Touring Club de France, for instance—besides differences we will also find a number of poignant similarities. In turn-of-the-century France, as "consistent with its nationalistic and solidarist convictions" the Touring Club "[strove] to recast French tourism as a redemptive experience of the national available to middle-class consumers. The sense of 'place' more commonly registered in the new tourism adduced both to the immediate agenda of republican nation-building, as well as to the broad need within the French and international bourgeoisie for always-updated markers of interior distinction."[72] Tourism in Hungary was as much a middle-class venture as anywhere else in Europe. What makes its comparison with the French situation important, however, is the key role centrally managed initiatives played in the development of tourism in both countries. The role of Budapest in the development of Hungarian tourism was similar to that of Paris, which acted as a central point from which French tourists were able to take a look deep into France, even if the Touring Club's interest in furthering the cause of regionalism might be invoked to the contrary.[73]

My third and last comparison is with literature on tourism in the French, British, Russian, and Soviet empires.[74] Travel and tourism in these empires was based on a culturally biased encounter between metropolitan travelers and indigenous peoples, an occasion used often by the former to impose their cultural habits, beliefs, and modes of conduct on the latter.[75] Although Austria-Hungary did not possess any overseas colonies, a comparison of the discursive construction of Hungarian tourism with colonial practices rooted in other imperial contexts might yield a number of significant insights. Until the 1880s and 1890s, Hungary's mountainous areas were so unknown to the newly invented Hungarian tourist as to create the same thrill and excitement as the exploration of terrae incognitae for colonial travelers. Another poignant similarity with colonial practices is that as exploration of Hungary's mountainous territories progressed, the encounter between tourists and locals was discursively reduced (and willingly distorted) to the trope of a "civilizational" en-

72. Patrick Young, "La Vieille France as Object of Bourgeois Desire: The Touring Club de France and the French Regions, 1890–1918," in *Histories of Leisure*, ed. Koshar, 170.

73. Ibid., 170–74.

74. John Barrell, "Death on the Nile: Fantasy and the Literature of Tourism, 1840–1860," in *Cultures of Empire: Colonizers in Britain and the Empire in the Nineteenth and the Twentieth Centuries*, ed. Catherine Hall (London, 2000), 187–206; Ellen Furlough, "*Un leçon des choses*: Tourism, Empire, and the Nation in Interwar France," *French Historical Studies*, 25, no. 3 (2002): 441–73.

75. See Inderpal Grewal, *Home and Harem: Nation, Gender, Empire, and the Cultures of Travel* (Durham, N.C., 1996); and Mary Louise Pratt, *Imperial Eyes: Travel Writing and Transculturation* (London, 1992).

counter between Hungarian tourists (as supposed agents of the cultural colonization of the locals called for by the nationalistically envisaged exigencies of the modern Hungarian nation) and the ethnically different locals appearing often in the guise of either active or passive resisters (i.e., the subaltern subjects) of their projected colonization.

The ideological construction of turn-of-the-century tourism in Hungary embodied all these aspects. What ultimately characterized Hungarian associational tourism in the period leading up to World War I, however, was its abandonment of its earlier goal, to admire nature in and of itself, for bellicose ends. The tourist-teachers' activity proved decisive in this regard. Their nationalization of Hungary's nature and geography through the wide array of educational channels at their disposal did not, however, lead to a Magyar national revival through the reinfusion of nature into civilization (as some of its early advocates expected), but instead to the affirmation of an uncontrolled militaristic impulse that finally succeeded in dismantling the earlier potential of Hungarian associational tourism.

CHAPTER 4

Slavic Emotion and Vernacular Cosmopolitanism

Yugoslav Travels to Czechoslovakia in the 1920s and 1930s

Noah W. Sobe

Describing the outset of a trip to Czechoslovakia in 1933, Nebojša Živanović, a high-school student from Belgrade, reported:

> Already in my childhood I had heard stories about the brave and peace-loving Slavs. I heard these from my mother's mouth, later from teachers, and I knew that we were brothers and that we had the same goals and that we strove toward the same ideals. This I knew, I knew it very well, however, at that moment when the train which was to carry us to our brothers the Czechoslovaks departed, it seemed to me that I was going into some sort of foreign land, where I would meet only unknown beings and things.[1]

The Slavic filiations that joined Yugoslavs and Czechoslovaks were prior knowledge, having been learned both from teachers and from "one's mother's mouth" [*iz majcinih usta*]. The experience of leaving "home," however, threw everything into disarray for this traveler. What was known became uncertain, and "our brothers the Czechoslovaks" began to appear as "some sort of foreign land" [*neku stranu zemlju*]. Nevertheless, by the end of Živanović's travelogue proper order had been restored. Živanović and the group of Yugoslav students on this excursion concluded their three-week tour with a visit to a Czechoslovak summer camp where, on one of the last evenings, he reported:

> Everyone gathered in front of our hut. We sang. Everyone together. One heard our words, one heard Czech words. It didn't matter. Everyone merged together in the divine melody of our brotherhood. It was the same the next day. In the evening there was a bonfire lit by the leader of our group and the leader of the other camp. More songs. But we had to leave. It was morning. Almost the entire camp was on its feet. Heartfelt saying of good-byes. After, sincere kisses. As if I were in the midst of my own. I felt that which once I had only known. Why did the Lord punish us so, by dividing two brothers?[2]

---

1. Letter dated 9 September 1933, from Nebojša J. Živanović to the minister of education, Arhiv Jugoslavije, 66–443–702.
   2. Ibid.

The foreignness of Czechoslovakia, which earlier in the text a source of apprehension, had by the end been eclipsed. In this instance, singing—with its suggestion of music as a universal language with unifying power—was one of the cultural practices making it possible that "everyone merged together." Živanović's report reveals shared collective belonging being constructed on an emotional plane. The social organization of individuals' emotional comportment is a cultural practice that is a regularly described feature of Czechoslovak-Yugoslav host-guest interactions in the interwar era. Both this high-school student's travelogue and other Yugoslav travel texts suggest that a normative style of emotional comportment, joined to notions of "hospitality" and "kinship," was central to a specific, local understanding of "the Slavic" and the construction of Pan-Slavic as well as national identity.

This chapter explores one set of the many intraregional travel and touristic encounters that took place in eastern Europe in the 1920s and 1930s. I examine the travels of Yugoslavs to Czechoslovakia, together with the Pan-Slavism that was expressed in and formed through these travel interactions. Travelogues and reports reveal that what it meant to be "Slavic" could be positioned as an important source of both Yugoslav national identity and individual self-identity. Looking at the construction of a "Slavic brotherhood" that would join Yugoslavs and Czechoslovaks provides a useful backdrop to the emergence of the "fraternal" features of socialist tourism within eastern Europe. A postwar culture of tourism in which fraternal solidarities were valued did not appear ex nihilo, but rather became possible partly due to antecedent styles of travel when tourism also intersected with a transnational political and cultural movement.

Yugoslav Pan-Slavism is a particularly interesting case because it represents a form of "thinking beyond the local"—a set of commitments and dispositions that might be called a "vernacular cosmopolitanism," as I discuss in the conclusion. In this configuration, Russia figures almost not at all. Soviet communism was officially not welcome in the Kingdom of the Serbs, Croats, and Slovenes, which meant that "mother Russia" could no longer operate as a viable organizing principle for the Pan-Slavic idea in southeastern/eastern Europe in the 1920s and 1930s. As it was viewed from the Yugoslav side, the Pan-Slavism of this period properly centered along a Yugoslav-Czechoslovak axis. Yugoslav travelers' accounts speak of Czechoslovakia as "the most advanced Slavic nation." The perception of a shared historical destiny, as well as of a shared Slavic nature, made brotherly Czechoslovakia an acceptable model of modern ways of being, acting, and organizing society.

The travelogues of Yugoslav students and teachers are the main sources for the present study.[3] The corpus of archival materials on which I rely includes

---

3. The travel literature of Yugoslav beekeepers about their beekeeping study tours reveals considerable homologies across the domains of education and apiculture in the impact that Pan-Slavism and foreign travel to Czechoslovakia had on visions of "modernity" in both areas. Quite

reports from travel stipend recipients [*ferijalne stipendiste*] that have been preserved in the archives of the Yugoslav Ministry of Education; articles and letters that were published in pedagogical journals and newspapers; and travelogues that appeared in books and annual school reports. That these are
student and teacher travel texts is significant to the extent that it defines the social field under study and allows for an examination of "official" social ideals
and the normative styles of emotional comportment moving through Yugoslavia in the 1920s and 1930s.

Emotional Comportment

Feeling and emotion were foregrounded in the intriguing statement Nebojša
Živanović offered on the completion of his travels to Czechoslovakia: "I *felt*
that which once I had only known" (emphasis added). Discernable in this, and
in other travelogues that I discuss in this section, is a historically and culturally
particular normative style of emotional comportment that can be characterized as one in which effusive enthusiasm and "deeply" held feelings played a
strong constitutive role in forming the self and fabricating national and ethnic
belonging. In contrast to the frequently cited analytic frame that John Urry has
elaborated around the tourist's gaze as a disciplinary ordering of objects of
knowledge though optics of seeing and being seen, the tourist culture of Yugoslavs traveling to Czechoslovakia in the 1920s and 1930s can be usefully an-
alyzed as centering less on the gaze than on emotions.[4]

The narrative trajectory of Živanović's 1933 text is of moving from "knowing" to "feeling," a transition presented as one of moving from the uncertainty
of received learning to the confident certainty that could come from empirical
confirmation achieved on an emotional plane. Pan-Slavism, of course, could be
expressed on multiple planes, and on this particular excursion it appears that
the Slavic joining of Yugoslavs and Czechoslovaks was also symbolically performed in a public fire-lighting ritual. This travel text, however, gave pride of
place to host-guest interactions that were more intimate than spectacular in
nature. With "heartfelt saying of good-byes" and "sincere kisses" among the
culminating features of the travel account, emotional closeness is positioned as
the signature feature of Yugoslav-Czechoslovak interactions. An expression of
emotional "fervor" even accompanies the writing itself. Although the entire
report appears to have been written after the trip ended, one can note a
marked difference in narrative style between the text's opening and closing

---

notable is that the norms of emotional comportment being discussed here in reference to student
and teacher travelogues have left a sharp imprint on beekeepers' travel accounts as well. See Noah
W. Sobe, "Cultivating a 'Slavic Modern': Yugoslav Beekeeping, Schooling, and Travel in the 1920s
and 1930s," *Paedagogica Historica* 41, no. 1–2 (2005): 143–58.

4. John Urry, *The Tourist Gaze: Leisure and Travel in Contemporary Societies* (London,
1990).

(the two excerpts above). The short, rapid-paced sentences at the end, "More songs. But we had to leave. It was morning," convey an intensity of experience. This as-if breathless enthusiasm, which emphasizes the extent to which these interactions affected the speaker, accords with what we find is a patterned style of emotional comportment among Yugoslav student and teacher travelers to Czechoslovakia.

Historicizing emotion can be seen to involve both an examination of the culturally shifting ways that people have reasoned about "feelings" and recognized something as "an emotion," as well as an examination of the shifting "neuro-psychological" makeup of these feelings/emotions. A recently proposed framework for writing histories of emotion draws on cognitive psychology to characterize affect as an "overlearned habit." William Reddy, a historian and cultural anthropologist, means by this that emotions have a neuro-chemical expression which over the long term can be manipulated, learned, and unlearned just as—he argues—social and cultural practices are in general.[5] Reddy's proposal is that collective and individual emotional unlearnings and relearnings vary with time and place. This can be accessed by historians who focus their attention on the various kinds of "emotional regimes" that have appeared in the past. In this chapter I am using the concept of "a style of emotional comportment" as a way of theorizing regulative consistencies within these discursive and nondiscursive formations.

The warm, cordial receptions that Yugoslavs received upon arrival in Czechoslovakia are regularly reported in student and teacher travelogues. Alongside Yugoslav descriptions of these outpourings of friendly welcome are frequent mentions of the travelers' own powerfully felt reactions to these greetings. Czechoslovak greetings and the Yugoslav reaction are, for example, recorded in the travelogue written by the leader of a 1933 Czechoslovak study-tour [naučno putovanje] of around thirty Yugoslav teachers. Salih Ljubunčić, professor of education from Zagreb, noted that a delegation of Czechoslovak teachers awaited the Yugoslav group at the border crossing from Austria, enthusiastically welcoming the travelers with "Vitame vas! Zdravo! Živjeli! Nazdar!" These were multilingual greetings and Ljubunčić commented "we were moved [ganuti] by this welcome."[6] The travelers' arrival in Czechoslovakia could, in fact, be construed to be a kind of homecoming. "We heard the Slovak language, soft and sweet and so close to ours. We saw Czechoslovak friends and immediately we drew close as though we had known each other before."[7] From this account, Slavic relatedness was established around linguistic com-

5. William M. Reddy, *The Navigation of Feeling: A Framework for the History of Emotions* (Cambridge, 2001). See also Anna Wierzbicka, *Emotions across Languages and Cultures: Diversity and Universals* (Cambridge, 1999); and James M. Wilce, "Passionate Scholarship: Recent Anthropologies of Emotion," *Reviews in Anthropology* 33, no. 1 (2004): 1–17.

6. Salih Ljubunčić, "Naučno putovanje naših učitelja u Čehoslovačku," *Napretka i Savremena Škole*, no. 5–10 (1933): 142.

7. Ibid., 141.

monalities and a shared Czechoslovak-Yugoslav vision of what a proper welcome ought to look and feel like.

Ceremonies of welcome continued for this expedition of educators. From the border, a special train car took them on to Bratislava where another reception awaited. There, a mass of schoolchildren and a teachers' choir greeted them with a rendition of the Yugoslav national anthem, a gesture that brought familiar elements of the Yugoslav national imaginary into an ostensibly non-Yugoslav space. Singing and ceremonies of greeting appear to have continued into the evening, and the Yugoslav trip leader mentioned the beautiful singing of a children's choir, noting "we all were brought to tears, particularly when we heard the little soloist."[8] These tears can be read as part and parcel of a certain normative style of emotional comportment—they can be seen as a physiological expression of the intimacy, closeness, and "depth" or "intensification" of feelings that accompanied Yugoslavs' arrivals in Czechoslovakia.

The emotional force of the welcome extended to Yugoslav travelers by Czechoslovaks is similarly reported in the travelogue of a participant in the Belgrade Women's Normal School's 1930 school excursion to Czechoslovakia. Fourth-year student Perka Vodanović discussed how her initial trepidations about foreign travel were assuaged, writing:

> The rigidity and fear in my soul from being in a foreign country [u tuđoj zemlji] and among foreign people [među stranim ljudima] quickly vanished and was replaced with a certain kind of joy which filled all of us when our Czechoslovak friends sang our national anthem, mentioning the name of our king. Their school director welcomed us with a heartfelt [srdačno] speech.[9]

As in the Živanović text with which this chapter began, uncertainty and initial apprehension were eclipsed through behaviors and the construction of collective belonging on an emotional plane. Vodanović noted the "heartfelt" speech of the school director who welcomed the group in Prague and added, "We were touched and our professor returned the greetings with warmth and sincerity such that we began to cry from the excitement."[10]

The emotional plane of Czechoslovak-Yugoslav host-guest interactions appears to have significantly contributed to the construction of a shared, collective Slavic belonging. The apprehension that Vodanović felt in such a physical way "quickly vanished" in the face of a warm Czechoslovak welcome. "Foreign people" rapidly become "our Czechoslovak friends." The Serbo-Croatian adjective used here for foreign, stran, carries the sense of the "unknown" and the "strange," both of which were overcome as Czechoslovaks became known

    8. Ibid., 142.
    9. Perka Vodanović, "Ekskurzija kroz Čehoslovačku i Austriju," in Izveštaj za 1925–26–27–28–29 i 30 godine, ed. Ženska učiteljska škola u Beogradu (Belgrade, 1930), 28.
    10. Ibid., 28–29.

and familiar to these Yugoslav travelers. The Serbo-Croatian adjective *tuđ*, which was used here to describe the "foreign land" that Czechoslovakia was initially, carries a sense of "belonging-to-others." This foreignness, too, appears to have been eclipsed. For Yugoslav students and teachers, Slavic belonging could be found in Czechoslovakia.

It is important to note that the concern of this chapter is with the correspondences and emotional reciprocity attached to Czechoslovak-Yugoslav host-guest interactions as they are recorded from the Yugoslav side. I am not examining Czechoslovak archival sources on the reception of Yugoslav travelers. However, as is indicated in nearly all the travel texts discussed above, these interactions and emotional behaviors were, to be sure, co-constructed. The style of emotional comportment that Yugoslavs perceived among Czechoslovaks was one that stood as a social norm for Yugoslavs as well; it required of them emotional enthusiasm, a consciously attended-to "depth" of feeling, and reasoning about the self-knowledge that could be generated through attention to the emotional domain.

Slavic Hospitality

Expectations for what welcome would be extended traveling Yugoslavs and how it would be received frequently appear in travelogues under the label of "Slavic hospitality" [*slovenska gostoljubost*]. In this section I argue that Slavic hospitality was the well-matched counterpart to the style of emotional comportment just described. Together the two produced a form of Slavic belonging that was at the core of the Pan-Slavism circulating through Yugoslavia in the 1920s and 1930s.

"Slavic hospitality" named the ritualized hosting practices and provided an organizer for thinking about the styles of emotional comportment that were expected from both guests and hosts. In Salih Ljubunčić's account of the 1933 teachers' study-tour visit to an apprenticeship/trade school in Bratislava we see how these elements were drawn together. Describing the visit, Ljubunčić effused: "And how they greeted us! Everyone was assembled: teachers and parents and then the children. From all sides affectionately and enthusiastically: *Vitame vas! Živjeli!* And then songs. Dances. Flowers. Snacks. Marching. And in all these expressions one felt a brotherly heart, one felt an open-armed Slavic hospitality."[11] Worth underscoring is that this Yugoslav report described a warmth of feeling coming from both sides. This perceived cultural alignment in how affection and enthusiasm were to be held and displayed was grouped under the term "hospitality." As *Slavic* hospitality, this conceptual organizer had the power to explain (and fabricate) a cultural connection accompanying linguistic commonalities between Czechoslovaks and Yugoslavs. Alongside

---

11. Ljubunčić, "Naučno putovanje," 142.

this, we can note that "Slavic hospitality" was also closely connected with the construction of non-Slavic "others."

Yugoslavs traveling to Czechoslovakia generally passed through Austria or Hungary en route. A common reference point in student and teacher travelogues is juxtapositions between the Germanic and the Czechoslovak/Slavic (much less frequent are juxtapositions between the Magyar and the Czechoslovak/Slavic). Yugoslav study-tours even visited schools in Vienna, though in the instance of the 1933 teacher expedition directed by Salih Ljubunčić the schools on the itinerary in Vienna were Czechoslovak schools. "Czechoslovaks have the prettiest and best-cared-for school buildings in Vienna. And, what's more, in these schools one finds the best methods used as well," noted Ljubunčić, who added that this commitment to education in diaspora stood as evidence of Czechoslovaks' "national perseverance."[12] Andrej Debenek, a Slovenian teacher participating in the study-tour, discussed the group's visits to these schools in a travel report that appeared in the journal *Učiteljski Tovariš* (Teacher's Companion). In reference to the Yugoslavs' visit to the Comenius School, Debenek remarked, "to begin with, we felt a Slavic hospitality [*slovanska gostoljubnost*] in the middle of this foreign existence. It warmed us."[13] The locale for this Slavic hospitality was not Czechoslovakia, yet it was with Czechoslovak-Yugoslav interactions that the "warmth" of a welcome was felt by these Yugoslavs in Germanic Austria.

The 1930 expedition from the Belgrade Women's Normal School also included Vienna on their itinerary, and similarly absent was any warmth of feeling connected with the welcomes or hospitality of Austrians. This group of Yugoslav students stayed in Vienna after their visit to Czechoslovakia and heard lectures at a Viennese teacher training institute, but it was only among fellow Slavs in the city that Perka Vodanović's text reported feelings of welcome. On arrival she noted, "again that feeling of dejection arose; I had some sort of fear in the face of this foreign world [*pred tim tuđim svetom*]." The Yugoslav high-school students were met at the train station and feted at a banquet by the president of a Vienna-based Yugoslav organization. Later, the Yugoslav ambassador and his wife invited the group to tea where they displayed a "parental warmth and cordiality," which, in Vodanović's view, was "evidence of the great love they have for young people."[14] The narrative parallel between this group's welcome in each country (the remark about the ambassador's "great love" should be mentioned in this respect as well) indicate once more that feeling and emotion were central among the registers through which these Yugoslav travelers brought sense and intelligibility to the foreign.

12. Salih Ljubunčić, *Školstvo i prosvjeta u Čehoslovačkoj: s osobitim obzirom na pedagošku i školsku reformu*, ed. Salih Ljubunčić (Zagreb, 1934), 44.

13. Andrej Debenak, "Vtisi iz učiteljske studijske ekskurzije po Čehoslovaški," *Učiteljski tovaris*, no. 10, 11 (1933).

14. Vodanović, "Ekskurzija kroz Čehoslovačku i Austriju," 29–30.

Evidence from these student and teacher travelogues suggests that the contrasts with a non-Slavic, Germanic "other" helped to give a crucial element of definition to the idea of "Slavic hospitality." As a conceptual organizer, Slavic hospitality meant that Yugoslavs were to have the ability to develop Slavic belongings in multiple locations; it also meant that in host-guest interactions it was commonplace activities—and not just elite ones—which formed the cultural patterns out of which a social collective cohered.

Nation Building in an Emotional Register

The patterns of emotional comportment seen in circulation along Yugoslav-Czechoslovak travel circuits, together with the concept of Slavic hospitality, are centrally related to the Yugoslav nation-building project. The travels of Yugoslav students and teachers Czechoslovakia in the 1920s and 1930s suggest that Pan-Slavic affections worked in a manner complementary to the emotional regulation that was to make "Yugoslavs" out of the citizens of the Kingdom of the Serbs, Croats, and Slovenes. Slavic emotion, in fact, I will argue in the following sections, imbued these cultural practices with a cosmopolitan, salvational humanism (albeit one bracketed along lines of "Slavic" filiations).

The regulation of feeling was openly discussed in Yugoslav pedagogical literature of the early 1920s. Woven into pedagogical writing about teaching methods and the desired aims of schooling were ideals of emotional comportment. One such statement, from Jovan P. Jovanović, one of the leaders of the Yugoslav Teachers' Association (Udruženje Jugoslovenskih Učiteljstva, UJU), claimed that a Yugoslavia could only be truly constituted through its schools:

> because only with the good upbringing and education of a young national generation is it possible to purge regional patriotism, tribal feelings, and separatist tendencies from our united region, so that in place of tribal feelings a national consciousness and national feelings rule, so that in place of regional patriotism there is general love toward the whole unified homeland, so that in this homeland everyone feels not only like the subject of a single state but like the sons of one nation.[15]

In this vision of the social role education could play, Jovanović conceptualized Yugoslavianism as a feeling [osećanje] that when held could lead to a more advanced consciousness. An objective of education was to encourage a "general love" and for Yugoslavs to *feel* as the "sons of one nation." This text, which appeared in *Učitelj* (The Teacher), the leading Yugoslav education journal of the interwar era, inscribed one of the key narratives of a modernity: the story

---

15. Jovan P. Jovanović, "Zadaci učiteljske organizacije u ujedinjenoj domovini Srba, Hrvata, i Slovenaca," *Učitelj* 3, no. 1 (1922): 7.

of a progressive arc in the development of societies and human behaviors toward increasing refinement and sophistication. Present here are echoes of what Norbert Elias called the "civilizing process," though in this instance it does not necessarily follow that "restraint" and "moderation" are what "rule" human emotional behavior, as is the case in Elias's analysis. Notable about the Yugoslav instance is that it was to be an expansive, laterally spreading "general love" that represented advancement.

Yugoslav travelers similarly viewed the Czechoslovak school as a site where national feelings could be normalized as proper human affections. In describing the schools in the industrial Czech city of Zlín, upon his return from leading the 1933 teacher study tour discussed above, Salih Ljubunčić noted the many educational innovations, including the involvement of teachers in monitoring the health, hygiene, and physical growth of students, as well as the regular organization of concerts and after-school student clubs. One thing in particular that strongly impressed Ljubunčić about the schools of Zlín were the school excursions, and he wrote in his travel report: "Students together with their teachers, or students by themselves, set up shorter and longer travels both through closer areas and areas farther away, as well as through the various regions of their homeland. . . . This collective travel instills the lesson in each young Czechoslovak of how and in what ways to travel."[16] An important feature of Czechoslovak school excursions was the reconfiguring of relations between teachers and students through shared decision making and planning, something that could be seen as a democratization of social relations and a model of social behavior appropriate to Czechoslovakia and Yugoslavia as new, independent, "democratic" nations.[17] Ljubunčić opined that this model of social relations produced a "social feeling" [socijalno osećanje] that enabled "future generations to enter into national life better able and better prepared."[18] Traveling helped to produce a national coherence that was at one and the same time both "natural" and in need of deliberate cultivation.

Any appearance of a paradox in the idea of needing to enhance innate national affections was resolved in Ljubunčić's text through reference to the claim of Czechoslovak president Tomaš Masaryk that while "youth by themselves are enthusiastic," one has to "give direction and order the direction of that enthusiasm." Analogously, according to Ljubunčić, "the love that is imbibed from mother's milk inspires Czechoslovaks to recognize [their homeland]." However, Ljubunčić wrote,

> It is not enough only to be a citizen of Czechoslovakia or just to bear the name Czechoslovak. Similarly, it is not enough just to carry in one's

16. Ljubunčić, Školstvo i prosvjeta u Čehoslovačkoj, 43.

17. For further discussion of the social relations that Yugoslav travelers witnessed in Zlín, particularly in reference to the concept of welfare and its connections to the idea of "agentic actorhood," see Sobe, "Cultivating a 'Slavic Modern.' "

18. Ljubunčić, Školstvo i prosvjeta u Čehoslovačkoj, 40, 43.

heart the unorganized and unclear feeling that connects a person through blood to one society. Rather, it is necessary to be conscious of all this, to understand it rationally and to devote oneself to the very end so that what is in the heart and in the nerves isn't destroyed and isn't lost.[19]

This cultivation of feeling through travel meant that Czechoslovaks were to become "conscious" of their bodily (e.g., "heart," "blood," and "nerves") connections to society. It is important to note that—parallel to Jovanović's call for the rule of national feelings over regional patriotism—the domain of affect is not something to be overruled. Even though the above observation discusses the development of "rational" [razumno] understandings, this is not a Lockean schema in which reason is to govern "passions" absolutely. Instead, the goal is the proper clarity and organization of feelings. In this vision, one can imagine the interlocked counterpart to Nebojša Živanović's acquisition of strengthened Slavic feelings discussed at the beginning of this chapter: the arc of transformations complementary to "feeling that which I already knew" was coming to know that which was already felt. Both share the sense that genuine belonging required individual activity and could not arise simply from the passive acceptance of received cultural authorities.

Slavic Love

The claim that in the 1920s and 1930s there was a distinctly Slavic style of emotional comportment is not an analytic anachronism. In the interwar era, various academic disciplines were involved in constructing a pan-Slavic sensibility; anthropological, sociological, and philosophical writing on "Slavic love" and "Slavic sympathy" imbued the "Slavic" with cosmopolitan commitments and equipped Yugoslavs with tools that could be used to make homes in the world.

A excellent representative of this literature is Paul Radosavljevich's 1918 *Who Are the Slavs?*. This two-volume work by a Serbian-born New York University professor of pedagogy synthesized a wide range of sources and was held up in the early twentieth century as an authoritative work on Slavs.[20] Many pages charted the accomplishments of various illustrious Slavs; and after reading the book, one would be inclined to conclude that every Slavic characteristic demonstrated nobility, or at least held some promise for improving the lot of humanity (e.g., the section titled "Slavic Humility and Lack of

19. Ibid., 44.
20. See, for example, Joseph S. Roucek, "The Development of Sociology in Yugoslavia," *American Sociological Review* 1, no. 6 (1936): 981–88.

Hypocrisy"). Regardless, for several decades the work appears to have been generally held in high regard for its scholarship. Radosavljevich adopted Tolstoy's line that love is "man's only rational activity," and argued that "the Slav has a craving to love and be loved, he would fain join the other European people as friend and brother."[21] The Slavic capacity to love is in actuality, according to Radosavljevich, a manifestation of "all-humanness." In the text, love is presented as a human universal with redemptive potential. Radosavljevich wrote: "Love abolishes the innate activity directed to filling on [sic] the bottomless tub of our bestial personality, does away with the foolish fight between beings that strive after their own happiness, gives a meaning independent of space, and time of life, which without it would flow off without meaning in the face of death."[22] This salvational conceptualization of love remakes the "natural," which here is cast as "bestial," into a transcendent universal ("independent of space and time") that has regenerative powers. Radosavljevich followed this dramatic description with the claim that "this faith is accepted both by the Slavic people and their great men and women,"[23] which is certainly something of an overstatement. Nonetheless, when this quote is read intertextually with Ljubunčić's description of the love that Czechoslovaks purportedly imbibed "with their mother's milk" and Vodanović's mention of the "great love" that the Yugoslav ambassador in Vienna showed toward the traveling Yugoslav student-teachers, it is possible to flesh out more convincingly the cultural significance that the concept of love had in Yugoslavia in the 1920s and 1930s. The archival material examined above suggests that a redemptive, humanist concept of "love" plausibly did serve as a normative meaning-giving and motivating factor in the organization of individuals' actions and reflection.

Radosavljevich specifically discussed the idea of "Slavic love," and it is important to note that this was neither romantic nor sexual love. It was not the chivalric love that has been construed to derive from the poet troubadours of eleventh-century Provence (this is the courtly romantic love that in Luisa Passerini's dexterous argument has served as an important touchstone in the development of a "European identity").[24] Slavic love as Radosavljevich discusses it is a form of general Christian sympathy that enables Slavs "to exercise a large tolerance toward the failings and foibles of their fellow-creatures, [and] to understand people different from themselves."[25] It was a social, or perhaps more properly put, a civic love.

21. Paul R. Radosavljevich, *Who Are the Slavs? A Contribution to Race Psychology*, 2 vols. (Boston, 1919), 1: 385.

22. Ibid.

23. Ibid., 386.

24. Luisa Passerini, *Europe in Love, Love in Europe: Imagination and Politics between the Wars* (New York, 1999).

25. Radosavljevich, *Who Are the Slavs?*, 1: 394.

The Traveling of Feeling and the Vernacular Cosmopolitanism of Yugoslav Pan-Slavism

One argument of this chapter is that the norms of emotional comportment which come into high resolution in interwar Yugoslav-Czechoslovak tourist interactions have the potential to enrich discussion of socialist-era tourism and in particular its "fraternal" features. Similarly, we can note that what occurs in the 1920s and 1930s also arises in conversation with antecedent cultures of tourism experienced in the region. The depth and "intensity" of feeling surrounding Slavic brotherhood is a long-standing trope that even before the interwar period, it could become an object of satire, as in Horvat-Kiš's comment on a 1911 Sokol calisthenics rally in Sofia: "Look, how the Serb and the Bulgarian hug and kiss! The two giants embrace one another. Good Lord above, is there anything sincere at all in those kisses?"[26] Horvat-Kiš's amused skepticism points to the linkage between emotional comportment and notions of Slavic fraternity being well worn by the time of the travels under examination here. However, I propose that in the interwar period these sets of cultural practices take on a new significance for Yugoslavs, both as increasingly widely dispersed social norms and as a vernacular cosmopolitanism that tied the traveler's socializing to knowing how to live properly in society.

In Yugoslavia, as throughout eastern Europe, the 1920s and 1930s were not a time of mass tourism as experienced in parts of western Europe or the United States in the same period.[27] Available documentation concerning the foreign travels of Yugoslav students and teachers suggests, however, that study tours and excursions to Czechoslovakia were being conducted on a scale large enough to be considered a form of purposeful tourism.[28] The annual reports of the "Educational Inspector" (*Prosvetni inspector* and *Prosvetni referent*) who was posted to the Yugoslav embassy in Prague provide some information about these visits. The 1927 report mentioned the amount of time he was having to spend greeting the "ever more numerous student excursions," and noted that in the spring of 1927 there had been twelve visits from secondary schools and universities "from various parts of the Kingdom of the Serbs, Croats, and Slovenians."[29]

26. I am grateful to Wendy Bracewell for bringing this passage to my attention. Franjo Horvat-Kiš, *Sabrana Djela* (Zagreb, 1943), 2: 32.

27. See Gorsuch and Koenker, in this volume.

28. This is not to assert a tourism/travel distinction as analytically key to this chapter but rather to treat the excursions under examination here as part of a conjoined "tourism and travel project." For discussion of this in the context of Russian tourism, travel, and leisure, see Diane P. Koenker, "Travel to Work, Travel to Play: On Russian Tourism, Travel and Leisure," *Slavic Review* 62, no. 4 (2003): 657–65.

29. Report dated 11 December 1927, with Prosvetni Inspektor number 203–I–1927, from Dragutin Prohaska to the minister of education, Arhiv Jugoslavije, 66–441–702.

Other sources indicate that individual groups could include as many as 350 student travelers.[30] The reports and publications of Yugoslav-Czechoslovak Friendship Leagues which were formed in nearly all the major Yugoslav and Czechoslovak cities make frequent mention of traveling groups of teachers, particularly during the summer months.[31] Encouraging the study-tour travel of teachers to Czechoslovakia was set as an institutional objective for the Yugoslav Teachers Association (UJU) at its inaugural meeting in June 1920, though the formally organized student and teacher excursions for which the most comprehensive documentation is available are the annual tours launched under the Yugoslav Ministry of Education's travel stipends program, which in the 1930s were sending groups of twenty to twenty-five secondary-school teachers, secondary-school students, and university students on monthlong summer study tours.[32] As noted earlier, the reports written by those who traveled through this program, as well as the travel reports that were published in school yearbooks and in the educational press, are particularly useful for the purposes of this chapter, as its objective has been to identify the "officially desirable" normative principles that structured the culture of Yugoslav-Czechoslovak tourism in the interwar era.

To understand these norms of emotional comportment as part of a vernacular cosmopolitanism it is useful to explore some of the ways in which the regulation of emotions can be linked to conditions of sociability. While the concept of *kosmopolitizm* was certainly known in Yugoslavia in the interwar period, I am not examining contemporary cultural representations of the "cosmopolitan" but rather am using cosmopolitanism as an analytic descriptor that can be applied to a historically shifting phenomenon appearing in multiple places and multiple times and in various guises.[33] As Radosavljevich's writings on "Slavic love" suggest, the emotional comportment that structured Yugoslav-Czechoslovak interactions possessed some of the qualities of a cosmopolitanism in that it specified techniques of living and forming solidarities outside the local. That these feelings were also tied to a system of inclusions and exclusions (as we saw in regard to Germanic non-Slavs) speaks less to something uniquely Slavic and more to the way in which transnational soli-

30. Letter dated 15 March 1930, with Foreign Affairs Ministry number 4833, from Ministry of Foreign Affairs to the Ministry of Education, Arhiv Jugoslavije, 66 POV–78–218.

31. See the discussion of these associations in Arnost Skoupy, "K Vyvoji Svazu Jihoslovansko-Československych Lig v Letech 1925–1938," *Acta Universitatis Palackianae Olomucensis—Historica* 24 (1988).

32. "Braća Česi u Beogradu," *Narodna Prosveta*, 1 August 1920.

33. Following the work of scholars such as Sheldon Pollock, K. Anthony Appiah, Carol Breckenridge, and Dipesh Chakrabarty, I consider it possible for cosmopolitanism to be considered a historical category "not pre-given or foreclosed by the definition of any particular society or discourse." See Carol A. Breckenridge et al., "Cosmopolitanisms," *Public Culture* 12, no. 3 (2000): 577–78. This makes it possible to speak of concepts like "Chinese cosmopolitanism," "Islamic cosmopolitanism," and the vernacular cosmopolitanism of Yugoslav Pan-Slavism.

darities are in general articulated in juxtaposition to certain "others" who fail to be sufficiently "global," "internationalist," or "fraternal."

Radosavljevich's view of the Slavic ability to sympathize as the torch bearer of a salvational humanism or "all-humanness" can be usefully viewed in the light of David Hume's arguments for the social significance of human emotion. In his *Treatise on Human Nature*, Hume presented a social theory in which socialized passions could be understood as the foundation of social order.[34] For Hume (at least in this early work) feelings and affections were not potentially divisive private desires, but instead were socially minded and, in essence, productive of society. Passions were "contagious," and it was their movement that Hume understood by the term "sympathy." He maintained that humans had a "propensity . . . to sympathize with others, and to receive by communication their inclinations and sentiments, however different from, or even contrary to our own."[35] This propensity meant that human beings could perform and reinforce their fundamental sociability through the encounters they had with others. Hume generalized particular, individual operations of sympathy (sympathy in the exchange of sentiments between particular individuals) to be a model that explained all social interactions (sympathy in the interest of society). The Humean model points out how features of a cosmopolitanism can be articulated on an emotional plane, something we have seen with the Yugoslav students and teachers who traveled to Czechoslovakia, who were emotionally "open" to and effused about their encounters with Czechoslovaks and held deep feelings of Slavic brotherhood. This emotional comportment enabled the establishment of solidarities outside the local and the cultivation of a vernacular cosmopolitanism.

In closing, we can note that in Yugoslav thinking about Czechoslovak schooling, an "enchanted," romantic understanding of the Slavic easily accompanied a "disenchanted," rationalized reasoning about the Slavic.[36] Above, we have seen a construction of the citizen through both the "enchanted" and the "disenchanted" in Ljubunčić's description of how Czechoslovaks—particularly in the city of Zlín—were taught to develop rational and organized understandings of a "love" that was their birth inheritance. These ways of expressing and cultivating the self embody the cosmopolitanism circulating in eastern Europe in the 1920s and 1930s. The amalgamation of these dispositions, sensitivities, conduct, and emotions are concisely captured in one Yugoslav student's travel-stipend report. Miloš Ilić, who traveled to Czechoslovakia in the

34. See David Hume, *A Treatise of Human Nature*, ed. L. A. Selby-Bigge (Oxford, 1978), bk. 2. My thinking about Hume has been helped by John Mullan, *Sentiment and Sociability: The Language of Feeling in the Eighteenth Century* (Oxford, 1988), 1–56; and Michael Bell, *Sentimentalism, Ethics, and the Culture of Feeling* (New York, 2000).

35. Hume, *Treatise of Human Nature*, 316.

36. On the problem of "enchantment" and "modernity," see Jane Bennett, "The Enchanted World of Modernity: Paracelsus, Kant, and Deleuze," *Cultural Values* 1, no. 1 (1997): 1–28.

summer of 1936, reported to the Ministry of Education in Belgrade: "We saw that the Czech nation is clear-headed and cultured, and that they are very fond of their Yugoslav brothers. In Czechoslovakia we felt as if we were in our second fatherland."[37] In pairing the Czechoslovak fondness for Yugoslavs with a clear-headedness and the notion of being "very fond of their Yugoslav brothers," Ilić, in this conclusion to his travelogue, described the proper balance and combination of "rationalism" and "romanticism" that Yugoslav travelers seem to have found in Czechoslovakia. These exemplary behaviors and traits helped to create belonging (here: the *feeling* of being in a "second fatherland"). For Yugoslav travelers, this suggested ways of being at-home in the world and transforming what belonged-to-others into their own belonging.

37. Undated letter (1936) from Miloš Ilić to the Minister of Education, Arhiv Jugoslavije, 66–444–702.

CHAPTER 5

"One Breath for Every Two Strides"

The State's Attempt to Construct Tourism and Identity in Interwar Latvia

Aldis Purs

Two admonitions for Latvian tourists written just over ten years apart capture the raisons d'être of tourism in two different eras. In 1926 Mārtiņš Celms wrote in his guidebook to the Latvian capital: "Let's begin our viewing of Riga at the Bastejs Hill . . . at its summit a string quartet plays in the summertime and you can get different kinds of refreshments." By 1939 such amusements no longer provided sufficient rationale for Kārlis Vanags, who counseled: "Everywhere and always travel not for rest and relaxation, but to learn, hear, and understand."[1] The first recommendation reflected parliamentary democracy and a market economy. Tourists were free to entertain themselves as they chose. The second was written after the coup of 1934 brought Kārlis Ulmanis to power. Under Ulmanis tourism aspired to something more total; it became one tool to transform the identity of Latvian citizens. As with most of the interwar east European regimes, there is considerable academic disagreement around which labels (conservative, authoritarian, or fascist) are most appropriate for Ulmanis-era Latvia. The Latvian historian Aivars Stranga has taken an important step beyond this vocabulary and examines whether the Ulmanis regime was transformational or pragmatic.[2] In Stranga's typology the common denominator of states such as Nazi Germany and Stalin's Soviet Union was their belief in applying all power to radically recreate the economy, society, and even the nature of the population. Within the regimes of eastern Europe there was a constant internal battle between the proponents of transformational change and those that took a more pragmatic approach. Regime leaders often played the divergent camps against each other to remain unquestionably supreme. In Ulmanis's Latvia, Stranga identifies Minister of Finance Alfreds Valdmanis as the pragmatic bureaucrat. Minister of Social Affairs Alfreds Bērziņš was the radical firebrand most eager to use the power of the state to serve a transformational ideology. Not surprisingly, the Department of Tourism within this ministry exemplified Bērziņš's approach. The "Travel

1. Mārtiņš Celms, *Rīga: Rokas Grāmata Ekskursantiem* (Riga, 1926), 33; Kārlis Vanags, ed., *Ceļvedis pa dzimto zemi: turistu ceļojumu maršruti Latvijā 2. daļa: Zemgale un Kurzeme* (Riga, 1939), 5–6.
2. Aivars Stranga, *LSDSP un 1934. gada 15. maija valsts apvērsums: demokrātijas likteni Latvijā* (Riga, 1998), 195–229.

around the Native Land" campaign was one of the ministry's many attempts
to invent a new Latvia.

The study of tourism is taking root in the historiography of the Baltic region. There are solid accounts of the history of tourism,[3] and recent general
works have incorporated tourism into a larger whole. These studies, however,
focus on what was seen, not why. A theoretically rich and nuanced approach
to what Rudy Koshar calls "travel cultures" is needed for Latvia.[4] Likewise,
Shelley Baranowski's studies of "tourism and national integration" in the
Third Reich suggest an approach for Ulmanis-era tourism.[5] The state manufactured and managed a tourist campaign revolving around identity; and its
successes, shortcomings, biases, and failures comment on the capabilities of
the state.

Tourist Beginnings

Before independence, tourism in the Baltic provinces of the Russian Empire revolved around the curative mud of Riga-Jurmala, also known as the Strand.[6]
With the construction of railroads, Jurmala attracted masses of tourists. By
1914 there were forty trains a day from Riga during peak season. Workers
could afford a day trip to the beach, while bourgeois visitors rented cabins and
other accommodations for longer stays. The wealthiest stayed in luxurious
spas or in their own summer villas. We know something of the demography of
this tourism and of its anecdotal side. If proscriptions hint at activity, for example, regulations in 1914 forbade nude bathing anywhere on the beach.[7]
Workers and peasants journeyed to a few other sites such as the castle and
river valley at Sigulda.[8] Religious pilgrimages to the basilica in Aglona and
trips to Riga were other important tourist variations. Tourism as an industry,
however, was in its infancy.

Leisure in Riga was more developed. In 1901 the city government decided
to create a large park on the outskirts of the city that included horse-drawn
and electric trams, bicycle paths, sports fields, and a restaurant by 1909. In
1912 a zoo opened on the park grounds with nearly eleven thousand visitors

3. Maija Rozite, "Tūrisma attīstība Latvijā" in *Latvijas arhīvi*, 1 (1999), 96–110; 20. *Gadsimta Latvijas Vēsture: I Latvija no gadsimta sākuma līdz neatkarības pasludināšanai 1900–1918*
(Riga, 2000).

4. Rudy Koshar, *German Travel Cultures* (Oxford, 2000), 6.

5. Shelley Baranowski, "Strength through Joy: Tourism and National Integration in the
Third Reich," in *Being Elsewhere: Tourism, Consumer Culture, and Identity in Modern Europe
and North America*, ed. Shelley Baranowski and Ellen Furlough (Ann Arbor, Mich., 2001), 213.

6. George F. Kennan, *Memoirs 1925–1950* (Toronto, 1967).

7. 20. *Gadsimta Latvijas Vēsture*, 526–27.

8. Unpublished diary of Līze Rungains (in author's possession) mentions a trip to Sigulda
around 1908.

on its busiest days. The popular Vermana Park and the Salomonski Circus also catered to Riga's inhabitants.[9]

War, revolution, and the beginnings of independence severely restricted all types of tourism and recreation. Riga-Jurmala, in particular, suffered extensive physical damage. With economic health, tourism began to recover and took on a vibrancy that mirrored Latvian society as a whole in the 1920s. Initially, ventures such as casinos catering to foreigners and the wealthiest were the most economically viable, but with time tourists returned to the old haunts. The tourist industry that emerged was, as prewar tourism had been, largely independent of the state. The cash-strapped government gave some limited subsidies to museums and tinkered with railroad tariffs but generally did not interfere or actively involve itself in this market-based tourism.

Riga, A Handbook for Excursions by Mārtiņš Celms, published in 1926, became an early definitive guide. To borrow from Koshar's description of the Baedeker guidebook's place in the "tourist cultures" of Germany, Celms's handbook "was the product of an age of liberalism" that revolved around "individualism." Like Baedeker, Celms's handbook "not only created a tangible image of . . . nationhood for the national liberal travel culture; it also created a self-image of cultured individuals consuming the nation."[10] Celms did so by splitting his guide into two parts: an overview of the history of Riga, and a series of walking tours through the contemporary city. In guiding tourists through Riga, Celms constructed a balanced and tolerant history of the city's turbulent social relations.[11] Although clearly a Latvian chauvinist, he drew attention to the Russian neighborhoods of the city that had existed from the early seventeenth century. Furthermore, Celms highlighted the civic work of the Russian governor, Prince Suvorov, and reveled in the colorful history of the German Blackheads Order. His description of the Doms Cathedral lacked the visceral hostility that surrounded the church in the late 1920s and early 1930s over German and Latvian congregation ownership rights.[12] Celms described Riga as a multiethnic organic whole; his history was not an early precursor of the nationalists' narrative of German and/or Russian domination over an oppressed, native Latvian population. Celms, for example, described the most recent war and revolution in the shortest, most nonjudgmental manner possible.

Celms favored the modern and technological city over the medieval. This presented a paradox: much of what he suggested should be seen were the physical symbols of bygone years. Yet as a whole, outside of the cathedrals and specific notable buildings, the past created in Celms's opinion, "an old medieval city with its oppressive influence, with a lack of sunlight and air."[13] To him it

9. 20. *Gadsimta Latvijas Vēsture*, 526–27.
10. Koshar, *German Travel Cultures*, 17.
11. Celms, *Rīga*, 18.
12. Ibid., 56–57.
13. Ibid., 65.

seemed as if the houses of Old Riga "would collapse on us and leave us buried under their ruins." Later, he described leaving the old city as "again feeling saved from the oppressive walls of Old Riga."[14] Similarly, during a discussion of the arrival of "all sorts of conveniences for the elementary needs of the inhabitants," Celms again contrasted the cramped, dark, narrow, stagnant, chaotic streets of the old town with the planned, tree-lined boulevards and parks of the new town.[15]

Celms's travel guide included occasional disdain and scorn for Russian traces in Riga. He wondered if Big Noise Street referred to the neighborhood's history as a Russian enclave.[16] He described the Russian Orthodox cathedral as an unwanted import from tsarist Russia, remarking approvingly that the bells had been evacuated during the war to "where they came from"; he wondered why "we leave this grim witness to an earlier time completely at peace."[17] He similarly hoped the evacuation of the bronze statues of Peter I and Barclay de Tolly would lead to their replacement with "a monument for someone who gave his life for a free Latvia."[18] In this same nationalist vein, Celms criticized the passivity of Latvians in Riga. He chastised the Riga Latvian Society (an important institution in the "National Awakening" of the nineteenth century) for renting assembly rooms to "Jews and [noted] that plays are performed in the hall in the Russian language."[19]

These anti-Russian sentiments and the bias for modernity came across as the author's opinion. Above all else his guidebook described what to see in Riga, the history behind these places, and how to get from one to the next. He also included information on restaurants, banks, museums, theaters, newspapers, and even the office hours of the president and the Cabinet of Ministers.[20] The guidebook, however, did not offer a direct nationalist message. There was no imperative to tour the city; the selection of a tourist itinerary was not a reflection on one's citizenship or identity. The open-ended nature of the book positioned itself well in a competitive book market by not alienating potential purchasers.[21] A vague sense of loose patriotism suggested that citizens should get to know their new country better, but where and how was left to their devices. This was neither duty nor obligation. The popular press also placed relatively little attention on promoting tourism within Latvia itself. Popularly weeklies such as *Jaunā Nedēļa* (The New Week), *Ilustrēts Schurnals 'Nedēļa'*

14. Ibid., 94.

15. Ibid., 97–99.

16. Ibid., 65.

17. Ibid., 79.

18. Ibid., 78, 94. The Freedom Monument was erected on the site of the Peter I monument. The Barclay de Tolly pedestal remains without a figure to this day.

19. Ibid., 83.

20. In a sign of how much some things have changed, Celms included the president's private number. Ibid., 105.

21. Atis Freinats, *Dzimtenes ārēs: Pa mājām, tirgiem un pilsētām* (Riga, 1939, repr. Brooklyn, N.Y., 1969).

(The Weekly Illustrated Journal) and *Zeltene* devoted the occasional article to "some of the beautiful places in our native land," but more frequently showcased the capitals and hot spots of Europe as travel destinations.[22]

Centralizing Tourism

Tourist societies sprouted throughout the 1920s and into the early 1930s. Some were loosely aligned with local government and/or business interests while others were ethnically based, such as Latvia's Jewish Tourist Society, or interest-based such as the sports society Native Lands Traveler. These societies organized trips and provided guides and maps. Ultimately most of these societies founded an umbrella organization for domestic and international tourism, Latvia's Central Tourist Society.[23] The society represented Latvia at international tourist conferences, opened a travel kiosk at Riga's central station, and operated several souvenir stands. The society also ran a lottery (an automobile was, appropriately, the grand prize) to supplement its income. The society seemed a perfect example of civil society taking root in the 1920s. The closing of this and all other tourist societies after the Ulmanis coup and their reorganization as a governmental department seems to add weight to the argument that the coup attacked and dismantled civil society in favor of governmental control. This, however, is only part of the story.

The leading lights of the independent tourist movement welcomed government control (a pattern replicated throughout Latvia's civil society). Kārlis Vanags and Otto Krolls, important founders of the tourist movement in independent Latvia, moved effortlessly into state service.[24] Vanags had edited the first tourist-theme magazine (*Turists*) and helped lead Latvia's Central Tourist Society. After the coup in 1934, he became director of the Tourist Department within the Ministry of the Interior, and later within the Ministry of Social Affairs. He did not view state control as a debilitating factor; rather he welcomed the increase in potential funds. The relationship of tourism with the state became symptomatic of a slide toward authoritarianism, a slide embraced by much of the nongovernmental establishment as a blessing or at worst a necessity in times of need.[25] Furthermore, this desire for greater state coordination as opposed to reliance on the vagaries of the market cut across

22. "Kahda no skaistakam dsimtenes weetam," *Ilustrēts Schurnals 'Nedēļa,'* 23 May 1924, 10, versus articles such as "Tschekoslowakijs peldu weetas un weselibas awoti," *Ilustrēts Schurnals 'Nedēļa',* 13 June 1924, 12; "Austrijas galvas pilsēta Vīne," *Jaunā Nedēļa,* 6 January 1928, 12; "Kanālu, tulpju, un hiacintu zeme," *Jaunā Nedēļa,* 5 August 1927, 14–15.

23. "Tūrisms," *Latvju enciklopēdija* (Stockholm, 1953), 2520–23.

24. Vanags was also credited for introducing *nedelas nogale* as opposed to the borrowed *vikends* for weekend. Alfreds Bērziņš, *Labie Gadi: Pirms un pēc 15. maija* (Brooklyn, N.Y., 1963), 236.

25. See Jānis Rogainis, "The Emergence of an Authoritarian Regime in Latvia, 1932–1934," *Lituanus* 17, no. 3 (1971): 61, for an early example of this idea.

hostile political lines. Social Democrats, Latvian nationalists, Latvian centrists, and a host of independent "specialists" encouraged state planning and control over market forces.[26] Moreover, as Koshar has suggested, tourism is an interpretative process; and the bourgeois, liberal Celms version, like Baedeker in 1930s Germany, "became brittle as new groups clamored for an updated hermeneutics."[27] In other words, by the time of the authoritarian coup the leaders of Latvian society saw the role of tourism, like the role of the state itself, differently.

After the entire tourist industry became an extension of the state, its capabilities expanded considerably. The Tourism Department built observation towers, coordinated cheap group rail rates, and offered tourist boat trips. The department ordered local administrators to delegate volunteers to look after the interests of tourists and worked with the Chamber of Labor to organize group excursions for workers. The department's largest single such event was a mass excursion for a thousand primarily female workers from Riga's textile factories to the World War I battlefield of Machine-Gun Hill. The department also organized tourist expeditions for workers to other factories, including visits to the Riga City Electrical Plant, the Smidts Cement Factory, and the Vildenbergs Leather Factory. Equally important, the state tracked tourism with detailed statistics.[28]

State control also altered the content and meaning, the hermeneutics, of tourism. The various guides the department produced leave no doubt that the new regime hoped to use tourism to shape national identity. Tourism was to inculcate the principles of the "Renewed Latvia" by promoting a united, purely Latvian Latvia obedient to the Leader, Kārlis Ulmanis. The "Travel around the Native Land" campaign underscored what tourism was supposed to accomplish, what the tourist was supposed to do, as well as how and why. The campaign tapped into a pan-European trend for discovering one's own country, not always solely through tourism. The long roots of this trend are anchored in the German concept of *Heimat*, which was introduced to Latvians by Atis Kronvalds in the second half of the nineteenth century.[29] The landscape and folk movement in England is another example of this conscious link developed between place and identity.[30] Throughout Europe, particularly in fascist states, autarchical efforts also encouraged domestic tourism.

26. Stranga, *LSDSP un 1934. gada 15. maija valsts apvērsums*.

27. Koshar, *German Travel Cultures*, 209.

28. A. Maldups, ed., *Latvija skaitļos* (Riga, 1937), 132–35.

29. See, for example, Elizabeth Boa and Rachel Palfreyman, eds., *Heimat: A German Dream: Regional Loyalties and National Identity in German Culture* (Oxford, 2000); and Katrina Schwartz, "The Occupation of Beauty: Imagining Nature and Nation in Latvia," *East European Politics and Societies*, forthcoming. Issues stemming from the concept of Heimat are also central to Moranda, in this volume.

30. David Matless, *Landscape and Englishness* (London, 1998).

Tourism in Ulmanis's Latvia also borrowed from Ulmanis's own experiences in the United States. After the 1905 revolution, Ulmanis spent several years studying at the University of Nebraska and working at farms across the prairies. He freely admitted to modeling his authoritarian youth alternative to the scouts, the *mazpulki*, on the 4-H Club. His time in the United States also coincided with the height of the "See America First" campaign, which exhorted Americans to spend their money in the American West, not Europe, and to develop an integrated American identity through their tourist vacations. Marguerite S. Shaffer described this as "narrating the nation":

> Tourist industries . . . created and marketed tourist landscapes as quintessentially American places, consciously highlighting certain meanings and myths while ignoring others, deliberately arranging historical events and anecdotes, intentionally framing certain scenes and views into a coherent national whole . . . defining an organic nationalism that linked national identity to a shared territory and history. And tourist interests insisted that by seeing the sights and scenes that embodied the essence of America, by consuming the nation through touring, tourists would become better Americans.[31]

The "Travel around the Native Land" campaign mimicked "See America First" in appearance, but its message became more transformational. The campaign mirrored its contemporary, the Strength through Joy leisure and tourism agency, which would serve as a vehicle to dissolve the social boundaries that internally divided Germany.

The Tourist Department took tentative steps toward this transformational mission soon after the coup of 15 May 1934. The first issue of an extensive Tourist Library of booklets, *Know Riga! A Short Guide for Tourists*, was compiled by Kārlis Vanags and published by the department in 1935.[32] *Know Riga* was rushed, borrowed heavily from pre-coup work, and only hinted at the transformational changes to come. In its introduction, *Know Riga* claimed to "tell the history of the visited sites, describe the most notable places, and give tourists practical advice on where to go, how to go, and what to see."[33] This same introduction advocated *Know Riga* for Riga's own inhabitants and particularly for the youth because "only one who truly knows his homeland can love it." *Know Riga* continued: "Riga cannot be for Latvians just a center of offices, schools, stores, and entertainment but must also be our nation's august historical and cultural monument, which can only be understood and felt by those that know Riga intimately."

31. Marguerite S. Shaffer, *See America First: Tourism and National Identity, 1880–1940* (Washington, D.C., 2001), 4.

32. K. L. Vanags, ed., *Pazīsti Rīgu! Īss Vadonis Tūristiem* (Riga, 1935).

33. Ibid., 3, 42.

Know Riga followed the format of Celms's guidebook with a detailed history of Riga and walking itineraries of the city. The history closely mirrored Celms's (borrowing particularly from the colorful history of the Blackheads Guild), except for its chronological bookends: *Know Riga* devoted more attention to the Teutonic conquest of Baltic tribes, and it presented a very partisan account of recent events. The Latvian defense of Riga in October and November 1919 was painted with the most patriotic brush strokes; and the coup of 1934 was described as "Riga's second liberation, this time from the onerous internal enemy—the yoke of political parties."[34] Similarly, the building that housed Latvia's parliament, prominently mentioned in Celms's account, was almost ignored in *Know Riga*.[35]

Within a year, "national tourism" became clearer in the Tourist Library's third title. Kārlis Vanags's *Guide for Tourists: Handbook for Travelers of the Native Land. The Ideology and Practice of National Tourism* broke from the pattern of standard tourist guides, instead instructing how to tour and how to be tourists. Whereas previous tour books were divided into history and itineraries, the two sections of the *Guide for Tourists* were "Travel around the Native Land," and "The Technique of Traveling around the Native Land." The extremely detailed instructions (always worded more forcefully than mere advice) included such minutiae as how many breaths to take per stride (one breath for two to three strides for a slow gait, one per one to two for a faster pace),[36] how to conserve time and energy by extending one's stride by two to five centimeters,[37] what to wear, what to pack, what to drink and eat and when, what songs to sing at the campfire (only patriotic ones), and how to sleep (snoring could be stopped through willpower).[38]

Far more central, however, was the emphasis in the *Guide for Tourists* on the "ideology" of national tourism. Throughout, Vanags detailed the role tourism was to play in shaping identity. To begin, he vigorously denounced traveling abroad. Part of the reason for this proscription was economic; "each lats taken abroad or spent there makes our nation and people poorer."[39] Traveling abroad was appropriate only for business, and most tolerable if it meant visits to our "brother land" of Lithuania or "our neighbor and ally" Estonia. Additionally, Latvian tourists abroad had to behave in an exemplary manner in order to leave a favorable impression of Latvia. In general, the desire to travel abroad was a "shameful stain on our country and nation."[40] Ultimately, the Latvian who learned to know Latvia would be happy nowhere else. There-

---

34. Ibid., 58–61, 40.
35. Ibid., 83.
36. Kārlis Vanags, ed., *Vadonis Tūristiem: Rokas Grāmata Dzimtenes Apceļotājiem, Nācionālā Tūrisma Ideoloģija un Prakse* (Riga, 1936), 139.
37. Ibid., 133.
38. Ibid., 153.
39. Ibid., 176.
40. Ibid., 178.

5.1. Tourists in Kandava in 1936 dressed in the "salon style" frowned upon by the national tourism campaign. Photograph in author's possession.

fore those that already knew Latvia would naturally continue to travel domestically, while those that had not yet were obliged to do so.

Throughout the *Guide for Tourists*, a clear, direct message was endlessly repeated: by traveling around the native land the national tourist would come to love his or her native land and understand it on a purer level. This love of the native land was in turn "the highest form of love on Earth."[41] Vanags mentioned that in the past year a new phenomenon had emerged, peasants engaging in tourism, but their closeness to the land already gave them a sense of their identity. The message of national tourism was intended particularly for urbanites who had lost touch with the foundations of their Latvian rural identity. As a result, the "national tourist" was a "true and just investigator of the native land," a "pilgrim," and not someone looking for entertainment or relaxation.[42]

The tourist pilgrimage to the nation included both Baltic German castles and natural landscapes. All these sights, however, had to be understood through the prism of looking "for the Latvian" in all things. "Every foreign construction on our land, even the [Teutonic] Order's castles hated by our fathers' fathers, has its Latvian side: they were built on land belonging to Lat-

41. Ibid., 9.
42. Ibid., 55–57.

vians, they were built to suppress the Latvian nation, they were built by Latvians themselves serving foreign masters."[43] Every inch of soil was instructive:
"Every footprint on our native land tells of great events: of our ancestors'
lives . . . as well as here Ulmanis was born . . . each step taken turns a new
page on the history of the Latvian people."[44] Clearly the language of national
tourism and of patriotic education was one and the same. The *Guide for
Tourists* consistently explained a simple moral behind traveling, that through
tourism "the nation is united and brought closer together."[45] Equally clear,
however, was that the city was to be brought closer to the country. By traveling, "the city dweller will come to realize that the peasant is the foundation of
our land, who clothes and feeds us . . . and who is still working when we are
sleeping."[46] Learning this lesson was most important for the young. The *Guide
for Tourists*, for example, asked rhetorically how university students could be
Latvia's "future advisors, social workers, teachers, bureaucrats, doctors,
judges and preachers" if they could not "differentiate among barley, rye, and
wheat or between ducks and geese."[47] As a result, the *Guide for Tourists* devoted considerable space to how the young should travel and what their teachers and chaperones should do during these educational field trips.[48]

The *Guide for Tourists* presaged two emerging metathemes in the development of the Ulmanis regime. One was the ascendancy of the cult of personality. In 1936 Kārlis Ulmanis was, at least in theory, only the first among equals
in his regime. The legally elected state president, Alberts Kviesis, had not yet
finished his term. The popular minister of war and co-conspirator General
Jānis Balodis was almost equal to Ulmanis, and Marģers Skujenieks, although
without real power, still held the impressive title of deputy minister president.
The regime may have been completely associated with Ulmanis, but a full-
blown cult of personality was not yet entrenched. The *Guide for Tourists*
demonstrates this cult in the making. Vanags used frequent quotations from
poets and writers to underline the pastoral beauty of Latvia's countryside, but
he most frequently quoted Ulmanis (ten times in total).[49] Tellingly, only Ulmanis's quotes received special italicization. Furthermore, Ulmanis's quotes did
not describe beauty (the job of poets) but explained, advised, and inspired.
Vanags even finished the chapter "Traveling the Native Land Means Being
Raised in the Nation" with a cleverly, ambiguous pronoun word play that
conflated land and king: If you want to be like this homesteader's son [Kārlis
Ulmanis], go to the native land's nature, learn to understand and love him [na-

43. Ibid., 20.
44. Ibid., 29.
45. Ibid., 15.
46. Ibid., 24–25.
47. Ibid., 29.
48. Ibid., 124.
49. Ibid., 27, 71.

ture or Ulmanis or both]!"[50] Within a year, the regime developed this cult even more explicitly.

The second metatheme that emerged in the *Guide for Tourists* was the incongruity between the claims that national tourism would craft Latvian identity and material reality on the ground. Essentially, the *Guide for Tourists* promised urbanites a transcendent experience if they traveled into the Latvian countryside. Could the countryside deliver? There were two problems: the physical conditions of the country were poor compared to the city, and the "national tourists" were going to need a great many places to see. On the first count, the *Guide for Tourists* attempted to forewarn urban tourists: they should stop and check if rural bridges would be able to bear the weight of their buses;[51] they should bring food with them because even butter and eggs could be difficult to come by;[52] they should not criticize or make fun of peasants' behavior, clothing, food, or ways of speaking.[53] Overall, the urbanites "should not ask for things to be like they are at home. They should satisfy themselves with country living (crickets, flies, and cockroaches)."[54] Accommodations proved equally challenging. Staying in hotels was discouraged because there were few in rural Latvia, they were too expensive for "national tourists" that looked for simplicity, and the hotels saw "their services only as goods through which to get more profit and gratuities from travelers." The preferred method of sleeping out in the field (in a tent or in the hay) was impractical as a mass solution. The *Guide for Tourists* hoped that a system of "national tourist" accommodations, similar to hostels, would take root.[55]

Equally troubling for "national tourism" was the number of sights to see. The *Guide for Tourists* suggested that tourists should begin "national tourism" at an early age and continue through their entire lives and through all seasons of the year on day trips, weekend trips, and weeklong trips. For 1936 alone, the *Guide for Tourists* estimated the average person would have forty-five days to pursue "national tourism."[56] Perhaps aware of this great strain on the relatively small country, the *Guide for Tourists* stated that it was "better to explore thoroughly a very small part of a province, seeing and comprehending everything unique and characteristic rather than crossing the province in a great hurry gaining only a general impression." Every parish had its "unique" beauty one only "needed to know how to see," and "even if some parishes did not have beautiful meandering rivers or hills bejeweled with

50. Ibid., 42.
51. Ibid., 80.
52. In the poorest regions, the *Guide* advised "tourists that real sustenance came from the sun and air, not eggs, butter, or ham." Ibid., 117.
53. Ibid., 162.
54. Ibid., 163.
55. Ibid., 148–56.
56. Ibid., 64.

groves of trees, they still had other things worth looking at: model farms, local industrial enterprises (coach houses, forges, starch factories, tar fires, mills, lime kilns, rock quarries), schools with wealthy libraries, [and so on]."[57] The job of the Tourist Department was set: to guarantee that national tourists would have the itineraries and guides for their travels and that while undertaking these learning events, national tourists would learn the correct things.

The "Travel around the Native Land" tourist campaign, like the state control that created it, aspired to manage the whole tourist experience. The various guides in the Tourist Library multiplied and overlapped one another. The maps that the guide suggested for use were released as postcards with a proposed itinerary on the reverse. Postal stamps highlighted the campaign and the popular media began more frequently to include photographs of groups at sights frequently mentioned in the growing national tourist litany.[58] Almost always, the idea of national tourism was a group activity and the individual's exploration of the native land was discouraged. Tourism cemented a fellowship between group members, between people from the country and the city. The entire campaign suggested instructional excursions whose aim was to instill the ideas, identity, and ideology of the new Latvia.

The leader principle, which demanded unswerving love and obedience to the Leader (the *Vadonis*), Kārlis Ulmanis, and to all other superiors as more immediate leaders, became increasingly central in tourism planning. National tourism needed particularly to sculpt this identity among the young and the workers. The "ideology and practice of national tourism," developed at the Tourist Department, trickled down to the young through the regime's control of education and extracurricular groups such as the mazpulki.[59] As in Nazi Germany, the working class was seen as an element potentially hostile to the regime that needed to be converted to loyalty.[60] To indoctrinate workers, the Tourist Department published *Summer's Travels*, distributed by the Chamber of Labor (inspired by Mussolini's Chamber system).[61]

Summer's Travels was intended for workers' leaders (and the requirements for the tour leader seem interchangeable with those for the 1960s Soviet guides discussed by Anne Gorsuch in this volume). The minutiae and the degree of planning, as always, border on the fantastic. Again the guide is divided in two, with the first part covering general advice on how to travel and the second pro-

57. Ibid., 70–71.

58. For general examples, see: "On a Bicycle along the Native Land's Roads," *Zeltene*, 1 July 1934, 9; photograph with the caption "Know Your Native Land! At the Renda Waterfall," *Zeltene*, 15 August 1935, 5; photograph with caption "The Pretty Castle Ruins at Koknese Await Guests during the Harvest Festival," *Zeltene*, 1 November 1935, 5.

59. For the regime's transformation of education, see Aldis Purs, "'Unsatisfactory National Identity': School Inspectors, Education, and National Identity in Interwar Latvia," *Journal of Baltic Studies* 35, no. 2 (2004): 97–125.

60. Baranowski, "Strength through Joy," 225.

61. Kārlis Vanags, ed., *Vasaras ceļojumi: Latvijas darba kameras rokas grāmata strādnieku arodbiedribu tūrisma kopu darbībai* (Riga, 1937).

5.2. The front cover of *Summer's Travels*, the workers' guidebook for national tourism. Kārlis Vanags, ed., *Vasaras ceļojumi: Latvijas darba kameras rokas grāmata strādnieku arodbiedribu tūrisma kopu darbībai* [Summer's Travels: Latvia's Chamber of Labour Handbook for the Work of Workers' Trade Union Tourist Cooperatives] (Riga, 1937).

viding very detailed itineraries. These detailed itineraries included "crib sheets" for the group leader on what to look at and why it was important. Castle mounds, resistance to Teutonic conquest in the thirteenth century, the battle sites of the recent war for independence, and important places in the life of the Vadonis, Kārlis Ulmanis (whose name was the only boldfaced type in the handbook) were particularly stressed. Like the Society of Proletarian Tourists in the USSR, the itineraries appealed to industrial workers with stops at local industries.

The first part of *Summer's Travels* followed the established patterns: how many kilometers to travel in an hour, how long to rest,[62] the importance of a detailed itinerary.[63] Specific emphasis, however, was placed on the moral, intellectual, and physical attributes of a good tour leader. The best leader was a workingman who knew his native land well, had already traveled it considerably, loved its nature, and was a true patriot. He furthermore had to have a good sense of humor and be intelligent, fearless, calm, composed, comradely, resourceful, persistent, polite, and tactful. His sacrifices for the group had to include waking first, falling asleep last, being the last to eat or drink, and in dangerous situations disregarding his own safety.[64] In parallel with the advice previously offered to Latvians traveling abroad, the group leader had to insure that the group's activity was a shining example of Latvian workers generally—a concern inherited by Soviet Latvian tourist specialists, who even prepared training films on etiquette.[65] A host of restrictions followed, such as remaining quiet in forest and towns, not littering, and respecting fences.[66] *Summer's Travels* also included the Chamber of Labor's regulations on how to choose a leader, what legal powers he enjoyed, and how he could be dismissed.[67]

Regardless of these closer controls over workers, the underlying raisons d'être of their tourist experience was the same as for middle-class Latvians. Kārlis Egle, the chairman of the Chamber of Labor, stated in the preface that by "traveling the hills and valleys of Latvia we will learn more fervently to love our fatherland."[68] In the section "Why Do We Have to Travel?" Kārlis Vanags returned to the leitmotifs of national tourism: it was not for enjoyment or relaxation, but had a "deep and meaningful goal . . . it creates new, unseen ties to the land, and it lights in them [workers] the spark of love for the fatherland." Furthermore, by taking the worker out of the unhealthy (morally and physically) city it provided a short-lived exposure to the countryside that would "help maintain a healthy spirit and a healthy body."[69]

62. Vanags, *Vasaras ceļojumi*, 26–27.
63. Ibid., 31.
64. Ibid., 30.
65. See Gorsuch, in this volume.
66. Vanags, *Vasaras ceļojumi*, 39–40.
67. "LDK instrukcija tūrisma kopām," in ibid., 7–9.
68. Ibid., i.
69. Ibid, 14–16.

The pinnacles of the "Travel around the Native Land" campaign were the massive two-part *Road Guide of the Native Land* and its visual equivalent in a popular, artistic map. The *Guide for Tourists* had lamented that Latvia did not yet have a comprehensive guide. The *Road Guide* overcame this shortcoming and spelled out everything to see in all of Latvia's parishes. The first volume, published in 1937, covered the provinces of Vidzeme and Latgale while the second volume, published in 1939, treated the provinces of Zemgale and Kurzeme. The two volumes together (933 pages!) combined meticulous attention to detail and the constant refrain of the importance of "national tourism."

According to the *Road Guide*, the most important sight for tourists to visit was the Pikšas homestead in Bērzmuiža: the birthplace of Kārlis Ulmanis.[70] If most parishes and villages received a page or two of attention, the childhood home of the Leader received eight. The *Road Guide* demanded that the tourist see the courtyard in which the Leader's swing had hung—and still did—the school he attended (where he learned that you had to look after yourself and not wait for others to do things for you), the church where the Leader went as a boy, the graves of his family members, the households of his relatives, the place where he gave his first public speech, and other minutiae of the president's boyhood. The praise was on a par with any cult of personality. The *Road Guide* even claimed that archeological evidence suggested that the area was one of the original homes of the Baltic peoples. The Leader's presence radiated out from this birthplace throughout the Latvia designated for national tourism: in Valmiera the tourist needed to see where a young Ulmanis worked as an agronomist,[71] in Valka where he discussed the need for Latvia's independence,[72] and so on ad infinitum. The list of Ulmanis sites included the trivial and the comical: a view of the hills outside of Dundaga, notable because Ulmanis said they were beautiful.

Beyond Ulmanis, the *Road Guide* repeatedly drew attention (often on spurious authority) to the ancient Latvian past of almost every region, more so than in the previous volumes of the Tourist Library. The constant discussion of castle mounds became more than repetitive; it suggested Latvians could claim a glorious mythic past. Along with the descriptions of recent model farms and small industrial enterprises, the *Road Guide* implied that the only things worthy of national tourism in Latvia were the distant, near mythic past and the near-miraculous accomplishments following Ulmanis's coup.

Finally the *Road Guide* continued the familiar refrains of etiquette and purpose. In interacting with "locals" the tourist should be simple, sincere, polite. Tourists should use simple language without a "salon style or overly intelligent words" (adding that mimicking dialect was not tactful). Littering was inap-

70. Vanags, *Ceļvedis pa dzimto zemi*, 89–97.

71. Kārlis Vanags, ed., *Ceļvedis pa dzimto zemi: turistu celojumu maršruti Latvijā 1. daļa: Vidzeme un Latgale* (Riga, 1937), 250.

72. Ibid., 239.

propriate (the book specifically mentioned paper, eggshells, bottles, and cigarette packages), as was trampling on plants and harvests and climbing over
fences or other barriers. Ultimately, tourists must be satisfied with rural conditions as they were. Only in this way could tourists overcome the "need to set
new records in the numbers of kilometers traveled, length of time in the sun or
surf." "Each trip around the Native Land required certain spiritual values"
and tourists should "travel to unknown corners to hear the steps of their nation's history, to get to know their land and nation and its life and work." National tourists should "everywhere and always travel not for relaxation or entertainment but to learn, see, and understand." They should return home "not
having seen sights, but with a spirit, heart, and sense" of the nation.[73]

A visual product of national tourism was an artistic map that depicted the
nation narrated in the orchestrated campaign. This narrated nation was ethnically Latvian (almost pure) as was its consciously highlighted history. The battlefields worth visiting as tourists commemorated when "Latvia lost its independence" in the thirteenth century, and when it regained it in 1919 and
1920. Even in these two cases only battles in which the Latvians were victori-
ous were commemorated. The imagined castle mounds of the twelfth century
were more prevalent and stressed than the castles of the Teutonic Knights.
Otherwise the map depicted happy, idealized peasants; painters; natural resources; modern accomplishments of the new state (a hydroelectric dam, war
monuments, bridges, radio towers, cement and paper factories); churches; and,
of course, the birthplace of Kārlis Ulmanis. The rest was absent. Essentially,
everything that did not fit into the Tourist Department's ideology of national
tourism was conveniently disregarded. As a result, the native land to be traveled had few minorities, even though more than a quarter of the population
was not ethnically Latvian. In the eastern province of Latgale almost 40 percent of the population was not Latvian. On the artistic map, however, where
the fewest Latvians lived, the map depicted wildlife. Ilukste district was not
swarming with Jews, Belorussians, Russians, and Poles but moose, lynx, and
geese. Parishes in Abrene district were not the home of overwhelming Russian
majorities but of sheep, horses, and foxes. Orthodox churches (too Russian),
synagogues (too Jewish), and most Catholic Churches (too Polish) were
equally underrepresented. The same absence held true in the written literature.

The itineraries, particularly in the exhaustive *Road Guide*, omitted, minimized, or radically interpreted almost all sites associated with Baltic Germans,
other minorities, or a socialist past. When the 1905 revolution was mentioned
at all, it was treated as an early national uprising. Anecdotes about Baltic German (and occasionally Russian and Polish) noblemen showcased some combination of cruelty and incompetence while emphasizing ethnic Latvians as the
real builders of castles and medieval towns. Religion was reduced to a poorly

73. Vanags, *Ceļvedis pa dzimto zemi: 1. daļa*, 3–6; Vanags, *Ceļvedis pa dzimto zemi: 2. daļa*,
5–6.

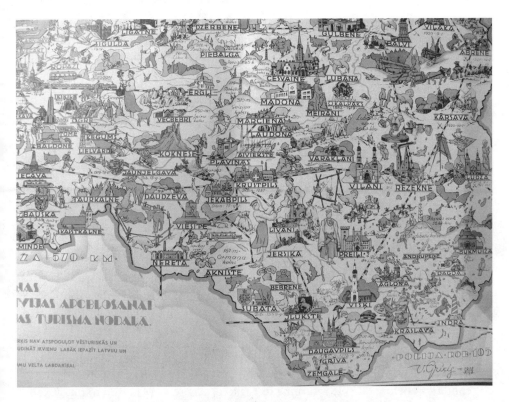

5.3. A detail of the Travel around Your Native Land poster centered on the town of Subata. Russians and Jews outnumbered Latvians in Subata, but in the poster the district is populated with moose and lynx. Tourism Department of the Ministry of Social Affairs, 1938.

explained division between Lutherans and Catholics, with frequent suggestions that Catholicism in Latgale was an unwelcome agent of Polonization. A more stark absence was the lack of non-Latvian communities, particularly in districts and parishes where Latvians were the minority. When mentioned, their presence was referred to as transient and impermanent. The descriptions for much of Ilukste District and Latgale Province, for example, anticipated potential future archeological discoveries to "prove" that Latvians lived in the area for at least six thousand years. Likewise, the *Road Guide* emphasized sights of the new order such as Unity Squares, 15 May Squares, and Home Guard Buildings in towns and cities with historic ethnic communities and corresponding significant architectural and historic treasures such as in Daugavpils (Dvinsk) and Krāslava.[74] The campaign ignored the parts of Latvia that contradicted the ideological message of national tourism.

74. Vanags, *Ceļvedis pa dzimto zemi:1. daļa*, 279.

How effective was this campaign? Quantitative measurements are difficult to assess and qualitative ones are notoriously elusive, but some generalizations are possible. The slogan "Travel around the Native Land" and the artistic map became and continue to be readily recognized and warmly received icons. Beyond that, however, the regime's relentless message about national tourism was often seemingly ignored or selectively digested. Tourists came primarily from urban areas (often Riga) and their trips into the countryside strengthened urban-rural divisions rather than cementing national unity. Although these tourists may have wanted unity, they assumed it would occur on urban terms. These assumptions spread to the very bureaucrat-nationalists that planned the tourist campaign and espoused the glory of Latvia's rural character. Their internal reports about trips into their idyllic countryside overwhelmingly described visits to dirty, grimy places with bad roads, limited hygiene, and few or no comforts.[75]

For the urban tourist, material shortcomings limited the appeal of national tourism. Departmental reviews repeatedly demanded that local governments improve accommodations, sanitation (from changing sheets to improving or installing plumbing), and service and respond to other needs of urban tourists. Local governments viewed these requests as emanating from a center that was out of touch with local needs. There was particularly little incentive to improve the tourist infrastructure because, with the exception of a few places, there were few tourists. As long as tourists planned day trips or one-night stays to economize and minimize their exposure to what they felt were substandard conditions before quickly returning to Riga, locals saw little reason to renovate hotels that were often empty. By 1939 even the Tourism Department began to shift its focus toward international tourists in transit to the Helsinki Olympics of 1940, as a *profitable* alternative to national tourism.[76]

There were more fundamental, structural reasons for the campaign's failures. Despite the remarkable economic performance of the interwar years and the rapid improvements in most qualities of life, Latvia, particularly rural Latvia, in the late 1930s was still a poor country. The state had grand designs, often borrowed and even plagiarized from western Europe and the United States, but the state still lacked the means to realize these aspirations. The regime hoped to build a tourist edifice on foundations that were only half poured. If the national tourism campaign's successes were limited due to material constraints, the campaign still tells us much about the regime that crafted it. The regime's attempted solution to the above-mentioned structural weaknesses was commonplace throughout eastern Europe and wherever states seek rapidly to overcome economic backwardness. If the foundations did not exist, the state would have to lay them, and in doing so it could not afford the lux-

75. Kārlis Vanags, "Ziņojums par provinces viesnīcu stāvokli," 5 April 1939, in Latvia's State Historical Archives, 3723, 2, 1893, 2–3.

76. Vanags, "Ziņojums par provinces viesnīcu stāvokli," 3.

ury of consensus building or opposition. In this light the national tourism campaign becomes a part of the debate about the nature of the Ulmanis regime.

The national tourism campaign strove to create a specific Latvian identity with unquestioning loyalty to Ulmanis and his regime, but by rigidly defining identity the regime undermined its attractiveness. There was no space for some within the nation (minorities and all but the most sycophantic), and the relationship between state and citizen was one-sided (the state ordered, subjects followed). In this way Latvia's national tourism campaign fundamentally differed from some of its models. The "See America First" campaign, for example, was a center-driven attempt to use tourism to mold national identity. There were, however, democratic mechanisms within the campaign that made it negotiated and its projected identity responsive and integrative.[77] In Latvia, there was no negotiation. The Department of Tourism in the Ministry of Social Affairs dictated policy. Local representatives of the state fulfilled directives and even the tourists were supposed to follow the dictates of the state down to the numbers of strides per breath. In spirit, this campaign was closer to transformational regimes like Hitler's Reich and its "Strength through Joy" campaign or Stalin's Soviet Union and its proletarian tourism of the 1930s discussed by Diane Koenker.[78] If the reality did not match the spirit, it was for two reasons. Ulmanis's Latvia did not have the human or material resources of the Third Reich and it was not willing (or not able) to employ extreme terror and coercion to enforce its prescriptions. Ulmanis's Latvia was more like Mussolini's Italy—a growing chasm emerged between what the state said and imagined and what happened. Another reason for this chasm may be the tourists. They went on vacation for leisure as much as for instruction. The national message may have been muted if not completely unheard. Despite living under a regime with a "fascist aesthetic"[79] in many things, including tourism, citizens may have taken as many steps per breath as they themselves chose.

77. Shaffer, *See America First*, 5–6, 169–220.
78. See Koenker, in this volume.
79. I am indebted to Vejas Liulevicius for this phrase describing Baltic authoritarian regimes that he argued had a fascist aesthetic but were essentially conservative (discussion at Fourth Association for the Study of Nationalities Conference, New York, 1999).

PART II

SOCIALIST TOURISM

CHAPTER 6

The Proletarian Tourist in the 1930s

Between Mass Excursion and Mass Escape

Diane P. Koenker

The Soviet project rested its appeal and legitimacy on the theory that under socialism, the contradictions of bourgeois life would disappear. Instead of a society in which one person's pleasure was bought at the expense of another's toil and in which toil, pleasure, and learning remained separate and mutually exclusive activities, socialism would allow every individual to share in every social activity. This was a totalist ambition: under Soviet socialism, everyone would work, everyone would engage in productive self-improvement, and everyday life would acquire new meaning because it would combine work, self-improvement, and pleasure in one. Among the arenas of everyday life in which this aspiration played itself out was the movement for proletarian tourism, which sought to use travel and tourism to create a new breed of Soviet citizen, and which sought to reward the hard toil of workers with the opportunity to travel outside the realm of their local everyday, to see spectacular mountains, bathe in the warm waters of the Black Sea, or explore the lakes and pristine beauties of Russia's Far North. But proletarian tourism would not replicate its bourgeois predecessors and appeal to romantic adventurers or the pursuit of idle pleasure. By marrying the term "proletarian" to the formerly bourgeois practice of "tourism," proletarian tourism would be simultaneously autonomous and collective, self-improving and socially constructive. As one publication put it, "While admiring the beauty of the Caucasus landscape, the [proletarian] tourist should at the same time investigate class struggle in the Chechen *aul*."[1] Proletarian tourism thus had a double mission: to admire the beauty of the sublime Caucasus mountains but also to make this task fundamentally a political one.

Travel, and in particular tourism, generated a lively debate in the Soviet press in the late 1920s and early 1930s about the meaning of tourism and the appropriate forms it should take. Acknowledging the pleasurable elements of travel and sightseeing, tourism activists argued that such delights should be made available to all citizens in the socialist republic. At the same time, how-

Research for this article was supported by a William and Flora Hewlett International Research Grant and the Research Board at the University of Illinois.

1. *Vecherniaia Moskva*, 24 April 1930.

ever, they insisted that tourism, under socialism, should serve to mobilize everyday life for the purposes of state. Proletarian tourism could serve to resolve the contradiction between compulsion and choice: the tourism movement would show Soviet citizens how to travel and why. As a consumer of travel experience rather than of commodities, the Soviet tourist would generate self-knowledge. Through voluntary and self-conscious participation in this personally enriching and socially useful activity, Soviet citizens would learn to value this citizenship and willingly meld their individuality with the good of the whole.

This chapter explores the dual mission of tourism discussions that were centered in the efforts of the Society for Proletarian Tourism and Excursions, debates that sought to define the meaning of proper proletarian travel from the late 1920s until the eve of World War II. Even within the "proletarian tourism" movement one can see conflicting elements of collectivism and individualism, between the function of the individual to serve the body social (production and patriotism) and to fulfill personal needs and desires (consumption and self). The regime's own institutional activists lacked a consensus about normative tourism, and this created a terrain on which consumers of Soviet tourism could carve out their own space within the system. By taking advantage of the movement for mass tourism, they could, in effect, escape from the mass.

The Politics of Proletarian Tourism

As Louise McReynolds shows, tourism had developed an enthusiastic following among the Russian middle classes by the beginning of the twentieth century. The Russian Society of Tourists (Rossiiskoe obshchestvo turistov—ROT) had emerged in the late nineteenth century to promote active touring, and the society continued to exist into the Soviet period. Its claim to represent Soviet tourists, however, was challenged in the 1920s by a series of new institutions. Local municipalities began to organize excursion bureaus to facilitate travel and outings that had become part of the staple repertory of proletarian leisure after the revolution. The Russian republic's Commissariat of Education also established programs to train excursion leaders and construct facilities for visitors to Petrograd and Moscow.[2] In late 1926 the Communist youth organization, Komsomol, seized the initiative to promote tourism as a method of cultural and physical uplift. In the midst of anxious reporting about deviant and aimless youth, epitomized in the trial of several dozen young Leningrad workers for the notorious gang rape in Chubarov Alley, the newspaper *Komsomol'skaia pravda* called for a new form of leisure travel, Soviet mass tourism:

2. G. P. Dolzhenko, *Istoriia turizma v dorevoliutsionnoi Rossii i SSSR* (Rostov-on-Don, 1988), 68–72.

"What is tourism? It is travel ... you see what you have never seen before, and this opens your eyes, you learn, you grow. .... And then you go back to the city, to work, to struggle, but the time has not passed in vain: you have become stronger and richer. This is tourism."[3] The organization's Central Committee devoted minimal attention to the project, but its tourism enthusiasts worked to propagate the idea of proletarian tourism through newspaper articles and handbooks. Trade union organizations also jumped on the tourism bandwagon.[4]

The Commissariat of Education sought to exercise hegemony over this movement and to profit from it: in September 1928 it created a joint-stock company, Sovetskii Turist (Sovtur), to operate organized tours and construct tourist facilities throughout the USSR.[5] With an eye on the potential foreign market, the agency published guidebooks, organized train tickets, and arranged accommodations for destinations across the Soviet Union.[6] Sovtur would soon emerge as the proletarian tourists' favorite whipping boy in their efforts to define proper proletarian travel. According to its critics, Sovtur functioned as a purely commercial agency interested only in providing a service, not in transforming culture. As a state agency, however, Sovtur enjoyed official protection. In search of an instrument for the "proletarianization" of tourism, Komsomol activists decided to utilize the Russian Society of Tourists. By the late 1920s, the society had become an allegedly small and narrow voluntary organization catering to Muscovite professionals and well-paid civil servants, a class physiognomy increasingly at odds with the strident new emphasis on proletarian purity. Komsomol and trade union activists sent aspiring proletarian tourists to flood this organization with new members; by the middle of 1928, they had succeeded in ousting the former leadership and claimed the society for their own, which they renamed the Society for Proletarian Tourism of the RSFSR (Obshchestvo proletarskogo turizma RSFSR—OPT).[7] The new organization took over the existing assets of the old ROT, in-

3. *Komsomol'skaia pravda*, 16 December 1926, 3. See Anne E. Gorsuch, *Youth in Revolutionary Russia: Enthusiasts, Bohemians, Delinquents* (Bloomington, Ind., 2000), 170–76. The Chubarov Alley trial began on 16 December 1926.

4. Rossiiskii gosudarstvennyi arkhiv sotsial'no-politicheskoi istorii (hereafter RGASPI), f. M-1, op. 4, d. 29 (meetings of the secretariat of the Komsomol Central Committee, 1927), ll. 97, 113–18, 126–32; G. Bergman, ed., *Pervaia kniga turista* (Moscow, 1927), was issued by the Komsomol publishing house. See Diane P. Koenker, *Republic of Labor: Russian Printers and Soviet Socialism, 1918–1930* (Ithaca, N.Y., 2005), 280–83, on the echoes of the movement in the trade union press.

5. Gosudarstvennyi arkhiv Rossiiskoi Federatsii (hereafter GARF), f. A-2306, op. 69, d. 2070 (correspondence of Sovetskii Turist, 1929), l. 10.

6. L. M. Loginov and Iu. V. Rukhlov, *Istoriia razvitiia turistsko-ekskursionnogo dela* (Moscow, 1989), 5–15; V. V. Dvornichenko, *Razvitie turizma v SSSR (1917–1983)* (Moscow, 1985), 11–12; *Na sushe i na more* (hereafter NSNM), no. 5 (1941): 20.

7. *Turist-aktivist*, no. 4 (1932): 9; NSNM, no. 11 (1930): 1; Dvornichenko, *Razvitie turizma*, 18.

cluding tourist hostels in prime mountain locations, and it signaled its intention to organize proletarian tourism on the ground, calling for the creation of factory-based cells across the country.

The OPT thus joined myriad other organizations competing for Soviet workers' time and dues money, from the Down with Illiteracy Society to International Aid to Political Prisoners. Like these organizations, it was wildly popular on paper. The evening Moscow daily, *Vecherniaia Moskva* (Evening Moscow), reported a rise in "participants in organized excursions" from 45,250 in 1928 to 661,502 in 1930.[8] By 1932 OPT would claim to have eight hundred thousand members and serve three million tourists.[9] As a voluntary society, the OPT plunged into the politics of cultural revolution and institutional rivalries, indicating that proletarian tourism was indeed a prize worth fighting over.

As in other arenas of the cultural revolution of 1928–1932, the players could not be distinguished on the basis of their class or even political positions.[10] Tourism radicals rallied to party organs like the Komsomol; state institutions like Sovtur's sponsoring Commissariat of Education emphasized their administrative credentials. The Moscow Communist party paper, *Vecherniaia Moskva*, took a populist line that minimized the importance of ideology. Sovtur attempted to limit OPT's role to propaganda and information, demanding for itself the exclusive right to organize tours, excursions, tourist bases, and ski stations.[11] Their battle replicated the intensifying "Great Turn" over Soviet economic and political policy. By the winter of 1929–1930, when the battle for all-out collectivization was raging in the countryside, OPT and Sovtur fought head-to-head for the monopoly over all tourist business in the USSR. The proletarian activists claimed the high ground:

> We were for a mass independent proletarian movement, Sovtur was for paid excursions. We were for cells in enterprises, as the basic center; Sovtur was for the center to be the excursion base. We were for subordinating administrative (*khoziaistvennye*) services to the political tasks of the movement, Sovtur in practice had raised administration to an end in itself.[12]

In March 1930, while Stalin warned his cadres not to become dizzy with the success of their collectivization effort, the Council of People's Commissars, encouraged by the Komsomol Central Committee, awarded victory on the tourist front on the principle of class. It ordered the state agency Sovtur to submit to the proletarian tourists, and henceforth tourism would be organized by

8. *Vecherniaia Moskva*, 19 August 1930.

9. *Turist-aktivist*, no. 5–6 (1932): 2.

10. See Sheila Fitzpatrick, ed., *Cultural Revolution in Russia, 1928–1931* (Bloomington, Ind., 1978).

11. GARF, f. A-2306, op. 69, d. 1826. ll. 1–40.

12. *Turist-aktivist*, no. 4 (1932): 10.

a new All-Union Voluntary Society for Proletarian Tourism and Excursions (Vsesoiuznoe dobrovol'noe obshchestvo proletarskogo turizma i ekskursii—OPTE).

The new organization launched an aggressive campaign to recruit new members through factory cells while at the same time struggling to fulfill the "administrative" functions of the tourist industry: providing services to tourists, expanding the network of tourist excursions, and keeping costs down.[13] Its own factory cells, on the other hand, spent less time touring than carrying out other Communist Party goals, such as fighting absenteeism at work, fulfilling the five-year plan, and studying Comrade Stalin's letter on Leninism.[14] To broadcast its message, the organization published two journals beginning in 1929. A biweekly popular magazine, *Na sushe i na more* (On Land and on Sea), featured a smorgasbord of photographs, fiction, exotica, travel advice, and politics. *Turist-aktivist*, a specialized monthly journal, provided instruction for dedicated proletarian tourism organizers. The organization held its first congress in 1932; that same year it opened three hundred new tourist bases and began construction on a six-story hostel for tourists visiting Moscow.[15] But already in 1933 and again in 1935 came ominous reports of inappropriate leadership from within the organization. In 1933 several members of the organization's central council were removed for "being cut off from tourist work"; in June 1935 *Na sushe i na more* revealed that the Leningrad organization had fallen victim to Trotsky-Zinov'ev oppositionists. In early 1936 came the final death knell for the voluntary society: the Soviet Central Executive Committee decreed that given the importance of tourism as part of the growth of physical culture, the existence of a separate tourism organization was no longer expedient. Henceforth, the work of tourism and management of all tourist property, as with the alpinists discussed by Eva Maurer, would be handled by the All-Union Central Council of Trade Unions (Vsesoiuznyi tsentral'nyi sovet professional'nykh soiuzov—VTsSPS) under the aegis of the All-Union Committee for Physical Culture and Sport of the Council of Peoples' Commissars of the USSR.[16]

It is difficult to disentangle the reasons behind the ongoing institutional struggle over the tourism project. Bureaucratic infighting over turf and assets surely played a role here as it did everywhere else in the state bureaucracy. The tourism battle might also have been a peripheral theater of operations in the larger leadership struggles at the apex of the Communist Party: once patrons fell, they generally brought their clients down with them. But it is also clear that there were ideological stakes involved in defining the nature of proletarian tourism: these were the terms in which public debate over proletarian tourism

13. Ibid., no. 5–6 (1932): 4, 12–14; no. 11–12 (1932): 23.
14. Ibid., no. 1 (1932): 7; no. 8 (1931): 15–16; no. 2 (1932): 20.
15. Ibid., no. 5–6 (1932); no. 7 (1932): 31; no. 10 (1932): 29.
16. NSNM, no. 5 (1936): 4.

was carried out in the press, and we must assume that whatever other factors affected the organization of tourism in the USSR, the struggle to define the proletarian tourist represented more than mere camouflage for some darker political struggle. At stake, after all, was defining the role that the citizen should play in laying claim to a democratic, multiethnic, and socialist nation.

Bad Trips and Good

In launching itself to the Soviet public in 1929, the new journal of the tourist movement, *Na sushe i na more*, took under its purview "travel and adventure, local study (*kraevedchestvo*) and ethnography, discoveries and inventions, achievements of science and technology, physical culture, and sport." Its purpose was to replace old bourgeois fantasy and the adventures of thinly disguised imperialism with "attentive and lively forms of local (*kraevedcheskii*) and touristic material, which exist in abundance in our wide multinational USSR, and we will acquaint [readers] with the life and customs of the numerous peoples of all five parts of the world."[17] In its opening manifesto, the journal aimed to establish for its Soviet readers the proper role of tourism and the proper aims of the Soviet tourist. From the outset, there seemed to be a fine line, however, between proper touristic endeavors and the inappropriate pursuit of the exotic for its own sake.[18]

Study of one's local region, *kraevedenie*, had long been an integral element of Russian intelligentsia culture, and tourism would include local study as one of its purposes, but local tourism presented particular problems. On the one hand, local sights and itineraries were readily accessible to the mass of tourists who could not afford to travel to distant destinations.[19] Tourism taught its participants to learn how to know, and study and understanding of one's own district was touted as a good place to develop this discipline. In the later years of the first five-year plan, local study by tourists was celebrated as a means to discover new sources of raw materials for the country's production goals.[20] On the other hand, and in the same breath, tourism activists warned against the "localist deviation." Some tourist organizations were too responsive to the influence of local lore societies, whose prerevolutionary origins signified a "class-alien" membership and mentality.[21]

17. Ibid., no. 1 (1929): 2.
18. Ibid.
19. *Biulleten' turista*, no. 4–5 (1930): 11; *NSNM*, no. 1 (1930): 15; no. 8 (1940): 4; no. 1 (1930): 14–15.
20. N. V. Krylenko, "Turizm i kraevedenie," *Turist-aktivist*, no. 5–6 (1932), 27–29; no. 1 (1932): 8–9.
21. Ibid., no. 7 (1931): 31; no. 12 (1931): 3. The kraevedenie movement also saw conflict on the class front, as rival organizations—one within Narkompros, another labeled "Kraeved-Marxists"—competed for the right to wear the mantle of kraevedenie (ibid., no. 1 [1932]: 8–9).

The most dangerous threat to proper proletarian tourism was a practice denounced as "tramping" (*brodiazhnichestvo*, also translated as "vagrancy").[22] "Tourism should not become purposeless tramping," warned the Komsomol Secretariat in 1927.[23] Proper tourists learned about their country and its economic achievements in collective and organized journeys, but under the guise of tourist travel, these tramps "gave up production, their factory, and their work and set out on long, round-the-world travels or a journey around the USSR," purposeless travel that valued only how many kilometers could be traversed.[24] Echoing west European contempt for worker-tramps who aspired to a "commoners' Grand Tour," *Na sushe i na more* denounced tramping as "petty-bourgeois" in February 1930, at the height of the regime's assault on the petty-bourgeois peasantry. The practice had dangerously spread from among the wrong sort—"counterrevolutionaries, people deprived of voting rights [*lishentsy*], criminals, spies, and adventurists"—to honest but misguided proletarian and student youth. Celebrated in newspaper articles with titles like "Three Thousand Kilometers on Foot," the "touring-tramp" [*turbrodiag*] enticed young people to give up their studies and hit the road in a quest for adventure, possibly fame, and even a questionable fortune. Full-time travelers could still make a living in the USSR of the five-year plan by selling their stories to the press or giving paid lectures on themes such as "From tourism to the beauty of the body."[25] Comrade Vrzhezhevskii drew extended and approving attention in *Vecherniaia Moskva* for his "12,000 kilometers on foot" around the USSR in 1929. In an interview with the paper, Vrzhezhevskii claimed his journey had improved his capacity to serve the Red Army, giving his adventures a patriotic veneer, but the proletarian tourist activists were suspicious of the true motives of self-made heroes like Vrzhezhevskii.[26] Proletarian tourism would discipline the unruly, chaotic, and risk-taking proclivities of Soviet youth, epitomized in the popularity of the Native American tales of Mayne Reid. "Strengthening the proletarian backbone will weaken the Mayne-Reid attitude in tourism, all this Indian-wigwam romanticizing, and strengthen its political purposefulness."[27]

Poor organization could also threaten the disciplinary value of tourism, and failure to plan trips carefully led to disasters just as damaging to the tourism movement as tramping. A mass excursion to the Caucasus allowed 650

22. *Komsomol'skaia pravda*, 4 March 1927.

23. RGASPI, f. M-1, op. 4, d. 29, l. 113 (policy on tourism adopted in the Komsomol Central Committee secretariat, 20 May 1927).

24. *Biulleten' turista*, no. 4–5 (1930), 5–6.

25. NSNM, no. 4 (1930), 1; V. Antonov-Saratovskii, "Doloi brodiazhnichestvo!" NSNM, no. 7 (1930), 1; Judith Adler, "Youth on the Road: Reflections on the History of Tramping," *Annals of Tourism Research* 12, no. 3 (1985): 341.

26. *Vecherniaia Moskva*, 18 July 1929.

27. Ibid., 24 April 1930.

Moscow tourists the opportunity to journey by foot along the famed Georgian Military Highway, but some participants had prepared for a "health spa, not a hike," and they walked the trails in high-heeled shoes and carrying purses and suitcases.[28] Host organizations arranged excursions so poorly that groups were forced to walk all night to reach their destinations, often found no meals available, and had to sleep on tables or on the floor.[29] Planning and accountability, exhorted the tourist activists, would protect novice tourists from mistakes like these.[30]

Planning would fight spontaneity (*samotek*) and tramping. It could also combat related bad practices. Physical culture groups and their misguided focus on "record breaking" (*rekordsmenstvo*) fed the tramping deviation. Tourism that focused on breaking barriers—days in the saddle, kilometers on foot—took the tourist's attention away from close and informed observation of the world he or she encountered.[31] "It is ridiculous to associate travel with attempts to set records," wrote *Komsomol'skaia pravda* in 1928. "Speeding along a route squanders the opportunity to carry out the fundamental task of the tourist—observation of a locality, nature, and the life of the local population."[32] The OPTE enumerated other "petty-bourgeois" deviations in its 1930 rules: bad travel was apolitical and seasonal, it was travel that privileged consumerism and rest.[33] Not that "rest" was entirely inappropriate for workers' vacation excursions: OPTE officials insisted that a healthy measure of rest days be factored into all organized and self-planned trips. Proletarian tourists could also take advantage of motorized transport to optimize their tourist experiences. The old slogan, "Our motor is a pair of strong legs," was excessively restrictive, wrote one activist in 1932.[34]

"Culturalism" (*kul'turnichestvo*) was likewise unproletarian: this was tourism with the politics left out.[35] Visitors to Leningrad and Moscow during the November holidays failed to appreciate or to celebrate the political significance of their visits, which followed a mainly recreational, or "at best," a culturalist agenda.[36] Later in the 1930s, at the height of the purges, concern about the apoliticalness of tourism resurfaced with accusations that tourist organiza-

---

28. *Proletarskii turizm (Iz opyta raboty baumanskogo otdeleniia obshchestva proletarskogo turizma). Materialy k X baumanskoi raikonferentsii VLKSM* (Moscow, 1929), 62; *Turist-aktivist*, no. 12 (1931): 30.

29. *Turist-aktivist*, no. 8–9 (1932): 21–22; no. 11–12 (1932): 44.

30. O. A. Arkhangel'skaia, *Rabota iacheiki OPTE po samodeiatel'nomu turizmu* (Moscow, 1935), 3; *Turist-aktivist*, no. 10–11 (1931): 21–22.

31. *NSNM*, no. 7 (1930): 1; *Turist-aktivist*, no. 3 (1932): 7.

32. *Komsomol'skaia pravda*, 7 July 1928.

33. GARF, f. R-9520, op. 1, d. 1 (rules for cells of OPTE), l. 2.

34. *Turist-aktivist*, no. 3 (1932), 31; no. 4 (1932): 21.

35. *NSNM*, no. 4 (1930): 1.

36. Ibid., no. 17–18 (1930): 1.

tions' indifference to political matters made them easy targets for penetration by enemies of the people.[37]

In denouncing practices like localism, tramping, and culturalism, tourist activists were working out the norms of proper socialist tourism. But good travel and authentically proletarian tourism could not be identified merely by inverting the signs indicated by the discussions cited above. The opposite of tramping was staying at home; if culturalism was bad, lack of culture was worse. So the promoters of proletarian tourism needed to carefully negotiate the narrow strait between the good thing and the good thing carried to inappropriate extremes or done for inappropriate reasons.

Intention was everything. Proletarian tourism had a purpose. Acquiring local knowledge, which motivated the kraevedchestvo movement, was therefore also a treasured goal of the tourist. The proletarian tourist was challenged to learn about the multinational USSR, to discover the variety and richness of the Soviet land—not out of casual curiosity, which would be the bourgeois form of tourism, but in order to produce knowledge. A tourist was celebrated in 1929 for having discovered a new ethnic group (*narodnost'*) in Turkmeniia.[38] Every tourist group, wrote *Turist-aktivist*, should plan to look for productive resources; it should query local residents about where to find them; it should collect specimens of local nature and plants. Every tourist itinerary should be designed to educate, to instruct tourists in political realities, and to show the five-year plan in action.[39] In this purposefulness, Soviet tourism conformed to state-building tourism projects elsewhere in Europe, as the chapters by Vari and Purs show.

Proletarian tourism incorporated rationality and science. Each tourist group would proceed only under the strictest monitoring by medical personnel, and "balneological tourism" along the seacoast was recommended not for pleasure but for the alleviation of stress, neurasthenia, and fatigue.[40] Tourist itineraries would be selected to suit the health and abilities of the travelers. Every trip required careful and elaborate preparation: choosing a route that optimized a group's abilities, time, and financial resources was an important element in the overall experience. As in Ulmanis's Latvia, experts advised on how many hours to walk, how often to stop, what to eat, and when to drink.[41] On the road, tourists would keep daily journals and carefully record their ob-

37. Ibid., no. 10 (1937): 34.
38. Ibid., no. 11 (1929); no. 2 (1929).
39. *Turist-aktivist*, no. 7 (1931): 20; no. 7 (1931): 32.
40. G. Bergman, *Otdykh letom* (Moscow-Leningrad, 1927); *Biulleten' turista*, no. 2–3 (1930): 33; *Turist-aktivist*, no. 8 (1931): 42; O. Arkhangel'skaia and N. Tiriutina, eds., *Puteshestvie po SSSR: Turistskie marshruty* (Moscow, 1938), 202; on medicalized leisure in nineteenth-century France, see Douglas Peter Mackaman, *Leisure Settings: Bourgeois Culture, Medicine, and the Spa in Modern France* (Chicago, 1998).
41. Bergman, *Pervaia kniga turista*, 66–67.

servations of the trip. Upon their return, they would file a report based on these journals, preferably illustrated with photographs and sketches that would collect, codify, and preserve the knowledge they had gained.[42]

Tourism was the best form of leisure because in exposing tourists to a rich panoply of impressions, it developed their intellects. By traveling to other industrial sites, tourists could observe how others worked and bring back new ideas for their own production endeavors.[43] Outside the Russian federation, they could observe the growth of the proletariat of all nationalities.[44] The good tourist would always keep eyes and mind open to new ideas and new impressions. By following itineraries dedicated to particular events or themes, such as the civil war, they could also improve their knowledge of their history and their country.[45] Tourist skills in themselves—map reading, use of a compass, pitching a tent, keeping safe in the mountains—prepared the nation for the potential requirements of military duty, a theme that became increasingly prominent in the second half of the 1930s.[46]

Proletarian tourists would also help to bring knowledge and culture to others. As ambassadors of socialism, they were encouraged to conduct cultural work among the inhabitants of the villages they passed through and to invite them to participate in their evenings of skits, music, and performances.[47] Members of the proletarian tourist society should go out on their tours armed with gifts of cultural significance—notebooks, pencils, pens, and primers in the local languages.[48] Tourists to Kareliia organized a children's nursery in one small village, with money sent from their tourist organization back home.[49] "Without cultural and socially purposeful tasks, tourism is empty amusement," instructed one OPTE branch.[50]

The French sociologist Jean-Didier Urbain has noted that among the ascribed differences between *travel* (good) and *tourism* (bad) is the inauthenticity of the tourist.[51] The traveler wishes to be the unique visitor to a site, to share the experience of discovery with no one else. The tourist, by definition, has already been commodified through the agency of the group tour and can only follow, never be a pioneer. The tourist is only a superficial observer who passes quickly through the prearranged items on the tourist agenda. Soviet discussions of good and bad travel turned this distinction around: the proletarian

42. L. L. Barkhash, *Sputnik turista* (Moscow-Leningrad, 1927), 21–22; Bergman, *Pervaia kniga turista*; Arkhangel'skaia, *Rabota iacheiki OPTE*, 32–34.
43. *Turist-aktivist*, no. 3 (1932): 7; NSNM, no. 12 (1929): 16.
44. NSNM, no. 13 (1931): 15; no. 3 (1929): 10; no. 1 (1938): 30.
45. Ibid., no. 25 (1931): 2.
46. Ibid., no. 12 (1935): 15; no. 2 (1937): 4; no. 7 (1940): 16–17; no. 5 (1941): 5.
47. NSNM, no. 12 (1929): 15–16; *Proletarskii turizm*, 24, 47–48.
48. NSNM, no. 1 (1930), 1–2.
49. *Proletarskii turizm*, 73–74.
50. Ibid., 50.
51. Jean-Didier Urbain, *L'idiot du voyage: Histoires de touristes* (Paris, 1991), esp. 204.

НА СУШЕ
НА МОРЕ

8

6.1. Cover of *Na sushe i na more*,
features one man and his bicycle.
Na sushe i na more, no. 8 (1936)

tourist was authentic; the bourgeois *traveler* merely sought fleeting sensation.
Thus the good proletarian tourist traveled by boat, horseback, bicycle, or on
foot; never by train or automobile.[52] "The railway passenger knows only one
street in a new city, the street from the train station to the hotel." A bicyclist,
by contrast, could observe all parts of a city, from its outskirts to its bridges,
from residential quarters to central districts.[53] The prescribed uniform of ruck-
sack, walking stick, and floppy hat to ward off the sun reinforced the image of
the tourist as a person who locomoted through nature and the nation under
his or her own power.[54] *Turist-aktivist* averred that small group tourism best
developed the individuality and independence of the Soviet subject; such independent tourism was much to be preferred over the packaged group tour.[55]

52. *Turist-aktivist*, no. 3 (1932): 31.
53. *Vecherniaia Moskva*, 5 August 1933.
54. NSNM, no. 4 (1929); *Turist-aktivist*, no. 10–11 (1931): 4–5. Such a figure emerged as the
icon of the "Tourist Corner" column of *Vecherniaia Moskva* beginning in 1929.
55. *Turist-aktivist, no.* 1 (1933): 4–8.

Conflicting Values in Proletarian Tourism

The shrill debates between the Society of Proletarian Tourists and its competitor Sovtur created a sharp sense of dichotomy between good proletarian tourism and bad that perhaps exceeded the actual preferences of consumers of tourist travel. But even these ideologically charged discussions reflected not just absolute values about proper proletarian tourist practice but also significant differences among the activists and writers themselves. This discussion about norms would in fact open up wide latitude for tourists to choose their own definitions of "good travel." One division concerned the choice between rugged travel and smooth. A second division related to the choice between collectivism and individualism in performing Soviet tourism. Finally, despite an ideology that aimed to create a society unmarked by class difference, tourist activists expressed concern that so few real proletarians were choosing to engage in proletarian tourism.

The emphasis on self-locomotion had been a basic tenet of proletarian tourism since the 1920s, and increasing attention to the military values of rigorous mountain touring only reinforced the high value placed on ruggedness and hard touring work: the chief pleasure of tourism, wrote one activist, was to travel by foot, boat, or bicycle ("My motor is two strong legs"). *Komsomol'skaia pravda* listed "dangerous" travel on its menu of tourism options, and a Moscow group of friends was renowned for their devotion to 40-kilometer weekend hikes.[56] There is a certain masculinist tone in some of the hardiness discussions that bears further exploration. At one Moscow factory, at any rate, men felt that women were too delicate to engage in real tourism: "They'll freeze in the tents!" But others insisted women, too, loved to battle the elements and encouraged tourist groups to include them, in part for their civilizing effect on men.[57] Still others insisted that the birth of children and the needs of young families were no impediment to strenuous touring, as the example of the Leningraders Maria and Mikhail Tsimbalist demonstrated. Avid cyclists, they toured with their five-year-old Kostia in a special bicycle seat. By age nine, Kostia had his own bike and toured with his parents along the Black Sea coast from Sevastopol to Tuapse, covering 523 kilometers in twenty-eight days.[58]

Yet these same normative sources also wrote in positive tones about the desire of proletarian tourists for comfort and ease. Travel by steamship, whether on the Volga River, along the new Moscow-Volga river canal system, or north to the Arctic Circle was not exactly self-locomotion, but would-be tourists were regularly encouraged to consider the pleasures of a cruise. In 1930, 257

56. Bergman, *Pervaia kniga turista*, 16; *Komsomol'skaia pravda*, 1 April 1927; *NSNM*, no. 8 (1940): 4.

57. *NSNM*, no. 5–6 (1931): 1; no. 5 (1935): 1; *Komsomol'skaia pravda*, 6 July 1928; Bergman, *Pervaia kniga turista*, 23.

58. *NSNM*, no. 1 (1940): 28.

select shock workers traveled aboard the newly commissioned *Abkhaziia*, their reward for hard work and political loyalty a berth on the vessel's maiden voyage from Leningrad to Odessa, via Hamburg, Naples, and Istanbul. White tablecloths, cleanliness, and filling three-course meals signified the reward of luxury they had earned.[59] A prize trip along the Black Sea for the Stakhanovites Nina and Zoia in 1936 celebrated the ease earned by these record-breaking workers: "The comfortable accommodations, a lively and gay company of tourists who had come from all the cities of the country, the astounding beauty of the shore, and the snowy peaks sparkling in the sky gave them rapture."[60] "River tourism has become one of the most popular forms of vacation," wrote *Vecherniaia Moskva* in 1937.[61] The failure of steamers to provide "comfortable accommodations" earned censure and a special investigation from the party control organization: all steamships ought to have linen on the dining-room tables, separate cabins, pleasant salons, covered decks, an area for sunbathing, a barber shop, chess, fresh newspapers, a book kiosk, and a telegraph office. But half of the steamers had no radios or bathing facilities, and on most boats, the newspapers were not only not "fresh" but were nonexistent.[62]

On land, tourists also expected a modicum of comfort. Some tourists may have spent their nights in tents, but many more availed themselves of beds in "tourist bases," or hostels. While simple, these hostels were not meant to be spartan, and they ought to provide facilities for washing and mending clothes, for warm baths and shaving.[63] The newly opened House of Tourists in Moscow boasted space for 450 travelers in 1936 and had a lobby, library, billiard room, and solarium on its eighth floor, but visitors had to wash in a neighborhood public bath. Tourists expected better amenities: not only were there no baths, they complained, but no hot water at all, no mirrors, no hooks to hang their clothes, no place to dress.[64] Proletarian tourism needed to provide for cultured travel with luggage and high heels as well as for rugged backpacking.

The proletarian tourist movement also reveals a surprising conflict between socialist collectivism and socialist individualism. One might expect that collectivism would be the default option for proletarian tourism: mass excursions

59. *Korabl' udarnikov* (Moscow, 1932).

60. NSNM, no. 8 (1936): 15. The link between Stakhanovism and cultured consumption has already been noted by Lewis H. Siegelbaum, *Stakhanovism and the Politics of Productivity in the USSR, 1935–1941* (Cambridge, 1988); see also Evgeny Dobrenko, "The Art of Social Navigation: The Cultural Topography of the Stalin Era," in *The Landscape of Stalinism: The Art and Ideology of Soviet Space*, ed. Evgeny Dobrenko and Eric Naiman (Seattle, 2003), 182.

61. *Vecherniaia Moskva*, 19 August 1937.

62. Ibid.; Rossiiskii gosudarstvennyi arkhiv ekonomiki, f. 7458, op. 1, d. 2885 (transcript of conference on passenger transport and passenger service, 11–14 September 1936).

63. *Turist-aktivist*, no. 1 (1933): 3–8, 28.

64. NSNM, no. 7 (1936): 25.

would forge group solidarity and wash away any residue of bourgeois individualism. The "tramp" could be a dangerous example because the man who traveled 2,000 kilometers on foot around the country celebrated his uniqueness, not a Soviet self that merged seamlessly with the collective. The whole point of proletarian tourism was that it would reach a mass audience through the economies of a mass scale: entire trains and boats could be reserved for the new mass tourist.[65] Collective strolls and hikes, insisted *Na sushe i na more* in 1931, would help to combat individualism.[66] Indeed, the OPTE's bill of indictment of the Sovtur organization included Sovtur's insistence on retaining a monopoly over mass excursions, leaving only consulting on independent travel to the new proletarian society.[67]

The mass excursion (*massovka*) represented a new socialist form of collective touring. More common and more popular was the packaged group tour (*operativnyi marshrut*), offered every summer by Sovtur and later the OPTE along itineraries long popular with the middle-class Russian tourists depicted by McReynolds; they also promoted tours to emerging new industrial destinations. But the group tour was far from hegemonic, and even at the start of the proletarian tourism movement, its activists stressed the importance of independent travel and individual initiative. The difference between excursions and tourism, wrote G. Bergman, is that "the participant in an excursion doesn't demonstrate any independence; he pays his money, and that's the extent of his 'independence.' The excursionist is 'carried' and 'led,' without any active participation."[68] *Turizm*, by contrast, "is travel in which the distance, itinerary, and even the means of locomotion (by foot, boat, etc.) are arranged by the tourist alone, based on his inclinations, material position, physical capabilities, and technical ability."[69] Independent tourism was especially suited for young people and workers because it required relatively little expenditure.[70] But in addition, only independent travel, activists argued, developed all the capabilities of the tourist: self-reliance, flexibility, autonomy, initiative, and self-knowledge.[71] Only the independent (*samodeiatel'nyi*) tourist was the truly authentic tourist. As Jochen Hellbeck and Igal Halfin have argued, Soviet selves realized their subjectivities through their own personal negotiations with the system.[72] Beginning in 1927 (and continuing well into the 1950s), handbooks

---

65. Ibid., no. 3 (1929): 10; no. 6 (1929); *Turist-aktivist*, no. 7 (1932): 16–17.

66. *NSNM*, no. 25 (1931): 14–15.

67. GARF, f. A-2306, op. 69, d. 1826 (materials on "Sovetskii turist"), ll. 14–16; *Turist-aktivist*, no. 4 (1932): 10.

68. Bergman, *Otdykh letom*, 55.

69. Barkhash, *Sputnik turista*, 7.

70. GARF, f. A-2306, op. 69, d. 2068, l. 22 (plan for cooperation between Sovtur and ROT); *Biulleten' turista*, no. 7–8 (1930): 8.

71. *Turist-aktivist*, no. 1 (1933): 4–5.

72. Jochen Hellbeck, "Fashioning the Stalinist Soul: The Diary of Stepan Podlubnyi (1931–1939)," *Jahrbücher für Geschichte Osteuropas* 44, no. 3 (1996): 233–73; Igal Halfin, "Looking into Oppositionists' Souls: Inquisition Communist Style," *Russian Review* 60, no. 3 (2001): 316–39.

told would-be tourists how to become self-activating tourists, advising on ways to form a small and harmonious group, select a destination, plan a budget, and carry out a trip.[73] For its part, the Society for Proletarian Tourism pledged to provide inexpensive lodging and transportation for these independent groups, and they lobbied for the production of touring equipment—tents, rucksacks, boats—to facilitate life on the road.[74]

If the independent tourist was the truly authentic Soviet tourist, however, such groups often found their plans thwarted by the priority given to the more predictable (and profitable) package tour. Tourist organizations continually chastised managers of tourist facilities for their unwillingness to cater to the independent traveler. Beds at hostels were too often filled with participants of group tours; independent tourists could not find meals or places on excursions.[75] Independent tourists found it difficult to obtain good local advice once they had arrived at a destination: consultants and guides reserved their services for groups.[76]

The class dimension of tourism colored the debates over proper forms of tourism: culturalism, physical culturism, and localism could be labeled "bourgeois" no matter who participated; "proletarian" tourism, by definition, was tourism with the right attitude. Were these just rhetorical flourishes? How "proletarian," in fact, was the Society for Proletarian Tourism; how many "proletarians"—factory, service, and craft workers—chose tourism as the mode of their annual paid vacations? When trade union leaders in 1926 were encouraged to consider putting tourism on their social agenda, the response was cool: Soviet tourism would appeal only to the bourgeoisie and intelligentsia, they felt.[77] *Komsomol'skaia pravda* acknowledged that until it began its campaign for proletarian tourism in 1927, "the word 'tourist' evoked laughter at most factories."[78] The Society for Proletarian Tourism admitted in early 1930 that "unfortunately, the desire of industrial workers for tourism remains weak, and the Society for Proletarian Tourism is not yet actually proletarian." It aimed in 1930 to recruit two hundred thousand members by October of that year, of whom 60 percent would be workers.[79]

The society would expand its proletarian base by organizing inside workplaces and especially in factories. Members joined the tourism society through enterprise cells; and all planning, education, and trips would arise from these basic units. As in the United States in this period, proponents of working-class

73. Barkhash, *Sputnik turista*; Bergman, *Pervaia kniga turista*; B. B. Kotel'nikov, *Sputnik turista* (Moscow, 1941); O. Arkhangel'skaia, *Kak organizovat' turistskoe puteshestvie* (Moscow, 1947); *Sputnik turista* (Moscow, 1959).

74. GARF, f. A-2306, op. 69, d. 1826, l. 14; d. 2068, ll. 6–7; *Biulleten' turista*, no. 7–8 (1930), 1; *Turist-aktivist*, no. 8 (1931): 42.

75. *Turist-aktivist*, no. 8–9 (1932): 21; no. 1 (1933): 4.

76. *NSNM*, no. 1 (1935): 4.

77. Bergman, *Pervaia kniga turista*, 182.

78. *Komsomol'skaia pravda*, 10 June 1927.

79. *Vecherniaia Moskva*, 24 April 1930.

tourism needed to overcome cultural barriers to tourism.[80] For most Soviet workers, Crimea represented a sunny place to recover from shattered nerves, not the start of a hiking adventure. Local cells raised consciousness and funds for travel through showing films, sponsoring entertainment, working overtime, giving up smoking, and by personal savings.[81]

The society also realized that touring needed to be affordable for workers, and the emphasis on independent travel was in part a response to the high cost of organized tours. Officials admitted that the "proletarian" component in package tours was 20 percent at best, but that 60 percent of independent tourists were "pure proletarians."[82] One solution was to offer discounted rail tickets to low-income tourists.[83] The Volga river fleet started a new line in 1928, featuring a "soft third class" that would "give tourists with very limited means the possibility to take a comfortable cruise on the Volga." A 1,000-kilometer trip in third class would cost 8 rubles 80 kopecks, compared to 22 rubles for the same trip in first class.[84] But the independent cruise was even cheaper. "Take your vacation by boat," announced the proletarianizing Russian Society of Tourists in 1928: teams of five or six people could rent a fully equipped boat, complete with sail and tent: the price for workers earning less than 60 rubles a month would be 4 rubles for two weeks.[85] At a time when the average worker earned around 125 rubles a month, these rates put touring vacations within the reach of everyone.[86] Even so, organized travel to destinations like the Caucasus and Crimea, where packages (without transportation) were advertised at 50 rubles and up, remained well beyond the means of the average worker.

From Mass Excursion to Mass Escape

The four aims of proletarian tourism—mass, collective, self-initiating, and purposeful—opened the door to multiple and sometimes conflicting definitions

80. Michael Berkowitz, "A 'New Deal' for Leisure: Making Mass Tourism during the Great Depression," in *Being Elsewhere: Tourism, Consumer Culture, and Identity in Modern Europe and North America*, ed. Shelley Baranowski and Ellen Furlough (Ann Arbor, Mich., 2001), 185–212; *Proletarskii turizm*, 22.

81. Bergman, *Pervaia kniga turista*, 197–98; *Proletarskii turizm*, 27, 42.

82. *Biulleten' turista*, no. 7–8 (1930): 9; *Pervyi vsesoiuznyi s"ezd OPTE v voprosakh i otvetakh* (Moscow, 1932), 67; GARF, f. A-2306, op. 69, d. 1826 (draft plan of tourism work of Polit-prosvet, 3 September 1928), l. 6.

83. *Biulleten' turista*, no. 2–3 (1930): 9–10; GARF, f. A-2306, op. 69, d. 1826, d. 2068.

84. *Povolzh'e: Spravochnik-putevoditel' 1930 g.* (Moscow, 1930), 243–44, 291–93.

85. *Komsomol'skaia pravda*, 28 July 1928.

86. Wage data from Elena Osokina, *Za fasadom "Stalinskoi izobiliia": Raspredelenie i rynok v snabzhenii naseleniia v gody industrializatsii, 1917–1941* (Moscow, 1998), 129 n. 2; Gert Meyer, *Sozialstruktur sowjetischer Industriearbeiter Ende der zwanziger Jahre* (Marburg, 1981), 155, citing A. G. Rashin, *Sostav fabrichno-zavodskogo proletariata SSSR v diagrammakh i tablitsakh* (Moscow, 1930).

of proper tourism, as we have seen. They also facilitated the emergence of a multitude of tourism practices. Tourists in the Soviet 1930s were offered a substantial variety of alternatives for engaging in this important and purposeful activity, and the very multiplicity of tourist destinations, regimens, and subcultures contributed to a fragmentation of disciplinary and state-building goals, permitting Soviet citizens to use tourism to shape a Soviet identity on their own terms, based on their own interests and desires.

There existed an inescapable tension between the purpose of tourism to develop independence and self-initiative and the activists' desire to instruct and to direct proper tourism activities. Tourists were encouraged to blaze their own *marshruty* into the socialist expanse, but they were also offered model itineraries that allowed the tourist to benefit from the collective experience of those who had gone before. The *First Book of the Tourist* in 1927 listed thirty-nine easy trips for aspiring tourists, advising on alternate routes and means of transport, and indicating the major attractions (*ob"ekty*) along the way.[87] The Society for Proletarian Tourism would provide the tools for the traveler, but the individual groups would choose their destinations and their goals.

Tourism's very essence consisted of flexibility, multiplicity, and plurality of destinations and of forms. Critics of tourism, argued *Turist-aktivist* in 1932, tried to subordinate tourism to their own particular institutions: the Commissariat of Education emphasized the enlightenment function of tourism, the physical culture movement insisted tourism was primarily about training the body. The beauty of tourism, continued the journal, was that its protean nature made any or all of these activities available.[88]

Domestically, the mountains and the sea continued to be the most widely advertised tourist destinations. Crimea remained for proletarian tourists the canonical goal. Soviet proletarian travelers eagerly sought to follow in the well-trodden footsteps of imperial tourists and soldiers alike. Both Sovtur and OPT competed to provide citizens and members with group tours to Crimean and other Black Sea destinations. The Caucasus Mountains had also long appealed to metropolitan Russians as an exotic and sublime destination, but the proletarian tourist movement sought to expand its accessibility. The region offered more than the famous Georgian military highways, wrote *Na sushe i na more* in 1929, and it extolled the attractions of the Kabardino-Balkariia Autonomous Oblast. Already in 1929, over one thousand tourists had made use of the tourist base in the oblast's capital, Nal'chik, many of them following OPT's "itinerary number 12" that took them from Nal'chik, skirting the slopes of Mount Elbrus, eventually reaching Sukhumi on the Black Sea coast.[89] But tourists could also choose to travel to the Soviet North, with ten-day itin-

87. Bergman, *Pervaia kniga turista*, 223–51.
88. *Turist-aktivist*, no. 4 (1932): 23.
89. NSNM, no. 12 (1929): 15.

Туристская ПУТЕВКА

ПУТЕШЕСТВИЕ — ЛУЧШИЙ ОТДЫХ

Советский туризм –
    мощное средство познания
    социалистической   родины

Туристско-экскурсионное управление ВЦСПС

организует в 1939 году

путешествия по СССР

Открыто 160 маршрутов

ВЦСПС ТУРИСТСКО-ЭКСКУРСИОННОЕ УПРАВЛЕНИЕ

6.2. Advertisement for VTsSPS excursions in 1940 depicts the range of tourism options on land and on sea. *Na sushe i na more*, no. 5 (1939): inside back cover.

eraries taking them from Leningrad to Murmansk, or to Ukraine, with a ten-day tour stopping at the Dneprostroi hydroelectric dam, Odessa, and Kiev.[90]

  As tourist practices developed in the 1930s, it became clear that tourists were subdividing into particular touring subcultures. In the early 1930s special arrangements for hunters and fishermen were offered to both foreign and domestic tourists.[91] "Fishing tourists" to Senezhskoe Lake could find accommodations at a new hotel in 1929, House of the Fisherman.[92] Combining tourism with hunting was one strategy to lure adult workers to the movement.[93] Soon the Society for Proletarian Tourism had generated individual sections for mountaineering, boating, cycling, and hiking. Controversy arose by the mid-1930s about whether such sections should exist at all, but they persisted as increasingly coherent units of tourist activity. In 1937 the OPTE's hikers challenged the boaters to a socialist competition for the best fulfillment of the cataloguing of itineraries.[94] The long-legged hikers of Moscow also attracted attention as almost a closed corporation of tourists: they developed their own customs surrounding their weekly 40-kilometer hikes, including special nicknames to indicate their distinctive pastime; when a child was born to one of them, the entire group helped to select a name.[95]

90. *Vecherniaia Moskva*, 28 June 1929.
91. Ibid., 12 June 1932; 9 July 1929.
92. Ibid., 1 June; 29 June 1929.
93. *Proletarskii turizm*, 19.
94. NSNM, no. 9 (1936): 2; no. 10 (1937): 34.
95. Ibid., no. 8 (1940): 4.

6.3. Prospective tourists receive kayak instruction from the OPTE in the Moscow Park of Culture and Rest, 1933. Rossiiskii gosudarstvennyi arkhiv kinofotodokumentov, no. 018460. Used with permission of the archive.

By 1938 a guidebook for independent tourists, enriched with reports from tourists themselves, offered elaborate descriptions of hundreds of itineraries, packaged in one volume so that tourists could select their program based on their own interests and desires.[96] Activists had warned in 1932 against the "bourgeois" practice of travel to "get away from people and daily cares," for one's self-interest exclusively, and yet, the proletarian tourist was encouraged to choose this activity and its destinations freely, "remembering that tourism will attract millions of people on the basis of their personal desires and interests."[97] This philosophy of Soviet tourism constituted a veritable license for independence, self-realization, and individuation. Under the guise of exploring and mapping out new routes, tourist activists became heroes of their own personal travel accounts, the travelogue itself the method of reinscribing their personal journeys as socially useful instruction for the larger collective.[98] The individual tourist could optimally combine personal pleasure with social purpose. The Vlasov couple undertook annual cycling trips around the Caucasus and the Urals; their articles in *Na sushe i na more* emphasized the practical knowledge they were now sharing with other potential tourists but could not disguise the sense of pure pleasure they enjoyed from the independence of bicycle touring.[99]

Reports from tourists celebrated the personal autonomy of life on the road. Among the letters sent to Moscow's Bauman district council of the OPTE, most emphasized two key tropes: adventures and good works.[100] Two aspiring teachers recounted a journey through the rivers and forests of the Urals in the summer of 1932, the group of six armed with five rifles and carrying food reserves for a month. (Tourists were advised in these years to carry their rations with them.) They had undertaken to collect animal furs for the biological museum in Moscow, but they took special care to describe the dangers of the trip and their adaptability in confronting unexpected situations.[101] A group of apprentices from a textile factory decided to spend their holiday rowing down the Volga. The OPTE delayed them for days with medical examinations and swimming tests; through their own initiative they managed to buy a boat from a fisherman, and only then did their "beautiful and successful" tour begin.[102] A fictionalized account of a Caucasus journey included the usual difficult mountain passes but also an encounter with a reformed local bandit, Seipul, com-

96. *Puteshestvie po SSSR*, 3. The press run was 9,300.

97. *Turist-aktivist*, no. 8–9 (1932): 35; no. 3 (1932): 7.

98. GARF, f. R-9520, op. 1, d. 5 (Reports of expeditionary groups in the Krasnaia Poliana-Gagra region, 1934), d. 6 (Reports of tourist groups in Abkhaziia, 1935).

99. See A. and M. Vlasov, "Na velosipede po Dagestanu," *NSNM*, no. 5 (1937): 5–7; no. 6 (1937): 4–6; "Po goram i stepiam Kavkaza," no. 3 (1938): 7; no. 4 (1938): 5–8; "V Dagestane," no. 5 (1939): 8–10; A. and I. Vlasov, "Po Uralu," no. 3 (1941): 6–8.

100. *Proletarskii turizm*, 22.

101. *Turist-aktivist, no.* 10 (1932), 14–15.

102. *Proletarskii turizm*, 78–80.

plete with the frisson of danger that came from eerie cries in the night and sharing a campfire with this "reformed" bandit.[103] A group of rather inexperienced tourists to Lake Ritsa in the Caucasus described some harrowing descents by moonlight, and their delight at stumbling across an alpine "corner of paradise," replete with waterfalls and bubbling springs. Theirs was a tale of survival and self-reliance, and of informing the local population about the international situation.[104]

Such accounts—and many more appeared in the pages of *Na sushe i na more* throughout the 1930s—invited aspiring tourists to reject the humdrum spa vacation and the tedium of the package tour. There were no fortresses Bolsheviks could not storm; there were no roads proletarians could not take. The best proletarian tourists rejected the beaten path and, in so doing, perfected the proletarian self-reliance of the new Soviet person.

The Meaning of Proletarian Tourism

It is important to consider not only prescriptive tourist practices and how tourists responded but also who exactly was creating the proletarian tourist in the USSR. The Soviet state was a coercive one, which experienced no crisis of doubt when it came to moving subjects around the nation for the purposes it deemed important: construction or correction, production or punishment, defense or discipline. With the demise of the prerevolutionary Russian Society of Tourists, the agencies organizing or reporting on tourism all fell under the supervision of the Communist Party if not the state apparatus itself. *Komsomol'skaia pravda*, which led the clamor for proletarian tourism beginning in 1926, was published by the Young Communist League; *Vecherniaia Moskva*, a leading culprit in the promotion of tramping instead of proper tourism, was the organ of the Communist Party Moscow Committee and the Moscow city soviet. The Society for Proletarian Tourism began life as a "voluntary" association, but one with the closest ties to the Communist Party; its journal continued to publish throughout the 1930s, whether its sponsor was the voluntary society, the trade union organization, or the state committee on sport. All belonged to what has been labeled the "party-state"; all participated in creating the Soviet tourist. But these organs spoke with different and sometimes contradictory voices. They provided, in their best moments, cheap tickets to picturesque and stimulating destinations; they could also supply room and board, consultants and guidebooks, and stories to dream on or to compare with one's own lived experiences.

The very cacophony of these competing voices provided cover for individuals to work out their own programs. The emphasis on individualism, authen-

103. GARF, f. R-9520, op. 1, d. 5, ll. 10–46.
104. *Proletarskii turizm*, 86–89.

ticity, and multiplicity suggests that the most important tourist was the self-creating tourist, and these party and state agencies significantly devoted their activities toward creating the space that would allow Soviet tourists—in groups, with friends, alone, or in families—to create themselves. In this way the meaning of proletarian tourism in the USSR was to enable the individual, through the medium of the mass tourism movement, to escape from the mass altogether and to forge a personal and independent path through the Soviet land.

CHAPTER 7

Al'pinizm as Mass Sport and Elite Recreation

Soviet Mountaineering Camps under Stalin

Eva Maurer

In 1958 a group of British mountaineers headed by the leader of the successful Everest expedition, Sir John Hunt, was permitted to climb in the Caucasus.[1] In the previous twenty years, not a single western mountaineer had set foot on a Soviet mountain, and information about the state of Soviet mountaineering was hard to come by. Now, the foreign party was invited to stay at one of the numerous state-owned mountaineering camps in the North Caucasus, close to Mount Elbrus. The British found "Russian mountains and mountaineers . . . very different from what we . . . had imagined." They acknowledged and even admired the high technical and physical standards of their Soviet fellow climbers, but the circumstances of their stay in the mountains often bewildered them. While the British visitors were still yawning in their pajamas, the Soviets were already up doing morning gymnastics. The Soviet mountaineers climbed in large parties, which made one of the visitors wonder whether they were "naturally more gregarious than we."[2] When a group of Soviet novice mountaineers (*al'pinisty*) came back after a three-day trip, the mountaineers entered their camp in a long row all dressed in the same green windbreakers, which made this look "like an army maneuver" to the foreign spectators—especially when the mountaineers reported the successful completion of their "mission."[3]

Not only work but leisure, too, was part of the all-embracing project of socialism, aimed at creating the New Man. While the Soviet regime rejected some ways of spending one's free time (such as excessive drinking), it strongly

This article is based on material from my dissertation project, "Pik Kommunizma: Mountaineering in the Soviet Union, 1928–1956." I am indebted to many people whose critical remarks helped me clarify my ideas, especially to the editors and fellow contributors to this volume and to Lothar Maier, Eva Honegger and Lisa Heller.

1. Official relations between the British and Soviet mountaineering associations began in 1954, when John Hunt held a lecture in Moscow. In the following years, Soviet mountaineers were invited to London as well. See Audrey Salkeld and José Luis Bermúdez, *On the Edge of Europe: Mountaineering in the Caucasus* (London, 1993), 169–71.

2. John Hunt and Christopher Brasher, *The Red Snows: An Account of the British-Caucasus Expedition, 1958* (London, 1960), 50–51, 57, 77, 132.

3. Ibid., 15, 55–56.

encouraged others (like reading or practicing physical culture).[4] Many forms of "appropriate" leisure, however, had been pastimes of the cultural and social elites under the tsarist regime and became accessible to a greater public only after the Russian revolution. Mountaineering (al'pinizm), combining elements of sports and turizm, was one of these activities which was ostentatiously "democratized," rose to prominence and popularity, and subsequently developed its own, specifically Soviet institutions and practices during the Stalin era.

This chapter explores mountaineering as a Soviet leisure practice by looking at mountaineering (training) camps (al'pinistskie (uchebnye) lageri, al'plageri for short), located in the Caucasus and other Soviet mountain ranges. While these state-financed institutions were at the periphery of the Soviet Union's geographical realms (and of Stalinist historiography), they constitute a specifically socialist place of leisure, an example of the space between public and private where so much of Soviet life took place. I discuss the establishment of mountaineering camps and their changing form and function within the context of the general rise of Soviet mountaineering, explore questions of access to this leisure space and mechanisms of exclusion, and look at visitors' use and experience of the space and its surroundings.

"Proletarian Mountaineering": The Search for Collective Leisure, 1928–1936

Although the Soviet Union boasted spectacular mountain ranges, including the Caucasus, Pamir, and Tian Shan, in 1929 mountaineering was still so unknown that the tourist journal Na sushe i na more (On Land and on Sea) had to explain that the word al'pinist meant mountain climber.[5] In tsarist Russia, the first mountaineering clubs had been founded only after 1890, considerably later than in western Europe.[6] As in other European countries, their members came mostly from the educated middle classes—a Bildungsbürgertum consisting of urban elites from science, trade, finance, and local politics.[7] Mountaineering's slow development in part echoed the restricted role and development of this cultural and social milieu in Russian society, but it also resulted from the enormous distances and challenges of transportation between urban

4. See especially Katharina Kucher, "Der Moskauer Kultur- und Erholungspark. Formen von Öffentlichkeit im Stalinismus der dreißiger Jahre," in Sphären von Öffentlichkeit in Gesellschaften sowjetischen Typs. Zwischen parteistaatlicher Selbstinszenierung und kirchlichen Gegenwelten, ed. Gábor T. Rittersporn, Malte Rolf, and Jan C. Behrends (Frankfurt am Main, 2003), 97–129.

5. Na sushe i na more (hereafter NSNM) no. 10 (1929): 16.

6. A short, reliable account of these clubs can be found in G. Dolzhenko, Istoriia turizma v dorevolutsionnoi Rossii i SSSR (Rostov-on-Don, 1988), 20–40.

7. Over the last decade, the development of mountaineering as a quintessentially bourgeois practice in western Europe has attracted historians' attention. A recent collection providing an overview is Claudio Ambrosi and Michael Wedekind, eds., L'invenzione di un cosmo borghese. Valori sociali e simboli culturali dell' alpinismo nei secoli XIX e XX (Trento, 2000).

centers and the mountainous periphery. On the eve of World War I, organized mountaineers in Russia could still be counted by hundreds, not thousands. They were a tiny minority not only on an international scale but also within the growing sector of Russian tourism. Considering that about a hundred thousand people visited the Caucasus each year, most Russians seem to have preferred to look at the mountains from spas and sanatoria rather than to climb them.[8]

Under the new regime, this was supposed to change. In the late 1920s the promotion of mountaineering was taken up by the Society for Proletarian Tourism (Obshchestvo proletarskogo turizma i ekskursii, hereafter OPTE), which became the only organization to represent the fast-growing Soviet "proletarian" tourist sector between 1928 and 1930.[9] The OPTE's mountaineering section, founded in 1929, provided the first institutional structures for Soviet al'pinizm, and its journal *Na sushe i na more* served as a popular platform to propagate its goals and achievements.[10]

As before the revolution, mountaineering was considered a form of tourism; indeed, the OPTE's chairman Nikolai Krylenko considered it as one of the most valuable forms of tourism, much to be preferred to organized mass trips on the "beaten tracks" of the Georgian or Ossetian military roads.[11] Now, however, mountaineering was no longer an "idle pastime," but "a weapon of workers' cultural development," to whom it should be universally accessible.[12] The Soviet citizen's individual self-improvement through mountain tourism at the same time served the greater good of socialism because tourists would return to their workplace physically and morally strengthened—and with a broadened knowledge and horizon: "Our Union . . . is not only a great forge of socialist construction but also a grandiose school for the visual instruction of the masses," one tourist ideologist stated.[13] As for other proletarian tourists, this process of individuation was supposed to take place within the bounds of

8. S. Anisimov, *Kavkazskii krai. Putevoditel'. Kniga dlia turistov i kurortnykh bol'nykh,* 3d rev. and exp. ed. (Moscow, Leningrad 1928), 5. The membership of all clubs together can be estimated at six hundred to nine hundred people at that time. Dolzhenko, *Istoriia turizma,* 38; *Zapiski Krimsko-Kavkazskogo Gornogo Kluba,* no. 2 (1913): 25; *Ezhegodnik Russkogo Gornogo Obshchestva* 12 (1915): 144.

9. The OPTE's discourses and practices are discussed in detail in Koenker, in this volume.

10. B. F. Kudinov and V. S. Nefedov, "Ot sporta odinochek k massovomu sovetskomu al'pinizmu," in *K vershinam sovetskoi zemli. Sbornik, posviashchennyi 25–letiiu sovetskogo al'pinizma,* ed. D. M. Zatulovskii (Moscow, 1949), 13.

11. N. Krylenko, "Sovetskii turizm," *Fizkul'tura i sport,* no. 6 (1928): 5. That the OPTE's chairman was an ardent mountaineer himself seems to have helped to give mountaineering substantial weight within the early tourism movement. Krylenko had climbed Elbrus in 1927: see *Fizkul'tura i sport,* no. 6 (1928): 5; no. 9 (1928): 9; and no. 10 (1928): 8–9. He co-organized and took part in the Pamir expeditions as well.

12. V. A. Elanchik and N. F. Tizengauzen, *Na vysochaishuiu vershinu Kavkaza. Ekspeditsiia S.-Kavkazskogo kraevogo otdeleniia OPT na vostochnuiu vershinu El'brusa v 1929 g.* (Rostov, 1930), 49.

13. A. Antonov-Saratovskii, *Osnovnye zadachi sovetskogo turizma* (Moscow, 1929), 5.

a collective. Group trips, not solo travels (*odinochki*) were the preferred form of proletarian tourism.

These new principles called for adequate forms of practice and training. Upper-class Russians traditionally had started their mountaineering careers on holiday in the Swiss Alps, but this was obviously no longer either possible or appropriate. Neither did independent climbing with local Caucasian guides seem fitting for a new generation of proletarian mountaineers.[14] Collective courses for mountaineers were therefore organized, the first by the OPTE's mountaineering section in 1929 for a group of young people from Moscow. Its participants first took a few theory lessons in the OPTE's headquarters and then participated in practical exercises in a small village outside the city, where one bank of the local river loomed up high enough to practice climbing up and roping down.[15] In the summer, the same group traveled to the Caucasus on what was humorously called a "workers' faculty on ice" (*rabfak vo l'dach*), completed their practice, and finally went on a few "easy" mountains in small independent groups. Lectures in geology and local studies (*kraevedenie*) complemented the instruction. Once they returned home, participants were actively to promote collective tourism and mountaineering among their colleagues at work or school.[16]

Soon, many other groups organized similar trips, some with financial help from the OPTE or from their trade union, and often combining newcomers with a few more experienced mountaineers. These marches (*pokhody*) usually proceeded along routes like the one organized by the Stalingrad OPTE in 1934. Starting in Nal'chik, the group walked up the Baksan Valley to the Elbrus region and then crossed over into Svanetiia. After hiking for several days, they put up their camp (*lager'*) while part of the group tried to climb Mount Tetnul'd. Often participants chose the southwestern slopes of the Caucasus for the end of their route, so they could spend the last days of their trip (sun)bathing on the Black Sea coast.[17] By the mid-1930s, most of these camps were still improvised tent camps, even if they were often put up in the same location every year. In 1933 the Moscow OPTE section gave advice on how to successfully organize such a *pokhod* or a camp. The group should always come from a single workplace or school to assure "group homogeneity," and participants should be selected in the year preceding the mountain trip—otherwise there might be "people who did not fit in" (*sluchainye liudi*). Experienced instructors should be included, and the participants should attend a the-

14. Proletarian mountaineering did not openly condemn guided climbing, however, and many independent groups still climbed with local guides well into the early 1930s.

15. *NSNM*, no. 7 (1929): 13–14.

16. Ibid., no. 10 (1929): 16.

17. Ibid., no. 11 (1934): 2; *Komsomol'skaia pravda* (hereafter KP), 11 May 1933. A detailed description of such a trip in 1930 is found in Ella Maillart, *Außer Kurs* (Munich, 1993, translated from *Parmi la jeunesse russe. De Moscou au Caucase* [Paris, 1932]).

oretical course before leaving for the mountains as well as a physical training program during the winter. However, the initiative for forming a group, choosing the route, selecting participants, and applying for financial aid lay with the mountaineers themselves. "Mass marches (*massovki*) and training camps are the best form of independent (samostoiatel'nyi) tourism," the article concluded.[18]

Beginning in 1931, permanent mountaineering camps also appeared—although in most cases only the main building was built of wood or stone.[19] They served between 50 and 250 people a season in two-to-three-week shifts. In 1935 the first camp outside the Caucasus was opened in the Altai, and over the next three years two more followed to serve mountaineers from Siberia.[20] Some camps were owned by OPTE regional or local sections, others by single large enterprises and schools like the Leningrad State University or the Stalin car factory in Moscow—model workplaces and schools whose employees had access not only to better food or housing but also to leisure facilities unknown to other people.[21] From this already privileged group, those sent on mountaineering trips were to include Komsomol members, politically active workers and shock workers.[22] While statistical source material for this period is rare, it seems safe to assume that a stay in a mountaineering camp during the early 1930s was often enough a reward for political loyalty and appropriate behavior.

The Integration of Mountaineering into the State System of Leisure and Sports, 1934–1936

The quick rise of mountaineering as a popular summer activity was paralleled and aided by the increasing prominence of climbing events in the public discourse of the media. The OPTE participated in joint events with both scientists

---

18. *NSNM*, no. 10 (1933): 14; *NSNM*, no. 9 (1943): 3–4.

19. *Krasnyi sport* (hereafter *KS*), 9 September 1939.

20. *KP*, 29 May 1938, 26 December 1938.

21. S. Rototaev, *K vershinam. Khronika sovetskogo al'pinizma* (Moscow, 1977), 52; *NSNM*, no. 12 (1933): 2; E. D. Simonov, "Pereval v podarok iubiliaru," *Turist*, no. 9 (1980): 4. On such privileges, see Jukka Gronow, *Caviar with Champagne: Common Luxury and the Ideals of the Good Life in Stalin's Russia* (Oxford, 2003), 128–34; Sheila Fitzpatrick, *Everyday Stalinism: Ordinary Life in Extraordinary Times. Soviet Russia in the 1930s* (New York, 1999), 95–105.

22. See, for example, *NSNM*, no. 17 (1934): 5–7; no. 18 (1934): 12–13; no. 19 (1934): 8–10 ("Udarniki idut v gorakh") or the regulations for the 1935 *al'piniada* of the VTsSPS (Gosudarstvennyi arkhiv Rossiiskoi Federatsii [hereafter GARF], f. 7710, op. 6, d. 58, ll. 78, 95). Descriptions of trip participants as "the best *shock workers*" are, however, repeated so regularly that this may well have been just an *epitheton ornans*, used to cover up other forms of privilege and connections.

7.1. Mountaineering trips as a reward for New Men and Women: Shock-workers from the Frunze works meet Nikolai Bukharin on their way up to Mt. Elbrus, 1934. Rossiiskii gosudarstvennyi arkhiv kinofotodokumentov, no. 19045/C. Used with permission of the archive.

and the military. Mountaineers took part in expeditions in Central Asia between 1928 and 1935, where the Bolsheviks established their presence not only by building roads but also by symbolically conquering the landscape.[23] In 1933 Soviet mountaineers climbed the highest Soviet peak, Pik Stalina, for the first time (followed by Pik Lenina in 1934).[24] Long marches in the Pamir and mass ascents—so-called *al'piniady*—to Elbrus were organized for Red Army officers from 1933 on.[25] While this strengthened aspects of militarization and scientific rationality within mountaineering's public image, climbers also prof-

23. These expeditions were usually financed by the OPTE, the Council of People's Commissars (Sovnarkom), and the Academy of Sciences. See N. V. Krylenko, D. I. Shcherbakov, and K. K. Markov, *Piat' let po Pamiru. Itogi pamirskikh ekspeditsii 1928, 1929, 1931, 1932, 1933 gg.* (Moscow, 1935).

24. The renaming of peaks, a process that transferred central hierarchies to the periphery, remained subject to political changes. Pik Stalina (7495 m) was renamed Pik Kommunizma in 1962 and is currently called Pik Ismoil Somoni. Pik Lenina (7134 m) was known as Pik Kaufmana (after the Russian governor-general of Turkestan) before the revolution.

25. The participants were organized into groups that often took different approaches and then converged to reach the top. Rototaev, *K vershinam*, 76–78, 84–86, 89.

ited from the popular iconography of the first half of the 1930s, which combined the fight against an inhospitable nature with the conquest of high altitudes. Mountaineers had to prove themselves in extreme cold and ice, just like Ivan Papanin's crew on board the icebreaker *Cheliuskin*,[26] in order to reach altitudes that during the same years were first conquered by Soviet airplanes.[27] Often, mountaineering events were visually or verbally linked to other symbolic victories over nature such as the car race to the Karakum Desert or the stratospheric balloons.[28]

Stories of such exploits attracted newcomers and provided them with ambitions and role models; mass mountaineering also profited from the increased willingness of state authorities to finance its infrastructure. In this process, mountaineering representatives willingly looked for state protection, went to lengths to prove the applied use of their activity, and readily rearranged their ideological alignment. Beginning in late 1934, mountaineering was included in the new all-union classification system for sports. In the same year, a badge called *Al'pinist SSSR* was introduced further to popularize mountaineering, but also to set standards for the training of beginning mountaineers in camps.[29] The number of badge holders was quickly to become the standard measuring unit in Soviet mountaineering statistics. *Massovost'*, mass character and mass participation, were now demanded of mountaineering, reflecting an emphasis on quantity visible in many other areas of Soviet life in this time period, culminating in the Stakhanovite movement. Reflecting the rising isolation of the Soviet Union in the international arena, massovost' was also constructed as a characteristic trait of Soviet mountaineering, which set it apart from the alleged individualism of western climbing.[30] Soviet al'pinizm was thus steadily becoming defined in opposition not only to the Russian past but also to the western present.[31] At the same time, massovost' contained an imperative to go

26. On the Soviet Far North, see John McCannon, *Red Arctic: Polar Exploration and the Myth of the North in the Soviet Union, 1932–1939* (New York, 1998).

27. Robert Kluge, *Der sowjetische Traum vom Fliegen. Analyseversuch eines gesellschaftlichen Phänomens* (Munich, 1997), especially 100–131; Hans Günther, *Der sozialistische Übermensch. M. Gor'kij und der sowjetische Heldenmythos* (Stuttgart, 1993), 155–78.

28. Mountaineers never achieved the same individual hero status awarded to pilots, however, contrary to some authors' assumptions. See Nina Sobol Levent, *Healthy Spirit in a Healthy Body: Representations of the Sports Body in Soviet Art of the 1920s and 1930s* (Frankfurt am Main, 2004), 72, based on Katerina Clark, *The Soviet Novel: History as Ritual* (Chicago, 1981), 121. Even top climbers seem to have been hardly known outside mountaineering circles, and they received only meager material rewards or expressions of gratitude from the side of the government.

29. *NSNM* no. 1 (1935): 10. On the other end of this new hierarchy, top mountaineers were awarded the title of "Master of Alpinism," equivalent to "Master of Sports" in other disciplines. See James Riordan, *Sport in Soviet Society: Development of Sport and Physical Education in Russia and the USSR* (Cambridge, 1977), 128–35.

30. See for example Zinaida Rikhter, *Shturm El'brusa. Vtoraia al'piniada RKKA* (Moscow, 1935), 8–9.

31. For a comparison see Elanchik and Tizengauzen, *Na visochaishuiu vershinu*, 48–49.

beyond the mere accessibility of mountaineering to "the masses"—explicitly to promote mountaineering and to "produce" as many mountaineers as possible.

Cultured and Controlled: The Growing Dominance of the Mountaineering Camp, 1936–1953

In April 1936 the OPTE was dissolved and mountaineering (together with tourism) was completely integrated into the Soviet state structures of sports and leisure.[32] A new All-Union Section of Mountaineering (Vsesoiuznaia sektsiia al'pinizma, hereafter VSA), uniting mostly experienced and active mountaineers, was established at the All-Union Committee for Physical Culture and Sports. It was supposed to supervise and direct all theoretical work on mountaineering.[33] The practical side—providing and financing camps and instructors—was to be taken over by the All-Union Central Council of Trade Unions (Vsesoiuznyi tsentral'nyi sovet professional'nykh soiuzov, hereafter VTsSPS) as the main workers' organization which provided leisure and vacation facilities.[34] Not only did this division of responsibilities lead to frequent friction, but the different aspects of Soviet al'pinizm—tourism, leisure, and sports—reflected in this arrangement were to remain in an often disputed balance.

After the "takeover," funding for mountaineering seems to have been greatly extended. In the second half of the 1930s, mountaineering camps illustrate the gap between Stalinist repression and everyday bleakness and the simultaneous promotion of leisure and luxury. While leading mountaineers fell victim to the Great Terror, the overall number of mountaineers almost tripled between 1936 and 1938 up to a new high of twenty-three thousand holders of the Al'pinist badge.[35] Even after the VSA was temporarily dissolved in late 1937 (due to the arrest of many of its members), mountaineering remained "in fashion," and much more so than "ordinary" tourism, as *Na sushe i na more* stated.[36]

32. On the closing down of mass organizations, see A. Kupaigorodskaia and N. B. Lebina, "Dobrovol'nye obshchestva Petrograda-Leningrada 1917–1937 gg. (Tendentsii razvitiia)," in *Dobrovol'nye obshchestva v Petrograde-Leningrade v 1917–1935 gg. Sbornik statei*, ed. A. Kupaigorodskaia et al., 5–16 (Leningrad, 1989).

33. In its initial composition, the VSA included most of the OPTE's top mountaineers; see GARF, f. 7576, op. 14, d. 25, ll. 40–41 (VSA, 1937).

34. For this purpose, the Tourist Excursion Bureau (Turistsko-ekskursionnoe upravlenie, TEU) was established in the same year, but at least initially, it did not seem to take any responsibility for independent tourists and mountaineers, even after a reprimand from *Pravda*. *Pravda*, 28 March 1937, 29 March 1937. See also *NSNM*, no. 4 (1938): 2.

35. Many of the former OPTE/VSA cadres were shot or arrested for long periods. The Russian mountaineer Iu. Pustovalov has created an impressive database containing names and short biographies of mountaineers who disappeared in the Great Terror. "Rasstrel'noe vremia" (retroobzor), URL. www.risk.ru/rus/mount/museum/pustovalov/ (last visited 13 December 2005). These and all the following statistics must be treated with the usual caution, even if the sharp overall rise is clearly discernable: *Pravda*, 5 April 1937; GARF, f. 7576, op. 14, d. 105, l. 38 (VSA statistics, 1939).

36. *NSNM*, no. 4 (1938): 2.

Massive investment in rebuilding and enlarging mountaineering camps made the dream of the Stalinist "good life" visible.[37] By 1938 the number of camps had risen to forty-three, and the al'plager had come a long way from being simply tents and a fireplace.[38] Seven years after its foundation, the extended camp Rot-Front was described as a model of this new, "cultured" leisure. Idyllically located in a small forest on terraced ground, it featured a natural pool filled by a spring nearby where climbers could dip in after a long day of climbing. Well-marked pathways led from the double-lined tents with wooden floors, where the visitors slept on camp beds, to the central structures: sanitary tracts, a large dining hall and—considered an exceptional luxury—a bathhouse built of stone instead of the customary wood. All the buildings and even the tents were electrically illuminated, thanks to the camp's own power station on the nearby Baksan River.[39]

Like other camps, Rot-Front also had a two-way radio station, but it was a pioneer in using it not only to receive broadcasts but also to stay in touch with its own mountaineers while they were on an ascent.[40] While this was propagated as a useful safety precaution, it also conformed with the radical tightening of control on mountaineers that was established by the new VSA in 1938. Camps were to open only after a thorough inspection, rescue stations were established where mountaineers had to register en route, and deadlines called "control times" were introduced. If a group was not back by a fixed date, a rescue team was sent up automatically. Breaking the control times if not in danger was a serious offense, as was climbing without the necessary permit.[41] Permits were given out according to the qualifications of the mountaineer and the difficulty of the planned ascent.[42] Moreover, at the beginning of the season of 1938, it was stated that "wild" (i.e., privately organized) camps, still common in the years before, "will not exist anymore."[43]

Mountaineering camps were thus no longer a form of "independent" tourism where, ideally, a self-chosen group defined its own leisure space and time. Since the former OPTE camps now belonged to the trade unions and their sport societies (*dobrovol'nye sportivnye obshchestva*, hereafter DSO), mountaineers had to apply for trip vouchers (*putevki*) at their local DSO—a centralized distribution system which was also used to assign places in sanatoria or rest homes. In 1939 the VSA tried to ban the usual practice by which ex-

37. See, for example, *KS*, 30 May 1940. I borrowed the term "good life" from Gronow's *Caviar with Champagne*.

38. GARF, f. 7576, op. 14, d. 105, l. 38.

39. *NSNM* portrayed Rot-Front in a two-part feature called "Kavkaz al'pinistskii": *NSNM*, no. 9 (1938): 5–8; no. 10 (1938): 20–23, 30.

40. Ibid., no. 10 (1938): 21.

41. In 1938 many mountaineers were severely punished for breaking these control times in what seems to be the first test of the VSA's sanctioning power (GARF, f. 7576, op. 14, dd. 72, 73).

42. All mountains had been classified in several categories of difficulty (from 1A to 5B) starting in 1935. This system is still in use today. *Federatsiia al'pinizma Rossii. Klassifikatsiia marshrutov na gornye vershiny*, 3d rev. and exp. ed. (Moscow, 2001).

43. *NSNM*, no. 5 (1938): 2.

perienced independent groups used camp facilities without a voucher.[44] Even if not all measures were realized immediately, the VSA's intention clearly reflected the period's obsession with control over its subjects and their movement. Within the camps, too, more emphasis was put on strict discipline and a hierarchical instruction system.

Independent mountaineering was further discouraged in other ways. Mountain gear, always a "deficit good," was first distributed to expeditions, camps, and DSO sections before being put on the open market. If available at all, items could be found only in the big cities.[45] To alleviate this problem, rental stations for all sorts of equipment existed, but their supply was small and unreliable. Accommodation for independent mountaineers was also difficult to find.[46] While in theory the DSO were supposed to assist independent groups, they often preferred to spend most or even all of their mountaineering funds on camp vouchers.[47] The hassle of dealing with many small groups who all wanted advice, equipment, and money—but also the fear of being held accountable if anything happened to "their" independent mountaineers—certainly influenced their preference for the al'plageri.[48] Although this development was never undisputed, mountaineering camps assumed an even more exclusive role in the immediate postwar years. Most of the camps in the western and central Caucasus were destroyed or severely damaged during World War II, and the efforts of the mountaineering sections in the late 1940s focused almost exclusively on their reconstruction.[49] The state's camp system had thus added much comfort and culture (*kul'turnost'*) to alpinism, but at the same time it restricted mountaineers' freedom of movement and their choice for alternative forms of mountaineering.[50]

From Cultural Outpost to Cultured Leisure: The Mountaineering Camp and Its Surroundings

As mountaineering camps became more permanent, they also gradually developed into clearly delineated spaces for a special purpose set apart from their

44. GARF, f. 7576, op. 1, d. 402, ll. 85, 90 (1939).

45. *NSNM*, no. 4 (1938): 2. In practice, though, camps often lacked equipment as well. See GARF, f. 9480, op. 22, d. 88, l. 6 (DSO Nauka, 1949); f. 5451, op.32, d. 469, ll. 65–67 (VTsSPS, 1954). Tourist journals therefore regularly printed sewing and construction patterns for tourist equipment.

46. *KP*, 22 June 1939; GARF, f. 9480, op. 22, d. 88, l. 25.

47. GARF, f. 7576, op. 14, d. 28-b, ll. 85–87 (VSA, 1940).

48. In 1939 several Moscow representatives of the TEU and a local DSO were held accountable after the death of three mountaineers on the grounds that they had not been given proper consultation before their ascent. The trial received extensive coverage in *KP*, 27 June 1939; 3, 5, 6 July 1939.

49. GARF, f. 7576, op. 14, d. 28, ll. 23–26, 32–34 (VSA, 1943).

50. Vadim Volkov, "The Concept of *Kul'turnost'*: Notes on the Stalinist Civilizing Process," in *Stalinism: New Directions*, ed. Sheila Fitzpatrick (London, 2000), 210–30.

surroundings. The changing relationship of the camp to its surroundings is, again, closely related to the role Soviet mountaineers were to assume within the "building of socialism." For the OPTE, disseminating new concepts of Soviet life in the more remote regions of the USSR was at least theoretically an essential part of its program.[51] Since proletarian mountaineers usually moved in remote, ethnically non-Russian fringes of the Soviet empire, they were supposed to act as cultural ambassadors of the new political power as well as mountaineers.[52] The lack of special tourist accommodation during the early 1930s often forced mountaineering groups to stay overnight in village schools or administrative buildings, which facilitated close contact with the local population.[53] One group of mountaineers, according to an official account, was said not only to have helped locals to repair their power station and sawmill but also to have held lectures about the work of *Osoaviakhim*, the Soviet Union's mass league for civil defense and aviation.[54] Countless tales about the wonders of Moscow were told, and women climbers were presented as the living proof of the all-embracing change the new order was to bring.[55] However, even official sources show that relations between locals and mountaineers did not always follow this patronizing official model. In the Pamirs, mountaineers were regularly accompanied by border troops because of threats from local rebels.[56] In the Caucasus, mountaineers depended on locals for directions and provisions but also competed for the same resources. When a group of instructors decided to put up a camp in a valley where arable land was scarce, a compromise with the local inhabitants was hard to find.[57]

As mountaineering camps became permanent, the agency of this cultural mission was transferred from the mountaineers to the camps, which were to serve as cultural outposts—replicating the Stalinist power-relation of center and periphery.[58] During the public campaign surrounding the elections in 1938, the mountaineering camp was represented as a patriotic bastion of Soviet internal harmony and unity. Camps were described as an "agitational base" where regular meetings with the locals could be held and tourists actively promoted the "new happiness of life in our country." They also served as polling places. "Russians, Ukrainians, Jews, Ossetians, Balkars, Belorus-

---

51. See also Koenker, in this volume, for a discussion of the OPTE's cultural mission.

52. N. N. Mikhailov, *Khan-Tengri* (Moscow, 1933), 33.

53. N. Nikolaeva, *Karaugom* (Moscow, 1931), 25–26.

54. This group was from Stalingrad, but the stories are to a certain extent interchangeable. See *NSNM*, no. 5 (1933): 13.

55. Mikhailov, *Khan-Tengri*, 38, 55–56.

56. Pawel Luknizki, *Gletscher, Räuber, blaue Steine. Gefährliche Reisen auf dem Pamir* (Leipzig, 1957, translated from *Puteshestviia po Pamiru* [Moscow 1955]), especially 35–68.

57. This dispute is mentioned in "Die Erinnerungen des Alpinistik-Instrukteurs Döberl," in *Österreicher im Exil. Sowjetunion 1934–35*, ed. Barry McLoughlin and Hans Schafranek (Vienna, 1999), 216.

58. See Katerina Clark, "Socialist Realism and the Sacralizing of Space," in *The Landscape of Stalinism: The Art and Ideology of Soviet Space*, ed. Eric Naiman and Evgeny Dobrenko (Seattle, 2003), 3–18.

sians—all have given their votes to the best sons of Kabardino-Balkariia."[59]
While thus propagating the unity and equality of all Soviet citizens, *Na sushe i
na more* at the same time asked Russian tourists to go into the local villages to
get a picture of the "hard and lawless past" of the North Caucasians.[60] Little
more than a museum of a gruesome history, a village in Balkariia left the visitors reassured that they came from a superior and much advanced world. Fit-
tingly, in 1940 a reporter wrote that the camps in the valley were "civilizing"
its "pristine wildness."[61]

The war years, during which the Balkars, like other peoples of the North
Caucasus, suffered from deportation and resettlement, put an end even to such
staged meetings with locals. After the war, no more effort was made to organize personal encounters in the Caucasus camps. Lectures like "Past and Present of Teberda Raion," "Twenty-Five Years of North Ossetian Autonomy" or
"The Friendship of the Peoples in the USSR" were the only projections of outside reality into the camp compound.[62] The ethnic and regional diversity of the
Soviet Union's mountain areas were reduced to a patriotic landscape representing all-embracing spatial claims. "Mountaineers' picturesque tent towns are
spread out at the foot of Elbrus, the icy giant (*velikan*), in the dreamy forests of
Svanetiia . . . on the shores of stormy Skaaz-don, in the remote valleys of the
high Tian Shan," an official account stated.[63] Roaming this idyllically depicted
countryside, however, was not encouraged anymore. After a young female
mountaineer hitching a ride to the camp was raped and murdered in 1949, the
VSA ordered that transport from the station to the camp should be organized
by the camps and that participants were to march and climb only in groups,
supervised by an instructor.[64] Real incidents mixed with persistent rumors
about banditry or the notoriously violent nature of certain local groups suggest
the persistence of older stereotypes about the Caucasus and its inhabitants.[65]
Together, they created an atmosphere in which the world outside the camp
was often perceived as dangerous and hostile, furthering the development of
the camp into an enclosed space with its own provisions and pastime.[66]

59. *NSNM*, no. 4 (1938): 4; no. 6 (1938), 4; no. 7 (1938): 4.

60. Ibid., no. 4 (1938): 4.

61. Ibid., no. 1 (1940): 16–17.

62. GARF, f. 9480, op. 12, d. 431, ll. 2–3 (DSO Krasnaia zvezda, 1953); f. 9480, op. 3, d.
193, ll. 18–19 (DSO Burevestnik, 1949).

63. B. F. Kudinov, "Piataia al'piniada profsoiuzov," in *Pobezhdennye vershiny: Ezhegodnik
sovetskogo al'pinizma. God 1949* (Moscow, 1949), 22. The Skaaz-don is a small river in North
Ossetia.

64. GARF, f. 5451, op. 32, d. 253, ll. 49, 75–77.

65. For the emergence and development of these stereotypes, see Susan Layton, *Russian Liter-
ature and Empire: Conquest of the Caucasus from Pushkin to Tolstoy* (Cambridge, 1994); and
Thomas M. Barrett, "Southern Living (in Captivity): The Caucasus in Russian Popular Culture,"
Journal of Popular Culture 31, no. 4 (1998): 75–94.

66. There are many stories of mountaineers traveling armed in remote areas of the Caucasus,
as in the Soviet mountaineering classic Vladimir Shataev, *Kategoriia trudnosti*, 3d exp. and corr.
ed. (Moscow, 2001), 25.

7.2. Camp life in the postwar years: Before leaving the camp, participants line up and report to their instructor. Mountaineering camp "Bolshevik" (Kabardian ASSR), June 1949. Rossiiskii gosudarstvennyi arkhiv kinofotodokumentov, no. 0171883. Used with permission of the archive.

Cultural outposts were no longer needed or wanted, as Moscow had emerged as the single center of authority and power within the Stalinist spatial hierarchy.[67] Camps were oriented toward that one center when they celebrated the capital's eight-hundredth anniversary in the summer of 1947.[68] Political lectures and "discussions" about current internal and foreign affairs connected the camp with the rest of the Soviet Union. Here, the regime could transmit its official viewpoint on the Nuremberg trials in 1949 or explain Beria's fall from power in 1953.[69] The mountaineers, former *kul'turtregeri* in a collective cultural mission, were thus themselves turned from agents into recipients of political instruction.

Access to a Privileged Space: Selection and Exclusion

In 1949 an official anniversary volume concluded that "in the USSR, the broad masses have for the first time received the opportunity to travel in the mountains"—"what is only accessible to the privileged classes in capitalist countries

67. See Clark, "Socialist Realism," and Jan Plamper, "The Spatial Poetics of the Personality Cult: Circles around Stalin," in *Landscape of Stalinism*, ed. Naiman and Dobrenko, 19–50.

68. GARF, f. 9480, op. 3, d. 69, l. 2 (DSO Burevestnik, 1947).

69. GARF, f. 9480, op. 3, d. 193, l. 19; op. 12, d. 431, l. 7.

has become possible for all people in our country."[70] After socialism had been officially attained, access to socialist leisure seemed to be part of the package. But by 1950 not even half of the camps were reconstructed, and their total capacity only amounted to about fifty-five hundred—certainly not enough to serve ten thousand to fifteen thousand active mountaineers in the Soviet Union.[71] Obviously, not everyone could enjoy these new leisure opportunities. Since camps dominated Soviet mountaineering, access to camps to a large extent coincided with access to mountaineering, and the discussion about selection criteria demonstrates regional and social lines of division within an alleged society of equals.

Already in the early 1930s, large cities like Moscow, Leningrad, and Gorky in Russia or Kharkov, Dnepropetrovsk, Kiev, and Odessa in Ukraine had established themselves as the centers of mountaineering. But even among them, resources were often hotly disputed. The all-union section and the Ukrainian section of the DSO Nauka constantly argued over the camp Nakra, which had belonged to Ukraine in the 1930s.[72] After the war, the all-union section had simply taken over the rebuilt camp, which had caused much resentment against "Moscow."[73] This was symptomatic, for the all-union sections were often—if not always justly—accused of primarily serving the needs of Moscow's mountaineers, a complaint that came from Leningrad as well as other urban centers.[74] As in many other areas of Soviet life, black marketeering and string pulling (*blat*) were commonly used to gain access to benefits, which added to the dominance of Moscow, the hub of voucher distribution.[75] In theory, smaller cities could send candidates to camps as well, but they often had no means of giving them instruction beforehand.[76]

Outside European Russia and Ukraine, only Georgia had its own strong mountaineering community, which seems to have been able to maintain a large degree of autonomy.[77] Most other union and autonomous republics suffered from a constant lack of funds. Their mountaineering sections were small, and vouchers were expensive (around 1,200–1,400 rubles after 1945), a prob-

---

70. The twenty-fifth anniversary celebration in 1948 relates to a Georgian group ascent of Kazbek in 1923, which was subsequently fixed as the birth of Soviet mountaineering (Zatulovskii, *K vershinam*, 7).

71. Statistics vary. See GARF, f. 7576, op. 14, d. 33, l. 22 (VSA, 1948), and d. 36, l. 7 (1950); f. 5451, op. 32, d. 183, l. 23 (VTsSPS, 1949); d. 253, ll. 43–49 (1950).

72. *NSNM*, no. 4 (1937), 12.

73. GARF, f. 9480, op. 22, d. 88, l. 30.

74. GARF, f. 7576, op. 14, d. 33, ll. 9–11.

75. GARF, f. 5451, op. 32, d. 253, ll. 81–83; see also d. 183, l. 23 (1951). In 1947 the camp Alibek proudly listed "the son of comrade Zhdanov" among its guests (GARF, f. 9480, op. 22, d. 20, l. 6).

76. GARF, f. 7576, op. 14, d. 27, l. 88 (VSA, 1938). Villagers and kolkhoz peasants were virtually excluded from tourism in the time period covered here.

77. In Georgia, mountaineers were united in a mountaineering club and not completely integrated into the sports system. See GARF, f. 7576, op. 14, d. 36, ll. 185–216 (VSA, 1950).

lem that was openly acknowledged by mountaineering representatives themselves.[78] Small republics could thus only afford to send a handful of people to the al'plageri, even if these camps were located on their own territory.[79] As a representative from Kyrgyzstan explained, before the war they had assembled groups and trained instructors themselves. "Independent mountaineering cost less than now, when we have to pay for the voucher and the train tickets for a ten-day trip."[80] Indeed, the camp's dominating role and the centralized division of mountaineering vouchers led to a situation where mountaineers from Central Asia, instead of climbing in their own republics, had to travel thousands of kilometers to learn mountaineering in the Caucasus.[81] Without the "unnecessary comfort" of camps, a Kazakh delegate argued, the training of a mountaineer would cost them only about 400 rubles.[82] But local independent mountaineering suffered from the fact that most of these regions lacked money, equipment, and cadres to train newcomers. In 1953 only one sports society in all of Uzbekistan owned a few sets of mountain gear.[83] The Moscow sections did make efforts to alleviate the situation, but local alternatives did not always win their approval. After returning from a new Armenian camp in 1952, a (Russian) representative complained that the local authorities were impervious to any critique, simply declaring it their "local practice" and "tradition" to lower the standards and cutting the program from twenty to six days. Armenia, he thought, had an "incorrect approach" toward mountaineering.[84] The Moscow-based mountaineering system, catering to the big cities in European Russia and focused on the Caucasus, was a standard imposed on all other regions in the Soviet empire and modified only slowly during the 1950s.

The social composition of camp visitors did not match the Soviet statistical average either. Age was the most obvious factor of social coherence. The overwhelming majority of camp visitors—84 percent in 1948—were seventeen to twenty-five years old, with only a few over the age of thirty.[85] This is not surprising, since youth and young adults were the most likely age group to engage in sports and had always been a prime target group of Soviet social engineering.[86] It was in the state's vital interest to provide leisure that was also useful

78. The participants usually had to pay a third of the sum plus the cost for transportation to the camp, but the rest was paid by the DSO. See GARF, f. 5451, op. 32, d. 183, l. 24; f. 9480, op. 9, d. 11, ll. 5, 9 (DSO Bol'shevik, 1947).

79. GARF, f. 9480, op. 22, d. 88, l. 11.

80. GARF, f. 5451, op. 32, d. 469, l. 35.

81. Ibid., l. 78

82. This sum covered the cost of training a mountaineer to take the first badge test (GARF, f. 7576, op. 14, d. 33, ll. 9–11).

83. GARF, f. 7576, op. 14, d. 48, l. 34 (VSA, 1953).

84. Ibid, ll. 63–68.

85. GARF, f. 7576, op. 14, d. 33, l. 23.

86. Anne E. Gorsuch, *Youth in Revolutionary Russia: Enthusiasts, Bohemians, Delinquents* (Bloomington, Ind., 2000); Corinna Kuhr-Korol'ev, Stephan Plaggenborg, and Monica Wellmann, eds., *Sowjetjugend 1917–1941. Generation zwischen Revolution und Resignation* (Essen, 2001).

as a preparatory training for its future soldiers. The social background of these young people was a much more delicate issue. A comparison of five different camps from 1939 to 1947 shows that students were by far the biggest group of all mountaineers, ranging between 41 and 63 percent, while workers never accounted for more than 20 percent, often much less.[87] Upholding the worker as the principal recipient of the Soviet Union's benefits system, the VSA officially complained about this trend, but many sport societies counteracted it by instructing their local collectives—as did the DSO Burevestnik—to choose camp candidates from their "badge holders" and "from students who have a month's vacation."[88] The latter argument explains, at least partly, the predominance of students and white-collar workers. All mountaineering vouchers, due to the VSA's own standardization drive in the late 1930s, lasted twenty days, but an ordinary worker received only twelve days of vacation a year.[89] But there were other factors, more difficult to trace, which contributed to the popularity of mountaineering with students. Universities and technical institutes often had very active climbing sections which were supported by their academic staff and therefore likely to build a strong feeling of community and tradition.[90] The DSO Nauka, uniting students and staff of high schools and state universities, received over 20 percent of all mountaineering trip vouchers in 1949 and was considered the single most important sports club in mountaineering.[91] In nonacademic workplaces there seems to have been much less interest in al'pinizm. The DSO Lokomotiv, for example, had a mountaineering section at every railway college and institute, but not a single one at the railways themselves, since the authorities there considered mountaineering "an appendage [*pridatok*], which does not appear at any competitions but still asks for money."[92] Among workers, competitive and spectator sports, especially soccer, were much more popular.[93] Obviously, the

87. This statistic is based on a comparison of five camps between 1939 and 1947. See GARF, f. 7576, op. 14, d. 104, ll. 33–41 (Stroitel', 1939); GARF, f. 7576, op. 30, d. 136, l. 9 (Molniia, Lokomotiv Iuga, and Energiia, 1940); and GARF, f. 9480, op. 9, d. 69, l. 20 (Burevestnik, 1947). Statistics of other camps confirm this trend.

88. In 1948 the VSA applauded the fact that the percentage of workers had climbed to 15 from 11.8 two years before (GARF, f. 7576, op. 14, d. 33, l. 23; f. 9480, op. 3, d. 69, l. 28).

89. See also GARF, f. 5451, op. 32, d. 469, l. 128. The postwar years saw the longest working hours in Soviet history. See Jiri Zuzanek, "Time-Budget Trends in the USSR: 1922–1970," *Soviet Studies* 31, no. 2 (1979): 188–213.

90. There are many examples of the high degree of support that university staff offered to "their" mountaineers—from tolerating their starting class late after the season to actively assigning them funds. See, for example, GARF, f. 9480, op. 22, d. 89, ll. 3–5, 11; and Anatolii Georgievich Ovchinnikov, *Al'pinisty MVTU imeni N. E. Baumana* (Moscow, 1998), 46.

91. GARF, f. 9480, op. 22, d. 88, l. 15; d. 89, l. 20.

92. To alleviate this situation, a quota of no more than 40 percent of students was therefore suggested (GARF, f. 7576, op. 14, d. 105, ll. 97–98).

93. Robert Edelman, *Serious Fun: A History of Spectator Sports in the USSR* (New York, 1993), 26–78.

later nimbus of Soviet mountaineering as the sport of intellectuals—which stems mostly from the 1960s, when such famous bards of mountaineering as Vladimir Vysotskii or Iurii Vizbor sang about it—has its roots in the early period of Soviet mountaineering.[94]

But the mountaineering associations approved of the fact that in 1948 more men (61 percent, as opposed to 47 percent a year before) than women visited the camps. This was an open reversal of the official policy during the OPTE years, when the equal rights of women in climbing had been an issue regularly advocated in *Na sushe i na more*. During the 1930s women's share in mountaineering had grown rapidly, and by 1940 women made up nearly 20 percent of all mountaineers in the USSR.[95] After the war, however, several sport societies even set internal quotas to limit the number of women in their camps.[96] At least in the short run, this policy seems to have met with more success than the attempt to restrict the number of students. In 1950 men's share in the camps had risen to 68 percent.[97]

This silent reinforcement of traditional gender roles follows a broader postwar trend. Although officially still "equal," women's radius of action was trimmed so that it would not threaten male superiority.[98] But instruments and discourses of exclusion can also be found within mountaineering itself. The militarization of mountaineering in the prewar decade and during the war had associated it principally with a male sphere of action and had contributed to a masculine and military stereotype of the mountaineer.[99] Shortly before the outbreak of war, women had even been excluded from becoming mountaineering instructors.[100] Meanwhile, massovost' as a target and the system of "socialist competition" between camps put the emphasis on quantitative "output." Camps competed not only in the number of "man-ascents" (*chelovekovos-*

94. In 1977 the quasi-official history of Soviet mountaineering openly prided itself in the high level of education among mountaineers—over 80 percent, it claimed, had a university degree, and almost 5 percent were professors (Rototaev, *K vershinam*, 7). See also Shataev, *Kategoriia trudnosti*, 15.

95. GARF, f. 7576, op. 30, d. 136, ll. 2–3 (VSA, 1939–1941). While the Soviet authorities boasted of the high qualifications of their women climbers to prove gender equality within the USSR (see the statistics in GARF, f. 7576, op. 1, d. 570, l. 52 and op. 14, d. 105, ll. 7–9; VSA 1939/1946), women's exploits received notably less publicity than men's.

96. GARF, f. 9480, op. 3, d. 193, l. 48; f. 9480, op. 22, d. 20, l. 6.

97. GARF, f. 5451, op. 32, d. 183, l. 21.

98. This process is described through the lens of Soviet fiction in Vera Dunham, *In Stalin's Time: Middleclass Values in Soviet Fiction* (Cambridge, 1976), 214–24. Unlike the non-Russian nationalities, women did not have a lobby or a quota at all-union meetings. The unwritten prohibition against questioning women's role in mountaineering may, in fact, have made it more difficult for women, since they had to fight against forms of exclusion whose very existence was denied.

99. In 1940 *NSNM* complained that there were too many girls but not enough recruits (*prizyvniki*) in the camps (no. 10 [1940]: 7).

100. GARF, f. 7576, op. 1, d. 427, l. 14 (VKFS, 1941).

khozhdeniia) but also in the percentage of people passing the norm of Al'pin-ist SSSR with as few rejects as possible.[101] Already before the war, some VSA members had proposed to send fewer women to the camps because they "make up a big part of the rejects."[102]

This last line of argument received additional support in the postwar years when militarization subsided, but mountaineering's voluntary involvement with the field of sports reached a new high. Soviet sport itself was in a process of redefinition after the war: no longer considered primarily a vehicle for mo-bilizing and training the population for work and war, it became a means of gaining international recognition with the openly acknowledged goal of beat-ing the West. The VSA latched on to this development, and in 1949 the Soviet Union was among the first nations to hold nationwide championships in rock climbing, thus turning aspects of mountaineering into a competitive sport.[103] The very notion of mountaineering as a sport focused on measurable, individ-ual performance clashed with the idea of universal accessibility. If read as a discourse of exclusion, it reduced participation opportunities for women, eld-erly people, amateurs, and those who did not have access to the necessary fa-cilities for preparatory training, especially in rural and remote areas.

Thus "sports" increasingly stood opposed to leisure (*otdykh*) in the post-war discussion about access to mountaineering; attempts to create a more ho-mogenous space were of limited success. The mountaineering authorities usu-ally blamed the shortcomings of the voucher system if their targets were not met and visitors did not show the desired enthusiasm. True, vouchers often ended up with the wrong people. Typhoid patients or a man whose left hand had been amputated were among the more strikingly ill-fitted people sent to mountaineering camps.[104] Rather resignedly, one end-of-season account stated that the "majority of camp visitors have come to relax" (*otdykhat'*).[105] The in-stitutional inclusion into the trade union's benefit system had placed the camps alongside other vacation resorts such as sanatoria, rest homes, or tourist bases. Given the constant shortage of organized vacation opportunities, Soviet citi-zens tended to take any voucher they could get. If they did not always know the difference between a mountaineering camp and a rest home, many moun-taineering camps did little to distinguish themselves.[106] While there were still rather spartan tent camps where all participants had to take on kitchen duties,

101. *Chelovekovoskhozhdeniia* were the total sum of every ascent by any camp participants or staff. Again, this was often held up as a sign of Soviet mountaineering's superiority over its cap-italist counterparts (GARF, f. 9480, op. 22, d. 20, ll. 21–23, 26–28).

102. GARF, f. 7576, op. 14, d. 28-b, ll. 8–12 (1940).

103. Mountaineering authorities went to great lengths to prove that mountaineering qualified as a sport. See, for example, GARF, f. 7576, op. 14, d. 33, ll. 9–11.

104. GARF, f. 7576, op. 14, d. 105, ll. 106–14; f. 9480, op. 3, d. 69, l. 13.

105. GARF, f. 9480, op. 22, d. 20, l. 11 (1947).

106. Even the official mountaineering yearbook declared camps "a place of rest for thousands of workers in our country" (Kudinov, "Piataia al'piniada profsoiuzov," 22).

7.3. Spaces of cultured leisure: one of the first pools in a mountaineering camp, 1953. *Fizkul'tura i sport*, no. 9 (1953): back cover page.

the camp Tsei had on its pay list over twenty-five people, including waitresses, a guard, and its own baker—rather like a sanatorium for the elite.[107] Facilities like swimming pools or tennis courts which became common in later years suggest that mountaineering camps rather deliberately sought to match the standards of other holiday resorts and to offer a varied leisure experience.[108]

Collectivism in Practice? Camp Visitors and Their Use of Space

Even officially, then, the Soviet mountaineering camp was a multidimensional space, with various discourses allowing for different ways of "using" it. While authorities had substantial means of selecting participants, they could only partly influence the relation and communication between them. By examining mountaineers' interactions with their "collective," their motives and experiences, I attempt a final look at the world of the camp from within.

107. GARF, f. 9480, op. 9, d. 11, l. 3. Many of the "simpler" camps were located in Central Asia and reminiscent of the early years of Caucasus mountaineering. See GARF, f. 9480, op. 3, d. 69, l. 1v.

108. Shataev, *Kategoriia trudnosti*, 30.

As in other Soviet places of education, work, and leisure, lectures on "the moral outlook of the Soviet sportsman," among other topics, were intended to shape the behavior of participants, strengthening discipline and discouraging drinking and other forms of hooliganism.[109] But in mountaineering camps, the usual ideological emphasis on collectivism could draw additionally on mountaineering's own ethical code of comradeship and mutual help, enhanced through the camp's isolated and closed situation in an unfamiliar environment. The collective return to the camps after a successful final ascent (such as the one the British guests had witnessed) was one of the most important moments of camp life, an event elevated to special prominence and turned into a collective ritual with a strong emotional appeal. For many, this became a memorable moment, as one mountaineer remembers such a return to camp in 1947: "The reception was very festive [torzhestvennyi]. On both sides of the path we walked on, many little fires had been lit. Everyone who had stayed behind in the camp stood in line to greet us. They congratulated us on our successful final ascent. Three times we heard the traditional 'Fizkul't-privet!' " Afterwards, dinner was held in the specially decorated dining hall. "Now they treated us like old hands in mountaineering (byvalye al'pinisty). That was flattering and made us cheerful."[110] The intensity of sharing one's life with many strangers for three weeks and the emotional stress of climbing also created a considerable degree of intimacy among participants. Now the young people belonged to "the great family of mountaineers," said another, thinking back on this rite of passage in the mid-1930s.[111]

Here friendships formed quickly, as a visitor to the camp Dombai noted in the camp's comment book of 1951.[112] The function of the camp as a meeting place was undoubtedly a main attraction to many of its visitors, not excluding the possibility of a romantic attachment—after all, it was one of the few places where the mostly young and unmarried visitors could meet persons of the opposite sex without the supervision of roommates or family members (especially considering the crowded living conditions of most urban dwellers in the postwar years).[113] That some camps reduced cultural work to dance evenings

109. GARF, f. 9480, op. 3, d. 193, ll. 18–19; f. 9480, op. 22, d. 88, l. 4; f. 7576, op. 14, d. 48, l. 41.

110. Ovchinnikov, Al'pinisty, 37–38.

111. B. F. Kudinov, El'brusskaia letopis' (Nal'chik, 1969), chap. 2: "Kavkaz predo mnoiu!" Available online: www.poxod.ru/narration/elle/print_p_elle_kavkazprodmdin_a.html (last visited 13 December 2005). However, recollections of camp life in the 1930s and 1940s were also shaped by the discourse of the post-Stalin era, when most of these memoirs were written—a factor that deserves further investigation.

112. GARF, f. 9480, op. 3, d. 457, l. 16 (DSO Burevestnik. Guestbook of the mountaineering camp Dombai, 1951).

113. See Anna Rotkirch, "Traveling Maidens and Men with Parallel Lives—Journeys as Private Space during Late Socialism," in Beyond the Limits: The Concept of Space in Russian History and Culture, ed. Jeremy Smith (Helsinki, 1999), 131–49.

only, as one inspector critically remarked, probably reflected the wishes of many of its guests.[114]

Not everyone, however, indulged in a spirit of collective harmony. Several visitors at the camp Dombai expressed their anger over colleagues who fell behind. "Mountaineering is the sport of the bold! Therefore I think that the selection and the dispatch of people to mountaineering camps should be more strict. . . . Very often the people who receive vouchers are unsuited in terms of their physical development and their health, which does not allow them to partake in this sport of the *bold*."[115] People who "infect others" with their "aversion" toward mountaineering, "have to be stamped out from the sports community," added another. "You need to fight for visitors who are not coming to the camp to relax and to get to know the beauty spots of the Dombai [region] but who truly thirst to be mountaineers."[116] These mountaineers identified themselves—and mountaineering—very much along the traditional line of masculinity, militarization, and sports by using the vocabulary of the official discourse (such as "the sport of the bold," a longtime slogan). The high group pressure this created is attested by many entries of young women who admitted to having a very hard time and being afraid of slowing down their colleagues.[117]

But for many people "thirsting to be mountaineers," it was precisely the "beauty spots of the Dombai" which had brought them to a mountaineering camp. Most of the young visitors from Russia and Ukraine had never seen mountains before, but they already had an image in their mind, shaped by literature, photographs, postcards, or tales from relatives and friends.[118] "Before my trip to the Caucasus, I heard and read much about it, from which a detailed impression had formed [in my mind], but when I saw it with my own eyes, I understood that my imagination had not come close," one participant wrote.[119] Given the recent rehabilitation of Russia's classical poets, a Soviet mountaineer could confess he had wanted to travel to the Caucasus ever since he had read Lermontov's "Prisoner of the Mountains."[120] The Caucasus these visitors were looking for was romantic, not revolutionary, and it was a landscape, not a living space; significantly, not one of the people writing in this comment book

---

114. "Torpedo," 1949 (GARF, f. 5451, op. 32, d. 253, ll. 63–64). Symptomatically, while the initiative for sexual relations was usually reported to come from the men's side (see, for example, GARF, f. 7710, op. 6, d. 58, ll. 139, 150; VTsSPS, 1935), it was women who were under the general suspicion of coming to the camp primarily to find husbands (Shataev, *Kategoriia trudnosti*, 29).

115. Emphasis in orig. GARF, f. 9480, op. 3, d. 457, l. 3.

116. Ibid., l. 17.

117. Ibid., ll. 3, 4, 18, v. 26.

118. Ibid., l. 15; Ovchinnikov, *Al'pinisty*, 30.

119. GARF, f. 9480, op. 3, d. 457, l. 3.

120. Ovchinnikov, *Al'pinisty*, 30.

mentioned the local inhabitants or their culture.[121] Landscape served as a background for their own, private and individual experience, be it contemplative and visual, or a more active and physical appropriation of nature.[122]

The nature of the Soviet mountaineering camp in the early 1950s reflects many significant trends in Soviet society. A belief in revolutionary self-improvement through group-oriented activities had subsided as the individual retreated into a more passive role vis-à-vis society and the state. Privileges and social stratification ruled over the goals of equality and accessibility, and connections often determined access to goods and services. Still, the typical Soviet mountaineer more than slightly resembled his prerevolutionary counterpart: an urban, male, university-educated member of the Soviet (upper) middle classes, dominated by the "specialists" of the new Soviet intelligentsia.[123] Not only education but also cultural markers such as a firm belief in the benefits of physical exercise and/or the aesthetic appropriation of landscape were necessary prerequisites to make use of this state-provided leisure space. As a cultural practice, mountaineering was based on self-control and self-discipline, exercise, and the notion of "limited risk." It thus perpetuated many of the qualities the Stalinist regime, as well as other modern societies, wanted to foster in its citizens as a means of helping to align private and state goals. Mediating these interests were the mountaineer's own associations, whose surprising degree of self-governance and influence in protecting their group interests deserves further investigation.

The mountaineering camp was a place at the borders of the Soviet realm— by its sheer physical distance, by the symbolical hierarchies of "pristine" nature and urban Moscow, and by its function as an "other world," all of which allowed for a temporary time-out from everyday life. It was not outside the Soviet realm, however. Not only were power hierarchies partly replicated inside the camp, but the all-embracing socialist discourse framed the experience of all participants. To some visitors, "collectivism" may have meant no more than a necessary evil or an instrument of control, intruding on one's privacy. Others, however, recalled it as an emotional connection with other people. For a group considered one of the regime's supporting pillars, the community of mountaineering may have well embodied values like comradeship, mutual help, and collectiveness in a way the Soviet state could postulate but never realize.

121. The reappraisal of landscape painting during the late 1930s is another aspect of that Stalinist landscape; see Mark Bassin, "'I object to rain that is cheerless': Landscape Art and the Stalinist Aesthetic Imagination," *Ecumene* 7, no. 3 (2000): 313–36.

122. This is equally true for landscape as a background in consumer advertisements. Randi Cox, "All This Can Be Yours! Soviet Commercial Advertising and the Social Construction of Space, 1928–1956," in *Landscape of Stalinism*, ed. Naiman and Dobrenko, 153–56.

123. On the evolution of the new Soviet intelligentsia and the *vydvyzhentsy*, see Sheila Fitzpatrick, *Education and Social Mobility in the Soviet Union, 1921–34* (New York, 1979). I rely on the broad definition of intelligentsia in Alex Inkeles, *Social Change in Soviet Russia* (Cambridge, Mass., 1968), 150–55.

CHAPTER 8

"Where Each Stone Is History"

Travel Guides in Sevastopol after World War II

Karl D. Qualls

"Sevastopol—City of Glory" and "Hero-City Sevastopol" adorn books, posters, buses and trolleys in the city of Sevastopol, Ukraine. The ubiquitous image of heroism and glory is neither new nor passively remembered. During two centuries of tremendous political change in Sevastopol, the city's image has changed little. Within the course of a century Sevastopol was part of the Russian Empire, of the Russian and then Ukrainian federations of the Soviet Union, and now of independent Ukraine. Into the twenty-first century, the population of Sevastopol has been overwhelmingly Russian by nationality, although it is now Ukrainian by citizenship. The shift in ruling ideologies and countries to which Sevastopol has belonged has done little to alter the dominant identity of the city.

Sevastopol has been, first and foremost, a Russian naval city. Peter the Great wanted to control the Black Sea for his new empire, but only in 1784 did Catherine the Great found the city on what used to be the ancient Greek city of Chersoneses (Khersones to Slavs) as an outpost against the Turks. In the nineteenth and twentieth centuries, Sevastopol and the rest of the Crimean peninsula played a vital role in defending imperial Russia in the Crimean War (1853–1856) and the Soviet Union in World War II (or the "two great defenses" as they are called in Sevastopol). Naval warfare and, especially, fighting against great odds and sacrificing for the Motherland became the hallmarks of Sevastopol and led to the Soviet "hero-city" designation.[1] The scuttling of ships to prevent Great Britain's entrance into the bays during the Crimean War and World War II soldiers who threw themselves under tanks and charged machine-gun nests became defining moments for the city's identity.[2] While the latter defense was fought during the Soviet period in which the regime declared all nationalities to be equal, the call to arms and the greatest praise was reserved for Russians. Thus the predominately Russian popula-

---

1. Sevastopol received the title "Hero-City" along with Odessa and Stalingrad in 1945. Nine other cities joined the list in the next forty years.

2. *The Heroic Defence of Sevastopol'* (Moscow, 1942); *Sevastopol': November, 1941–July, 1942: Articles, Stories and Eye-Witness Accounts by Soviet War Correspondents* (London, 1943); Karl D. Qualls, "Imagining Sevastopol: History and Postwar Community Construction, 1942–1953," *National Identities* 5, no. 2 (2003): 123–39.

8.1. Khersones Archeological Preserve. Sevastopol, Ukraine, November 2005. Photographed by Karl D. Qualls.

tion in Sevastopol could continue its fight for the Motherland—Russia—and thereby maintain an affinity with the city's past.[3] The last fifty years of travel guide literature and tourism has reinforced the image of the Russian defender, although Sevastopol has been part of independent Ukraine since 1991.

Sevastopol has developed in a way unlike most other cities. Sevastopol was not a resort city like nearby Yalta; rather, it had become an open-air museum of monuments, memorials, and plaques even before World War II. The war catalyzed a resurgence of mythmaking during the second half of the twentieth century, so that the city has roughly 2,015 monuments today. Moreover, for six decades ending in 1996, Sevastopol was a closed city, open only to those who gained permission from the Ministry of Internal Affairs. Residents' relatives or tour groups of veterans, workers, or party activists could visit the city, but armed border guards at the military city's outskirts hindered the "wild tourism" of individual or small groups outside official channels.[4] Just as au-

3. As of 2001, 74 percent of Sevastopol's population was Russian, 21 percent Ukrainian, and 5 percent Belorussian, Crimean Tatar, Jewish, Armenian, Greek, German, Moldovan, Polish, and more. See Alexander Dobry and Irina Borisova, *Welcome to Sevastopol* (Simferopol, 2001), 5.

4. Of course, deviations from planned itineraries could still happen, even in Sevastopol. For more on "wild" tourists, see the chapters by Noack, Maurer, and Moranda in this volume. The

thorities circumscribed tourism in the highly sensitive military city, so, too, guidebooks circumscribed the "reading" of the city. Few stayed within the city boundaries, so guidebooks did not have to include information about hotels and other conveniences. Outsiders came to the city either to visit family or to celebrate the city's history and traditions. Sevastopol had been marked as a city of Russian military valor since the mid-nineteenth century; therefore, guidebooks directed readers to sites of memory and not frivolity. With further research on other cities, we might conclude that Soviet tourism mirrored the specialization of Soviet industrial development; each region or city served a specific function in the larger system. Whereas Yalta and Sochi became resorts, Sevastopol became an outdoor museum of military history.

Wartime propaganda and postwar reconstruction built on prerevolutionary images of the city. Leo Tolstoy's famous Crimean War sketches, *Sevastopol Tales*, provided generations of readers with a portrayal of the hero-city. An 1857 travel guide noted that the "subject and source of inquisitiveness of visitors in Sevastopol is its defense [during the Crimean War]."[5] The tragic and heroic military past assumed center stage instead of the beautiful bays and beaches of the city. As World War II raged, newspapers carried stories of the new heroes and linked them to the heroes of a century earlier. After the 97 percent destruction of World War II, toponyms highlighted the foundation of Sevastopol's nineteenth-century legacy; and renaming streets, parks, and squares aided urban identification.[6] Central streets and squares after World War II were more often named for nineteenth-century admirals than for revolutionary leaders. Tourists today, however, can still find Vladimir Lenin, whose name marks the central region and one of its main streets.

Why has the identity of Sevastopol persisted despite ongoing political and economic turmoil, and what role have guidebooks played in maintaining the city's identity? Travel guidebooks were one medium for transmitting an official image of the city to readers throughout the USSR. Guidebooks instructed readers where to look and how to interpret what they saw and how it fit into a larger urban and national biography. Because World War II destruction and dislocation—physical, psychological, and ideological—was of the highest magnitude in cities like Sevastopol and Stalingrad, it was imperative in the postwar decade to rebuild not only structures but also ties that bound state and society. The regime's legitimacy and power had been questioned during

---

historian and guidebook author Emiliia Doronina claimed that three million people visited the city each year by the 1980s, but she gave no indication of how many were individual tourists and how many came with organized groups. Likely the largest visitation period would have been the May holidays of Victory Day and Liberation Day when thousands of veterans descended on the city. See Emiliia Doronina and Alexander Liakhovich, *Po ulitsam Sevastopol'ia* (Simferopol, 1983), 4.

5. D. Afanas'ev, *Putevoditel' po Sevastopol'iu* (Nikolaev, 1857), 1. See also A. N. Popov, *Pervaia uchebnaia ekskursiia simferopol'skoi muzhskoi gimnazii: Sevastopol'* (Simferopol, 1889); and Anna Petrovna (Munt) Valueva, *Sevastopol' i ego slavnoe proshloe*, 2 (St. Petersburg, 1904).

6. For a comparative perspective of other Soviet name changes, see John Murray, *Politics and Place-Names: Changing Names in the Late Soviet Period* (Birmingham, UK, 2000).

N

A. Nakhimov Square
B. Lazarev Square
C. Ushakov Square
D. Historical Boulevard
E. Primorksii Boulevard
F. Vladimir Square
G. Petropavlovskaia Square

1. Nakhimov Street
2. Bolshaia Morskaia
3. Lenin Street

Korabelnaia due east
Severnaia due north
Black Sea outlet northwest

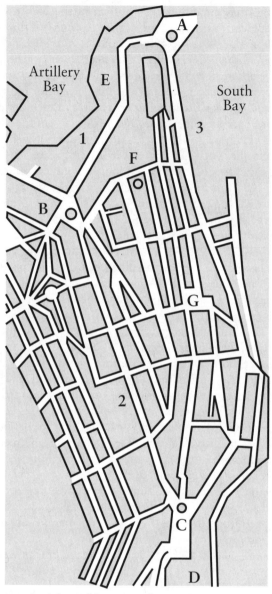

Map of Sevastopol's city center

8.2. Map of Sevastopol city center. Drawn in Adobe Illustrator by Karl D. Qualls. Used by permission of University of Pittsburgh Press.

the war, and it was imperative that new identities be (re)constructed to restore allegiance. The rebuilding process restored the necessities of life, but monuments, toponyms, and the travel guidebooks that discussed them also reoriented people's thinking about a city's place within the Soviet world.[7] Although much of the postwar architectural style varied little from one urban area to the next, guidebooks clearly delineated a unique history and contribution for each city.[8] This was a paradoxical attempt to reimpose authority by celebrating uniqueness. For Sevastopol, this also meant disaggregating the city's naval character from the image of Crimea as a peninsula of pleasure and resorts and thereby giving residents a special role.[9] The "individuality" of a given city supported and complemented the greater Soviet identity and helped to reestablish authority and traditional culture. While some cities, like Magnitogorsk, had primarily an economic identity, others, like Novgorod, based their myth primarily on their heritage. Whether as a center of mining and metallurgy or of ancient Russian culture, each city served as a component of the larger Soviet whole. Thus city residents could celebrate the unique and special role of their locale while still supporting central Soviet ideals of labor and culture.

This study of Sevastopol's travel guides since World War II continues the work of scholars investigating other cities and countries, but in many ways it highlights the particularities of Soviet (and Sevastopol's) guidebooks. Soviet guidebooks in general promoted knowledge-based travel, especially to cities not known as resorts. Local history, in a truncated and politically selective form, dominated. When authors addressed leisure they usually focused on cultural pursuits, and rarely did readers find much discussion of the restaurants and shops, a feature that clearly separates Soviet guides from their capitalist counterparts. In Sevastopol's guidebooks, entertainment was almost completely absent. Local history made the entire city into a museum to valor, sacrifice, and heroism. The blood of fallen soldiers and sailors had sanctified the soil for two centuries, thereby making Sevastopol a city of reverence, not revelry, for visitors.[10]

7. Iuliia Kosenkova, *Sovetskii gorod 1940-kh–pervoi poloviny 1950-kh godov: ot tvorcheskikh poiskov k praktike stroitel'stvo* (Moscow, 2000); Karl D. Qualls, "Local-Outsider Negotiations in Sevastopol's Postwar Reconstruction, 1944–53," in *Provincial Landscapes: The Local Dimensions of Soviet Power*, ed. Donald J. Raleigh (Pittsburgh, 2001), 276–98.

8. In addition to the books under investigation here, the author has found strong similarities in Smolensk and Novgorod. For example, see *Novgorod: putevoditel'* (Leningrad, 1966); I. A. Zaitsev and I. I. Kushnir, *Ulitsy Novgoroda: spravochnik* (Leningrad, 1975); I. Belogortsev and I. Sofinskii, *Smolensk* (Moscow, 1952); and *Smolensk: spravochnik-putevoditel'* (Smolensk, 1960).

9. In this volume Layton shows Crimea as part of the "pleasure periphery" in nineteenth-century military tourism.

10. V. Khapaev and M. Zolotarev, *Legendarnyi Sevastopol': uvlekatel'nyi putevoditel'* (Sevastopol, 2002), 37. On battlefields as sacred spaces, see Stephen L. Harp, *Marketing Michelin: Advertising and Cultural Identity in Twentieth Century France* (Baltimore, 2001); David W. Lloyd, *Battlefield Tourism: Pilgrimage and the Commemoration of the Great War in Britain, Australia, and Canada, 1913–1939* (New York, 1998); Catherine Merridale, *Night of Stone: Death and*

This volume is one of the first forays into the history of tourism in eastern Europe, but scholars of tourism elsewhere have framed a discussion of important issues. Dean MacCannell, Rudy Koshar, and Stephen Harp advance one interpretation of tourists' motives that suggests tourism was essentially a quest for knowledge and/or an authentic experience.[11] John Urry, however, argues that the quest for pleasure and an escape from the everyday is at the heart of the tourist urge.[12] The obsession with Soviet workers' "active leisure" based on knowledge and culture ironically links it with the turn-of-the-century bourgeoisie in Europe. Only in the last decade has pure pleasure tourism emerged in Sevastopol and the former USSR.

Scholars also have debated the relationship between modernity and tourism. MacCannell argued that the dislocation of modernity leads to a "search for authenticity" and that tourism is a process of "self discovery."[13] As research on World War I has shown, the dislocation and dissociation of the "Great War" led many people to travel to battlefields searching for meaning and for collective mourning.[14] Travel guides directed visitors to "what ought to be seen" on pilgrimages to near-sacred sites.[15] Authorial selectivity created a set of shared sites and experiences but in no way represented the full range of events and interpretations about the war experience. Even when visitors followed the same path to memorial space, their assumptions, expectations, and experiences led them to different understandings.

The effectiveness of travel guides in creating a unified experience or identity is also open to debate. MacCannell's assertion that attempts to create a unified experience are "doomed to eventual failure" because of the need to create uniqueness is suspect.[16] It is true that Koshar has shown that the success of the Baedeker guides in Germany bred competing "travel cultures" from people who felt that their travel desires had been unmet. But Harp has also shown how the Michelin gastronomic guides that celebrated French regions actually supported nation building.[17] Battlefields and monu-

Memory in Twentieth Century Russia (New York, 2001); George Mosse, *Fallen Soldiers: Reshaping the Memory of the World Wars* (New York, 1990); and Jay Winter and Sivan Emmanuel, eds., *War and Remembrance in the Twentieth Century* (Cambridge, 1999).

11. Developing from discussions of the search for "authenticity" in Dean MacCannell, *The Tourist: A New Theory of the Leisure Class* (New York, 1976), 3–5, Rudy Koshar (*German Travel Cultures* [Oxford, 2000]) argues against John Urry, *The Tourist Gaze: Leisure and Travel in Contemporary Societies* (London, 1990) and the supposition that tourists only seek novelty. Harp, *Marketing Michelin*, 101, argues that French battlefield tourists were seeking "supposed authenticity."

12. Urry, *Tourist Gaze*.

13. MacCannell, *Tourist*, 3–5.

14. John Gillis, *Commemorations: The Politics of National Identity* (Princeton, N.J., 1994); Mosse, *Fallen Soldiers*; Winter and Sivan, *War and Remembrance*.

15. Rudy Koshar, " 'What Ought to be Seen': Tourists' Guidebooks and National Identities in Modern Germany and Europe," *Journal of Contemporary History* 33, no. 3 (1998): 323–40. On the use of the model of religious pilgrimages, see Lloyd, *Battlefield Tourism*.

16. MacCannell, *Tourist*, 13.

17. Harp, *Marketing Michelin*; Koshar, *German Travel Cultures*.

ments are central in much of this research on identity in the interwar period, but the research generally investigates national identity rather than local. When repeated and reinforced (as in highly ritualized Soviet travel, obligatory wedding-day visits to monuments and school trips with veterans to memorial sites), it can become part of a larger collective memory. Whether in the didacticism of Soviet guidebooks or the free press of capitalism, the past is always reimagined and constructed both intentionally and by the selectivity necessary for a portable guidebook. Modern mass production and consumption (travel included) have led to "mass deception" of populations searching for authentic experiences even in democratic, capitalist societies.[18] The instructive nature of Soviet travel in general and the didactic motives of its guidebooks created a mythologized world into which the reader/traveler could write him- or herself. Travel guidebooks showed an eternal past and future, which provided the comfort of continuity and a sense of belonging during turbulent times. Guidebooks generally balance past and present, but Soviet guidebooks devoted more attention to orienting visitors to the usable past.

The Soviet censorship regime complicated issues of authorship and intent. In the Soviet model, powerful institutions at the national, republic, and local levels were able to craft much of the urban biography. Authors wrote texts understanding the censorship regime. We do not know if guidebook authors had to follow a model or provide multiple revised versions like tour group leaders, but there is a high degree of consistency across time and authors.[19] This makes those variations that do exist, important, and it is in part the nature and significance of these that I explore in this chapter. Guidebooks helped readers to navigate their way through cities, but the same books also helped readers navigate a sometimes shifting past by educating, commemorating, and mythologizing the city and its image. They told readers what was important about the city and why visitors should visit.

The Expository Soviet Travel Guidebook

The vast majority of Soviet travel guidebooks written after World War II followed the expository model of introduction, body of evidence, and conclusion. This model provided the reader with a quick and efficient way of learning what was most important, according to the authors, about Sevastopol's past and how that past informed the present and future. The expository guidebook

18. Max Horkheimer and Theodor W. Adorno, *Dialectic of Enlightenment* (New York, 1999), 121.

19. For more on Soviet travel, see Anne E. Gorsuch, " 'There's No Place Like Home': Soviet Tourism in Late Stalinism," *Slavic Review* 62, no. 4 (2003): 760–85; and Diane P. Koenker, "Travel to Work, Travel to Play: On Russian Tourism, Travel, and Leisure," ibid.: 657–65. Gorsuch provides information on the editing process of the scripts for tour leaders.

presented the argument, used "evidence" from the monuments and sites, and concluded with suggested excursions that reinforced the portrayal of the city's special heritage. In this way, the reader was supposed to be convinced that the argument was true and that there was only one understanding of the past. The density and clarity of presentation and seeming completeness of the text lent an air of authority, and the mostly black-and-white editions provided a documentary feel. In short, the very form of the guidebooks suggested that there was no need to look for alternate explanations.[20]

Introductions, although often quite different in length and style, consistently highlighted a number of topics that authors deemed central to the city's identity. In Sevastopol's guidebooks the "hero-city" formed the foundation for all other reporting on the city and its history. Sevastopol's naval exploits in defending Russia and the Soviet Union during the Turkish Wars, the Crimean War, and World War II dominated. This selective presentation of the past that omitted peaceful times projected continuity and causality; focus on Sevastopol's exploits during times of national emergency suggested a preordained fate to stand at the ready and sacrifice to protect the Motherland.

Most guidebooks concluded with a suggested set of excursions that reinforced themes and allowed one to understand the city's heritage and identity without ever visiting. In the concluding sections, precise directions about where to turn and when and at what one should look further circumscribed the "reading" of the city. Excursions varied among guidebooks, but all show a conscious attempt through descriptions or the order of the excursions to relate the sites of one period to another, especially the "two great defenses." In doing so, guidebooks reinforced the idea of continuity in the hero-city and aided remembering, forgetting, and recapturing.

In addressing the issue of continuity and change over time, this chapter analyzes the most prolific authors of the postwar period, Zakhar Chebaniuk and Emiliia Doronina and her co-authors, and three recent post-Soviet texts. The frequency with which Chebaniuk published in the 1950s and 1960s made him the primary voice on travel in Sevastopol. Likewise, Emiliia Doronina and her co-authors dominated the travel literature of the late 1970s until the end of the Soviet period. They became, in essence, the official voices of two generations. Although other authors published at this time, the nature of Soviet publication led to a standard model illustrated most often by Chebaniuk and Doronina. The post-Soviet era's free press has led to a multiplicity of voices, three of which are discussed below because their approaches differ more than the Soviet texts. The following examples thus address the presentation of Sevastopol in three eras roughly bounded by the reigns of Khrushchev and the interregnum (Chebaniuk), Brezhnev (Doronina), and independent Ukraine.

20. For more on the aesthetics of guidebooks as a method of persuasion, see Anne Bush, "Reviewing Rome: The Guidebook as Liminal Space," *Visual Communication* 1, no. 3 (2002): 369–74; Harp, *Marketing Michelin*, chap. 3; Koshar, *German Travel Cultures*.

Forgetting

Although monuments, plaques, and other common foci of guidebooks evoke remembering, they also enable "forgetting" through an active process of omission when an author excludes a landmark from the text or removes material from subsequent editions.[21] Forgetting about leaders who fell from favor is but one example of rescripting the political past in Soviet guidebooks. Discussion of present politics is rare, but mention of the regime's leaders alongside the author's introduction of the "proper" understanding of the city's identity equated the political leadership with the city's glory. While one could pass this off as the Soviet norm of refashioning history, a more balanced interpretation could see it as part of a normal process of inventing tradition and history common in capitalist democracies, too.[22]

The multiple editions of Zakhar Chebaniuk's *Sevastopol': istoricheskie mesta i pamiatniki* (1955, 1957, 1962, 1966) offer the best example of "forgetting." In the chapter "Hero-City Sevastopol," Chebaniuk set out the general framework for understanding the city's past. In the 1955 edition he noted Stalin's approval of the "selfless struggle of the Sevastopol residents [who] serve as an example of heroism for all the Red Army and Soviet people."[23] Despite Stalin's praise of Sevastopol's heroism, the 1956 "Secret Speech" of his successor Nikita Khrushchev, in which he denounced Stalin's cult of personality and numerous crimes against the party, necessitated the omission of any direct reference to Stalin in the 1957 edition.[24] We may never know if censors demanded the change, but Chebaniuk likely exercised internal censorship rather than risk running afoul of authorities.

In 1955 Khrushchev, Voroshilov, and others attended the city soviet meeting celebrating the centenary of the Crimean War. Voroshilov celebrated the "city of glorious warriors and revolutionary traditions" that "personifies the greatness and glory of our people." Khrushchev praised the military feats of the "glorious sons of our great Motherland" but also the "glorious activity of laborers in the struggle for the restoration of the city . . . and further strengthening of the military forces of the Black Sea Fleet."[25] Khrushchev thus linked the military feats with the equally daunting reconstruction tasks of the postwar decade and the ongoing need for military strength during the Cold War.

21. Pierre Nora, "Between Memory and History: Les Lieux de Memoire," *Representations*, no. 26 (1989): 7–25.

22. David Lowenthal, *The Past Is a Foreign Country* (Cambridge, 1985). Harp has also shown that the Michelin guides declared their "authenticity" in presenting World War I battlefields in opposition to the alleged lies of the German guidebooks like Baedeker. Michelin, however, "offered readers a very specific, politically loaded interpretation of the recent past." Harp, *Marketing Michelin*, 115. On Baedeker, see Koshar, *German Travel Cultures*.

23. Zakhar Chebaniuk, *Sevastopol': istoricheskie mesta i pamiatniki* (Simferopol, 1955), 27.

24. Zakhar Chebaniuk, *Sevastopol': istoricheskie mesta i pamiatniki* (Simferopol, 1957), 26–27.

25. Ibid., 30–31.

In the 1962 edition only Khrushchev remained, and the text enumerated the numerous economic and industrial changes in the city, which reminded the reader that Khrushchev's economic decentralization would make Sevastopol even more prosperous in the near future and "transform hometown Sevastopol into a city of communist labor, of exemplary order and high culture."[26] Readers found that the new political elite were mindful of Sevastopol's importance to the larger Soviet Union and recognized the city's special mission, traditions and heritage of sacrifice, hard work, and high culture.

Chebaniuk's 1966 edition, following Khrushchev's ouster two years earlier, merely eliminated reference to Khrushchev and Stalin and refrained from taking sides in the struggle for power eventually won by Leonid Brezhnev. Greater elaboration on local cultural institutions and opportunities replaced paeans from and to the political leadership. Chebaniuk's discussion of increased housing construction in the 1960s failed to note the efficacy of Khrushchev's campaign to eliminate the much-hated communal apartment in favor of private space. He concluded the section with a generic declaration of Sevastopol's latest awards. Rather than note that Anastas Mikoian—one of Khrushchev's possible successors and a leading functionary under both Stalin and Khrushchev—signed the award decree, Chebaniuk merely told the reader that the Presidium of the Supreme Soviet, an institution he believed would outlive its membership, bestowed the honor on the city.

Although no one likely read these editions side by side, the reader of any given volume except the 1966 edition found the leader du jour lauding Sevastopol's heroic past and its long history of selflessly serving the Motherland. Statements praising Sevastopol's past served to legitimize the city's importance to residents and nonresidents alike and to provide a context for the newly arrived workers and sailors. How readers actually understood and interpreted the signals is impossible to tell. Because descriptions of the historical sites and their meanings remained intact in Chebaniuk's multiple editions, political changes must have necessitated reprinting in order to legitimize the new leader and discredit his predecessor. Political leaders functioned as constantly changing window dressing; Sevastopol's role and place in history remained consistent while the leaders who praised it fell from favor. When we see such changes over time yet key themes persist, it reinforces the central importance of ever-present sacrifice and heroism.

Remembering

While guidebooks reinforced the process of forgetting discredited leaders, they also actively created a selective "remembering" of the past based on the needs

---

26. Zakhar Chebaniuk, *Sevastopol': istoricheskie mesta i pamiatniki* (Simferopol, 1962), 32.

of the present. In addressing the Turkish Wars and the Crimean War, authors across the decades could remain consistent in the types of sites they highlighted and the language they used to describe the themes of heroism and sacrifice. Coverage of the revolutionary period and World War II, however, varied dramatically among guidebooks as the World War II generation moved into and out of power.

Post-World War II guidebooks emphasized sacrifice, teamwork, unity, and symbolic defiance against great odds in describing Sevastopol's earliest monument.[27] In May 1829 Captain Alexander Kazarskii decided to blow up his ship's magazine rather than surrender to two Turkish battleships. Chebaniuk reminded his readers that "in an uneven fight an eighteen-gun Russian brig won a victory over an enemy that had more than a tenfold superiority in artillery."[28] Likewise, Emiliia Doronina, writing in the late 1970s and 1980s, called Kazarskii's feat an "example of fortitude to the warriors of the two defenses," which the Soviet Black Sea Fleet was continuing.[29] Doronina not only consciously connected her readers to the past but showed the continuity of behavior from Kazarskii to the present. A 2001 guidebook noted that the inscription "An example for posterity" on Kazarskii's pedestal came from Tsar Nicholas I, an admission unthinkable in Soviet times.[30] Moreover, Kazarskii now represented a democratic choice because the city's first monument was "dedicated not to an emperor or an admiral, but to a captain-lieutenant!"[31]

Veneration of the Crimean War became the first full-scale memorialization project in Sevastopol with three sites of memory dominating guidebooks: the Monument to Scuttled Ships, Malakhov Kurgan, and the Panorama and Museum of the Great Defense. The monument to ships scuttled to prevent the British and French navies from entering Sevastopol Bay, although not the first monument, is undoubtedly the most beloved in Sevastopol. It is the "emblem of the city of Russia glory—Sevastopol," and it "reminds everybody of the sorrowful but important event."[32] It continued the legacy of "the sailors [who]

27. For more, see Petr Garmash, *Gorod-geroi Sevastopol': ocherk putevoditel'* (Simferopol, 1972); Vitalii Olshevskii, *Sevastopol': spravochnik* (Simferopol, 1977); Vitalii Olshevskii, *Sevastopol': putevoditel'* (Simferopol, 1981); Nikolai Orlov and Igor Gassko, *Gorod-geroi Sevastopol': fotoal'bom* (Simferopol, 1985); Boris Rosseikin, *Sevastopol': al'bom* (Simferopol, 1960); Boris Rosseikin and Georgii Semin, *Sevastopol': putevoditel'-spravochnik* (Simferopol, 1961); Boris Rosseikin, Georgii Semin, and Zakhar Chebaniuk, *Sevastopol': putevoditel'-spravochnik* (Simferopol, 1959); and E. V. Venikeev, *Arkhitektura Sevastopol'ia: putevoditel'* (Simferopol, 1983).

28. Chebaniuk, *Sevastopol'* (1957), 34.

29. Emiliia Nikolaevna Doronina and Tamara Ivanovna Iakovleva, *Pamiatniki Sevastopol'ia* (Simferopol, 1978), 22–24.

30. Alexander Dobry and Irina Borisova, *Welcome to Sevastopol* (Simferopol, 2001), 74. The Russian-language edition is A. Dobryi, *Dobro pozhalovat' v Sevastopol'* (Simferopol, 2000).

31. Khapaev and Zolotarev, *Legendarnyi Sevastopol'*, 102.

32. Chebaniuk, *Sevastopol'* (1957), 61.

8.3. Monument to Scuttled Ships, Sevastopol, Ukraine. November 2004. Photographed by Karl D. Qualls.

served as examples for all participants in the defense" and has become "the emblem of Sevastopol, its visiting card."[33] Whether on book covers, postcards, Web sites, or the many canvases of artists, this picturesque monument has remained the symbol of the city.

The gates of Malakhov Kurgan, the hilltop scene of bloody fighting in and the death of several Russian military leaders during the Crimean War, appeared on the cover of Chebaniuk's 1955 text. The hill's Crimean War complex remained "one of the most famous places of Sevastopol."[34] Doronina validated the importance of the World War II memorial space at Sapun Hill by noting that its eternal flame was lit from that at Malakhov Kurgan, thereby "symbolizing the continuity of glorious combat traditions."[35] In this way, Malakhov Kurgan and the Crimean War gave legitimacy to World War II veneration.

The Panorama building and painting, a "monumental memorial to the heroism of Sevastopol's defenders in the Crimean War" and "the national

33. Doronina and Iakovleva, *Pamiatniki Sevastopol'ia*, 45; Dobry and Borisova, *Welcome to Sevastopol*, 54.

34. Khapaev and Zolotarev, *Legendarnyi Sevastopol'*, 126.

35. Doronina and Iakovleva, *Pamiatniki Sevastopol'ia*, 123.

8.4. Sapun Hill Museum and memorial complex. Sevastopol, Ukraine. May 1997. Photographed by Karl D. Qualls.

pride of this country and its people," drew forty million visitors from 1905 to 2004 and received extensive coverage in all guides.[36] The authors were consistent in describing the events memorialized in the panorama, its construction, the Nazis' devastation of it, and the postwar reconstruction of the building and the panoramic painting on the interior. It is the "main noteworthy site of our city," claimed one post-Soviet author, and "many tourists come more than once to touch the great art and history."[37] As one of the great military feats of the nineteenth century, along with the Napoleonic invasion, the Crimean defense became a defining moment for Russian military and political power, identity, and literature (such as the career of Leo Tolstoy).

Like Kazarskii, the scuttling of the fleet and other Crimean War tales served explicitly as "examples" of fortitude and sacrifice against a superior force. The focus on heroes as examples, however, also omits mention of cowardice; the necessity for examples implies a fear that in future conflicts not all will respond with such valor. Here, then, is a process of both "forgetting" and "remembering." How would one "read" what could be an ambiguous message? Because most people would rather be part of something heroic rather than

36. *Sevastopol': putevoditel'* (Simferopol, 2004), 35; Dobry and Borisova, *Welcome to Sevastopol*, 46–47.
37. Khapaev and Zolotarev, *Legendarnyi Sevastopol'*, 111–20.

cowardly, Soviet tourists likely chose not to ask whether all sailors lived up to examples of heroism and sacrifice. Visitors today may see it much differently. Would Ukrainian sailors stationed in Sevastopol relate to past Russian heroism and sacrifice? Would German, British, and American tourists see scuttling as folly, failure, or fortitude? Even in the Soviet period each viewer interpreted through the lenses of gender, age, profession, and more, but now international visitors come from backgrounds that rarely have recognized Russian/Soviet valor and therefore make multiple or muddled understandings more likely.

Unlike the Crimean War, the city's revolutionary heritage played a remarkably minor role in guidebooks despite the centrality of many local events to the Soviet revolutionary mythology. The 1905 revolution and the "Battleship *Potemkin*" are an important part of the city's biography and the residents' heritage, but coverage varied greatly among guidebooks. The November 1905 uprising, in which the monarchy arrested and punished hundreds without a trial, led to the bloody execution of the leaders. Chebaniuk, writing during the transition between Stalin and Khrushchev, was uncertain about the official interpretation of the revolutionary period, so much of which Stalin had rewritten to give himself a more prominent role. Chebaniuk felt compelled to show that some of the Bolshevik Party's opponents, the "Menshevik ringleaders," were the cause of failure and that the revolutionaries stood in court with "fortitude . . . knowing the deep feeling of the masses, millions strong, who were on their side."[38] Doronina, writing well after Stalin's version of history had been overturned, gave considerably more attention to the revolutionary period, but it still occupied quite a small portion of the book (only 23 of 143 pages). She noted that the First Sevastopol Soviet "endured a drubbing, but the revolutionary spirit of the people remained unbroken."[39] Thus death was a perfectly acceptable fate when it led to greater good. Guidebooks recast momentary losses as ultimate victories and presented courageous men and women who gladly sacrificed for the cause. This understanding of the past also served as a protection against current and future setbacks during the cold war. When times got hard, residents needed only remember the actions of their forebears.

In post-Soviet Ukraine, authors have further marginalized the revolutionary tradition, which has lost most of its importance. Alexander Dobry lamented that children in 2001 knew little about the revolutionary movement, but by devoting only three pages to it Dobry contributed further to its marginalization. Other post-Soviet authors have rejected the revolutionary past entirely, noting how it ushered in "one of the most excruciating periods" of Russian history—the Soviet Union.[40] Another author went further and called the 1917 revolution and civil war "a microscopic, laughable segment of time in the scale

38. Chebaniuk, *Sevastopol'* (1957), 98–101.
39. Doronina and Iakovleva, *Pamiatniki Sevastopol'ia*, 65.
40. Khapaev and Zolotarev, *Legendarnyi Sevastopol'*, 42.

of history. . . . Horrible! . . . Bloody! . . . Destructive!"[41] After the end of the USSR, there was no editorial pressure to include what for many likely appeared as an anomaly (and a negative one) in Russian history. Of the only forty-six monuments, plaques, and memorial places dedicated to the events and people of these uprisings, most were erected only after World War II, which suggests that memorialization of the events had been an afterthought and not a deeply felt part of the city's character. Erected during a time in which the party was trying to recapture its dominance and recentralize authority, monuments to revolutionary heroes seemed both hollow and suspect.[42]

As other scholars have noted, World War II became the defining event for a new generation of Soviet citizens, and guidebooks bear this out.[43] Two-thirds of the sites to World War II activities were erected in the 1960s and 1970s as the war generation moved into power and began to shift the use of the war myth.[44] Whereas Khrushchev had promoted a populist understanding of the war as the work of millions of heroic individuals in order to counter Stalin's "cult of personality," Brezhnev mobilized a "cult of the Great Patriotic War" in order to counteract youth culture, the Prague Spring, and other events that threatened to destabilize the regime. The mythic unity of Lenin and the revolution found less resonance after the war.[45] Not surprisingly, guidebooks began to place greater emphasis on the war during the Brezhnev years. Post-Soviet guidebooks, while still noting the importance of the war in Sevastopol's history, place World War II exploits in context as some of many moments of valor rather than the most important ones, as the war generation texts suggested.

Chebaniuk focused primarily on individual heroes and thereby personalized the war for his audience. In the first days of the 1941–1942 defense, Chebaniuk noted, five members of the naval infantry initiated an "unparalleled duel" as they destroyed sixteen tanks by themselves. In Chebaniuk's favorite phrase they "fulfilled their debt" as they fought to their death.[46] Doronina also recounted the feats of the "five daring Black Sea sailors" and their ability twice to repel the German advance against all odds.[47] The seven Communist Youth League members and three communists in Pillbox No. 11 likewise staged a valiant defense against all odds. Bombarded from the air and on the ground, they held out for more than three days until all but one were dead. Both

41. *Sevastopol': putevoditel'*, 22.

42. Doronina and Iakovleva, *Pamiatniki Sevastopol'ia*, 64.

43. Amir Weiner, "The Making of a Dominant Myth: The Second World War and the Construction of Political Identities within the Soviet Polity," *Russian Review* 55, no. 4 (1996): 638–60.

44. Dobry and Borisova, *Welcome to Sevastopol*, 64.

45. Nina Tumarkin, *The Living and the Dead: The Rise and Fall of the Cult of World War II in Russia* (New York, 1994).

46. Chebaniuk, *Sevastopol'* (1957), 113–14.

47. Doronina and Iakovleva, *Pamiatniki Sevastopol'ia*, 103–4.

Chebaniuk and Doronina highlighted their feat and included their oath. Chebaniuk reported the full oath, but Doronina distilled it to its three main points: "Under no condition surrender to captivity. Fight the enemy the Black Sea way (po-chernomorski), to the last drop of blood. Be brave, masculine to the end." She conveniently omitted point one of the oath which repeated Stalin's infamous directive to take "not one step back."

Disregarding signs of compulsion and relating these stories of heroic deeds and others like them obscured the fact that many acts of heroism may have been resignation to fate. Knowing that blocking units would kill them if they retreated and hoping that their deaths would not be in vain, some Soviet soldiers likely sacrificed their lives hoping to kill some of the enemy. The World War II generation wanted to ignore the fact that those too frightened to fight had been compelled to do so. The younger generations reading these texts were to be told that all were brave and all were heroes and that when the time came, Sevastopol and its defenders would emulate those feats and fulfill their debt to future generations like a dying soldier named Kaliuzhnyi who wrote "My Motherland! Russian land! . . . I kept my oath. Kaliuzhnyi."[48] Not surprisingly for a city already near the center of Russian national identity for two great defenses in one century, Kaliuzhnyi's sacrifice was for his "Russian land."

Doronina and Dobry generally omitted detailed discussion of individual heroes and instead directed readers' attention to the larger complexes of communal remembrance that became more common during Brezhnev's reign. Perhaps as a reaction against the cult of personality of the Stalin years, monuments since the 1960s highlighted groups more often than individuals. Doronina and the post-Soviet authors followed suit and spread the umbrella of heroism over a broad audience. Doronina focused on monuments to military divisions; post-Soviet guides concentrated mainly on even larger groups. The most recent guides have omitted all monuments to individual World War II heroes and even the multiethnic rifle divisions discussed by Doronina. The individual still matters, however, because nineteenth-century naval heroes are discussed at length. Perhaps the location of the monuments Chebaniuk favored, which are located at the site of action in the city's outskirts, are too far off the beaten path for today's tourists. Also, authors may judge that contemporary tourists are too detached from the war to know or care much about individual feats. Instead, twenty-first-century guides have accommodated the time-sensitive tourist by including centrally located monuments. The Memorial to the Heroes of the Defense on the chief square and traffic node of the city lists various heroes of the Soviet Union, but with its eternal flame it honors all who fought and died for Sevastopol. The Hero-City Obelisk and Monument to Victory honor the city and all who fought for it. The Sapun Hill complex is the

48. Ibid., 104–5.

only World War II site outside the city center to merit inclusion in post-Soviet guidebooks.

Why this shift? It could be that the luster of hagiographic images of heroes has dulled and that guidebook authors are content with providing a few examples. Without state censorship authors are freer to include what they choose. Rather than laboriously cover each example of heroism, guidebook authors have opted for portraying the overall collective heroism of the defenders of World War II. The explosion of commemoration in the last quarter-century that added roughly five hundred monuments to the city landscape made comprehensive coverage impossible and likely seemed excessive for generations with no direct contact to the war.[49] Besides, as one guidebook noted: "one must judge that many monuments are either excessively grandiose or simplistic (*prostovaty*)."[50] With the war generation long out of power, post-Soviet monument construction has slowed, and authors are taking a more balanced approach to the city's military past. Therefore, recent guidebooks honor the war and the valor of fighting, but individual heroes have less meaning for them and their readers. With the passing of many World War II veterans, municipal officials have decided it is time to honor other servicemen in a collective fashion. For example, in 1999 a large cross atop a star represented the Sevastopol citizens who fought in Afghanistan.[51]

Recapturing the Past

After almost a decade of post-Soviet economic stagnation, the Ukrainian economy started to strengthen rapidly beginning in 1999.[52] With this boom came more attention from the outside world and an investment in infrastructure (e.g., hotels and restaurants) catering to tourists. Sevastopol and much of the Ukrainian hinterland have developed more slowly than Kiev, but relative prosperity may be in sight. At the dawn of the twenty-first century, Sevastopol and the surrounding region began what could be a new economic industry to complement the fishing, wine-making, and ship construction and repair industries that have been central to the region for so long. In 1996, after roughly six decades as a closed city, Sevastopol began to welcome tourists from the former Soviet Union and further abroad, which caused a recent guidebook author to title his first chapter "Sevastopol-Open City!"[53] Approximately five hundred

49. In 1978 Doronina counted 739 monuments, and in 1999 there were 2,015 monuments registered with the city. See Doronina and Iakovleva, *Pamiatniki Sevastopol'ia*, 3; and Dobry and Borisova, *Welcome to Sevastopol*, 46.

50. *Sevastopol': putevoditel'*, 37.

51. Ibid., 37; Khapaev and Zolotarev, *Legendarnyi Sevastopol'*, 95.

52. Jason Bush, "Will the Boom Last in Ukraine?" *Business Week*, 8 November 2004, 62.

53. *Sevastopol': putevoditel'*.

thousand tourists visit Sevastopol each year; about fifteen thousand visitors came from outside the former Soviet Union.[54] Although the gains so far have been modest, Sevastopol appears ready to tap into several tourism markets.

Early twenty-first century guidebooks, while retaining the focus on the city's heroic past, have started to cater to a new audience. As one guidebook notes, "Sevastopol is neither only a fleet nor only a museum. It is an incomparably beautiful and affable city, welcoming guests with its glow."[55] Three things separate most post-Soviet guidebooks from their predecessors: less attention to the individual heroes of World War II, greater elaboration on opportunities for leisure beyond historical tourism including renewed attention to the city's beauty, and slightly more discussion of ethnic and religious diversity.

The city's premiere symbols like the Monument to Scuttled Ships, Kazarskii's memorial, and the Crimean War Panorama remain the focal points of post-Soviet guidebooks and carry on the tradition of noting the heroism, courage, and sacrifice of the city's defenders. The trends continue of placing sacrifice at the center of Sevastopol's mythology, while avoiding mention of disasters that could not be redeemed by leading to an ultimate victory or greater good.[56]

The change to profit-driven publication also has greatly decreased the length of guidebooks, which necessitates an even more selective portrayal of the past. Tourist-consumers are likely demanding more attention to the comforts that they now associate with vacations. With the opening of the city came a need for guidebooks to tell nonresidents about transportation, accommodations, and leisure. Some guides reproduce extensive train schedules and maps of train, trolleybus, and fixed-route taxi lines.[57] Rarely does one find this level of detail in postwar Soviet-era guides, because a touring agency arranged transport. The list of excursions in Sevastopol's Soviet-era guidebooks often included trolley numbers for various destinations, but as a rule these guides contained no detailed maps for reasons of military security.

In a shift from "active leisure," post-Soviet guidebooks also provide much more attention to restful places, like beaches, and highlight the natural beauty of the city and region as is common in general descriptions of Crimea. With a nod to more consumer-driven tourism, guidebooks provide locations and working hours for markets, souvenir stands, restaurants, and stores.[58] Several guidebooks tell the readers about vineyards and retailers.[59] Authors note the

54. "Travel Ukraine" (2004), www.ukrtravel.com/Sevastopol/main.htm (last consulted 21 December 2005).

55. Khapaev and Zolotarev, *Legendarnyi Sevastopol'*, 3.

56. Ibid., 46–48.

57. Ibid., 152–57.

58. *Sevastopol': putevoditel'*; Dobry and Borisova, *Welcome to Sevastopol*; Khapaev and Zolotarev, *Legendarnyi Sevastopol'*.

59. For example, see *Sevastopol': putevoditel'*, 88–89; and Dobry and Borisova, *Welcome to Sevastopol*, 118–22.

location, sometimes with maps, of the city's various beaches and enumerate some of the amenities of each. Beaches in Sevastopol were wildly popular in Soviet times for locals, but they were rarely mentioned in guidebooks because the focus remained on knowledge, not pure pleasure in Sevastopol.[60] Post-Soviet authors seem to understand that many tourists want to relax and therefore promote Sevastopol's beaches in an attempt to lure tourists away from Yalta. The city government has acted in concert to beautify recreation areas to appeal to the foreign visitor. For example, in 2004 city officials began the process of demilitarizing Balaklava, the site of much Crimean War tourism, and cleaning up ordinance and other ecological dangers "for further development of Balaklava as a resort-recreation zone."[61]

From the outset, post-Soviet guides made natural beauty a complement to the city's historical attractions. After noting that "Sevastopol, 'where each stone is history,' is a unique museum under an open sky," one publisher asserted that it has everything for "any taste and purse."[62] He described the bays, hills, numerous cafes and shops, tree-lined streets and more. Not wasting a chance for hyperbole, another author concluded that "Sevastopol is one of the most beautiful cities in the world. . . . It is right to consider Crimea the most museum-like (*muzeinyi*) region of Ukraine, and in Crimea—Sevastopol."[63] The chance for romance was a new lure for tourists, too: "The incomparably romantic aura of this city penetrates the soul and remains there forever. It wants to come back to breathe this velvet air, dip into the waves of the tender sea, and look at the silhouettes of the ships."[64] This type of boosterism was imperative as Sevastopol fought for tourist dollars. "Sevastopol," asserted one guidebook, "is almost unknown to the wider resort public." Most view it as a "military city, the great port of Crimea, a city of ships and sailors. Not more than two people out of a hundred identify Sevastopol as a resort."[65] The author even tried to personify the city, asking the reader to "feel its pulse, its vibration, its breathing."[66]

The most striking changes in the twenty-first century, outside of topics dealing with Soviet-era politics, have come in the treatment of Sevastopol's multiethnic past. Whereas Soviet guidebooks minimized or excluded the understanding of the city's ethnic past, post-Soviet guidebooks have embraced much of it and even expanded the perceived borders of the city to incorporate nearby

---

60. Beach restoration and maintenance were key points in the accommodation plans of postwar reconstruction. For one such discussion see Rossiiskii gosudarstvennyi arkhiv ekonomii, f. 9432, op. 1, d. 387, ll. 371–75.

61. "Demilitarizatsiia Balaklavskoi bukhty uspeshno vypolniaetsia," *Sevastopol'skaia gazeta*, 28 October 2004.

62. Khapaev and Zolotarev, *Legendarnyi Sevastopol'*, 1.

63. *Sevastopol': putevoditel'*, 26.

64. Khapaev and Zolotarev, *Legendarnyi Sevastopol'*, 1.

65. *Sevastopol': putevoditel'*, 76.

66. Ibid., 26.

Tatar and Karaite sites. While this could be seen as finally admitting the non-Slavic past of the region, it appears to be more profit motivated than a step toward reconciliation. Guidebooks, in short, began to meet the needs of the developing capitalist tourist industry and the various travel cultures it has engendered. Renewed attention to non-Slavs may draw visitors hoping to reclaim some of their own past and others who desire a sense of the exotic, for which Crimea has been known since Pushkin's famous poem "The Fountain of Bakhchisarai."

Most post-Soviet guides recognize the city's multiethnic, multidenominational character. Taking advantage of the near absence of the ethnic "other" after the slaughter of Jews and the repression and deportation of Tatars, Greeks, and others in World War II, authors initially omitted or at least minimized the past influence of non-Slavic groups. It was only after the collapse of the Soviet Union that many people rediscovered Sevastopol's multiethnic past. "The history of the defense of the city," according to a 1995 memorial book, "is full of examples of massive heroism of its defenders—sons and daughters of various peoples."[67] Post-Soviet guidebooks have become more explicit in retelling part of the history of the "small peoples" of Sevastopol and its region. One book, for example, includes a discussion of the Crimean Khanate in its "Great History" section. Moreover, the authors provide an extended discussion of Sevastopol's Karaite tradition, even noting that several prerevolutionary Karaites "played a significant role in the fate of the city, becoming honorific citizens."[68]

Persistence of Memory

Over a decade after the collapse of the Soviet Union, many of the images created during the Soviet period and the guidebooks it produced should have faded as the generation that survived the war and supported the Soviet Union dies out. Because much of the postwar cult of victory was orchestrated to bolster support of the regime, World War II has started to lose some of its power, although sixtieth anniversary celebrations of Victory Day (9 May) still find their way into political discourse. Just as the memory of the Crimean War persisted into the Soviet period, so, too, the images of the Soviet Union and World War II persist in now independent Ukraine. A giant statue of Lenin still towers over the city from the high central hill, and his name still graces one of the streets that make up the central ring road and the central administrative region. The street named for his brother remains near the ancient ruins of Khersones. Heroes from the Crimean War, the revolutionary period and World War

67. *Gorod-geroi Sevastopol': kniga pamiati*, 2 vols. (Simferopol, 1995), 2: 14–15.
68. On the Crimean Khanate, see Khapaev and Zolotarev, *Legendarnyi Sevastopol'*, 17–19, 86–87.

II continue to be honored with streets in their names as Sevastopol has shunned the iconoclasm so common in eastern Europe in the 1990s.

The persistence and perpetuation of memory reached a crescendo in 2003–2004. As Sevastopol turned 220 years old, it celebrated the 150th anniversary of the Crimean War and the 60th anniversary of the liberation of Sevastopol (May) and Ukraine (October). Tourists, including Prince Phillip of Great Britain, flocked to the city to commemorate various events. Newspapers from the communist *Sevastopol'skaia pravda* to the more mainstream *Slava Sevastopol'* (Glory to Sevastopol) and *Sevastopol'skaia gazeta* carried historical articles about the two mid-century defenses and remembrances from veterans of the latter one. Television channels also aired reports on the various celebrations as well as brief documentaries. Posters lined store windows, and publications on the Crimean War and World War II filled bookstore shelves. The interested buyer could even buy multilingual postcards celebrating the 150th anniversary of the Crimean War. The fold-out cards had historical images adjacent to the same scene from the present.[69] Thus the education of the traveler about Sevastopol's past continues.

At least a dozen private tour agencies have established an international presence and actively promote the city as a tourist center. But although there may be economic benefits, some residents also see problems. The communist newspaper notes that the city is "advertising Sevastopol as a tourist center. Despite that, the city cannot arrange to pick up the trash in the city center."[70] The question that only time can answer is whether tourism will continue to increase after this momentous anniversary year, and if so, will it have a positive or negative effect on the persistence of memory? Will, for example, the need to attract foreign tourists begin to turn the city's history into a "greatest hits" package that can easily be consumed in a two- or three-day stay? Guidebooks have already distilled the city's history; focused tourism could further narrow the scope. The advent of ecological and extreme tourism could also draw visitors away from the central naval identity of the city that has persisted for two centuries. Conversely, some events deemed politically taboo in Soviet times (like Tatar deportations) may be discussed more openly and engender more tourism. Will increased tourism bring the past closer to the younger generation of residents who have grown up without the proximity of the war that their great-grandparents fought? The city's history is still taught in school and young couples still make the obligatory tour of monuments on their wedding day, but do they understand them with the same depth as their elders?

Interest in local history is still prominent, but the depth of remembrance may indeed be giving way. In 2004 forty-two teams of students from the city

69. "Sevastopol': 150–letiiu Krymskoi (Vostochnoi) voiny" (n.d.).
70. "Pochemu pod rukovoditeliam lomaiutsia stul'ia," *Sevastopol'skaia pravda*, 18 October 2004.

matched wits in "intellectual games" about ancient and medieval Khersones, the Crimean War, and the region's nature.[71] Over seven hundred young students from Donets Oblast "visited historical and memorial places, [and] placed flowers at the Memorial of Hero Defenders of Sevastopol in 1941–1942."[72] The naval news program "Reflection" also reported on the visit of a school group from St. Petersburg studying the city as a Russian naval outpost and the birthplace of Orthodox Christianity for the East Slavs.[73] Despite these events, teenagers interviewed at various sites of memory around the city generally recognized the names of some of the prominent events and people in the city's history like those discussed above, but few could elaborate on why they had been honored with monuments. Conversely, most residents in their mid-thirties and older provided detailed (if not always completely accurate) synopses of the events in question.[74] For visitors, however, there can only be positive benefits from greater openness.

One also wonders whether the further "Ukrainianization" of the city will change attitudes. At the beginning of the new millennium, at almost the same time that Presidents Putin and Kuchma appeared at the reopening of St. Vladimir Cathedral, the city placed a statue to the Ukrainian literary hero Taras Shevchenko in front of the Gagarin regional administration building. Local citizens, the overwhelming majority of whom do not speak Ukrainian, were less than happy about a monument to someone with no connection to the city. Several people explained that this was more than Russophilia or Ukrainophobia because they fully accepted monuments to Ukrainians, Armenians, Georgians, and more who fought and died defending the city. What they resent, they say, is a revered Ukrainian artist standing figuratively alongside military heroes simply because he has become the one clear symbol of the Ukrainian nation.

One plausible explanation for this persistence of memory is that the repetition of a standard set of images over five decades has created an indelible mark on public remembrance. Guidebooks surely played a role in educating residents and nonresidents alike. Whereas schools and local newspapers reinforced the central images, nonresidents had to rely on guidebooks as one of their main sources for understanding Sevastopol and its role in Russian and Soviet history. Even faced with the momentous collapse of the Soviet Union, the city's identity has changed little. Of course, it is no longer defender of the Soviet Union, and many of the Russian nationalists would say that it should not defend Ukraine either. Much like in the guidebooks themselves, politics

71. "Nachinaiutsia turniry znatokov-kraevedov," *Slava Sevastopol'ia*, 23 October 2004.

72. "Spetspoezd s donetskimi det'mi," *Sevastopol'skaia gazeta*, 28 October 2004.

73. "Otrazhenie," NTS (Independent Television of Sevastopol), 22 October 2004.

74. The author conducted informal interviews with teenagers at memorial sites, as well as some formal interviews with adults. Interview with Mikhail Mironov (Sevastopol, Ukraine, 2004); interview with Vladimir Semenov (Sevastopol, Ukraine, 2004); interview with Liliia Korchinskaia (Sevastopol, Ukraine, 2004).

was a mere veneer over the more deeply felt affinities. Some specific events like World War II may rise and fall in prominence as the generation in power changes, but the heritage of courage, valor, and sacrifice, despite the city's peaceful present, will continue.

Guidebooks changed with the times. World War II valor became a new chapter in invented tradition; and by the 1960s the frontline soldiers had become political leaders, and sites of memory to the war proliferated at a staggering rate. Likewise, guidebook authors began to shift the war to the foreground in their retelling of local histories, but the prewar and prerevolutionary past remained strong currents in urban biographies during and after the Soviet period. The collapse of the Soviet Union ushered in the greatest change in guidebooks with the birth of a profit-driven tourist industry that must cater to the demands of the market. While capitalism and democracy in independent Ukraine have led to changes in the balance between past and present, knowledge and entertainment, much of Sevastopol's identity as a hero-city has remained intact while city and business leaders try to layer on a new image of resort par excellence to rival Yalta and other more familiar Crimean attractions. Sevastopol's guidebooks created or reaffirmed its image as the defender-city of heroism and sacrifice, but for whom?[75] How readers made sense of what they read and saw, we can only speculate.

Sevastopol is in the midst of reinventing itself as a tourist resort destination. While the sacred heroes of World War II have not yet had their hagiographies questioned, they are being marginalized in current guidebooks and Web sites. Although we cannot predict how Sevastopol's identity might change in the future, the repetition of heroic myths certainly created an identity for the city that is still strong and will likely remain for some time, especially if the population remains three-fourths Russian by nationality.

75. Bush, "Reviewing Rome." Francine Hirsch calls this "virtual travel" in "Getting to Know 'The Peoples of the USSR': Ethnographic Exhibits as Soviet Virtual Tourism, 1923–1934," *Slavic Review* 62, no. 4 (2003): 683–709.

CHAPTER 9

Marketing Socialism

Inturist in the Late 1950s and Early 1960s

Shawn Salmon

"My new guide wanted my shoes," writes the young British tourist James Kirkup in an account of his travels to the Soviet Union in 1966. Having visited the Hermitage with this "fashionably dressed" and "refreshingly decadent" young man, Kirkup realizes that he and his western compatriots have supplied much of the clothing (an "American nylon shirt and one of those awful American bow ties" as well as a "Beatle haircut") worn by the local host.

Not to his surprise, at the end of the tour, a series of offers is made: first rubles for the shoes, which Kirkup rejects; then U.S. dollars, which he also refuses. The guide's "thin gaunt face seemed to grow even thinner with hidden anguish, cunning, and greed. He was like a spoilt child who is denied a sweet or a toy," Kirkup writes. There is a proposal to change dollars for rubles at a rate very advantageous to the British tourist; another rejection. Then, "without saying a word," according to Kirkup, "I slipped off my shoes and gave them to him. I did not want his money. I wanted to show him that outside of Russia there are people who will do something for nothing, who despise money and who are not always seeking their own advantage. I walked away in my stockinged feet."[1]

Numerous such stories from this period depict western visitors to the Soviet Union returning home, like Kirkup, more scantily clad than when they arrived. In most instances, they are described as having been "fleeced," "scalped," or just "stripped" of their goods.[2] Whatever the object, through theft or trade, bargaining, buying or direct giving, tourists often left the country lighter than they came. It was a law of the day that if the tourist sold everything the Russian wanted to buy, he would continue his journey "naked

---

1. James Kirkup, *One Man's Russia* (London, 1968), 121.

2. See, for example, Yuri Brokhin, *Hustling on Gorky Street: Sex and Crime in Russia Today*, trans. E. B. Kane (New York, 1975), 10. Reports sent by the minister of foreign affairs to the Communist Party Central Committee list instances of theft or trade where the tourist was often left without any clothes; see, for example, Perevertkin, "Pis'mo TsK KPSS," 29 June 1956, Gosudarstvennyi arkhiv Rossiiskoi Federatsii (hereafter GARF), f. 9401, op. 2, d. 465, l. 146 (follow-up report l. 270). Sometimes the "fleecing" was a reference to the low quality of service in relation to the price charged for the tour by Inturist; see, for example, James Drane, *Pilgrimage to Utopia* (Milwaukee, 1965), 7.

as a jaybird."[3] In contrast, according to most travelers, the Soviets walked away from such deals with their clothing "lumpy with books and butts."[4]

What distinguishes Kirkup's remarks from many others of its kind, however, is the tourist's disdain for the trade, his joy in snubbing the Soviet by dismissing the market itself. Indeed, trade was the name of the game played by the *fartsovshchiki* of the day.[5] In travelogues and popular magazines, visitors relate endless tales of being chased by black marketers and harassed by "easy women" who hoped to profit from an evening of entertainment.[6] Some, as in Kirkup's case, found nothing more offensive than to be reduced in character from a well-traveled gentleman to a nameless representative of British mass consumer society.

Inturist, the Soviet state administration for foreign tourism, considered all of this activity a scourge to its operations. Its representatives publicly denied the existence of a black market while focusing internally on the negative impressions these encounters might create.[7] It was more than just a question of social ills, however: the black market inspired fear among Inturist officials as their work grew increasingly commercial during this period. Competing against the street traders for a limited supply of available dollars proved a difficult venture.[8] Just as fartsovshchiki looked to foreigners as a source of supply for their own deals, Inturist leaders at this time maintained high hopes that western tourists would do what was expected of them: they would consume socialism in whatever form Inturist offered it. For this is what Inturist was selling.

3. Edward Diedrich, "The Rose-Colored World of Intourist," *National Review* 19, no. 23 (1967): 638. In later years, tourists comment instead on how they packed extra clothes and goods in anticipation of black marketers.

4. E. J. Kahn, "Recollections of an Intourist Tourist," *New Yorker* no. 34 (20 December 1958): 44.

5. The term "fartsovshchik" is typically translated as "black marketeer" or just "trader." A. Panov, *Fartsovshchiki* (London, 1971), 34.

6. See, for example, Drane, *Pilgrimage to Utopia*, 42, 48–50; Ludmila Koehler, "A Cultural Encounter: U.S. Students Visit the USSR," *Russian Review* 29, no. 4 (1970): 443; and Diedrich, "Rose-Colored World," 638. In the archives, see L. Seregina, "Soobshchenie o rabote narodnoi druzhiny po okhrane obshchestvennogo poriadka v gostinitse Turisty za 1959 g.," 1959, Tsentral'nyi munitsipal'nyi arkhiv Moskvy (hereafter TsMAM), f. 496, op. 1, d. 396, l. 1. The problem of prostitution in Soviet hotels where foreigners stayed gained widespread attention among Soviet citizens in 1988 with the publication of the book (later adapted for film) by Vladimir Kunin, *Interdevochka* (Moscow, 1988). Space constraints do not permit a separate discussion of this important topic or of the black market to which it was so fundamentally tied.

7. "Spravka o besede Predsedatelia Pravleniia VAO Inturist tov. Ankudinova, V. M. s gruppoi predstavitelei turistskikh firm i zhurnalistov iz SShA, Frantsii i Bel'gii," 9 April 1960, GARF, f. 9518, op. 1, d. 632, l. 293; "Stenogramma zasedaniia Komissii po inostrannym delam Prezidiuma Verkhovnogo Soveta RSFSR," 7 October 1964, GARF, f. 385, op. 13, d. 1755, l. 73.

8. Annual notes on the black market in the Soviet Union can be found in *Pick's Currency Yearbook* (New York). See also Gregory Grossman, *A Tonsorial View of the Soviet Second Economy*, Berkeley-Duke Occasional Papers on the Second Economy in the USSR, no. 4 (December 1985).

To date, the emphasis in much of the literature on foreign tourism in the Soviet Union has been to frame it as a uniquely political endeavor and to dismiss questions of Inturist's business as secondary or even extraneous. Such arguments are rooted in a conceptualization of tourism as a subset of cultural exchange rather than a unique proposition rooted in the context of the international travel market. Though the economics of tourism to the Soviet Union have recently garnered some attention from scholars,[9] those who have written about cultural relations argue that tourism was primarily a way to influence foreign opinion abroad.[10] Inturist in all accounts appears alternatively as an institution shepherding the pilgrims of the sympathetic, left-leaning western elite or as an institutional arm of the Soviet security apparatus, employing various "techniques of hospitality" to ensure that visitors drew the right conclusions about Soviet society.[11]

A close study of Inturist's archives and the papers of several related institutions suggests, however, that from the start of its work, Inturist was deemed (and its leaders referred to it as) a "commercial" institution with tasks tied closely to the financial needs of the state.[12] Certainly, as Diane Koenker argues in her discussion of the joint-stock company Sovetskii Turist, the question of profit was present and problematic even in early attempts to define proletarian tourism within the Soviet Union. In these debates, "commerce" and "politics" functioned as proxies for one ideological position (those willing to cater to any social segment/"market" for the sake of income) or the other (those for "proletarian purity"). Inturist took a strong stance on the issue, arguing from the start that unlike other groups working with foreign visitors—such as VOKS, the All-Union Society for Cultural Relations—it had been given the responsibility of fulfilling "economic" (*khoziaistvennye*) goals.[13] Officials thus re-

9. Matthias Heeke, *Reisen zu den Sowjets: Der ausländische Tourismus in Rußland 1921–1941* (Münster, 2003).

10. See M. S. Kuz'min, *Deiatel'nost' partii i Sovetskogo gosudarstva po razvitiiu mezhdunarodnykh i kul'turnykh sviazei SSSR 1917–1932* (Leningrad, 1971), 32; A. E. Ioffe, *Internatsional'nye, nauchnye i kul'turnye sviazi Sovetskogo Soiuza 1928–1932* (Moscow, 1969); and G. P. Dolzhenko, *Istoriia turizma v dorevoliutsionnoi Rossii i SSSR* (Rostov-on-Don, 1988), 150.

11. Sylvia Margulies, *Pilgrimage to Russia: The Soviet Union and the Treatment of Foreigners, 1924–1937* (Madison, Wisc., 1968); Frederick Barghoorn, *The Soviet Cultural Offensive: The Role of Cultural Diplomacy in Soviet Foreign Policy* (Princeton, N.J., 1960); Paul Hollander, *Political Pilgrims: Travels of Western Intellectuals to the Soviet Union, China, and Cuba, 1928–1978* (New York, 1981). On selective perceptions by western intellectuals of the "costs" of Soviet modernization, see also David Engerman, *Modernization from the Other Shore: American Intellectuals and the Romance of Russian Development* (Cambridge, Mass., 2004).

12. Inturist was officially founded as a joint-stock company which had the right to function as a market-based institution. For a good discussion of this type of Soviet organization, see John Quigley, *The Soviet Foreign Trade Monopoly: Institutions and Laws* (Columbus, Ohio, 1974), 105–12. Declassified files from Inturist's highly sensitive "first department" include hard-currency plans for the organization from 1932 to 1963. See, for example, GARF, f. 9612, op. 2, d. 10.

13. Most scholars have distinguished the organizations in terms of the types of visitors they served. This is true, but one senses early on that responsibilities were divided more fundamentally

solved what otherwise seemed an essential paradox of Soviet socialism; this dependency on international capital—which was nevertheless acquired in monopolistic fashion through government bodies—was critical to the construction of the new state.[14]

This chapter explores the significance of trade in Inturist's operations in the late 1950s and early 1960s. It suggests that though the receipt of foreign currency had always been central to Inturist's work, this became a top concern—one might say even an obsession—among officials at this time. The intensive reevaluation of what Inturist should sell to foreign visitors was primarily the result of new principles in Soviet economics, though also shaped by trends in contemporary political culture. Indeed, insofar as the Cold War was fought "in the kitchen," the shift to considering tourists' consumer desires is somewhat to be expected.[15] Nor is it surprising given that the type of tourist and foreign travelers' vision of Soviet life had changed since the 1930s; though certainly just as curious about the great experiment in the "East," tourists to the Soviet Union came in greater numbers, were more predominantly middle-class, and, in the context of the Cold War, were less sympathetic to Soviet socialism by the 1960s.[16] Inturist officials were sophisticated in their ability to detect that a visitor's eye for material goods (as opposed to more blatantly "socialist" symbols like factories) was now an important factor in the judgments they would make about the new superpower. What could Inturist offer beyond the traditional package tour of hotel accommodation, guides, cultural excursions, and tickets to various events, meals, and transportation? Rather than discussing the "proper" socialist sites to show guests, officials began to question the possibility of offering an entirely original suite of consumer goods and services. As with the Yugoslav officials described by Wendy Bracewell, however, Inturist officials were never sure how best to capture this audience. This

---

over the issue of whether the institution was able to act in international markets. See Margulies, *Pilgrimage to Russia*, 33.

14. In her study of Torgsin, Elena Osokina makes a similar argument that sales of goods in hard currency to foreigners in the 1930s helped to fund industrialization: E. A. Osokina, "Za zerkal'noi dver'iu Torgsina," *Otechestvennaia istoriia*, no. 2 (1995): 86–104. For a discussion of the role of international capital in the Soviet economy by an early policy maker, see L. N. Yurovsky, *Currency Problems and Policy of the Soviet Union* (London, 1925).

15. Susan Reid, "Cold War in the Kitchen: Gender and the De-Stalinization of Consumer Taste in the Soviet Union under Khrushchev," *Slavic Review* 61, no. 2 (2002): 211–52.

16. These assertions are based on my own readings of British and American travelogues, some of which are discussed in this chapter. Inturist's archive contains surprisingly little sociological research about its own visitors with a few critical exceptions such as A. M. Rumiantsev, "Ob otnoshenii amerikanskikh turistov k SSSR do i posle poezdki v nashu stranu," 24 September 1968, Rossiiskii gosudarstvennyi arkhiv noveishei istorii (hereafter RGANI), f. 5, op. 60, d. 43, ll. 60–71. This report suggests that the majority of Americans were working professionals, businessmen, or students. Part of the difficulty of making generalizations about tourist demographics is that Inturist's system for tracking visitors changed in the postwar period from one that was class-based to one that categorized visitors by the purpose of their trip (travel for religious purposes, health, business, etc.).

same movement toward catering to guests' (assumed) desires exposed internal doubt about who Inturist's visitors were and what expectations they had about their experience in the country.

Inturist and the Soviet Economy

Efforts to reconstruct Soviet tourist infrastructure in the wake of World War II were rooted in the simultaneous transformation of Soviet economic values.[17] Not only did the war reshape ideas about the movement of people across borders, but questions of trade were also given new attention as various European governments sought to rebuild economies. Already by 1945 the idea that tourism would solve balance-of-trade payment problems was recirculated in the Soviet press.[18] Inturist officials were quick to adopt it again in their own official pronunciations about the importance of work in the travel industry.[19] By 1959 they publicly declared the "doors to the USSR" to be open again for visitors of all countries.[20] New relationships with tourist firms abroad were swiftly brokered. By 1957 Inturist began to see roughly five times the number of annual visitors as in the prewar period. Though still small compared to traffic to the major European tourist centers, this number would double again to roughly one million between 1957 and 1965.[21]

The shift in thinking about Soviet trade with foreign countries was symbolized in part by the reorganization of banking structures in the early 1960s with Vneshtorgbank, the bank of foreign trade, now responsible for managing the financing of ventures abroad.[22] Public pronouncements by figures like Nikita Khrushchev also pointed to this change.[23] Not only was foreign trade sanctioned, but the higher costs of fighting the Cold War—especially those associated with the opening of military and intelligence outposts abroad—required

17. Inturist's postwar work was outlined in a decree "on measures to further develop tourism" from the Council of Ministers in May 1956. V. Ankudinov, "Prikaz no. 6 po Pravleniiu VAO Inturist," 29 May 1956, GARF, f. 9612, op. 2, d. 228, ll. 13–16.

18. A. Gorchakov, "Ob inostrannom turizme," *Vneshniaia torgovlia* no. 10 (1945): 22–26.

19. V. Ankudinov, "Strana prinimaet gostei: turizm—delo interesnoe i vygodnoe," *Izvestiia* article as clipped in GARF, f. 9612, op. 3, d. 9.

20. G. Bulgakov and V. Ankudinov, "Dveri v SSSR shiroko otkryty dlia turistov vsekh stran," *Vneshniaia torgovlia* no. 6 (1959): 26–27.

21. "Statistika v"ezda inostrannykh grazhdan v SSSR za 1956–1975 gg.," 1977, GARF, f. 9612, op. 3, d. 1119, l. 3. Though tourism statistics vary as much as the methodologies used to calculate them, it appears that more Americans traveled to France in 1960 than did the total number of international tourists to the Soviet Union the same year. See Christopher Endy, *Cold War Holidays: American Tourism to France* (Chapel Hill, N.C., 2004), 8.

22. George Garvy, *Money, Financial Flows, and Credit in the Soviet Union* (Cambridge, Mass., 1977), 151–52.

23. N. S. Khrushchev, "Vneshniaia torgovlia—zdorovaia i prochnaia osnova mirnogo sosushchestvovaniia gosudarstv," *Vneshniaia torgovlia* no. 3 (1959): 1–8.

new sources of hard-currency income and a new method of planning for this growing sector of economic activity.[24]

Indeed, the Soviet state was trading vastly more than it had been in the pre-World War II years. The average annual volume of imports (in millions of rubles) was roughly fourteen times greater in the 1955–1965 period than it had been between 1930 and 1940. Moreover, trade with capitalist countries, though hovering only between 20 percent and 30 percent of the total volume in the postwar years, consistently increased in absolute terms on an annual basis beginning in 1954, when it first crossed the billion ruble mark. By 1966 this number would be more than four times what it had been just a decade earlier.[25]

Finally, though many of the changes proposed by Inturist leaders were inspired by Khrushchev-era policies, it is clear that the more radical shift in thinking happened with the onset of the Evsei Liberman and Aleksei Kosygin reforms of 1964–1965. Liberman, a Soviet economist who as early as 1956 had begun arguing for revisions to enterprise planning, stirred debate in western circles by suggesting that the primary indicator of efficient planning and operations should be profit (surplus). While western specialists of Soviet policy were convinced that this move indicated a weakening of socialist principles in favor of a market model, Liberman defended the proposal with a rebuttal that profit itself was not antithetical to either system; rather each depended on and strove for economic efficiency and should use profit as an indicator of that efficiency. Under capitalism, however, profit was the goal and the "satisfaction of the needs of the population" was the means; in socialism, he argued, the opposite was true.[26] The language of the Liberman reforms, with its emphasis on efficiency, profits, and incentives for performance strongly biased the nature of Inturist's internal discussions about how to organize service for tourists.

Vladimir Ankudinov, head of Inturist from 1947 to 1968, was one of the most vocal supporters of the new focus on profits from tourism. Across count-

---

24. I. Grishin, "Spravka o valiutnom plane Ministerstva vneshnei torgovli po torgovo-nakladnym raskhodam v svobodno-konvertiruemoi valiute na 1962 god i o vozmozhnostiiakh sokrashchenii torgovo-nakladnykh raskhodov," 27 November 1962, RGANI, f. 5, op. 20, d. 219, ll. 8–11; M. Sveshchnikov, "Pis'ma Gosbanka v Sovet Ministrov SSSR ot 8 aprelia 1960 o merakh po uluchsheniiu valiutnogo planirovaniia," 19 August 1961, RGANI, f. 5, op. 20, d. 210, ll. 62–63. Hard currency mattered because the ruble was a nonconvertible, "internal accounting unit" (Garvy, *Money, Financial Flows, and Credit*, 135).

25. *Vneshniaia torgovlia SSSR: statisticheskii sbornik, 1918–1966* (Moscow, 1967), 9, 62–63. These numbers are likely skewed by the currency reform of 1961 when the ruble was denominated and devalued. Ultimately the percent of foreign trade relative to Soviet gross national product remained low (roughly 4 percent). See Garvy, *Money, Financial Flows, and Credit*, 137.

26. Evsei Liberman, "Profits and 'profits,' " *Soviet Life* article as reprinted in Evsei Liberman, *Theory of Profit in Socialist Economy: A Discussion on the Recent Economic Reforms in the USSR* (New Delhi, 1966), 18.

less publications within the USSR and abroad, Ankudinov argued that tourism was a miracle industry with "colossal" possibilities to spur Soviet economic growth.[27] Tourism, he argued, should be considered its own branch of the socialist economy, one that he was sure would bring millions of dollars annually to the country.[28] In this sense, the postwar context and, in particular, new lines of thinking about trade and the economy helped to shape the way the leaders of Inturist positioned their work. Officials were encouraged to engage with the market in order to sell socialism.

Marketing *Matreshki* and Martinis

Just what this focus on the market and profitability meant to Inturist was a more complicated question, however. Officials spent the better portion of the 1960s mapping out the specifics of their new vision. Not surprisingly, they grew concerned with finding ways to cut costs within the organization. Still more prominent in their discussions were questions about the range of consumer goods and services Inturist should now sell to foreign tourists. Yet those talks were rooted in a relatively narrow understanding of the "average" tourist from the West who, it was assumed, literally embodied the values of capitalist consumption. For the same reason, officials quickly fell into a conceptual trap. What would tourists want to buy? Would they want foreign things? What exactly did it mean to package and sell socialism? Among Inturist officials, there was little consensus about what the Soviet product was and what tourists expected to receive in exchange for the money they spent in this socialist paradise.

The decision to offer tourists more than what until then had been part of the standard suite of services in the package tour was decreed from the highest levels. According to Kosygin, who became chairman of the Council of Ministers in October 1964, 50 percent of Inturist's receipts in foreign currency were now to come from the sale of souvenirs and provisions to travelers.[29] Goods were to be sold in all areas visited by foreign tourists but especially in the newly opened Berezka stores.[30] The design and production of goods were to be

27. V. Ankudinov and V. Rozen, "Turizm kak otrasl' ekonomiki," *Novoe vremia* no. 34 (1966): 21–22.

28. "Discover Russia for Yourself," *Soviet Life* (March 1965): 52. In this interview, Ankudinov refers to "profit" in both senses of the term: as a function of gross receipts and of net values. My sense is that the latter usage of the term "profit" was becoming more popular in the 1960s and especially during the Liberman reforms.

29. As quoted in V. Isaev, "Reshenie o merakh po obespecheniiu razvitiia inostrannogo turizma v Leningrade," 7 August 1964, GARF, f. 10004, op. 1, d. 2, l. 12.

30. The first Berezka was opened in Moscow in January 1962. The stores were organized and managed by Vneshposyltorg under the Ministry of Foreign Trade. See S. Selivankin, "Pust' rastut Berezki," *Sovetskaia torgovlia* no. 3 (1962): 40–44. Selivankin's article hails the modern organization and style of trade practiced in the Berezka store while also making it clear that the chain was

managed by the Ministry of Trade at the level of the republic.[31] Plans for souvenir manufacturing in 1965–1966 within the Russian Federation, however, tapped into a wide range of official representations of Soviet life.[32] Instructions suggested that "inexpensive" but popular goods (key chains and cigarette lighters) should be sold, but luxury items such as perfumes, jewelry, and shot glasses were also to be made.[33] Images of Russian national culture gained expression through lacquer miniatures painted in the village of Fedoskino, while Russian factories were instructed to produce dolls in "national costume" and Central Asian skullcaps (*tiubeteiki*). Even objects of everyday use (souvenir soaps, razor blades, and men's ties) were to be manufactured for the foreign tourist market.

Similarly complicated was the range of experiences Inturist hoped to make available to guests. Central to the 1964 decrees "on the organization of trade in foreign currency" was a provision that called for the establishment of bars and cafés in the main Inturist hotels throughout the Soviet Union.[34] By the start of the 1965 season, hotels in Moscow, Leningrad, Kiev, Odessa, Sochi, Yalta, Tallinn, and Erevan were to be stocked with "high-quality wines and other types of vodka and cognac—some of which should be imported—as well as desserts, coffee, cocktails, and other goods produced within the country," all of which were to be sold for foreign currency. Instructions on the opening of bars made clear that they were designed "exclusively" for the service of foreigners but especially for those from the leisure-loving societies of the West. Borrowing heavily from European and American models, Inturist's bars were

---

designed for tourists. See also "Berezka," *Stroitel'stvo i arkhitektura Moskvy* no. 2 (1962): 14; and O. Paramonov, "Berezkiny den'gi," *Rodina*, no. 4 (1999): 74–75.

31. On the process of designing and producing souvenirs see G. Voronov, "Rasporiazhenie no. 4302r," 6 November 1964, GARF, f. 259, op. 45, d. 2322, ll. 1–11; "Rasporiazhenie," June 1965, GARF, f. 10004, op. 1, d. 11, ll. 121–22; I. Kaplan, "Bol'she suvenirov, khoroshikh i raznykh," *Sovetskaia torgovlia* no. 3 (1969): 23–26. There is a small but growing body of new work on souvenir production in the former Soviet Union. See Theresa Sabonis-Chafee, "Communism as Kitsch: Soviet Symbols in Post-Soviet Society," in *Consuming Russia: Popular Culture, Sex, and Society since Gorbachev*, ed. Adele Marie Barker (Durham, N.C., 1999), 362–81, and Stephanie Bunn, "Stealing Souls for Souvenirs or Why Tourists Want the 'Real' Thing?" in *Souvenirs: The Material Culture of Tourism*, ed. M. Hitchcock (Aldershot, UK, 2000), 166–85.

32. By far the strangest object in the RSFSR plans for 1965–1966 was a "slide rule in a case with souvenir design."

33. Indeed, the question of whether to sell tourists luxury items or affordable trinkets plagued officials. See V. Saburov, "Pis'mo nachal'niku upravleniia po inostrannomu turizmu pri Sovete Ministrov RSFSR tov. Krupinu, K. V.," 27 March 1965, GARF, f. 10004, op. 1, d. 11, l. 12; and V. Palavandishvili, "Pis'mo nachal'niku organizatsionno-metodicheskogo otdela Pravleniia VAO Inturist tov. Baranovu, P. N.," 28 January 1964, GARF, f. 9612, op. 1, d. 558, l. 23.

34. V. Ankudinov, "Prikaz po upravleniiu po inostrannomu turizmu pri Sovete Ministrov SSSR no. 24," 19 November 1964, GARF, f. 9612, op. 1, d. 598, l. 66. Note that there were bars in hotels in the prewar period, notably in the Natsional' in Moscow. Tat'iana Nikolaevskaia, *Isskustvo zhit' v Moskve: istoriia gostinitsy Natsional' 1903–2003* (Moscow, 2000), 149.

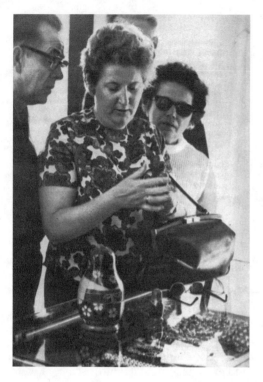

9.1. Shoppers examine souvenirs at a Berezka foreign currency shop. *Greater Sochi* (Moscow, 1968), 204.

to be "easy to relax in" and well stocked with ice for drinking water, a necessity for the average American tourist of the day.[35] Prices were to be listed in dollars, and the hours of operation were set from 6 pm to 2 am.[36]

   In spite of these efforts, some officials argued that to be successful, Inturist's offerings should be rooted even more overtly in western experience. Already by March 1965, for example, they decided that Abrau-Durso (a south Russian wine dating from the tsarist era), "Benediktin" liqueur, and cocktails prepared from recipes in a 1955 Russian collection were not all that popular among foreigners. Instead, it was suggested, "cocktails of European standards like the

---

   35. In the 1950s and 1960s, ice for drinking water was the clearest sign that a hotel was catering to American tourists. See Annabel Jane Wharton, *Building the Cold War: Hilton International Hotels and Modern Architecture* (Chicago, 2001), 2, 28, 97, and Endy, *Cold War Holidays*, 91.
   36. V. Ankudinov, "Prilozhenie No. 1 k prikazu po upravleniiu po inostrannomu turizmu pri Sovete Ministrov SSSR ot 19.11.64: Vremennaia instruktsiia po organizatsii torgovli prodovol'stvennymi tovarami na inostrannuiu valiutu," GARF, f. 9612, 1, d. 598, ll. 67–72. V. Vishniakov, "Prikaz po pravleniiu VAO Inturist no. 2b," 22 January 1965, GARF, f. 9612, op. 3, d. 6, l. 2.

Manhattan and Martini" should be studied and introduced in Inturist bars.[37] Similarly, Leonid Khodorkov argued that it was wrong to create new bars "based on the tastes and needs [*vkusy i potrebnosti*] of Soviet people while completely ignoring those of foreigners. Take cigarettes. To date we have no foreign brands of cigarettes. We could make a lot of money if we sold these," he argued.[38] The reality, of course, was that there was no coherent set of "foreign tastes," no instruction kit on international consumption practices. Originally American jazz was played in restaurants and bars. Then it was decided that Russian classics should be played. Similarly, meals were not considered "national"—that is, Russian—enough, and restaurants were eventually ordered to localize and thematize their offerings. Officials were caught in a bind as they attempted to capture a market about which they had only surface knowledge while still conveying key messages about Soviet life to foreign guests.

Indeed, the focus on generating sales gradually moved beyond the question of consumer goods as officials discussed an array of new services that the organization might offer tourists. Proposals were floated about forming a subdivision within Inturist that would organize congresses and symposia in Moscow and Leningrad, a sort of special events group.[39] Others suggested that investing in the construction of a concert hall where various events might be hosted in one of the larger Inturist hotels, such as the Aurora in Leningrad, might yield valuable returns.[40] The most successful catchword of the day, however, was far more general than either of these. "Additional services" (*dopolnitel'nye uslugi*)—which referred in Inturist's internal vocabulary to anything from hotel guest telephone calls to theater tickets to individual excursions that were purchased in addition to the original package tour—ultimately became the most trusted method of ensuring that tourists on the ground would spend just a bit more than they had originally planned.[41] By 1966 in Moscow, where the vast

37. "Dokumenty k protokolu no. 5 zasedanii kollegii upravleniia o vypolnenii postanovleniia Soveta Ministrov SSSR ot 16 aprelia 1964 g. po razvertyvaniiu torgovli na inostrannuiu valiutu v restoranakh Inturista," 22 March 1965, GARF, f. 9612, op. 3, d. 2, l. 113.

38. Leonid Khodorkov, "Protokol no. 12 zasedaniia pravleniia VAO Inturist," 18 December 1964, GARF, f. 9612, op. 1, d. 596, l. 11. Khodorkov was a prominent member of Inturist's board and served as vice-chairman of the organization in the late 1960s.

39. Interestingly enough, the idea was considered only after a "sharply competitive struggle" among several western firms to obtain exclusive rights to manage large congresses in the Soviet Union. Inturist took this as a sign that there was some money to be made here. See "Spravka o gruppe kongressov," 16 November 1964, GARF, f. 9612, op. 2, d. 596, ll. 32–40.

40. A. Anikin, "Pis'mo v Sovet Ministrov SSSR po voprosam stroitel'stva ob"ektov," June 1965, GARF, f. 9612, op. 3, d. 1, l. 13.

41. Representatives of foreign tour firms had regularly urged Inturist to change its price structure to enable greater profits and allow visitors more flexibility in their choice of services. The root of the problem was that Inturist's packaged tours cost too much, they argued. By reducing the total price and allowing visitors to purchase services on the ground in foreign currency, the total

9.2. Inturist brochure aimed at the international consumer of nested dolls and western cocktails.

majority of tourists stayed at some point during their trip, such additional services were offered via the Moscow Excursion Bureau and, in other cities, at the so-called Service Bureaus.[42]

Having studied western tour firms, Inturist officials recognized that none of these changes would pay off without concerted efforts to attract customers. For that reason, in addition to developing new service plans, they focused on creating more aggressive and smarter advertisements targeted to western markets. The first issue of the glossy color magazine *Puteshestvie v Sovetskii Soiuz* (Travel to the USSR)—clearly intended to reach a mass audience of lovers of travel and Soviet culture—appeared in 1966 and quickly became Inturist's primary advertising platform. Printed in Italy and translated into English, French, and German, the magazine included logistical information, historical descriptions of key cities on the tourist map, notes on Soviet fashion, and romantic tales of the far-off sites and exotic tastes one might experience while traveling in the USSR.[43] Similarly, Inturist became a regular presence in Soviet stands at exhibits abroad where representatives could be found handing out brochures, chatting with local businessmen, and displaying the latest in Soviet champagne, perfume, and cognac.[44] Even tourists themselves were seen as valuable material for more per-

number of tourists and revenues per tourist would increase. See, for example, "Zapis' Besedy Torgpreda SSSR v Norvegii t. Artem'eva M.K. s predsedatelem bergenskogo filiala firmy Norshk Fol'ke Ferie g-nom Khal'vorsenom," 14 August 1959, GARF, f. 9612, op. 1, d. 425, ll. 22–23.

42. I. Stepura and N. Sheviakov, "O merakh po obespecheniiu postupleniia inostrannoi valiuty ot prodazhi dopolnitel'nykh uslug," 7 February 1966, GARF, f. 9612, op. 3, d. 81, ll. 49–53. V. Ankudinov, "Prikaz nachal'nika upravleniia po inostrannomu turizmu pri Sovete Ministov SSSR no. 35," 30 March 1966, GARF, f. 9612, op. 3, d. 82, l. 61.

43. V. Ankudinov, "O merakh po obespecheniiu vypuska ezhekvartal'nogo informatsionno-reklamnogo prospekta zhurnal'nogo tipa—Puteshestvie v SSSR," January 1965, GARF, f. 9612, op. 3, d. 2, l. 6.

44. S. Safronov, "Pis'mo nachal'niku otdela reklamy i pechati upravleniia inostrannogo turizma pri Sovete Ministrov SSSR tov. Chernovu V. T." 15 June 1967, GARF, f. 9612, op. 3, d. 194, l. 23. "Dokumenty ob uchastii upravleniia v vystavkakh-iarmarkakh v FRG, Frantsii," October–

suasive ads. The deputy chairman of Inturist, Vladimir Boichenko, chided his colleagues in an October 1964 meeting for not taking advantage of the visit by a French parliamentary delegation to Moscow to generate ads for the western press.[45] Inturist had an effective monopoly on the organization of such groups. Why, Boichenko asked, had they not used it to attract more well-connected westerners to the Soviet Union?

If tourists were now valued for how much they could spend, Inturist officials were encouraged and encouraged others within the organization to reduce their costs. Tour leaders in Moscow and Leningrad were to plan their itineraries better in an effort to avoid excessive and expensive telegraphs between the center and periphery.[46] Additionally, it was suggested that guides should be penalized for bringing their tour groups late to the airport. Delayed or missed flights had led to consistently big losses for Inturist, so guides should cover these losses themselves, some argued.[47] (Likewise, the idea was proposed that guides and service bureau employees be financially rewarded when they successfully overfulfilled the plan for currency receipts.)[48] Finally, in areas of Inturist's work where income fell far below expected levels, officials investigated and made recommendations for improvements. When it was discovered in 1965 that tourists were not spending money at the restaurant in the Sheremet'evo international airport because only rubles were accepted there—and the restaurant was physically located beyond the customs point where foreigners were required to surrender any remaining Soviet currency—Inturist's chairman ordered that the situation be fixed.[49]

It was Inturist's task to obtain foreign currency. But to what lengths would it go to achieve this goal? The range of proposals that circulated in the organization's board meetings over the course of the early 1960s was almost dizzying and occasionally verged on the absurd. E. Faitel'son, one of the board's economists, suggested that tourists should be charged for watching hotel tele-

November 1965, GARF, f. 9612, op. 3, d. 33, ll. 1–6. Program to the Salon International du Tourisme et des Sports, February–March 1965, GARF, f. 9612, op. 3, d. 34, ll. 20–21. Success at these events was usually measured by the sheer volume of brochures given out to interested visitors.

45. V. Boichenko, "Protokol zasedaniia no. 9 pravleniia VAO Inturist," 16 October 1964, GARF, f. 9612, op. 1, d. 596, ll. 58–66.

46. Z. P. Kochugovoi, "Predlozheniia o chastichnoi ekonomiki finansovykh sredstv i nekotorom uluchshenii raboty pravleniia VAO Inturist," October 1964, GARF, f. 9612, op. 3, d. 49, ll. 69–74.

47. V. Boichenko, "Prikaz po pravleniiu VAO Inturist no. 85b," 10 September 1962, GARF, f. 9612, op. 1, d. 516, l. 172.

48. Tsvetkov first suggested workers of the service and excursion bureaus should see $50 for every $1,000 received via sales. "Protokol No. 11 zasedaniia pravleniia VAO Inturist," 7 October 1965. The idea was discussed again later that year: "Protokol no. 13 zasedaniia Pravleniia VAO Inturist," 23 December 1964, GARF, f. 9612, op. 1, d. 596, l. 1.

49. V. Boichenko, "Prikaz no. 12 po osnovnoi deiatel'nosti upravleniia," 16 January 1965, GARF, f. 9612, op. 3, d. 4, l. 36.

visions. This suggestion was proffered in 1965, however, a time when the vast majority of hotel rooms still lacked this accoutrement. Nor was it clear, admitted Faitel'son, how exactly one would even charge for such a service if there were televisions.[50] Furthermore, absent in all these discussions is any mention of the role of negotiations with noncapitalist countries. According to one relatively senior Inturist official, for example, "tourists from socialist countries are not very profitable (*vygodny*) for us as we don't receive from them the currency we need."[51] Given that visitors from socialist countries annually outnumbered those from capitalist countries (by the late 1960s at a ratio of roughly 2 to 1), it is moderately surprising that Inturist officials did not devote more attention to this part of their business. At the same time, the statement reflects a very serious adherence to the state's mandate in the early 1960s. Indeed, in light of the Liberman reforms and a new emphasis on profitability within Soviet enterprises, the project of selling socialism was hardly distinguishable from that of buying capital. At the same time, capturing the western tourist market proved an elusive task. For the desires, tastes, and habits of the average tourist to the Soviet Union in the early 1960s were hardly well known.

Unsatisfied Demand

Judging the relative success or failure of these ventures based on quantitative data is difficult first and foremost because the annual reports on currency plans and their fulfillment have been declassified only through the year 1963.[52] Additionally, Inturist reconciled its receipts in a fairly complex way. Moreover, with the passing of the 1964 decrees, Inturist agencies within the Soviet Union had the right to spend a certain amount of the hard currency earned from tourists for the purchase of imported goods such as food, furniture, and refrigerators for its hotels and restaurants.[53] Extrapolating from smaller pieces

50. E. Faitel'son, "Protokol no. 4 zasedaniia Pravleniia VAO Inturist," 25 February 1965, GARF, f. 9612, op. 3, d. 49, l. 38.

51. I. Stepura, "Protokol no. 5 zasedaniia Pravleniia VAO Inturist," 28 August 1964, GARF, f. 9612, op. 1, d. 596, l. 151.

52. These files are usually titled "otchet o rabote" or "otchet o vypolnenii valiutnogo plana" for a given year. They are relatively well maintained for the early part of Inturist's work in the *spetskhranilishche* at GARF. Documents for 1964 on are kept in opis' 4c. Another way to answer this question would be to study the archive of Vneshposyltorg, the organization that managed the Berezka stores where tourists shopped. However, those files were closed during the time research was being conducted for this chapter.

53. S. S. Nikitin, "Pis'mo v Sovet Ministrov," 9 September 1966, GARF, f. 9612, op. 3, d. 80, l. 32. V. Ankudinov, "Instruktsiia o poriadke otchislenii VAO Inturist, ucheta i ispol'zovaniia inostrannoi valiuty, perevodimoi Sovetam Ministrov Soiuznykh respublik i VTsSPS ot valiutnykh postuplenii za priem i obsluzhivanie inostrannykh turistov v podvedomstvennykh im predpriatiiakh," 10 April 1969, GARF, f. 10004, op. 1, d. 85, ll. 105–10.

of data such as the annual sales of the Berezka filial at GUM would suggest, perhaps not surprisingly, that the total income from things like souvenirs remained quite low, especially in the early part of the 1960s.[54] Whether the numbers were positive, negative, or nonexistent, there were fundamental problems establishing and ensuring the success of Inturist's commercial offerings at this time. Not only did officials lack the know-how with which to approach this new work but their efforts were equally hampered by foundational aspects of the Soviet economy.

Bartending proved to be particularly daunting to Inturist officials. An April 1965 meeting of the Inturist board suggests that there was much discomfort in charting this unknown territory. First, there was the issue of the materials necessary to open new bars. As one member declared, "none of us really knows what's needed for a bar. I myself don't know what exactly this bar equipment [*barmenskii instrument*] is." Then came the issue of bartenders. Officials asked: where was one to find such specialists in the Soviet Union? Were they to be men or women? What kind of character and skills were they to have? As Boichenko himself acknowledged, "this problem of bartenders is very serious." Admittedly, bars were a "completely new area of work for Inturist." But it was unfortunate, as Erokhin argued, that the board was trying to find solutions to the problem in such a "primitive" (*kustarno*) way. He acknowledged, "we don't even have people who could tell us what we should do. And perhaps it's too late now to send two or three workers abroad to study how all this is done there or to invite a few foreigners here to help us."[55]

Moreover, even if officials had found a solution to this question, problems endemic to Soviet trade complicated the issue. Production and distribution, for example, caused endless hassles. When by August 1965 only 18 percent of supplies were received in the Russian Federation Berezka stores, the head of the Russian Ministry of Trade pleaded to the Council of Ministers for help. The summer months, with the increased flow of tourists, led to "serious difficulties satisfying the demands of foreigners for a number of items. . . . The unsatisfied orders for supply of the Berezka stores will be the cause of huge losses in currency returns," he warned.[56] Tourists wanted to spend their money, many Inturist officials argued. Often, though, the goods just were not to be had.

Occasionally, too, problems of distribution and supply were compounded by issues with labor, frequently a source of grief during board meetings. The average salesperson in a Berezka store and Inturist restaurant was not highly educated or fluent in foreign languages, in spite of the organization's varied at-

54. The total income from the souvenir department in 1964 at GUM was 214 rubles (about $240 at the official rate) (Spravka o prodazhe tovarov Vneshposyltorga za 1964 god v tys. rub, TsMAM, f. 474, op. 1, d. 258, ll. 5–6).

55. Erokhin, "Protokol no. 5 zasedaniia Pravleniia VAO Inturist," 3 April 1965, GARF, f. 9612, op. 3, d. 49, l. 52.

56. D. Pavlov, "Pis'mo v Sovet Ministrov RSFSR," 30 August 1965, GARF, f. 259, op. 45, d. 3803, l. 48.

tempts to force this development.[57] It was unlikely that the stores would realize much income if salespeople were rude with customers, as many really were,
the organization's officials feared.[58] The head of the Russian branch of Inturist
reported the following in a republican-level meeting where many of the organization's leaders were present:

> We've received complaints from some East German tourists about the
> restaurant in Sheremet'evo where they were served rotten meat which
> had an unpleasant smell. The tourists refused to eat it. The senior chef
> was called to the table and he tried to show that the meat was of good
> quality, even eating a piece to prove this. But such "resourcefulness"
> didn't save the situation; the scallop was actually made of low-quality
> meat.[59]

Properly educated chef or not, the question among officials remained: when
would such "resourcefulness" no longer be necessary? Should the head of the
Irkutsk office ever expect to serve his guests fresh fish?

Although it is difficult to judge the economic success of Inturist's use of new
methods of planning during the 1960s, we do know that officials never reversed this movement to sell consumer goods, even though they did gradually
reposition their justifications for it. In the meantime, constraints inherent in
the Soviet system combined with a lack of deep knowledge about western markets made for difficult work on Inturist's part. And the numerous comparisons
with more developed service industries abroad left a long-standing residue of
frustration among members of the board.[60]

Consuming Socialism

"Shopping in Russia can be hard work," writes one tourist to the Soviet Union
in the late 1950s.[61] Others suggested more simply that "much effort" was

57. Inturist workers received a bonus for knowledge of a foreign language. This was the case
as early as 1935, the same year that the training school called the Institute of Foreign Tourism was
established in Leningrad. V. Kurts, "Prikaz no. 115b po VAO Inturist," 27 September 1965,
GARF, f. 9612, op. 1, d. 26, l. 98. Knowledge of foreign languages was consistently a problem for
the organization, however. Additionally, most restaurant workers and sales clerks were hired
through the local city councils or the Ministry of Trade, making it more difficult to ensure that
they were properly trained.

58. Khodorkov, "Stenogramma k protokolu no. 12 zasedanii Pravleniia VAO Inturist," 11
January 1965, GARF, f. 9612, op. 3, d. 49, l. 10.

59. K. Krupin, "Doklad o sostoianii i zadachakh po razvitiiu inostrannogo turizma v RSFSR
na respublikanskom soveshchanii po inostrannomu turizmu," 20 April 1965, GARF, f. 10004, op.
1, d. 15, l. 20.

60. This theme is echoed in Gorsuch and Bracewell, in this volume.

61. E. J. Kahn, "Recollections of an Intourist Tourist II," New Yorker no. 34 (27 December
1958): 37.

needed to find anything worth buying.[62] Indeed, for a group of people expected to spend, guests and hosts alike were often disappointed by the meager
amounts of currency left behind. In spite of Inturist's efforts and the serious-
ness with which its officials approached the task of increasing receipts of foreign currency, the matter was not solved quickly. By 1970 the head of Inturist
was still arguing for increased production of souvenirs. Because there was so
little for visitors to buy, according to Sergei Nikitin, "tourists complain that
from nowhere else do they return so wealthy (*takimi bogatymi*) as from the Soviet Union."[63] Visitors were returning home with just as much money as they
had brought. And, as most travelogues detail, basic acts of consumption in the
Soviet Union required labor. Contrary to most sociological theory, tourism to
this land was not always a form of leisure. But ultimately and ironically, this
experience was part of what Inturist offered up for sale.

Or so the tourists wrote. Indeed, regardless of how accurately such comments reflected Soviet reality, the fact that most travelogues from visitors to
the Soviet Union detail the range of goods or services available to them while
traveling is of interest. Acts of popular consumption were more visible to
tourists because, in the context of the Cold War, they were of greater import
than ever before. Tourists' reflections must be considered in light of the new
role of consumer culture that was at the heart of postwar judgments about Soviet socialism and American capitalism.

Most often tourists' complaints focused on the poor quality of goods.
Whether this meant portraying Russia's consumer goods sector as "inferior,"
"behind" that of the West, "scarcely desirable," or just "scarce," the message
was consistent: there was not anything worth buying.[64] For some tourists, that
fact alone was valuable. As a souvenir of the trip, some preferred to bring
home everyday objects, especially those of low quality. As one visitor relates,
"I bought two different brands of safety razor blades at the little kiosk on the
ground floor [of the hotel]. . . . Both kinds have rough jagged edges and are
much worse than the used blades which Americans discard. Russian blades
will make good souvenirs."[65]

More distressing than the shopping, though, were the awkward moments
that emerged in the act of exchanging hard currency for goods. On the one
hand, Inturist managed food distribution by giving out meal coupons to
tourists at the start of the trip. These were required for anyone buying the standard travel package. On the other, only cash was accepted in the newly opened
hard-currency bars and stores. Thus "the hungry or thirsty devil clutching his

62. Hans Koningsberger, *Along the Roads of the New Russia* (New York, 1968), 139.

63. Stenogramma zasedaniia Komissii po inostrannym delam Verkhovnogo Soveta RSFSR, 29
June 1970, GARF, f. 385, op. 13, d. 2570, l. 33.

64. See, for example, Koningsberger, *Along the Roads*, 137, 139; M. Phillips Price, *Russia
Forty Years On* (London, 1961), 42, 118.

65. James Robinson, *Americanski Journalist: Ten Thousand Miles of Russia through the Eyes
of an American Observer* (Los Angeles, 1969), 202.

№ 064516

„ИНТУРИСТ"

Талон
на одну экскурсию

Coupon
for one excursion

Coupon
für einen Ausflug

Coupon
pour une excursion

9.3. Inturist coupon good for one city
excursion. Similar coupons were
issued for prepaid meals.

meal coupons (which he has bought with hard currency of course, for no other money will get them for him) will not be allowed into these places."[66] Similarly frustrating was the absence of any possibility to get change for items one bought. Bartenders and store clerks frequently claimed that they could only return money in Russian currency. As James Kirkup describes, while trying to order a drink one night, he protested this move. "As I had paid him in dollars the least he could do was to give me change in American currency. But he refused. He said he had no American money to give for change. I offered him Polish currency instead, but this he looked at with contemptuous sneers and then pushed over my change in Russian currency."[67]

The full range of western tourist responses to the experience of seeing the Soviet Union was, of course, great and complicated. Indeed, even individual travelogues contained internal contradictions. Just as Kirkup denounces the bartender for not accepting socialist banknotes, he brags about the ability to buy off Inturist workers for services and ticket salesmen for access to concerts and the theater.[68] Some tourists poked fun at their compatriots for falling for Inturist's cheap tricks and imagining that the "rough deal" was "simply part of the system." Traveling to the Soviet Union, in this sense, was just a taste of life under communism.[69] Others wrote glorifying tales of encounters with their guides (said to be more valuable in influencing opinion abroad "than all the sputniks in the world")[70] who patently refused to accept tips or monetary rewards. The signed letter of thanks from one tour group to its host was, nevertheless, accepted "as though we had given him something worth many dollars."[71] Tourists found a range of meanings in their visits, be they in cheap consumer goods, the "human capital" of guides or the wealth of an experience of life in nonmarket conditions.

66. Koningsberger, *Along the Roads*, 144.
67. Kirkup, *One Man's Russia*, 98.
68. Ibid., 96.
69. Koningsberger, *Along the Roads*, 146.
70. Price, *Russia Forty Years On*, 36.
71. Ben Haden, *I See their Faces* (Johnson City, Tenn., 1963), 7.

Н.4. Inturist souvenir folder, depicting activities and regions of foreign tourism to the USSR.

Between objects and experiences, the market and socialism, producers and consumers, a study of Inturist in the postwar years suggests numerous ways in which hosts and guests understood and made sense of two worlds. While Inturist officials maintained high hopes that tourists would act like the consumers they had researched in meetings with international travel organizations, upon returning home westerners often described the wealth of the experience of being in a nonmarket space (or the relief of witnessing the poverty of socialism). Ultimately, the ability to cross the imaginary "curtain" dividing East and West was itself among the more valuable things Inturist provided tourists in the Cold War. Buying socialism was more than touring factories and fancying a Central Asian skullcap: it was also acquiring the opportunity to tell the story of how one got access to an otherwise closed world.

Selling socialism was equally complex insofar as Inturist officials genuinely struggled with the question of satisfying tourists' everyday needs. The fact that this now meant providing a range of goods, some of which were thoroughly Soviet and others not, is as indicative of changes in postwar shifts in internal economics as in international politics. Foreign tourism to the Soviet Union was a business, of course, but it was one that was critical to the socialist project. Inturist's work, however awkward it may have been, was done in the service of the state. After a period of relative isolation in the 1930s and 1940s, with little direct insight into how foreign markets operated and what the typical lifestyle of their visitors was, Inturist officials faced a nearly impossible task of instituting new practices under the constraints of socialism. Its leaders encouraged an odd combination of study and emulation of foreign firms that led to all-too-direct comparisons and regular frustration. By the early 1970s, having established a greater dependence on income from the sale of arms and oil, the state seemed to call upon Inturist in a less harried fashion for receipts of foreign currency.[72] Yet many of the problems Inturist struggled with so much in 1960s did not go away at that time. These were, in fact, part of the organization's history from beginning to end.

72. Stephen Kotkin, for one, argues that the Soviet state would surely have collapsed decades earlier than 1991 if it had not discovered oil. According to him, oil exports between 1973 and 1985 accounted for 80 percent of the USSR's hard-currency income. Kotkin, *Armageddon Averted: The Soviet Collapse, 1970–2000* (Oxford, 2001). See also Central Intelligence Agency, *USSR: Hard Currency Trade and Payments, 1977–1978* (Washington, D.C., 1977).

CHAPTER 10

Time Travelers

Soviet Tourists to Eastern Europe

Anne E. Gorsuch

In 1956 the residents of the city of Gorky heard the following "advertisement" on the local radio: "At the height of the summer season every worker in Gorky dreams of how best to spend his holiday. One dreams of going to the Crimea; another of the southern shores of the Caucasus; and the third, choosing a different path for his vacation, goes on a tourist trip abroad."[1] The previous year, Inturist, together with the Tourist Excursion Bureau (Turistsko-ekskursionnoe upravlenie) of the All-Union Central Council of Trade Unions (Vsesoiuznyi tsentral'nyi sovet professional'nykh soiuzov), had begun sending small numbers of Soviet tourists to east European countries.[2] In 1962, just seven years later, the vice-chairman of Inturist would proudly declare: "There is not a single region of the Soviet Union that has not sent a Soviet tourist abroad, and no corner of the earth where Soviet people have not been."[3] Some of the travel of the Khrushchev era was international, some was domestic, and some was imaginary (the armchair travel of the reader, moviegoer, or stamp collector), but much was driven by a new sense of expansion and exploration, of being able to examine new topics and new places, and of extending Soviet power (via the tourist) into new spaces. In late Stalinism, in contrast, the regime had prohibited most travel abroad, nourished ignorance about foreign countries, and encouraged instead domestic tourism. Tourists were told that it was only within the borders of the Soviet Union that they could be confident of a warm welcome.[4] Under Khrushchev, however, to travel now also meant leaving home for someplace else. "Every worker in our motherland can take his vacation on a fascinating tour abroad," the newspaper *Trud* (Labor) cheerfully

I would like to thank Diane Koenker and the other contributors to this book for their insightful comments. Special thanks to Bob Allen for his advice about matters economic and to Valeriia Emmanuilovna Kunina for sharing her memories and photographs with me.

1. Gosudarstvennyi arkhiv Rossiiskoi Federatsii (hereafter GARF), f. 9520, op. 1, d. 316, l. 48 (Text for a radio announcement on tourist trips abroad).

2. V. V. Dvornichenko, *Razvitie turizma v SSSR (1917–1983 gg.)* (Moscow, 1985), 48–49.

3. GARF, f. 9520, op. 1, d. 468, l. 29 (Report by Erokhin, vice-chairman of Inturist, at a Tourist Excursion Bureau meeting on international travel, March 1962).

4. Anne E. Gorsuch, "'There's No Place Like Home': Soviet Tourism in Late Stalinism," *Slavic Review* 62, no. 4 (2003): 657.

instructed its readers in 1956. Soviet tourists can expect a "warm, friendly reception everywhere."[5]

This chapter explores Soviet tourism to eastern Europe, the most common destination for the Soviet international tourist.[6] In 1963 over fifty thousand Soviet citizens traveled to eastern Europe via Inturist and trade union organizations.[7] Another approximately ten thousand traveled via Sputnik, the Komsomol youth tourism organization.[8] Although front-page stories in the Soviet press described with evident pride the number of new and exotic countries Soviet citizens could now visit—Iceland, Luxembourg, and Thailand, to mention only a few—many of these destinations were still open only to members of the Soviet political, scientific, athletic, and cultural elite.[9] "Travelers" of this kind had long been allowed to cross international borders, even if not previously in such great numbers.[10] In contrast, eastern Europe was now available to a new category of tourists who, if still largely "from the middle" rather than "from below," nonetheless represented a sea change in regime attitudes toward international travel and evidence of tentative democratization of previously elite experience.[11]

This chapter investigates sightseeing, consumption, and debates about the "cultured" (or not) behavior of the Soviet tourist as ways to explore two broad themes. First, what was the relationship between seeing the foreign and Khrushchevian constructs of nation, of self, and of other? Because travel by its very nature crosses boundaries, tourism to eastern Europe is an especially good vantage point from which to examine understandings (both personal and official) about "difference" and about transgressions of borders both actual and symbolic. We will see that although the regime encouraged foreign travel, it also limited the number of people traveling through careful vetting before departure and through close monitoring while away. Khrushchev was not afraid to institute significant changes—travel abroad, increased freedom of expression, greater attention to the satisfaction of consumer desire, the renuncia-

5. "Every worker can spend his leave abroad," *Trud*, 6 May 1956, in *Current Digest of the Soviet Press* (hereafter *CDSP*) 8, no. 18 (1956): 20.

6. GARF, f. 9520, op. 1, d. 430, l. 171 (On sending Soviet tourists abroad in 1959–1960).

7. GARF, f. 9520, op. 1, d. 613, l. 18 (Report on international tourism, 1963).

8. Rossiiskii gosudarstvennyi arkhiv sotsial'no-politicheskoi istorii (hereafter RGASPI), f. M-5, op. 1, d. 161, l. 3 (Soviet tourists traveling with the Komsomol by year).

9. "International Tourism on a New Scale," *Literaturnaia gazeta*, 6 May 1958, in *CDSP* 10, no. 18 (1958): 25.

10. See Michael David-Fox, "Stalinist Westernizer? Aleksandr Arosev's Literary and Political Depictions of Europe," *Slavic Review* 62, no. 4 (2003): 733–59; and David Caute, *The Dancer Defects: The Struggle for Cultural Supremacy during the Cold War* (Oxford, 2003).

11. On travel from east European Soviet-bloc countries to Yugoslavia, see the article by Patrick Hyder Patterson, "Dangerous Liaisons: Soviet-Bloc Tourists and the Temptations of the Yugoslav Good Life in the 1960s and 1970s," in *The Business of Tourism*, ed. Philip Scranton (Philadelphia, forthcoming).

tion of terror.[12] But these very changes permitted, even encouraged, behaviors and beliefs which threatened to outrun the regime. How to institute de-Stalinization without challenging the very legitimacy of the state? Which experiences of "difference" were Soviet citizens permitted, even encouraged to have, and which were regulated or forbidden?[13] What, in sum, can tourism tell us about what it meant to be "Soviet" in a country no longer defined as Stalinist?

Second, what was the relationship between Soviet center and east European periphery? Soviet tourists traveling to capitalist countries were still expected to defend themselves and the reputation of the Soviet Union against clearly articulated differences. But what about east European countries: were tourists traveling to an Other or to an extension of the Soviet Self? In the official imagination, as presented in published travel accounts, eastern Europe was presented as a younger and less advanced version of the Soviet Self. The experience of travel challenged this perspective as tourists discovered that the "colonies" were in fact more developed than the center. In other words, when they crossed the border tourists crossed not only a physical border, but a temporal one. They were told that they were going back in time to visit an imaginary, younger, historical Self—an imagining that was used to help to justify Soviet domination over the socialist periphery. But tourists were also, contradictorily, moving forward in time to experience what the Soviet Union might become. They were time travelers as well as tourists.

"We Always Know about the Behavior of Our Tourists"

Soviet travel accounts and guidebooks are good sources for exploring official meanings. Archival materials, including the transcripts of yearly conferences held by Inturist and the Trade Union Tourist Excursion Bureau, as well as more frequent reports by local tourist authorities and organizations, are even better given what they reveal about conflicts and doubts as well as enthusiasms. It is difficult on the basis of these sources alone, however, to say much about the experiences of Soviet tourists abroad. The best, if not unproblematic, sources of "experience" are the trip reports filed by Soviet group leaders with Inturist and the Tourist Excursion Bureau after each trip abroad. These sources are also far from private. But the intimate, everyday details of travel—both positive and negative—are useful. The difficulties were often organiza-

12. For a discussion of these changes, and limits to them, see William Taubman, *Khrushchev: The Man and His Era* (New York, 2003); and William Taubman, Sergei Khrushchev, and Abbott Gleason, eds., *Nikita Khrushchev* (New Haven, 2000).

13. For a discussion of difference versus deviance in the Khrushchev era, see Ted Hopf, *Social Construction of International Politics: Identities and Foreign Policies, Moscow, 1955 and 1999* (Ithaca, N.Y., 2002), 92–98.

tional; trip leaders complained about the many missed connections, challenging conditions, and poorly trained local guides. Trip leaders also described the many tourists who violated accepted "norms of behavior" for the Soviet tourist abroad. Because these reports are a key source for this chapter, it is worth pausing briefly to consider the role and writings of the trip leader.

Each trip leader had to fulfill the multiple, and sometimes untenable, roles of cultural guide, political leader, and informant. The job of trip leader was not simple; even before departure, leaders working for the Komsomol were supposed to learn about the economy, history, culture, and politics of the country they would be visiting; familiarize themselves with every aspect of their charges' biographies; "guarantee" the participation of their tourists at pre-trip informational and educational sessions; and retrieve the necessary trip documents for every tourist from the regional authorities.[14] Most trip leaders were party members, and many were also party or trade union activists.[15] But their authority as trip leader was sometimes undermined by the greater "authority" of their privileged tourists who sometimes refused to do as told.[16] To add to this confusion, trip leaders were participants as well as leaders, an ambiguous position suggested by the fact that some trip leaders had to use vacation time, rather than work time, to lead a trip.[17] In this sense, their reports can be read as travel diaries (a window on their own experience) as well as a report on the experience of others. Trip reports varied in their composition, in their formality, in their attention to detail. Some appear to have been dashed off quickly, while others are lengthy and labored. Some are factual in tone, others more literary. But all trip leaders must have known that any possibilities for future trips, as well perhaps as possibilities for advancement at home, depended on their own behavior and that of their charges while abroad. Indeed, group leaders were themselves a point of anxiety for tourist authorities. How to find enough experienced guides with the requisite languages for tours when so few Soviet citizens had traveled and/or were politically acceptable?[18] That everyone, including the trip leader, was considered vulnerable is suggested by the multiple layers of surveillance on international trips. Some groups were accompanied by a leader (*starosta*) from a local trade union who was of stature equal to the group leader and who would also report to the trade union upon

14. RGASPI, f. M-5, op. 1, d. 52, ll. 26–27 (Instructions for group leaders of Soviet youth traveling abroad).

15. GARF, f. 9520, op. 1, d. 391, l. 94 (Report to Tourism Excursion Bureau conference on international travel, 1961).

16. See, for example, GARF, f. 9612, op. 1, d. 563, l. 36 (Report on trip to Poland and Czechoslovakia, 1963); and GARF, f. 9520, op. 1, d. 430, ll. 105–6 (On the inadequate behavior of Soviet tourists abroad in 1960).

17. GARF, f. 9520, op. 1, d. 468, l. 17 (Report by Alekseeva to a Tourist Excursion Bureau meeting on international tourism, May 1962).

18. GARF, f. 9520, op. 1, d. 391, l. 172.

his return about the behavior of the tourists.[19] KGB agents also traveled abroad with some groups for the purposes of surveillance (especially to capitalist countries), a fact widely known as suggested by the use of the colloquial term *nian'ka* (nanny) to denote such a person.[20] "We know everything," a trade union delegate from Irkutsk claimed. "We always know about the behavior of our tourists."[21]

Finally, a note about terminology. Throughout this chapter I use the term "eastern Europe" to refer to those countries between the USSR and western Europe that were in the Soviet sphere. Soviet sources on international tourism, in contrast, most often referred to these nations as "socialist countries" in pointed contrast to tourism to and from "capitalist countries." Soviet tourism to both Poland and England was considered tourism to a "foreign" (*zarubezhnyi*) country, but Poland was less foreign by virtue of being "socialist." I have not adopted this terminology in part for the practical reason that by the end of the Khrushchev era, "socialist" tourism also included travel to places like Cuba, but also because I do not want to privilege the ideological definition of this liminal space. But by so often referring to "eastern Europe" as a whole, I recognize that I do risk (as in so many Soviet sources) suggesting that it was a single, undifferentiated entity. In reality, of course, the construction of an "east European" and/or socialist identity was a gradual and often contested process, as the chapters by Wendy Bracewell and Scott Moranda in this volume demonstrate.

"Travel to Foreign Countries . . . How Easy It Has Become!"[22]

In a 1956 interview, a resident of Kamchatka in the Soviet Far East described his surprise at ending up on a trip abroad. "It happened completely unexpectedly. We were talking with a woman who turned out to work for the regional trade union soviet. Talk turned to tourist trips. She told us that going on a tourist trip really was possible."[23] The Kamchatka interviewee was not the only person to question the idea of travel abroad after so many years of living behind closed borders. Indeed, this interview was part of a 1956 propaganda

19. See, for example, GARF, f. 9520, op. 1, d. 468, l. 22 (Report by Skupova, a senior instructor for the Irkutsk soviet of trade unions to a Tourist Excursion Bureau meeting on international travel, March 1962).

20. Irina H. Corten, *Vocabulary of Soviet Society and Culture: A Selected Guide to Russian Words, Idioms, and Expressions of the Post-Stalin Era, 1953–1991* (Durham, N.C., 1992), 90–91.

21. GARF, f. 9520, op. 1, d. 468, l. 22 (Report by Skupova).

22. This quote is from the journalist interviewing the Kamchatka tourist described below. GARF, f. 9520, op. 1, d. 316, ll. 128–29 (Transcript of broadcast: Kamchatka tourists go to China and Korea, 1956).

23. GARF, f. 9520, op. 1, d. 316, l. 129 (Transcript of broadcast).

campaign launched because the new plan for international tourism had not been fulfilled the previous year.[24] International travelers were encouraged to re-present their trips at lectures in factories, at universities, in contributions to wall newspapers, in photo exhibitions, and on radio and television.[25]

These propaganda efforts were successful. In 1960 the Inturist plan for numbers of people sent abroad was almost fulfilled and the Komsomol plan overfulfilled, reflecting the increasing numbers of people wanting (and now able) to travel.[26] That said, the majority of Soviet tourists to eastern Europe were still from privileged groups: academics, cultural workers, factory managers, party functionaries, housewives.[27] Still, tourists to eastern Europe were far more diverse than those to capitalist countries, particularly the United States. In 1961, 228 Soviet citizens traveled as "tourists" to the United States—of whom close to 70 percent were party members, almost all were white-collar workers, and just 6 travelers were of Komsomol age.[28] In contrast, of the tens of thousands of tourists traveling via Inturist to eastern Europe in 1961, only about 40 percent were party members, almost 17 percent were workers, and 18 percent were Komsomol members.[29]

The non-working-class nature of international tourism was problematic for a regime which understood its own identity and that of other nations in terms of class-based social systems. The main problem, according to tourist officials at both the local and national level, was the high cost of travel abroad.[30] In 1959 an excursion to Romania cost 1,122 rubles and to the German Democratic Republic (GDR) 1,376 rubles.[31] (A fourteen-day itinerary to New York,

24. GARF, f. 9520, op. 1, d. 316, l. 41 (On fulfilling the plan for sending Soviet tourists abroad in 1956, Gorky Oblast); GARF, f. 9520, op. 1, d. 317, l. 16 (On the fulfillment of plans for travel abroad, 1956, Leningrad Oblast). Also see GARF, f. 9520, op. 1, d. 317, l. 1 (On fulfilling the plan for sending Soviet tourists abroad in 1956, L'vov Oblast) and Dvornichenko, *Razvitie turizma v SSSR*, 49.

25. GARF, f. 9520, op. 1, d. 468, l. 75 (Report by Serov from the Novosibirsk trade union soviet to a Tourist Excursion Bureau meeting on foreign travel, March 1961).

26. GARF, f. 9520, op. 1, d. 430, l. 165 (On the fulfillment of the plan for international tourism, 1960); RGASPI, f. M-5, op. 1, d. 52, l. 34 (On tourist trips by Soviet youth abroad in 1960 and in the plan for 1961).

27. See, for example, the discussions in GARF, f. 9520, op. 1, d. 390, l. 34 (Report by Shafieva at a conference on international tourism, March 1961); GARF, f. 9520, op. 1, d. 319, l. 86 (Report by Buianov at a conference on international tourism, May 1961).

28. GARF. f. 9520, op. 1, d. 432, ll. 3, 29 (Lists of numbers and categories of tourists going abroad in 1960 and 1961).

29. Ibid. Over twenty-six thousand tourists traveled via Inturist in the first half of 1961.

30. For just a few of the many examples, see GARF, f. 9520, op. 1, d. 316, ll. 13, 17 (Reports on sending tourists abroad from the Astrakhan' and Briansk Oblasts, 1956).

31. GARF, f. 9520, op. 1, d. 430, l. 187 (Report on the cost of trips abroad). Fares included the cost of the travel, food, and lodging abroad, as well as the cost of travel to Moscow from the traveler's home town. Not included was the cost of a passport for travel abroad or rubles exchanged for hard currency. See GARF, f. 9520, op. 1, d. 316, l. 45 (Form for tourists traveling abroad, Gorky Oblast).

Washington, Chicago, Dearborn, and Niagara Falls cost over 6,000 rubles!).[32] When the average wage of a Soviet industrial worker in 1955 was just over 9,500 rubles a year, a trip to eastern Europe could be well out of reach.[33] Due to an increase in the minimum wage in 1957, and to a relatively constant cost of living, the real wages of Soviet workers increased in the mid- to late 1950s, and people had slightly more discretionary income to spend on luxuries such as tourism, but still not enough to enable many ordinary workers to travel.[34] On Inturist-organized trips the number of *rabochie* (blue-collar workers) was still far less than officials desired.[35] An additional problem was the limited number of vacation days.[36] (The problems were different for agricultural workers, who were the least likely to travel, as they could only travel in the winter when there were few excursions.)[37] This said, more rabochie did travel to eastern Europe on less expensive non-hard-currency exchanges arranged by the Trade Union Excursion Bureau with east European counterparts beginning in 1958.[38] These tourists received a significant discount on the cost of the trip as well as on train travel to Moscow. By the early 1960s, between 50 to 85 percent of the participants sent to eastern Europe each year on non-hard-currency exchanges or for "relaxation and healing" were workers.[39]

Of course, the fulfillment of a plan for tourism reflected how many people the regime wanted to have travel, not how many might have wanted to but could not. Foreign travel was not a right, but still a privilege to be dispensed by the state. In the 1950s and early 1960s, tourism authorities fretted that not

32. *Spravochnik: Ob usloviiakh i marshrutakh puteshestvii sovetskikh turistov za granitsu* (Moscow, 1960), 28, 156.

33. On the average wage, see Abram Bergson, *The Real National Income of Soviet Russia since 1928* (Cambridge, Mass., 1961), 422.

34. Janet G. Chapman, *Real Wages in Soviet Russia since 1928* (Cambridge, Mass., 1963), 181–84.

35. In 1963 authorities tried to "fix" this problem by arguing that the percentage of workers increased to 43 percent if one included engineers and technical workers (GARF, f. 9520, op. 1, d. 613, l. 18). Also see RGASPI, f. M-5, op. 1, d. 52, l. 33 (List of the composition of Soviet youth tourists abroad, 1959); and RGASPI, f. M-5, op. 1, d. 158, l. 119 (On international tourist trips of Soviet youth in 1958–1962).

36. In 1958 approximately 40 percent of workers still had just twelve days of vacation a year, which meant that many were unable to go on trips abroad, as they were often more than two weeks long. See GARF, f. 9520, op. 1, d. 438, l. 101 (Report by Vatsar, Senior Instructor and Estonian representative to a Tourist Excursion Bureau meeting on international travel, March 1961). Some 12 percent of Soviet citizens, presumably the higher-ranking ones, had more than twice as much vacation: over twenty-four days a year. See *Trud v SSSR: Statisticheskii sbornik* (Moscow, 1988), 106.

37. GARF, f. 9520, op. 1, d. 438, l. 162. Also see GARF, f. 9520, op. 1, d. 390, l. 31.

38. Dvornichenko, *Razvitie turizma v SSSR*, 50.

39. GARF, f. 9520, op. 1, d. 422, ll. 3, 4, 6, 54 (On Soviet tourists traveling for rest and healing to socialist countries in 1961); GARF, f. 9520, op. 2, d. 26, l. 17 (Report on sending Soviet workers abroad for healing and rest to socialist countries, 1964); GARF, f. 9520, op. 1, d. 613, l. 18; GARF, f. 9520, op. 1, d. 432, l. 4.

enough people were traveling abroad, but they also turned away some potential tourists as unsuitable. Soviet citizens who wanted to travel abroad had to
apply to the trade union organization of their local enterprise or place of work,
or to the regional trade union.[40] Potential tourists were vetted before departure
to ensure their proper "political understanding and moral quality," their "relationship to work," and their "participation in social life."[41] In addition to
providing a "character" reference from local party authorities and filling out a
medical form, those hoping to travel to east European countries in 1957 had to
fill out three pages of forms about their personal and work history.[42] A delegate from the Moscow oblast soviet to a Tourist Excursion Bureau conference
in 1961 admitted that there were many people who wanted to travel, but "we
don't take all who so desire."[43]

"Our Heart Is One Heart"

Like most tourists anywhere, Soviet tourists to eastern Europe spent most of
their time seeing the sights.[44] East European tourist destinations frequently
confirmed conservative discourses about a fraternal but unequal relationship
between a superior imperial metropolis and the socialist periphery. The obligatory excursion in Berlin was to Treptow Park where travelers visited the Soviet Soldiers' Monument. "Of course, the most impressive place we saw [on
our tour of Berlin] was the monument to the Soviet war," wrote one enthusiastic Komsomol trip leader in 1963. "Our delegates brought wreathes to lay
down. Around us we saw many, many tourists, Germans from other cities,
children. They were all coming to pay honor, to respect and grieve."[45] Tourism
was also used to confirm the industrial prowess of a modern Soviet Union as
exemplified by large construction projects of postwar rebuilding. Tourists to
Warsaw visited the enormous skyscraper, the Palace of Culture and Science,
which was said by L. Kudrevatykh in his 1956 account of Soviet tourism to

40. GARF, f. 9612, op. 1, d. 387, ll. 25–26 (Report on rules for foreign documents for Soviet
citizens traveling abroad).

41. GARF, f. 9612, op. 1, d. 387, l. 33 (What is required in a character recommendation for a
tourist desiring to go abroad, 1957).

42. GARF, f. 9612, op. 1, d. 387, ll. 34, 37–39 (Copies of questionnaires for travel abroad,
1957). On the character assessment, see also GARF, f. 9520, op. 1, d. 391, ll. 104–5.

43. GARF, f. 9520, op. 1, d. 391, l. 145.

44. For a more developed discussion of these issues, see Gorsuch, " 'There's No Place Like
Home'," 764–65. See also the description of *turizm* as both sport and sightseeing in *Kratkaia
entsiklopediia domashnego khoziaistva*, vol. 2 (Moscow, 1962): 1486–98.

45. RGASPI, f. M-5, op. 1, d. 171, l. 46 (Reports on youth trip to the GDR, 1963). See also
Turistskaia poezdka v Germanskuiu Demokraticheskuiu Respubliku (Moscow, 1959), 3. In countries other than Germany, local heroes were sometimes honored alongside Soviet ones. See GARF,
f. 9520, op. 1, d. 405, l. 11 (Tourist Excursion Bureau trip leader report, Bulgaria 1961); and
GARF, f. 9520, op. 1, d. 405, l. 61 (Tourist Excursion Bureau trip leader report, Hungary 1961).

Poland to embody all the Soviet Union's many gifts to Poland, as well as its brotherly superiority. The concert halls demonstrated Soviet concern for the cultural life of Polish citizens; the meeting rooms provided a space for political gatherings, including the meetings of the Polish communist party.[46] Throughout eastern Europe, tours typically combined visits to cultural and historical sites with more determinedly "socialist" excursions. On a twenty-day cruise on the Danube (Dunav) River, tourists breakfasted on board the ship, and then bused (sometimes over 250 kilometers) to various points of interest including the historical and architectural monuments of Bucharest, Sofia, Vienna, and Prague, the tomb of Bulgarian leader Georgi Dimitrov, a cemetery of Soviet soldiers killed in the liberation of Belgrade, and a Prague museum dedicated to Lenin.[47] Many of these sites were Stalinist. The Soviet "time traveler" visited two kinds of Soviet pasts: the heroic past of revolutionary construction, and a more recent Stalinist past visible in those countries, such as the GDR, that had resisted de-Stalinization.

Soviet "strategies of representation" in which military and economic domination were re-presented as liberation and rebuilding, resemble what Mary Louise Pratt has called "anti-conquest" or the strategies "whereby [colonial powers] seek to secure their innocence in the same moment as they assert [their] hegemony."[48] Pratt is referring to travel and travel writing by the European bourgeoisie, but Soviet travel writing served much the same purpose: instructing citizens at home and abroad that the Soviet domination of eastern Europe was both necessary and just. "It's good that Russians again come to our country!" one Yugoslav citizen was said to have exclaimed in a 1956 travel account published in the Soviet weekly Ogonek (Spark): "Your country is big, powerful, while ours is small. But our heart is one heart, a Slavic heart, and between us, as between brothers, there is much that is shared, much as if between relations."[49] For armchair travelers back home, travel accounts such as this one were meant to reinforce lessons about relationships between east European countries and the Soviet Union that were consistent with official policy. In 1955 the USSR reestablished relations with Yugoslavia, a political reversal which was explained in part to Soviet readers through travel accounts. Sunny travel essays about Bulgaria can be understood similarly as differently worded versions of more conventional articles on Soviet-Bulgarian relations, the Soviet tourist receiving in miniaturized form the wildly enthusiastic greeting

46. L. Kudrevatykh, "Na ulitsakh Varshavy," Ogonek, no. 16 (April 1956): 6.

47. GARF, f. 9520, op. 1, d. 954, l. 20 (Printed program for tourists on Danube cruise, 1966).

48. Mary Louise Pratt, Imperial Eyes: Travel Writing and Transculturation (New York, 1992), 7.

49. K. Cherevkov, "Leningradtsy v Iugoslavii," Ogonek, no. 25 (June 1956): 4. That this rhetoric was only partially successful is suggested by the fact that in 1960 Yugoslavia was still classified as a capitalist country in a list of Komsomol travel destinations. See RGASPI, f. M-5, op. 1, d. 52, l. 9 (List of the composition of Soviet youth tourists to capitalist countries in 1960).

10.1. Soviet tourists visiting a memorial to Soviet soldiers in Belgrade, ca. early 1960s.
Photograph loaned to author.

Khrushchev was said in newspaper reports to have received in his 1962 trip to Bulgaria.[50]

In these travel accounts, east European regimes were presented not as Other but as younger, less advanced, versions of a Soviet Self. Indeed, so much was said to be shared between the older and wiser Soviet Union and its younger, less experienced "blood brother" that any significant expression of ethnic or national difference was often eclipsed in favor of a shared socialist/working-class identity.[51] It is as if these accounts were trying to soften not only existing differences, which might get in the way of fraternal relations, but also older ethnic (Slav/non-Slav) and historical differences and perceptions. The experience of travel, however, often challenged Soviet narratives of military and industrial superiority, willing subordination and socialist fraternalism. For one thing, itineraries for Soviet tourists were set in significant part by east Euro-

50. "Dobre doshli, sovetskie brat'ia!" *Ogonek*, no. 21 (May 1962): 2–3.

51. The term "blood brother" was a common one. See, for example, M. Bugaeva, "U Bolgarskikh druzhei," *Ogonek*, no. 27 (September 1956): 5. Sometimes they were "sisters" as in the case of the book, *Sestra moia Bolgariia* (Moscow, 1963).

pean tourist organizations. East European organizations generally wrote the texts for advertisements and brochures about travel in their country which were then translated into Russian to be distributed to Soviet tourists. They hired local guides to accompany Soviet tourists. Although the chairman of Inturist defended this practice ("Only the country which takes our tourists can guarantee what it is in a position to show"), others complained that east European tourist agencies did not exert sufficient "control" over either guides or itineraries.[52] For some Soviet authorities there was too much attention paid to historical and religious sites of the presocialist Other and not enough visits to the "modern" products of socialist industrialism.[53] Trip leaders also complained about young guides who emphasized their presocialist heritage as a way to deny the authority of the USSR.[54]

As this suggests, of particular threat to Soviet strategies of representation was the infiltration of local guides who were necessary as "translators" of local sites and experience. While published travelogues emphasized east Europeans' warm welcome of their Soviet visitors (they often began with a rhapsody to the unseasonably warm weather or to the spring flowers "greeting" their arrival), in reality, Soviet tourists were voyaging among people who sometimes had a more negative understanding of what it meant to be "Soviet."[55] A local Czech guide openly expressed his preference for capitalist countries because of their "higher standard of living," and because capitalist countries were "fighting for peace," while the USSR had "acted aggressively for many years."[56] A Romanian train conductor forced Soviet tourists with assigned seats to give up their places to Romanians saying that they also wanted to travel: "It's our territory, our power."[57] Tourists were reminded that east Europeans often preferred capitalist visitors to socialist ones. On the Romanian Black Sea coast, visitors from each country were allotted their own hotel—"the Yalta for the Russians, the Palace for the Finns, the Modern for the British."[58] The hotels for British travelers were "up-to-date," and "modernistic," "situated amid cool green lawns and thickly blooming flower beds."[59] Such was not the case for Soviet travelers. "What kind of friendship is this," one tourist to Albania muttered, "All it means is that they don't give a damn about taking care of us."[60]

52. GARF, f. 9612, op. 1, d. 561, l. 5 (Report from P. M. Gritsenko, Inturist representative in Bulgaria, 1962); GARF, f. 9520, op. 1, d. 391, l. 170.

53. GARF f. 9520, op. 1, d. 391, l. 43.

54. GARF, f. 9520, op. 1, d. 504, l. 88.

55. On the warm greetings, see, for example, K. Cherevkov, "Leningradtsy v Iugoslavii," *Ogonek*, no. 25 (June 1956): 4, and V. Soloukhin, "Bolgarskie vstrechi," *Ogonek*, no. 51 (December 1956): 15.

56. GARF, f. 9520, op. 1, d. 504, l. 89 (A "critical remark" on improving work in international tourism, Ukrainian section report).

57. GARF, f. 9520, op. 1, d. 405, l. 16.

58. Mary Kay MacKintosh, *Rumania* (London, 1963), 94.

59. Ibid., 47.

60. GARF, f. 9612, op. 1, d. 372, l. 8.

10.2. Photograph of Dubrovnik tourist hotels taken from onboard a Soviet cruise ship, ca. early 1960s. Photograph loaned to author.

Of course, tourism was not only a site of official meaning, be it optimistic or oppositional; it also offered the possibility of time and space "apart" for the traveler him- or herself. This was despite the fact that a tourist's time was highly structured ("bus here, bus there," observed one former tourist) and always in a group. Official "evenings of friendship" were encouraged, but this was still "friendship" at a distance: after one evening party a worker was censured for sitting with the Hungarian musicians rather than staying with his own group.[61] Nonetheless, some tourists managed to explore "off the beaten track." Trip leaders complained about tourists who "met up with the wrong people," and slipped out at night to go to night bars or restaurants.[62] Travel to

61. GARF, f. 9520, op. 1, d. 422, l. 10. Also see GARF, f. 9520, op. 1, d. 430, ll. 111–12. The quote "bus here, bus there" is from an interview with Valeriia Emmanuilovna Kunina, who although thrilled to have traveled abroad noted that her time was highly structured (Interview, Moscow, July 2004).

62. GARF, f. 9612, op. 1, d. 561, l. 79 (Report by Inturist representative to Bulgaria, N. Gubakina, 1963).

eastern Europe also provided opportunities for encounters with west European items and ideas, particularly in Poland, Czechoslovakia, and East Germany. In Poland, for example, tourists could "consume" magazines that reported on western culture, including French fashion and American jazz, or listen to Polish radio stations that played French and American jazz.[63]

Not every official was opposed to this exposure to difference. After all, despite the controls, Soviet citizens were being permitted, indeed even encouraged, to see what they had previously been so forcefully kept from seeing. Challenges to Soviet ideological and political superiority were disturbing, but the benefits of travel were thought to outweigh potential risks, at least for some members of the citizenry. Indeed, the vice-chairman of Inturist warned tourists against the dangers not of difference and deviance but of thinking oneself superior. We have to guard against the know-it-alls, Aleksei Erokhin argued in 1962, the "tourist who upon arrival in a country, takes on the role of a person who doesn't ask questions, but only answers them."[64] Travel accounts, too, sometimes reflected this openness. There were things to learn even from younger "brothers," especially, as we will see below, in the realms of consumption and culture. If in a 1957 issue of *Vokrug sveta* (Around the World), Vadim Safonov began his account of a trip to Bulgaria with a recitation of the pleasures of home, he also described the excitement of crossing previously closed borders into a new country, and possibly a new way of thinking.[65] Exposure to difference, even at a distance, was part of what made a good Soviet citizen.

Shopping Adventures

One of the major attractions of travel abroad was the opportunities it provided for viewing and purchasing goods unavailable at home. Socialist tourism was supposed to be purposeful, but tourists to eastern Europe added their own consumerist agendas to the more socially constructive agendas of the regime. It was in the street market and the clothing store that Soviet tourists traveled most definitively to the "future" of a "modernizing" socialist society. The tourist Karpeikina wandered though one store in Poland with "wide-open eyes." "We don't have the kind of children's goods that they have in Poland," she remarked.[66] Thirty years after a trip to the GDR, the Soviet cardiologist V. I. Metelitsa still remembered mistakenly trying to buy a dress for a ten-year-

---

63. David Crowley, "Warsaw's Shops, Stalinism and the Thaw," in *Style and Socialism: Modernity and Material Culture in Post-War Eastern Europe*, ed. Susan E. Reid and David Crowley (Oxford, 2000), 41; K. S. Karol, *Visa for Poland* (London, 1959), 178; and John Kenneth Galbraith, *Journey to Poland and Yugoslavia* (Cambridge, Mass., 1958), 72.

64. GARF, f. 9520, op. 1, d. 468, l. 55 (Report by Erokhin). Also see GARF, f. 9612, op. 1, d. 387, l. 4 (Statement by Inturist department of Soviet tourism, April 1957).

65. Vadim Safonov, "U bolgarskikh brat'ev," *Vokrug sveta*, no. 9 (1957): 4.

66. GARF, f. 9520, op. 1, d. 425, l. 7 (Report on a trip to Poland, 1961).

10.3. Dubrovnik street market for tourists, ca. early 1960s. Photograph loaned to author.

old daughter in a maternity shop: "In our country I couldn't even imagine that such a specialized shop could exist."[67] Some of the most enticing material was available on the black market. Soviet tourists to Poland could shop for black-market goods (everything from cosmetics to dinner jackets to razor blades) at Warsaw street markets.[68] Most Warsaw stores were state run, but as described in a 1956 travel article in *Ogonek*, there were also "private shops, hidden away in small lanes, that sold all kinds of things."[69] In Germany, before the construction of the Berlin Wall in 1961, American food, clothing, and music circulated on both sides of a divided country.[70]

All this was despite the fact that the "democratic" part of Berlin, for example, suffered from shortages in comparison to its capitalist neighbor, as did

67. V. I. Metelitsa, *Stranitsy zhizni* (Moscow, 2001), 317. This trip took place in 1971.
68. Crowley, "Warsaw's Shops, Stalinism and the Thaw," 37. Also see Karol, *Visa for Poland*, 180.
69. Kudrevatykh, "Na ulitsakh Varshavy," 7.
70. Uta G. Poiger, *Jazz, Rock, and Rebels: Cold War Politics and American Culture in a Divided Germany* (Berkeley, Calif., 2000), 2; Bernard Newman, *Berlin and Back* (London, 1954), 121.

other east European countries.[71] But even if the material goods they sold were limited, east European stores still offered possibilities for shopping adventures different from those at home. As David Crowley has argued: "Not only did the [Polish] street market offer the opportunity to engage the senses in direct and prohibited ways—fingers to touch, eyes to range over and compare all the goods on display—but it was an 'adventure' made up of chance encounters with things. The fact that many of these things came from 'beyond the iron curtain' added to their appeal as 'forbidden fruit.' "[72] Indeed, spectatorship of material goods was often a Soviet tourist's only form of consumption. "Our tourists behave badly in stores, looking at everything, pricing it, and buying nothing," reported the Soviet embassy in Prague. "All this creates a very bad impression among those nearby and among salespeople."[73]

Soviet tourists looked rather than bought because they received only a small amount of hard currency with which to make purchases. Tourists on a twelve-day Inturist excursion to the GDR could withdraw 84 German marks from the State Bank foreign exchange post in Brest before crossing into eastern Europe, the equivalent of about 217 rubles.[74] This was enough to buy two pairs of ny-lons, or one lesser-quality wool dress, or three or four linen sheets, but not enough to buy a watch and far too little for a radio set (which cost between 375 to 490 marks in 1964).[75] To increase how much they could buy, tourists sometimes brought items of their own to sell or trade, most often Soviet watches or cameras; Comrade Galkina from Moscow sold her camera in Austria and used the money to buy two blouses.[76] The exchange may not have made sense financially: in 1954 a new portable camera of the Leika type cost 713 rubles, while a silk blouse cost 138 rubles.[77] But cameras had become readily available in the USSR beginning in the mid-1930s (indeed, the cameras tourists sold may have been older models), while good-quality blouses may not have been easy to find even in the 1950s.[78] Some tourists were accused by Soviet officials of traveling for the sole purpose of speculating: for example, one Comrade Mikhailova from Leningrad Oblast was said to have traveled to Poland to make money from selling watches.[79]

71. Bernard Newman, *Behind the Berlin Wall* (London, 1964), 78. Also see Iu. Korol'kov, "V Germanii cherez desiat' let," *Novyi mir*, no. 5 (1961): 133.

72. Crowley, "Warsaw's Shops, Stalinism and the Thaw," 39.

73. GARF, f. 9520, op. 1, d. 580, l. 128 (as reported in a speech by Bulgakov, the head of the department for travel in socialist countries at a seminar on international tourism).

74. *Spravochnik: Ob usloviiakh i marshrutakh*, 39, 89. Also see GARF, f. 9520, op. 1, d. 438, l. 93, on where tourists could receive their hard currency.

75. Newman, *Behind the Berlin Wall*, 29. The prices of items in the GDR are from 1964.

76. GARF, f. 9520, op. 1, d. 430, l. 11.

77. Chapman, *Real Wages in Soviet Russia*, 193, 195.

78. Jukka Gronow, *Caviar with Champagne: Common Luxury and the Ideals of the Good Life in Stalin's Russia* (Oxford, 2003), 61.

79. GARF, f. 9520, op. 1, d. 430, l. 111 (On the inadequate behavior of Soviet tourists abroad in 1960). See also GARF, f. 9520, op. 1, d. 438, l. 118 (Report by Elizarov, Saratov trade union representative to Tourist Excursion Bureau conference, March 1961).

It is not surprising that Soviet officials condemned "profiteering," but they were also anxious about other, less marginal forms of consumption. "The majority of [problems abroad] happen in connection with the incorrect expenditure of foreign currency and inappropriate behavior in stores," argued Comrade Serov, a representative from Novosibirsk to a Trade Union Excursion Bureau meeting on foreign travel.[80] Serov gave as an example a young female researcher who bought "some kind of curtain in Germany" which she carried along with her "for the entire itinerary."[81] Serov's chosen target—a young woman—is illustrative of the type of tourist thought most likely to consume at the expense of other activities. Young people in general were often considered a risk in trips abroad, when "in view of the absence of certain life experiences" they "sometimes wrongly value[d] foreign lifestyles."[82] But it was women who were believed especially likely to abandon the ideologically appropriate group excursion for the glitter of the shop window. Anxieties about women's supposedly "natural" and uncontrollable urge to consume are not exclusive to tourism, of course, nor to the Soviet Union.[83] But, according to Susan Reid, in this period of some ambiguity about satisfying consumer demand, Soviet authorities were especially worried about "Soviet citizens', and especially *women's*, potential for excessive, unwarranted consumerism."[84] As the historian Mary Louise Roberts has reminded us, "commodities do not, in themselves, encourage one to be accountable or responsible to any set of political ideals."[85] But for the Khrushchev regime, according to Reid, "once unleashed," women's "insatiable desire" to consume threatened to become "the Achilles' heel of socialism."[86] With this in mind, it is not surprising perhaps that there was more anxiety about consumption on trips to eastern Europe than on trips to western Europe or North America: in 1961 close to 60 percent of tourists on hard-currency trips to eastern Europe were female.[87] So, too, on Sputnik trips, where often 70 to 80 percent of the participants were female.[88] On trips to capitalist countries, in contrast, there were almost always more men than women (most so in trips to the United States).[89]

80. GARF, f. 9520, op. 1, d. 468, l. 78 (Report by Serov).

81. Ibid.

82. GARF, f. 9520, op. 1, d. 438, l. 185.

83. See Mary Louise Roberts, "Gender, Consumption, and Commodity Culture," *American Historical Review* 103, no. 3 (1998): 817–44.

84. Susan E. Reid, "Cold War in the Kitchen: Gender and the De-Stalinization of Consumer Taste in the Soviet Union under Khrushchev," *Slavic Review* 61, no. 2 (2002): 240. Emphasis in the original.

85. Roberts, "Gender, Consumption, and Commodity Culture," 842.

86. Reid, "Cold War in the Kitchen," 240.

87. GARF, f. 9520, op. 1, d. 432, ll. 2–3; GARF, f. 9520, op. 1, d. 375, l. 8 (from a speech by Orfanitskii at a meeting on international tourism, September 1960).

88. RGASPI, f. M-5, op. 1, d. 158, l. 121 (On international tourist trips of Soviet youth in 1958–1962).

89. Of 228 tourists to the United States in 1961 traveling with Inturist, 144 were men and 84 women. To "capitalist" countries as a whole in 1960, 51.7 percent of travelers were men and 48.3 percent women. See GARF, f. 9520, op. 1, d. 432, ll. 1, 29. The same was true for youth travel.

It is not surprising that the high-ranking party members and elite scientific and cultural figures who went on trips to capitalist countries were usually male. It is less obvious why there were more women than men on trips to eastern Europe. Galina Mikhailovna Tokareva, a longtime Komsomol member and now archivist, has argued that more women traveled to eastern Europe because they were more likely to be party and Komsomol activists.[90] As an example, she described her own frequent excursions to eastern Europe as a trip leader for children and youth traveling to international youth camps. Her enthusiastic portrayal of *turizm* as a form of activism is consistent with official Soviet understandings of tourism as purposeful. Trade union and tourism officials emphasized, for example, the professional contacts Soviet worker-tourists could make with workers in foreign enterprises such as the Czech factory Motor.[91] And yet, tourism was also a nod to individual consumer desire. Indeed, it is also possible that more women traveled to eastern Europe precisely because it was such a good place to shop. There is some suggestion in the sources that men preferred more sporting forms of tourism including hiking and camping. This difference was satirized in a 1959 cartoon which showed an unhappy woman sheltering with her husband under a tent in the rain. The caption ran: "Travel with you again to the south? Never!"[92] Consumption reveals the contradictions inherent in sending people abroad to further the collective cause of Soviet socialism and then giving them hard currency (even if in limited amounts) to satisfy individual desires while there.

"Greasy Beaver Coats [and] Hats with Ear Flaps": The Challenges of Selling the Soviet Union

Soviet tourists were not only consuming eastern Europe but selling the Soviet Union. "With their words, conversations, and personal contacts, [tourists] are invaluable propagandists for our successes, our politics, and our Marxist-Leninist ideology," argued one Inturist representative to Bulgaria.[93] Soviet tourists did not always live up to expectations, however. Tourist authorities were ambivalent about sending Soviet citizens abroad not only because of the potential for unregulated experiences, but because of the "uncultured" impressions Soviet tourists sometimes conveyed of themselves and, by extension, of the Soviet Union.

Much of the behavior condemned by Soviet authorities violated cultural norms (*kul'turnost'*). Catriona Kelly has described the virtual "torrent" of advice books appearing in the Khrushchev era prescribing appropriate forms of

RGASPI, f. M-5, op. 1, d. 52, l. 9 (List of the composition of Soviet youth tourists to capitalist countries in 1960).

90. Interview with Galina Mikhailovna Tokareva, Moscow, July 2004.

91. GARF, f. 9520, op. 1, d. 391, l. 45.

92. *Krokodil*, no. 21 (30 July 1959): back page.

93. GARF, f. 9612, op. 1, d. 561, l. 82.

"cultured behavior" in an ever-widening arena of subjects.[94] As portrayed in these books, the ideal Soviet man or woman of the 1950s had "a developed taste in curtains and wallpaper, an eye for elegant dress, good table manners, and refined speech."[95] The cultured individual also knew how to dress and behave while traveling abroad. Proper behavior and dress were described in articles such as one called "Happy Trails" that ran in a Moscow fashion magazine in the early 1960s.[96] In large part, there was little specifically "Soviet" about this advice, which often resembled Europe-wide advice about appropriate behavior. In a report to a Tourist Excursion Bureau meeting about international travel, Alekseeva, a Latvian tourist expert, was dismayed, for example, by ill-mannered Soviet tourists to eastern Europe who did not know what to do with the lemon on their fish.[97]

But a long history of Russian and Soviet assumptions about native inferiority in comparison to European standards of cultured behavior increased expert anxiety about the behavior of "our" tourists in comparison with others. Clothing was a particularly important marker of cultural sophistication or ignorance, a point of some irony given official anxiety about excess consumption (often of clothing) as described above. In a report to a 1962 meeting on international travel, Aleksei Erokhin, the vice-chairman of Inturist, fretted about the poor dress of Soviet tourists: "Our tourists, arriving for vacation, were dressed such that we felt badly for Soviet man, not because he doesn't have the money necessary to purchase a swimming suit, but because although literate and cultured in all other ways, he does not know how to dress or conduct himself properly."[98] "There was an exceptionally good group that went to Czechoslovakia; it was obvious that they were all working people," Erokhin continued, "but some arrived in greasy beaver coats, hats with ear flaps, and boots with the trousers tucked in. They looked like illustrated caricatures of the typical Soviet man."[99] Despite the exceptional "goodness" of these working-class tourists, their working-class style was embarrassing. Articles in the popular *Concise Encyclopedia of Home Economy* (1962) advocated simple blouses for women with loose, comfortable skirts, or, as an option for outdoor activities, capris.[100] Alekseeva complained about Soviet women who ignored such advice. "How can you figure out who are our tourists in a foreign country?" she asked. Our "women waste lots of money sewing dresses [and] expensive silk dressing gowns, when maybe a simple cotton dress would be better."[101] The ideal tourist-citizen dressed in a measured but modern style,

94. Catriona Kelly, *Refining Russia: Advice Literature, Polite Culture, and Gender from Catherine to Yeltsin* (Oxford, 2001), 320.

95. Ibid., 321.

96. As described in GARF, f. 9520, op. 1, d. 468, l. 14 (Report by Alekseeva).

97. Ibid., ll. 12–13 (Report by Alekseeva).

98. Ibid., l. 82 (Report by Erokhin).

99. Ibid., l. 84.

100. *Kratkaia entsiklopediia*, 977.

101. GARF, f. 9520, op. 1, d. 468, l. 15 (Report by Alekseeva).

avoiding both the "Soviet" dress of the obviously working class and the vulgarity of the aspiring elite.

Tourists who dressed inappropriately posed multiple threats to Soviet attempts to sell the superiority of the Soviet Union. In part, their inattention to "modern" styles suggested the cultural backwardness of the USSR. Their clothes also challenged the Soviet presentation of self as economically prosperous. "The men wore some kind of knitted underwear," Erokhin wrote about one group to eastern Europe, "It had once been black, but had faded to gray; one end hung below the knees, and the other rode up God knows where."[102] Erokhin worried about the impact of such dubious costumes on non-Soviet observers: "At this same moment, tourists from Poland and the GDR arrived; and we felt pained to the depths of our souls looking at our good, deserving people who for their work, their role in the world, deserve to be looked at with admiration, not with ridicule."[103] By showing up in their underwear, tourists revealed the dirty reality of life in the Soviet Union where it could be difficult to buy a swimsuit or new underwear. Concerned about the international reputation of the USSR, as well as the personal dignity of the Soviet tourist, Erokhin admitted that consumer conditions were less than adequate and suggested that tourist organizations should sell swimsuits to departing travelers so that "our people aren't left in such bad straits."[104] Better pre-trip education which would discuss appropriate "norms of behavior for Soviet people" was an additional solution.[105] Tourist officials in Latvia produced a film on "etiquette" meant to help to prepare Soviet tourists to go abroad; it demonstrated, among other skills, "how to behave while eating, how to use a spoon, fork, and knife."[106] Once abroad, less worldly tourists were also encouraged to "watch the group leader, [and] watch the guide," and to "keep a close eye on what experienced comrades are doing."[107] In these reports, we hear the voice of the educated Soviet member of the intelligentsia embarrassed by Soviet citizens less "cultured" than he or she. Unwittingly they also replicate the superior voices of western travelers to the Soviet Union, who in their travel accounts often commented on poor service in Soviet restaurants and hotels and on the "truly pathetic dresses and shoes" Russian women wore.[108]

It is notable that all the examples of uncultured behavior provided by Erokhin and Alekseeva were about tourism to socialist countries. This may have been because those traveling to capitalist countries were more likely to be from highly educated classes presumed to be more cultured. Opening up new possibilities for tourism to a wider spectrum of people led to increased anxiety

102. Ibid., l. 82.

103. Ibid.

104. Ibid., l. 83 (Report by Erokhin).

105. GARF, f. 9520, op. 1, d. 391, l. 94; GARF, f. 9520, op. 1, d. 405, l. 2 (Tourist Excursion Bureau trip leader report, 1961).

106. GARF, f. 9520, op. 1, d. 468, ll. 12–13.

107. Ibid., l. 13.

108. Gunnar D. Kumlien, "Fashion à la Russe," *The Commonweal*, 17 January 1958: 402.

about these people when they traveled. The Soviet project of ideological and economic domination in eastern Europe also made authorities sensitive to the cultural position of tourists in countries under Soviet control. To preserve Soviet moral and cultural authority, tourists from the USSR needed to appear at least as cultured as those they were visiting. It was "uncomfortable," Alekseeva reported, when Soviet tourists did not have any money to pay for a coat check at theaters: "We aren't so poor that we can't pay for the coat check." Trip leaders need a little change, she concluded, so that "our tourists can freely use the things that tourists from other countries are able to use."[109] The Soviet Union was not alone among colonizers in its effort to look good in front of the "natives."[110] The difference is that eastern Europe was constructed by Soviet observers as more "West" (and thus more "modern") than the USSR even as it was politically dominated and economically plundered. Suggestively, in Soviet travel accounts the most positive "differences" mentioned about eastern Europe were the "cultured" behaviors of modernity which had long been positively associated with the "West."[111] A travelogue in *Ogonek* described the streets of Warsaw as admirably quiet and "disciplined." Pedestrians were said to cross the road "only at crosswalks and only with a green light."[112] A 1960 article in *Novyi mir* (New World) described with loving enthusiasm the "attentive," "calm," and "attractive cordiality" of a café waiter in Czechoslovakia.[113] The Soviet Union was, by implicit if unstated comparison, understood to be less decorous, less polite, and less "civilized," even as these qualities were now central to what it meant to be Soviet.

Soviet experts assumed that Soviet tourists were embarrassed by their lack of knowledge about how to behave and dress. But how did Soviet tourists themselves feel about what was appropriate? Were the workers wearing hats with ear flaps embarrassed, wearing the hats because they had no other alternative? Or did they think these hats warm, comfortable, and perfectly suitable? Some tourists surely tried their best to imitate foreign fashions as suggested by the kind of purchases they made. But we know that others actively refused the recommendations of their superiors. "One woman, large, middle-aged, went out in a tight skirt, high-heeled shoes, a black hat and gloves. It was summer time. She was told to 'take off the hat,' but she just responded, 'Let them go ahead and look at us.' " The tourist was not bothered, but Alekseeva was. "If tourists wear modest clothes even to the theater, then that won't be noticed," Alekseeva concluded. "But if a large woman wears a dress with a

109. GARF, f. 9520, op. 1, d. 468, l. 16.

110. Inderpal Grewel, *Home and Harem: Nation, Gender, Empire, and the Cultures of Travel* (Durham, N.C., 1996), 93.

111. For a discussion of the West's dual role under Stalin as both "capitalist enemy and exemplar of civilized modernity," see David-Fox, "Stalinist Westernizer?" 734.

112. Kudrevatykh, "Na ulitsakh Varshavy," 7; and Ia. Fomenko, "Predvesenii Budapesht," *Ogonek*, no. 13 (March 1958): 4.

113. I. Radvolina, "K druz'iam v Chekhoslovakiiu!" *Novyi mir*, no. 5 (1960): 146.

ruffle, overly adorned, then people will laugh at her."[114] Erokhin argued that wearing the "wrong" clothes reduced the mood of a "good, kind man" to "some kind of clodhopper who feels ashamed, deteriorates."[115] But we need not assume that travel experts were correct about this. Perhaps the resistance to changing clothes was a defiant assertion of self in the face of comparative poverty and desperation? Maybe the "large, middle-aged woman" in a "tight skirt" was resisting not "bourgeois" norms but the sometimes self-serving notions of polite and cultured behavior imposed from above? We know that tourists sometimes resented the authority of trip leaders, who were said to sometimes rebuke comrades "in inappropriate and untactful ways, often yelling loudly."[116] One group sent a letter of complaint to Inturist about their trip leader who, upon meeting them, belligerently declared: "I am considered an important worker at MOSPS [the Moscow Soviet of Trade Unions] and can purge and clear each of you out thoroughly."[117] "We constantly felt as if we were dangerous characters, if not almost criminals, thanks to the sick fantasies of our leader!"[118]

Demi-Sovietism

Tourism did not always confirm Soviet superiority or erase difference, but it sometimes encouraged the consumption of items and experiences thought by many (including some authorities) to be better than those in the USSR. In *Inventing Eastern Europe: The Map of Civilization on the Mind of the Enlightenment,* Larry Wolff has argued that the invention of eastern Europe by west Europeans during the Enlightenment might be described "as an intellectual project of demi-Orientalism."[119] We might want to consider the Soviet "invention of eastern Europe" as a project (and not only an intellectual one) of "demi-Sovietism." If for west Europeans during the Enlightenment, eastern Europe was "a paradox of simultaneous inclusion and exclusion, Europe but not Europe," for Soviet citizens, eastern Europe was "a paradox of simultaneous inclusion and exclusion," Soviet but not Soviet.[120]

Sending Soviet citizens to this ambiguous space had both advantages and risks. The regime had long acknowledged that there was much to be learned from the technological achievements of the "West." (In the 1930s Stalinist government officials returned from trips to capitalist countries praising paper cups

---

114. GARF, f. 9520, op. 1, d. 468, l. 15 (Report by Alekseeva).

115. Ibid., l. 84.

116. GARF, f. 9520, op. 1, d. 430, l. 98 (Letter of complaint to Inturist).

117. Ibid.

118. Ibid.

119. Larry Wolff, *Inventing Eastern Europe: The Map of Civilization on the Mind of the Enlightenment* (Stanford, Calif., 1996), 7.

120. Ibid.

and plates, American hamburgers and ketchup, and the design of shop windows.)[121] What was significantly different in the 1950s was that this possibility
for experiencing the "demi-Other" became available to a wider range of almost ordinary people. Of course, the risk was believed limited in that those
sent abroad were supposed to be "suitable people" who would "uphold the
prestige and interests of their government."[122] We have seen that this was not
always the case. We should not assume, however, that all Soviet tourists returned home feeling their country to be worse than that which they had visited. Robert English has argued that experiencing the Other contributed to reformist impulses among Soviet diplomats and journalists who lived abroad for
long periods.[123] But reformism did not necessarily mean rejection in the 1950s
and early 1960s, when most tourists were still privileged members of a Soviet
citizenry. Many tourists may have combined enthusiasm for a regime now allowing them to travel with pleasure at what they could consume. In the
Khrushchev era, "Sovietness" meant tolerating, even encouraging, the experience of (controlled) difference. A tourist trip to socialist eastern Europe was a
trip to just the right amount of "demi-Other."

121. Gronow, *Caviar with Champagne*, 70, 75.
122. GARF, f. 9520, op. 1, d. 390, l. 9.
123. Robert D. English, *Russia and the Idea of the West: Gorbachev, Intellectuals, and the
End of the Cold War* (New York, 2000). Also see John Bushnell, "The 'New Soviet Man' Turns
Pessimist," in *The Soviet Union since Stalin*, ed. Stephen Cohen, Alexander Rabinowitch, and
Robert Sharlet (Bloomington, Ind., 1986), 179–99.

CHAPTER 11

Books and Borders

Sergei Obraztsov and Soviet Travels to London in the 1950s

Eleonory Gilburd

The mid-1950s were a moment of unprecedented, government-initiated, and government-sponsored opening of Soviet cultural as well as physical borders to western products and people. Radical expansion of foreign tourism was a centerpiece of the new policy from the summer of 1955, when Nikita Khrushchev returned from the Geneva summit with redoubled confidence in Soviet international prestige. The earliest resolution drafts concerned primarily the presence of foreigners in the Soviet Union and restricted Soviet citizens' foreign travel to socialist countries, at least for 1955. There were no provisions for tourism to capitalist countries, but vague wording allowed for the possibility of such trips "in the years to come."[1] This initial indecision would prove formative: while every year, tourism to eastern Europe continued to expand dramatically, travel to western Europe remained largely the domain of the cultural elite and specialized, carefully selected, delegations. They went to represent the Soviet Union in their various professional capacities, and along the way, some of them assumed a self-ascribed mission of mediators, capable of representing European capitals and cultures to Soviet audiences.

Cultural mediators were luminaries in their fifties and sixties, who had stood at the origins of the Soviet cultural establishment, traveled widely in the 1920s, but since then had not been to western Europe. Traveling to the West was a professional, personal, and material value unto itself; they put on their best faces and best shows abroad, taking both professional and patriotic pride

An earlier version of this article was presented at the University of Chicago Russian Studies Workshop, and I am grateful to the participants for engaging questions. Many thanks to Wendy Bracewell, Sheila Fitzpatrick, Klaus Gestwa, Emma Gilligan, Anne Gorsuch, Diane Koenker, Elizabeth McGuire, Shawn Salmon, Noah Sobe, and Yuri Slezkine for conversations and useful suggestions. I am especially indebted to Julia Gilburd and Denis Kozlov for reading many drafts and for most helpful comments, stylistic and substantive.

1. Rossiiskii gosudarstvennyi arkhiv noveishei istorii (hereafter RGANI) f. 5, op. 30, d. 113, ll. 32–36, esp. 35; Gosudarstvennyi arkhiv Rossiiskoi Federatsii (hereafter GARF), f. 9612, op. 1, d. 359, ll. 11, 36. On travel to eastern Europe, see Gorsuch, in this volume. On Khrushchev's emerging confidence after the Geneva summit, see Vladislav M. Zubok, "Soviet Policy Aims at the Geneva Conference, 1955," in *Cold War Respite: The Geneva Summit of 1955*, ed. Günter Bischof and Saki Dockrill (Baton Rouge, 2000), 61–64, 72–73.

in their accomplishments. But the return gave meaning to the experience of travel, for that is when the travelers had a chance to tell about their trips.

While most people did not physically travel to the West, insofar as going abroad entails seeing, experiencing, and perhaps believing, many visited European capitals nonetheless—vicariously, by reading travel accounts. In a society where travel abroad was so restricted, such accounts were as important as physical border-crossing. Written by cultural mediators, travelogues about the West proliferated in the 1950s. Many of them had one thing in common: recognition. For cultural mediators, these first trips abroad were long-awaited journeys of return: as they rejoined their old friends and colleagues abroad, they also reclaimed European culture for Soviet audiences. At the same time, the landscapes they described, photographed, or filmed were already familiar to Soviet readers and viewers who did not have a chance to travel. Having read European literary classics, the intelligentsia lived with the images of European street corners, cafés, and palaces; for many, traveling abroad and reading travelogues was as much a rendezvous with their adolescent readings of Great Books as an encounter with actual cities.

Like all texts, travelogues have a social life: they are shaped by previous texts and, in turn, shape other trips and travel accounts. They are produced for a certain audience whose responses derive from earlier readings, experiences, and memories. Close attention to multiple dimensions of a single text allows for contextualization of Soviet travel within the imaginative universe of literary pilgrimage, knowledge, and nostalgia. This chapter examines one such travelogue, Sergei Obraztsov's *What I Saw, Learned, and Understood during Two Trips to London*, its crystallization from various artistic media into a coherent text, its reception, and its functions as a narrative and as a material artifact. The focus is on the process of domestication, on the transformation of foreign places into familiar ones through various means of erasing differences, from mapmaking to co-opting and appropriating western literary classics.

Sergei Obraztsov (1901–1992) was a perfect cultural mediator, for he believed in the societal relevance of his personal travel experiences. No trip was complete until he shared its mementos, be they maps or music records, with the whole country through mass media, in print, or in public lectures, putting his many talents to the task. A puppeteer and somewhat of a Renaissance man, Obraztsov wrote books, sang heartbreaking Gypsy romances, made movies, collected curiosities, and painted. In the 1920s he studied art at VKhUTEMAS (an acronym for the Higher State Art and Technical Workshops), at the same time acting at the Musical Studio of the Moscow Art Theater. In 1931 he founded the Russian Puppet Theater, which still carries his name and his legacy. He was born to a famous Moscow intelligentsia family, liberal missionaries of education and progress. Predictably, his childhood was just like other happy childhoods of Russian lore; or rather, that is how he remembered it: a comfortable and cultured life, with quiet family singing around the dinner table, trips to the opera in a cab and to his godmother's Potapovo estate (a

Chekhovian house with a mezzanine and a cherry orchard), and Petrushka street shows.[2] These biographical facts and the atmosphere they evoke are important for understanding Obraztsov's travelogue, for just as his memoir reproduced some of the most enduring tropes of Russian autobiographical writing, so, too, his travel account drew on the classics of European realist literature.[3]

The Politics of Travel Writing

Inspired by two trips to London in 1953 and 1954, Obraztsov's travelogue was one of the first sympathetic Soviet accounts of the West since World War II. From 1954–1955 on, writers and journalists persistently evoked the war in their conceptualization of "peaceful coexistence," "suddenly" remembering that Britain had recently been a Soviet ally. In this spirit, Obraztsov's travelogue was an attempt to effect a "personal [friendly] meeting" between Soviet readers and Londoners, literary characters and, presumably, real people as well.[4] Bearing a cumbersome title that highlights the subjectivity (the "I") of his account, the book went through five editions in three years (1954–1957)—three printed ones, a radio broadcast, and a film. It first appeared in *Novyi mir* (New World) in 1955, the brief heyday of Soviet-British relations, when, following the Geneva summit, the Communist Party Central Committee passed a series of nearly identical resolutions on the "expansion of cultural ties" with various capitalist countries. The resolution on Soviet-British cultural exchange framed the preparations for Khrushchev's trip to Britain in April 1956.[5] Under its mandate, the USSR Ministry of Culture directed a comprehensive effort at propagating British culture to Soviet audiences: in the spring of 1956, Soviet information space was inundated with things British.[6]

The *Novyi mir* publication, the most exuberant among all the editions of Obraztsov's book, was central to these efforts.[7] In March 1956, the Sovetskii pisatel' (Soviet Writer) publishing house decided to issue the travelogue in

2. Obraztsov, *Po stupen'kam pamiati* (Moscow, 2001), 16, 18–19, 26–29.

3. On the subgenre of travel accounts about England, see *"Ia bereg pokidal tumannyi Al'biona..." Russkie pisateli ob Anglii, 1646–1945* (Moscow, 2001); and O. Kazina, "Angliia glazami russkikh," in ibid., 3–24.

4. Sergei Obraztsov, *O tom, chto ia uvidel, uznal i ponial vo vremia dvukh poezdok v London* (Moscow, 1957), 33–34 [all citations are from this edition].

5. RGANI, f. 5, op. 36, d. 11, ll. 17–20.

6. RGANI, f. 5, op. 36, d. 11, ll. 17–21, 86–87; Rossiiskii gosudarstvennyi arkhiv literatury i iskusstva (hereafter RGALI), f. 2329, op. 8, d. 235, ll. 123–26; ibid., d. 239, ll. 39, 40, 44, 130–32, 134–35; Marietta Shaginian, "Na vystavke angliiskoi knigi," *Pravda*, 24 March 1956; Shaginian, "Na vystavke angliiskogo iskusstva," *Pravda*, 25 March 1956; Samuil Marshak, "Dorogi druzhby," *Pravda*, 1 April 1956; David Oistrakh, "Dvadtsat' dnei v Londone," *Literaturnaia gazeta*, 10 April 1956; V. Iakovlev, "Pogovorim o druzhbe," *Trud*, 8 April 1956.

7. Sergei Obraztsov, "Dve poezdki v London," *Novyi mir* no. 6 (1955).

book format. Along the way, the editors toned down Obraztsov's excitement and admiration, because "indulging in" such "tender emotions toward the English is erroneous and, of course, inappropriate in our press."[8] The print run was small, although the demand was enormous; like all important books of the period, this one was snatched from libraries immediately, read during barely a night, and passed from hand to hand, as new readers waited for their turn. The book became a bibliographic rarity, going for incredible prices at the Kuznetskii Most black market and from under the counter in used bookstores.[9] Despite the book's superimposed moderation, Obraztsov's affection, warmth, and light humor remained and resounded across the country a month later, in April 1956, when he shared his travel impressions in three radio broadcasts based on the book.[10] His radio talks were timed to Khrushchev's British trip, an occasion that called for a congenial pitch.

Obraztsov's travelogue actually served not merely as a cultural background but also as a script and an itinerary for the crew of cameramen who went to film Khrushchev's visit. They took the book with them to England, and while following the official delegation and producing *The Mission of Friendship and Peace*, they also checked their cinematic impressions against the travelogue and filmed another documentary, *In London*. Upon returning, they invited Obraztsov to write the offscreen text, but he was so taken by the work that the final product became his own: he edited 9,000 meters of film, wrote the text, and recited it on and off the screen.[11]

Obraztsov envisioned the film's purpose as a chance for everybody to visit London and make personal friends. That is why, instead of a landscape film featuring monuments, he chose shots of everyday life and ordinary people.[12] With the same goal of creating an aura of authentic intimacy, he illustrated his book with his own sketches "from life" and photographs but did not include postcards. Obraztsov took particular care to highlight his authorship of the photographs: the inside cover notifies the reader that "the design of the book, the drawings and photographs are the author's," each photograph comes with a factual or humorous authorial inscription, and throughout the book, there are tidbits of conversations about camera models, film quality, and other photographic matters.[13] These were no technicalities. Obraztsov frequently declared his own inexperience with photography, and, by implication, his inability to make artful and arranged representations. In this, he followed the

8. RGALI, f. 1234, op. 18, d. 866, ll. 3–4.

9. RGALI, f. 2732, op. 1, d. 1078, ll. 220b, 320b, 40, 42, 590b, 72, 82–84; ibid., d. 1082, ll. 9, 11–110b, 13, 34, 35, 37; ibid., d. 1130, ll. 17–170b, 25–250b, 29, 32, 36, 39, 40, 42, 48, 50, 52, 55, 57, 58, 64, 70, 72, 73, 75, 78, 87, 94, 98; ibid., d. 1364, l. 36.

10. GARF, f. 6903, op. 15, d. 235; see also ibid., op. 12, d. 350.

11. Obraztsov, *Po stupen'kam*, 209; RGALI f. 2487, op. 1, d. 194, ll. 97, 109.

12. RGALI, f. 2487, op. 1, d. 194, ll. 97–98.

13. Obraztsov, *O tom*, 38, 72, 197.

traditional distinction between travelers and tourists. For him, tourists, who purchase postcards with iconic representations, were exposed only to superficial aspects of a culture. Tourists as unwitting consumers of sites proffered specifically for consumption were contrasted with his own self-positioning as a cultural (not to mention cultured) traveler, capable of penetrating beyond the façade—quite literally, photographing familiar places at unusual angles, from the side or the back of buildings.[14]

In his conceptualization of the film, Obraztsov abandoned "the narrative epic" for "a conversational, personal" account told in the first person. Ironically, although montage obeyed the logic of the political moment, the film was unusual among Soviet documentaries of those years. While the Soviet documentary customarily cherished fact and the offscreen narrator's voice laid claims to detached objectivity, Obraztsov replaced fact with a "novella," and thus created an unabashedly subjective account.[15] He appeared on the screen in the beginning and the end, announcing both the project and his presence, against the background of drawn curtains, as if on stage. His lifelong engagement with theaters gave an additional level of meaning to the film's theatricality. But it was the voice, above all, that made for the account's distinctiveness: unlike remarks by a detached observer, Obraztsov's stories were embedded within the images and emanated from the perspective of an insider, a participant.[16]

As in the book, he planned to open the film with a statement on viewers as participants, on the importance of personal experiences of foreign places for mutual understanding, and on the new possibilities for "hundreds of people" to tour England. But between the spring/summer of 1956 when the film was made, and late 1956 when it was scored for sound and the commentary went through censorship, domestic and international politics changed, and the statement was expunged. So, too, was the declaration of the film's purpose to show London "to millions, not hundreds, of Soviet people."[17] *In London* came out in 1956, the year when the dual crises of Hungary and Suez forestalled further cultural initiatives.

14. Ibid., 91, 197. For a discussion of "authenticity" in the making of tourists and travelers, see Jonathan Culler, "The Semiotics of Tourism," in *Framing the Sign: Criticism and Its Institutions* (Oxford, 1988).

15. On Soviet documentary, see L. Iu. Mal'kova, *Sovremennost' kak istoriia: Realizatsiia mifa v dokumental'nom kino* (Moscow, 2002), 11–39, 47–53, 59–71, 78–91; RGALI, f. 2487, op. 1, d. 194, ll. 97–98.

16. RGALI, f. 2487, op. 1, d. 194, l. 98; Rossiiskii gosudarstvennyi arkhiv kinofotodokumentov (hereafter RGAKFD), no. 10298. For a discussion of commentary versus perspective in documentary film, see Bill Nichols, *Representing Reality: Issues and Concepts in Documentary* (Bloomington, Ind., 1991), 118–33.

17. RGALI, f. 2487, op. 1, d. 194, ll. 7, 109; the statement was reduced to one sentence with no reference to travel.

Overcoming Distance

Britain was one of Obraztsov's lifelong causes, and he would become one of its most prominent spokesmen in the Soviet Union, but in 1953–1954, when he went there for the first time, it was a country he remembered as unreachable. In 1925, on the way to and from New York, the young Obraztsov caught a glimpse of the British shore at Southampton. Like other actors in the Soviet troupe, he was not allowed to disembark, and for the next twenty-five years the inaccessible city would remain a mirage. Hence, distance—more precisely, overcoming distance—became the leitmotif of his travelogue.

He sought to overcome distance by exposing difference as false consciousness.[18] The first two chapters, in which we find the narrator en route, outline two itineraries, one mostly above eastern Europe by plane (1953), the other around western Europe by ship (1954). Neither one provides for a direct trip from Russia to England; along the way, Obraztsov makes stops and changes planes in various European capitals, visits or recalls noteworthy sights, using the occasions for self-reflective commentary on distance and proximity. These itineraries habituate readers to foreign places and prepare them for an encounter with London that is not altogether strange. As the last stopovers and the first capitalist cities, Amsterdam and Stockholm give a taste of things to come: medieval quarters, kings' palaces, art galleries, and stock exchanges.[19] The two chapters serve another purpose as well; they establish commonalities through the shared experience of World War II. For example, the ruins of London echo those of Warsaw, and Obraztsov's book was one of first to remind Soviet readers of their recent ally: "fascist bombs . . . were flying and houses in London were falling, as if exploding within. . . . Could this be forgotten?"[20] In the film, the reminder is a stark series of images: overlapping, alternating, displacing each other and reappearing, the debris of buildings is paired with shots of contemporary children.[21]

Children are the most poignant illustration of proximity-as-similarity between England and Russia, and the most frequent characters in Obraztsov's written and visual travelogues. Images of children account for much of the film's congeniality, intimacy, and familiarity, for bringing foreign sites and rituals home. For example, the Changing of the Guard—in Obraztsov's words, "the most astonishing and theatrical" ritual—is preceded and followed by shots of children. The mounted guards line up but for a brief moment, to be displaced by children hanging over a fence to get a better view, and then a boy on tiptoes trying to catch a glimpse of the procession, his attempts frustrated

---

18. For a discussion of various degrees of permissible difference at this time, see Gorsuch in this volume; and Ted Hopf, *Social Construction of International Politics: Identities and Foreign Policies, Moscow, 1955 and 1999* (Ithaca, N.Y., 2002), 70, 74, 79, 80, 92–98, 113.

19. Obraztsov, *O tom*, 14–23.

20. Ibid., 11–12, 14–15, 17–18.

21. RGALI, f. 2487, op. 1, d. 194, ll. 48, 107; RGAKFD, no. 10298.

by a forest of legs. With a smile in his voice, Obraztsov devotes most of the commentary to the little boy, rather than the procession.[22] The old exotic ritual is a colorful parade, and boys climb up the highest spots, just as they would in Moscow. In the end, children move to the forefront and become the film's main protagonists. Here Obraztsov explicitly rejects differences: a girl's face rushes toward the screen, then darts back from the camera, and "Look!"—he exclaims—"here they are swinging back and forth just like that, only in Moscow, not in London." The screen reveals similar views in succession: a glimmering carousel in London and a wooden merry-go-round in Moscow, and boulevards packed with children in both capitals.[23] This finale was particularly distressing for the Main Administration of Motion Pictures and its overlord, the Ministry of Culture. Yet Obraztsov held stubbornly to his emphasis on similarities, even in little things.[24]

For distinctions were precisely what he argued against both in the film and the book. Upon arrival in London, alone in his hotel room, he rewinds his trip in his mind while the city sleeps. The kaleidoscope of impressions upsets the tranquility of the night as Obraztsov restlessly measures the distance between Moscow and London. Beyond the mirage of the conceited London emerges an innocuous sleeping kingdom. Surprisingly, London is tangible, almost mundane: "Is it possible that the ceiling above my head and the unfamiliar window curtains are London? So, Moscow and London are that close?" With some gentleman snoring in a neighboring room, the hotel becomes a metaphor for geopolitical space: "Our doors open onto the same hallway, and our windows look out onto the same park. We are so close."[25]

Obraztsov measures proximity in real time: a two-day journey by train, a few hours by plane. Distance, by contrast, is measured in imaginary units. Partitions are unreal because he does not come across an "iron curtain" on the way, nor a red-and-white striped bar in the skies, only a meridian in the seas, but meridians, as we know from geography textbooks, are "imaginary lines of longitude."[26] He summons geography, the science of distances, to support his calculations. The book's inside cover contains a map of Europe that fortifies Obraztsov's project by minimizing the geographical space between Moscow and London. This map is a backbone outline, more of a silhouette. It has no countries, and only bodies of water are shaded and distinct. The rest is undifferentiated empty space; suggestive thin lines go off in all directions and never intersect to form a boundary or an enclosed place. Obraztsov writes his journey upon this blank space. The map bears no printed words, no country names, no scale; the only designations are his writings in cursive, the only handwritten inscriptions are the names of cities he had visited or passed

22. RGALI, f. 2487, op. 1, d. 194, l. 14; RGAKFD, no. 10298.
23. RGALI, f. 2487, op. 1, d. 194, ll. 48, 107, 108; RGAKFD, no. 10298.
24. RGALI, f. 2487, op. 1, d. 194, ll. 52, 112.
25. Obraztsov, O tom, 30–32.
26. Ibid., 31–32, 46.

through. The only lines that structure the map's space and text are two thick diagonals connecting Russia and Britain. One line curves in and out, resembling waves: this is the sea route between Leningrad and London. The other goes straight from Moscow to London, through Minsk, Warsaw, Prague, and Amsterdam. Both represent a continuous path—no bars, borders, divisions. Or, as Obraztsov himself put it, referring to socialist Prague and capitalist Amsterdam, "I take out a pocket atlas and mark in pencil a straight line."[27]

Capitalist London

He did not succeed in erasing all differences. There still remains the capitalist London, and capitalism at once marks its distinction from the Soviet world and makes for its similarity to any other capitalist city. Capitalism determines London's appearance, dividing the city into neighborhoods so different that Obraztsov wonders whether it is not several unrelated cities coexisting within the metropolis. He describes capitalism through the concept of "incommensurability"—between the East End and the West End; between comprehensive children's encyclopedias and "comics"; between the National Gallery and Madame Tussaud's Wax Museum. "It is as if people live in different worlds. This incommensurability of different social strata, different groups, and even different people is characteristic of any capitalist city; and you will experience it in London, too. This is what will astonish you at the outset."[28] And, of course, the press, which distorts the scales of all things, is the most inconsistent part of capitalist life. Obraztsov devotes a separate chapter to the press, all of it yellow by definition; and in the film, he conveys the sensationalism of the press through movement. In quick succession follow newspaper flags; cars with newspaper markings scurry about, against the background of bustling street traffic. Above all, it is the image of an eager, perhaps a bit gullible, reader that makes for the commotion on the screen. Simultaneously, in different places, men buy papers and delve into them on the spot.[29] For Obraztsov, what the newspapers and Madame Tussaud's museum have in common is the principle of commercialization for the sake of entertainment, sensationalism, and, ultimately, profit. He offers a cultural critique of capitalism: "poisonous" comics and horror films; bizarre orators in Hyde Park, prostitutes twiddling keys, and wandering musicians earning their pitiful living—a lonely crowd. "There is nothing more frightening in the world than to be alone among the many. . . . A man would perish in the crowd of people similarly isolated from

27. Ibid., inside cover, 20. For a similar approach, see Andrew Thacket, "Journey with Maps: Travel Theory, Geography and the Syntax of Space," in *Cultural Encounters: European Travel Writing in the 1930s*, ed. Charles Burdett and Derek Duncan (New York, 2002), 11–28.
28. Obraztsov, *O tom*, 52, 104–5, 124–28, 136–39, 141–43.
29. Ibid., 117–22; RGAKFD, no. 10298.

each other, lonely in their happiness and in their grief, because people's destinies are stratified, estranged. . . . They are incommensurate."[30]

Very little of his assessment, however, concerns politics: there are no slums here, no starving people, no "fascistic thugs"—all a standard fare in Soviet travel writings about the West. There are only: "a dirty yard," a "multi-apartment house . . . that looks much like a corrugated can cut vertically into halves," "pubs or small snack bars where workers eat their modest lunch," and a man with "a dark, almost black face and curly metallic hair" who credits his hands with making Britain rich. To be sure, these are variations on standard themes, but the tone is more restrained, while the colors are brighter. The difference is not only a matter of shades: completely missing from Obraztsov's account is a sense of crisis, the impending crisis of capitalism, which was a central tenet of Soviet journalism. On the contrary, East Enders are proud Londoners and celebrate bank holidays along with everybody else. In Hyde Park, the same black man shouts: "I love London, I so much love London!"[31]

Even commerce, which bears the brunt of Obraztsov's criticism, has something attractive about it. He certainly qualifies his descriptions with references to prohibitive prices, but he also relishes it all: Lincoln cars "proudly displaying their shiny, smooth sides," "remarkable ball dresses of brocade and gauze," "these rugs and this chintz upholstery." The film presents close-ups of shoes, jewelry, dresses, wedding gowns, and elegantly poised mannequins.[32] In the book, a chapter on a West End commercial district recreates the shopping fever and the noise by personifying inanimate objects. Things have taken on a life of their own: "cotton skirts, straw hats, and bathing suits are *screaming* in unison," "colorful advertisement stripes *moan*," "commercial banners *call on*," and "neon signs *twinkle*." Advertisement is coercive and omnipresent, and its colors, "green, red, blue, yellow," "running, jumping, turning about, changing," generate the same feeling of rush, uneasiness.[33]

But somewhere along the way, his narrative slips from the confines of cultural critique, and the "bustle of lights at the Piccadilly Circus" turns into the lights of the big city, or simply, "city lights."[34] Dusk falls and the lights blaze up: "Guinness time," movie theaters, plays, revues, and restaurants. In the film, illuminated signs are not static images; inscriptions, taking the viewer by

30. Obraztsov, *O tom*, 106–14, quote 115–16; on alienation as an important theme in European travel writing about London, see Roy Porter, "Visitors' Visions: Travellers' Tales of Georgian London," in *Transports: Travel, Pleasure, and Imaginative Geography, 1600–1830*, ed. Chloe Chard and Helen Langdon (New Haven, 1996), 40.

31. Obraztsov, *O tom*, 82–83, 85, 109–10.

32. Ibid., 61–65; RGAKFD, no. 10298.

33. Obraztsov, *O tom*, 61–70; the passages that recreated the feeling of rush and hysteria were omitted from the radio presentation; see GARF, f. 6903, op. 15, d. 235, per. 1, ll. 10–11; on consumerism, traffic, and the feeling of rush as themes in European travel writing about London, see Porter, "Visitors' Visions."

34. Chaplin's *City Lights* was rendered in Russian as *Ogni bol'shogo goroda*.

surprise, emerge from the darkness of the screen and disappear effortlessly. Lights glimmer to the tempo of fast-paced jazz accompanying these sequences offscreen. "The colorful streets of the West End will keep shining and flickering for much longer, and plastic ladies in the windows, with glittering gauze and spangles of evening gowns, will keep spinning in a silent waltz."[35] Night falls and the lights go out—only a few that are still flickering "cover the street with wide, bright stripes, as if someone spread out silver-yellowish runners." Then "the noisy West End fell asleep and became mysterious like any sleeping city."[36] Especially like Charlie Chaplin's mythical city in Jazz-Age America.

For, indeed, that is how Obraztsov's nighttime London looks from the screen. Chaplin's *City Lights* opens with a neon sign spelling the title over the background of flickering lights, "as if part of a modern Broadway marquee," to the tunes of jazz; then lights fade into the darkness. There is an underside to this city of skyscrapers, cars, stylish women, and millionaires, of entertainment and glamour: the lone Tramp and the blind flower girl. In 1925 Obraztsov had lived in New York, and on his way home via Broadway, he was repeatedly struck by the mad dance of lights and the loneliness of this city. New York was his reference point for discussing "a big capitalist city." America intrudes into Obraztsov's description of London at several junctures, everywhere striking the eye disagreeably. Coca-Cola has the biggest billboard; American television and cinema are ruining the old English music hall, while American comics are destroying the minds of British children. The brightest shirt and the most offensive tie (always with a monkey or a naked woman) inevitably belong to an American, such as the one who rudely interrupts the proud black man in Hyde Park: "No reason to brag about your black hands!" It was America that accounted for much of the differences Obraztsov did not tone down, and it was in comparison to American metropolises, that London gained in old-world familiarity and charm.[37]

The concept of "peaceful coexistence" presented an entirely new problem for Soviet propagandists: how to represent capitalism? For almost forty years there was but one way to talk about it—in abusive language forecasting its imminent and violent collapse. "Peaceful coexistence" meant that capitalism was

35. RGAKFD, no. 10298; RGALI, f. 2487, op. 1, d. 194, l. 28.

36. Obraztsov, *O tom*, 71, 74; for similar images, see a documentary filmed by an agricultural delegation in 1956, in RGALI, f. 2487, op. 1, d. 610, and RGAKFD, no. 10756.

37. Obraztsov, *O tom*, 70, 104, 110, 127, 148, 153–54, 159–60; GARF, f. 6903, op. 15, d. 235, per. 1, ll. 1–2. On Obraztsov's impressions of New York, see *Po stupen'kam*, 93. Originally modeled on Paris, Chaplin's city soon became "no city on earth and . . . all cities," above all, American metropolises ca. 1930. Chaplin's American city might have been a variation of London, where he grew up in destitution, in workhouses, garrets, and Poor Law schools. Chaplin scholars have noted that the blind flower girl, a paradigm of virtue, is associated with a European landscape. See Gerard Molyneaux, *Charles Chaplin's "City Lights": Its Production and Dialectical Structure* (New York, 1983), 201–8, 211–22; the quote about Broadway marquee is on 207, and the script of the film's opening is on 250. For the composite city, see David Robinson, *Chaplin: His Life and Art* (London, 1985), 395; and for Chaplin's London childhood, ibid., 10–41.

here to stay for a while; the idea of peaceful competition necessitated open comparisons and acknowledged borrowings. A new language for talking about capitalism would have to be found. And it was found—in westerners' commentaries on their societies. As a result, losing some of the vehemence of their earlier critique, Soviet authors began to replicate the imagery and language of western self-representations, cinematic and literary. In their portraits of the West, there was now the wistfulness and sadness of the ordinary folk, a Tramp's longing for the glitter of the rich man's world.

Familiar London

If Obraztsov did not altogether erase differences, he did succeed in domesticating Britain. He did so by bringing back the London long familiar to Soviet audiences from English literature—the London of Russian childhood readings. He posited two types of memory and opened the travelogue with a discussion of two corresponding artifacts: "the memory of knowledge," akin to a notebook or an address book with dates, numbers, maps, and "the memory of feelings," resembling a scrapbook, "an album with pictures." "All the pictures are colored, many pages contain various smells, and some even make sounds" in this scrapbook that works Proustian magic in the Soviet world. Indeed, double the magic: the scrapbook effected a dual transference into a time lost and a place unreachable. However useful "the memory of knowledge" was, it failed Obraztsov when he tried to picture London before his first trip. Not so the "album of the memory of feelings" packed with portraits:

> Its very first page made me smile. It depicted a boy with long curly hair dressed in a black velvet suit with big, white, starched collar. This is my first English friend—*The Little Lord Fauntleroy*. Like he, I was eight years old when we met.
>
> Then he is replaced by *The Prince and the Pauper*. Medieval London. In the album of memory I see the big, noisy bridge across the Thames and the gloomy prison, the Tower. Dickens. The London of the nineteenth century. The frightening city of Oliver Twist. The city of moneylenders, slave labor, and debtors' prisons. The somewhat sentimental city of *The Cricket on the Hearth* with the traditional happiness of the family fireplace. Pickwick's ironic city, populated with merry, kind, witty people.
>
> London of the Forsytes. As I sit in the plane, I enter, along with Soames, the old house of the Forsyte Aunts, or make my way through the blinding fog, catching up with Irene's unfortunate beloved.
>
> This is almost present-day London. Probably, if one were to sit for a while on a bench in Hyde Park, one could see how Lord Essex, following the son of the young Forsyte along the riding trail, rides by, patting his chestnut mare with a riding crop.

Surely, Aldridge's heroes have come across the heirs of Galsworthy's characters. Which means that I, too, will meet them in London.[38]

And he does meet them in London. The Forsyte Aunts are practically the first people Obraztsov and his readers encounter upon arriving at his hotel, just as they are among the first ones Galsworthy introduces to his readers. In *The Saga*, the sisters epitomize the idea of permanence—of the Forsyte clan, of the bourgeoisie, of proprietorship as a way of life, and of London itself, which came to bid its last farewell to Aunt Ann, bending "a hundred thousand spires and houses . . . before the grave of this, the oldest Forsyte of them all."[39] In the mid-twentieth century, "the old ladies, who live in this hotel permanently, as if it were a boardinghouse, and who look very much like the Forsyte Aunts, are sitting in the drawing room, still reading that same *Christian Monitor*, and knitting. When they see us, they smile in surprise and nod their heads affably."[40]

Obraztsov takes Galsworthy as his travel companion from the start of his journey, offering his audience a vicarious choice of reading *The Saga* en route.[41] Throughout the travelogue, and presumably throughout his stay in London, he repeatedly runs into Galsworthy's protagonists in the City, where passers-by remind him of "the first generation of the Forsytes," on the train, and in Hyde Park.[42] Of course, the story would not be complete without Irene, *The Saga*'s embodiment of beauty, with whom Obraztsov fell in love.[43] In his travelogue, English women are modeled on Irene's image: "young, tall, . . . slender, well built, with a head beautifully set, hair curling freely."[44] This is the portrait of a young mother he meets, true to form, in Hyde Park one "breezy morning."[45] It must be Irene, and it is—that turns out to be her baby's name. His love is finally consummated: the young woman has nicknamed her baby after Obraztsov's famous puppet, Tiapa.[46]

Galsworthy's characters thus structured Obraztsov's street encounters. But it was Charles Dickens who provided the mimetic devices and the chronotope for Obraztsov's travelogue and readers. In the Soviet Union, Dickens was instantly recognizable because of how he was read. Reading Dickens was a refrain in the intelligentsia's nostalgic recollections of growing up. Dickens was published in millions of copies and acclaimed by Soviet literary critics for depicting the dehumanizing and downtrodden London of early capitalism, replete with debtors' prisons, child labor, malicious strangers, and strange crea-

38. Obraztsov, *O tom*, 8–10.
39. John Galsworthy, *The Forsyte Saga* (London, 1950), 92.
40. Obraztsov, *O tom*, 50.
41. Ibid., 37.
42. Ibid., 58, 186–87.
43. Galsworthy, vii–ix; Obraztsov, *O tom*, 196.
44. Obraztsov, *O tom*, 192.
45. Ibid., cf., for example, Galsworthy, 8, 37, 58, 99, 102–5.
46. Obraztsov, *O tom*, 195–96; GARF, f. 6903, op. 15, d. 235, per. 3, l. 10.

tures, all of which encroach upon the safety of the domicile.[47] Yet, it was the safety associated with childhood that resonated with Soviet memoirists and Obraztsov's readers.

Dickens's novels are fairy tales writ large, with plots frequently motivated by quests and journeys, with resolutions resembling the Cinderella story, and with a world populated by kind fairies and eerie ogres.[48] Most of Dickens's heroes are children who lead the lives of grown-ups—beg, wander about, take care of adults more infantile and fragile than themselves—but who never quite grow up; they chance upon bad people but remain uncorrupted and innocent. These are transitional characters that readers encounter at a transitional age. In memoirs of Soviet readings, Dickens's name hinted at a special bond with a parent: mothers read him to their children, his novels were the "first 'grown-up' books" fathers brought home from libraries.[49]

Dickens's books are drawn out, with many characters, plots, and subplots, which extend the pleasure of reading almost infinitely, or at least for as long as childhood lasts. "For an infinitely long time," recalled the art historian Mikhail German, "as if reading a cozy fairy tale, I read one of the most charming novels in the world—*The Pickwick Papers*, an amazing book, where there already exist Dickens in his entirety, his England, his unique unhurried humor, the divinely shy sentimentality."[50] Dickens was also an introduction to the English language: sometimes people made their way through the original, with a dictionary, "copying down all the unknown words," memorizing them, "stumbling, of course," yet learning the language nonetheless—Dickens's English.[51] But more than a country and a language, for Kseniia Atarova, who grew up in the late 1940s and 1950s among the literary and artistic elite, Dickens was "an entire world into which [she] would immerse with pleasure. . . . [She] read and re-read, remembered some episodes almost by heart, knew all the characters, even incidental ones, adored Dickens's humor, forgave him the saccharine sentimentality of positive heroes for the unsurpassed eccentrics."[52]

Dickens smelled of thyme and wormwood, perhaps of medication, and also, of old papers in Father's bookcase. His name evoked long summer dacha evenings, "the sea and gray cliffs," "aromatic, dark garden at night," first at-

47. For a more detailed treatment of Soviet critical response to Dickens's anti-capitalism, see Maurice Friedberg, *A Decade of Euphoria: Western Literature in Post-Stalin Russia, 1954–64* (Bloomington, Ind., 1977), 158–61, and for Galsworthy, 163–64.

48. For an analysis of fairy-tale plots in Dickens, see Harry Stone's classic *Dickens and the Invisible World: Fairy Tales, Fantasy, and Novel-Making* (Bloomington, Ind., 1979); and Elaine Ostry, *Social Dreaming: Dickens and the Fairy Tale* (New York, 2002), 17–27, 63–78.

49. Revekka Frumkina, *Vnutri istorii. Esse, stat'i, memuarnye ocherki* (Moscow, 2002), 242; Kseniia Atarova, *Vcherashnii den'* (Moscow, 2001), 309–10; Kornei Chukovskii and Lidiia Chukovskaia, *Perepiska, 1912–1969* (Moscow, 2003), 24.

50. Mikhail German, *Slozhnoe proshedshee* (St. Petersburg, 2000), 98.

51. Chukovskii and Chukovskaia, *Perepiska,* 58, 287; German, *Slozhnoe,* 254.

52. Atarova, *Vcherashnii,* 310.

tempts to write poetry, and the first "bookish" love.[53] Dickens was read during similarly long winter evenings, and during long illnesses. During the war, he brought the feeling of home to evacuee children.[54] And for children, as well as for adults, his name denoted a measure of safety amidst Stalin-era arrests, or at least, this is how he entered contemporary Russian prose. In Liudmila Ulitskaia's story about a teenage girl's (and the whole country's) awakening in March 1953, Dickens's name is a shelter from the ugly world of the "doctors' plot"—Dickens, together with Biblical tales, classical music, a secluded dacha, and an old apartment full of antiquarian things. While the storm rages outside, the story's elderly intelligentsia couple continues to read Dickens, play the piano, and protect their granddaughter by simply remaining innocent as children.[55] "Even now, as I look at Dickens's collected works in thirty volumes, calm thoughts of old age, with a deep armchair and glasses, descend upon me. Thoughts of how Oliver Twist, David Copperfield, and Little Dorrit, the kind and unfortunate heroes of my childhood, will surround me again," wrote Raisa Orlova, identifying Dickens with respite.[56]

Obraztsov brought back Dickens's London that Soviet armchair travelers had grown up with. In the travelogue, Dickens is the designation for places and the measure of time. His name becomes an adjective (*dikkensovskii*) for old cars that look like cabbies, for entire districts and streets, for buildings and stagecoaches, for humor, and for London itself—"an old curiosity shop."[57] It turned out that capitalism in twentieth-century Britain looked much the same as it did in "Dickens's times": "sturdy, heavy" banks were built in the second half of the nineteenth century, and clerks, carrying long umbrellas with bent handles, were dressed just like their nineteenth-century predecessors, in narrow striped pants, black suits, and derbies.[58] "Dickens's times" have left another legacy: the slums of the East End, eternally inhabited by David Copperfield. On his walk through "the labyrinth of narrow black yards, passages, low arches, and dark, iron staircases" of the East End, Obraztsov expects "the thin little figure of David Copperfield to emerge from just around this very corner, and Mister Scrooge to walk on the other side of the street."[59]

The paradigm of "the old curiosity shop" shaped much of Obraztsov's conception of London. If the shop "was one of those receptacles for old and curi-

53. Lidiia Libedinskaia, "*Zelenaia lampa*" i mnogoe drugoe (Moscow, 2000), 104; German, *Slozhnoe*, 152–53.

54. German, *Slozhnoe*, 15–16, 89–101.

55. Liudmila Ulitskaia, "Vtorogo marta togo zhe goda . . ." in *Lialin dom: povest' i rasskazy* (Moscow, 1999).

56. Raisa Orlova, *Vospominaniia o neproshedshem vremeni* (Ann Arbor, Mich., 1983), 131.

57. Obraztsov, *O tom*, 58, 80, 158–59, 162, 197.

58. Ibid., 58–59; GARF, f. 6903, op. 15, d. 235, per. 1, l. 6 (same text, but with a preface that Dickens is, indeed, a valid paradigm—in response to the British Ambassador's argument that contemporary England cannot be "defined by Dickens." "Vystuplenie angliiskogo posla po moskovskomu televideniiu," *Pravda*, 20 March 1956.)

59. Obraztsov, *O tom*, 80; Mister Scrooge is the miser from *A Christmas Carol*.

ous things which seem to crouch in odd corners of this town . . . suits of mail standing like ghosts in armour here and there, . . . rusty weapons of various kinds,"[60] then London is another such receptacle. It is filled with old curiosities—some picturesque, some absurd, and some simply amusing. There are useless and even harmful laws, preserved, together with the appropriate regalia, "white horsehair wigs and medieval black gowns," from times immemorial.[61] There are fantastic figures (such as the "winged griffin"), the armor, and the rusty weaponry, too. In Westminster, for instance,

> If [the horses] did not move their feet and did not wave their tired heads, one could mistake them for agate sculptures. The horses bear riders in bright red, sleeveless vests and golden helmets, showing no signs of life.[62]

Within this huge curiosity shop called London there are smaller ones, but all are noteworthy for the rarities contained therein: a storefront exhibiting two-hundred-year-old hats, or a pub called the Tiger, where Queen Elizabeth had her ale, and other such places that, Obraztsov explains, the English like to preserve and exhibit as symbols of "good old England."[63] He also builds his own "curiosity shop"—a chapter on "Traditions," in which he criticizes the propensity toward "conserving the everyday," from Cambridge colleges to fireplaces. The fireplaces especially exasperated Obraztsov for their wastefulness of human labor and resources, for the smog and illnesses they caused, for their sheer inefficiency.[64] Despite the criticism and the sarcasm, however, he recreates the ideal of English domesticity: fireplace, armchair, five-o'clock tea, and garden.[65] The home centered on the hearth and the celebration of the family are, of course, the cornerstones of Dickens's world, with its endless domestic scenes and relations that offer refuge from the rain, fog, cold, and the towering steeples of the great and gray city.[66] Even as Obraztsov is ironic about the hearth and the paraphernalia of jurisprudence, he situates his own sarcasm within the conventions of Dickens's satire, English puns, parodies, and the Punch show. "The English themselves like to chaff at these traditions. This ironic folk [narodnyi] humor created funny names and little witty stories about London's curiosities. . . . The humor of the Pickwick Club is not only Dickens himself; it is, first and foremost, the English. This is their humor. Humor that is always self-consciously ironic and polemical toward the interlocutor."[67]

---

60. Charles Dickens, *The Old Curiosity Shop* (Oxford, 1998), 11, 20.

61. Obraztsov, *O tom*, 53, 170–71; GARF, f. 6903, op. 15, d. 235, per. 1, l. 3.

62. Obraztsov, *O tom*, 94, 96.

63. Ibid., 162–66.

64. Ibid., 167–69, 172–75, 179–80.

65. Ibid., 85, 160, 172. For smog, fog, and fireplace as prominent tropes in European writings about London, see Porter, "Visitors' Visions."

66. On hearth and home, see Alexander Welsh, *The City of Dickens* (Oxford, 1971), 141–63.

67. Obraztsov, *O tom*, 197, 201.

Dickens's London is the city of children's imaginary universe, of long-forgotten objects, stories, and dreams. "Childhood" and "youth" are Obraztsov's most frequent temporal reference points: Stratford-on-Avon, Shakespeare's birthplace, is the "town that seemed a fairy tale in my adolescence"; the first train, the Rocket, is "a fairy-tale heroine of my childhood"; the statue of Homer in the British Museum is the one "whose copy I drew so many times when I was a child."[68] Time stands still in this kingdom from childhood books: "To walk around the Tower is to read a long historical novel." Or, perhaps, a fairy tale, for London is no ordinary kingdom—horses are immobile sculptures, mannequins freeze in their waltz, and guardsmen stand still in this "enchanted kingdom of sleeping beauty," where magic happens every night:

> Wait for the night! Large searchlights will illuminate the roofs of Westminster Abbey and Big Ben, which, at once, will become transparently waxen. Green and yellow lights will transform that big administrative building on the other shore into an enchanted castle. . . . The hands of the clock meet and peer into the skies. Midnight.[69]

Obraztsov's Fellow Travelers

Obraztsov claimed reality for this familiar fairy tale, and his audience was willing to suspend disbelief. So readily and self-indulgently did readers give him credence as an eyewitness to magic, that they deliberately surrendered their own agency. In their letters to Obraztsov, readers represented the book as an active subject that "casts a spell," "captures" as if by surprise, and described themselves as co-opted, even seduced by the irresistible travelogue.[70] The radio talks magnetized them: "we listened with my son, afraid to miss even one word," and (from a different letter), "when you finished, I sat benumbed for a long, long time, and scene after scene ran before my eyes."[71]

Judging by numerous literary and historical references in the travelogue, Obraztsov's implied audience was well-read and erudite. The real audience, whether for the book, the film, or the radio broadcast, indeed consisted largely of the intelligentsia, in the Soviet sense of well-educated professionals. The evidence is inevitably fragmentary, coming as it does from a self-selected group of letter writers, but a sketch of the audience's social profile is possible. Of the letter writers who indicated their professions, over 80 percent were teachers, students, engineers, librarians, scientists, and various others with a higher ed-

---

68. Ibid., 130–31, 135.
69. Ibid., 95, 100–102.
70. For example: RGALI, f. 2732, op. 1, d. 1078, ll. 19, 62, 69; ibid., d. 1081, ll. 5, 102; ibid., d. 1364, ll. 16, 51.
71. RGALI, f. 2732, op. 1, d. 1081, ll. 17, 83–830b; ibid., d. 1364, l. 19.

ucation, while factory workers, soldiers, and sailors made up merely one-fifth. Almost half of the students envisioned themselves as future educators and librarians. Perhaps it is not surprising, given the subject matter, that at least 43 percent of all teachers and 21 percent of all students claimed to know foreign languages. Nor is it surprising that a third of the letters came from Moscow and Leningrad. What is remarkable about the geography of the audience is the prominence of provincial centers, small towns, and even rural settlements, "backwoods with no railroad and no electricity," where a librarian or young teacher constituted an avid and grateful readership.[72]

In response to his book, radio talk, and film, Obraztsov received laudatory mail, with the overwhelming majority of letters phrased in terms of "true pleasure."[73] In these letters, references to sentiments abound: feelings exalted, wistful emotions, a sense of proximity (*chuvstvo blizosti*) both to the author and to faraway places.[74] Effusive "delight" was the most widespread condition of reading the travelogue: "How sad . . . how much joy . . . it is impossible not to be delighted."[75] "Such a book must awaken in people the purest of feelings," because of its "mood," "effortless and gentle," its manner, "truthful, noble, and delicate," and its "warm and friendly feelings."[76] A reader from Leningrad "was involuntarily seized by a feeling of subconscious charm," and when she went out, "the air felt purer, the sun brighter, and there, behind . . . the trees of brilliant green, I imagined blue sea and light boat sails." While this landscape was entirely possible in summertime Leningrad, the reader found herself "in an unknown country" as "the old and new England emerged from a hazy distance, like a mysterious sorceress, whimsical and beautiful in a new way."[77]

Thus, doubly the transports: delight and the feeling of being elsewhere, linked explicitly as well as structurally in the letters. The sensation of transference must have been intense and startling because letter writers returned to it, again and again, searching for the right words to express "this feeling of visibility . . . vividness."[78] Their letters recreate the illusion of presence with much immediacy. A teacher of English, who spent much of her time experiencing the country through books, finally "felt that England and London became so close to us as if we ourselves had just spoken with real Londoners, and only two

72. Calculations based on 173 letters in RGALI, f. 2732, op. 1, dd. 1078, 1081, 1082, 1130, 1364.

73. For example: RGALI, f. 2732, op. 1, d. 1364, ll. 2, 9, 15, 19, 23, 48, 59, 85; ibid., d. 1130, ll. 47, 93, 95ob; ibid., d. 1078, ll. 19, 200b, 220b, 28, 32, 61, 85; ibid., d. 1082, ll. 9, 32, 460b.

74. On emotions as central to travel experiences and writing, see Sobe in this volume.

75. RGALI, f. 2732, op. 1, d. 1078, l. 78; ibid., d. 1081, ll. 36–36ob; ibid., d. 1082, ll. 60b, 11, 67–68; ibid., d. 1130, l. 68; ibid., d. 1364, ll. 100b, 25, 51–51ob, 86.

76. RGALI, f. 2732, op. 1, d. 1130, l. 93; ibid., d. 1364, ll. 25, 51–51ob, 64–64ob, 88; ibid., d. 1082, l. 11; for "so many feelings at once," see ibid., d. 1078, l. 32.

77. RGALI, f. 2732, op. 1, d. 1082, ll. 28–28ob; see also ibid., d. 1364, l. 38.

78. RGALI, f. 2732, op. 1, d. 1081, l. 50b; ibid., d. 1078, ll. 9, 28, 40; ibid., d. 1130, ll. 93, 95; ibid., d. 1364, ll. 45, 73, 94; ibid., d. 1082, l. 70.

days ago stood under the gloomy vaults of the Tower and saw Westminster's white-and-black columns."[79] "I have been under the sway of such moods," confessed a letter writer from Moscow, because "you have the gift of leading the reader with you, along the streets of London, into its museums, its gardens, of showing . . . and making visible, really tangible what we read about. . . . With great pleasure I accompanied you."[80] The end of the book spelled the end of the trip, and letters are tinged with sadness even as they speak of delight.

It was Obraztsov's voice (the offscreen voice in the film, the narrative voice in the book) and, importantly, his marginalia—all those photos, drawings, and maps—that made foreign places tangible. Obraztsov addressed his audience directly, in colloquial language and an informal manner, generating intimate conversation—not exactly an exchange, but a familial atmosphere for telling familiar tales. During the mid-1950s, when "sincerity" became a public motto, "truth" equaled "simplicity," and purifying language from clichés was an urgent task, readers and viewers were especially receptive to Obraztsov's unhurried, effortless talk and quotations from childhood.[81] Letter writers frequently commented on his *zadushevnost'*, which connotes both intimacy and sincerity; he was entirely convincing (thus *doverie, pravda, iskrennost'* are refrains in the letters). This was Obraztsov's project from the start, as he turned his camera to the backsides of buildings in pursuit of authenticity; and readers granted him this, too, admiring his "rare and wondrous ability to see, to perceive."[82]

Photographs and maps enhanced veracity; at once they transported readers to London and Obraztsov into readers' homes. For some, it was as if an old friend had brought a photo album; others peered into photographs with their spouses in private moments of imaginary romantic getaways.[83] Still others sought to render public the private experiences of the photo album, requesting photographs for club newspapers and class demonstrations "through an epidiascope."[84] The maps were another item in the scrapbook of memory. Besides the route diagram, the inside cover contained a "Sightseers' Map of London" with the layout of streets and parks, and the plan of the underground, everything labeled in English—an authentic artifact travelers bring home as a token for themselves and evidence for their friends. Obraztsov appropriated this map for himself and his readers with his own bold handwritten scribbles,

79. RGALI, f. 2732, op. 1, d. 1081, ll. 17, 83; ibid., d. 1078, l. 150b; ibid., d. 1364, ll. 2, 15, 79, 87.

80. RGALI, f. 2732, op. 1, d. 1078, ll. 19–200b; ibid., d. 1364, ll. 45, 75, 85, 87; ibid., d. 1082, ll. 38, 460b, 57.

81. RGALI, f. 2732, op. 1, d. 1082, ll. 13, 16, 38; ibid., d. 1081, l. 980b; ibid., d. 1364, ll. 64–640b, 75, 79, 85.

82. RGALI, f. 2732, op. 1, d. 1081, ll. 50, 52, 98–980b; ibid., d. 1078, ll. 150b, 49; ibid., d. 1082, ll. 13–130b, 16, 17 (quote), 28, 570b, 74, 76–760b; ibid., d. 1130, ll. 30, 93; ibid., d. 1364, ll. 34, 75.

83. RGALI, f. 2732, op. 1, d. 1081, l. 50b; ibid., d. 1082, ll. 13–130b, 160b–17; ibid., d. 1130, l. 20; ibid., d. 1364, ll. 2, 110b, 23, 51–510b, 520b, 850b, 87, 91.

84. RGALI, f. 2732, op. 1, d. 1130, ll. 6, 7, 56–560b, 910b, 98, 99.

arrows, circles, and inscriptions, all saying "I was here" in so many ways and in Russian.[85] The readers used this map, flipping back and forth from the text to the inside cover, mentally strolling along London streets, and searching for still other signposts they had read about: South Square, for example, where Galsworthy's Fleur lived, or Baker Street, immortalized by Conan Doyle.[86] Nor did the letter writers overlook the book jacket designed as a diary—the drawing of a laced colorful notepad, with an attached pencil, the title in cursive—entailing subjectivity Obraztsov underscored and authenticity the audience yearned for.[87] Hence the occasional confusion of genres: readers sometimes mistook the travelogue for a memoir.[88]

They spoke of the travelogue as touching, sweetly and sadly poignant, moving, even to tears; their epistolary record might well have belonged to the Victorians.[89] Some were quite self-conscious and a bit embarrassed: "Perhaps this is a really bizarre exaltation—not for young ladies"; "Perhaps I have still preserved the impressionability of youth."[90] Their attempts to explain their own sensibilities with references to youth are key to understanding the reception of Obraztsov's travelogue, because the readers responded to his image of London as the city of Dickens, Galsworthy, and adolescent readings.[91]

For many readers, the travelogue was a madeleine that sent them in search of lost time. For a sixty-year-old teacher, who had been educated in Warsaw and Petersburg before the Revolution, the travelogue excavated a whole world lying dormant: "Oh, how many memories, thoughts, and moods your book stirs! Since childhood, *The Little Lord Fauntleroy* has been implanted in my memory so vividly. Here he is riding in a coach along a shady park alley; here he is standing in his velvet suit before his grandfather." The travelogue prompted this reader to write a letter-memoir about her family decimated during wars and revolutions—about her father, her brothers killed during world wars, and her husband killed in 1917. She stored the book "in a special place," "in the desk drawer," rather than on the bookshelf, to emphasize its distinctiveness and to reach out for it "again and again." "Often, I examine the familiar pictures and photographs, the map, the cover . . . I love [this book], I want to stroke it. I [cannot] part with it."[92]

"For a long time I could not part with it," another woman wrote almost in the same words. She grew up in a very different time and place, during the So-

85. Obraztsov, *O tom*, inside cover.

86. RGALI, f. 2732, op. 1, d. 1364, ll. 90b, 19, 340b, 48, 640b, 73, 91; ibid., d. 1082, ll. 5, 16, 320b, 52.

87. RGALI, f. 2732, op. 1, d. 1082, ll. 6, 320b; ibid., d. 1078, ll. 59, 62, 67; ibid., d. 1130, l. 71; ibid., d. 1364, ll. 48, 73, 900b, 91.

88. RGALI, f. 2732, op. 1, d. 1078, l. 85 ("Vashi memuary"); ibid., d. 1082, l. 76.

89. RGALI f. 2732, op. 1, d. 1082, l. 4.

90. RGALI, f. 2732, op. 1, d. 1082, ll. 40b, 110b; ibid., d. 1078, ll. 49–50.

91. On "childhood" and "youth," see, e.g.: RGALI, f. 2732, op. 1, d. 1078, l. 780b; ibid., d. 1081, ll. 43, 52; ibid., d. 1082, ll. 28, 53, 67–68, 70; ibid., d. 1130, l. 20; ibid., d. 1364, l. 59.

92. RGALI, f. 2732, op. 1, d. 1082, ll. 48–55.

viet 1930s, but the book reminded her, too, about her father arrested in 1937. When, in 1957, she was summoned by the Ministry of Internal Affairs to learn of her father's fate, she took the travelogue with her as a "dear friend," and kept reading it literally "until the last second, until I was called into the office." The book protected her: her father, who had played classical music, staged fairy tales as home puppet shows, and ensured the innocence of her childhood, was rehabilitated.[93] The travelogue's and the letters' association with fathers, with families threatened, destroyed, and reclaimed from death, was not accidental: recall, again, Father's choice of first "serious books," the smell of Father's bookcase, where stood the European classics, Galsworthy and Dickens.

The two authors, their heroes and settings, as well as recollections of reading their books, constituted a common cultural heritage. While some readers praised the travelogue for presenting new information about contemporary England,[94] others fell in love again with " 'the good old England' so familiar since childhood," with the England of "quaint traditions, of firesides dating back to Dickens's times."[95] Obraztsov's travelogue extorted a confession of love from his contemporaries:

> I myself have never been to England, but, without seeing it, I love the England of Dickens (whom I love very, very much), the England of the Forsytes. I learned English to have the lucky opportunity to read English literature in the original. You captivated me from the very first pages of your book, because you perceived the approaching London as the London of Dickens and the Forsytes. I have always felt them to be my friends.[96]

This was the England—or rather, the memory of oneself as a child associated with it—that inspired in readers the "feeling of subconscious charm."

At the end of his life, Obraztsov turned to another audience, offering his memoir, *Up the Staircase of Memory*, to the young generation of the 1980s. His memoir, perhaps the ultimate memory scrapbook, is loosely structured as momentary snapshots, each representing a step in the lifelong staircase. While his travels all over the world contributed many a step, the London trips have a unique place in the structure of the memoir. Not only does London take more steps than any other place, but also this part of the account belongs to an entirely different text: it is an abridged replica of the 1950s travelogue, with many film episodes reproduced directly from the script and examples of English humor duplicated from the book. After those 1953–1954 trips, Obraztsov traveled to England many more times, but, despite subsequent first-

93. Ibid., ll. 21–25ob.
94. RGALI, f. 2732, op. 1, d. 1364, ll. 38–38ob, 48; ibid., d. 1081, ll. 13, 17, 31; ibid., d. 1078, ll. 19ob, 20, 38, 39.
95. RGALI, f. 2732, op. 1, d. 1082, l. 28ob; ibid., d. 1078, l. 15.
96. RGALI, f. 2732, op. 1, d. 1082, ll. 4–4ob; ibid., d. 1081, ll. 52–52ob, 59–59ob.

hand experiences, and no matter what audiences he addressed, for the next forty years he would largely retell the same story, stubbornly disregarding differences ("simply put, they are people, just like us") and revisiting English literary classics.[97] His travelogue, so profoundly shaped by literary images, became formative for all his subsequent trips and recollections. European literature—a shared cultural language of the intelligentsia and the core of their childhood readings—dictated the expectations and sensibilities with which many Soviet travelogues of the 1950s were written and read.

97. RGALI, f. 2732, op. 1, d. 203, ll. 1–16; Obraztsov, *Po stupen'kam*, 200, 201, 209–14.

CHAPTER 12

Adventures in the Marketplace

Yugoslav Travel Writing and Tourism in the 1950s–1960s

Wendy Bracewell

What did it mean to be a Yugoslav tourist in the 1950s and 1960s? Access to the wide world after years of war and political isolationism? Encounters with ideological difference? "Getting to know cultural monuments and enjoying the natural beauties of a sun-drenched country," as suggested in one of the first Yugoslav-published foreign guidebooks?[1] All these experiences played their part, but one theme runs through discussions of travel abroad in this period. As much as anything else, Yugoslav tourism seemed to be about shopping.

Memories of travel abroad are made of this. Ljerka Damjanov-Pintar's account of her first trip to London in 1955 is typical in its loving recollections:

> I felt everything, and even tried things here and there. One whole hall was stuffed with coats. There must have been several thousand. In another hall hundreds of hats scattered on tables with mirrors. . . . I sold some of my things: a ring, a bracelet, two little pieces of Herend porcelain. I bought a winter coat, then I went to Harrods for some beautiful fabric for an evening gown, a handbag, shoes, gloves and other trifles. . . . When I unpacked everything at home, the whole family gathered round and wondered at the quantity and admired the quality. So I decided that next year I would repeat my travels.[2]

Damjanov-Pintar remembers her shopping travels as subversive of the Yugoslav comrades' values. In contrast, contributors to a current Web-based compendium of Yugoslav popular culture record memories of shopping trips to Trieste and elsewhere as an aspect of everyday life, an occasion for Yugo-nostalgia.[3] These contrasting evaluations are nothing new. In the 1950s Milovan Djilas denounced Yugoslavia's "new class" of party functionaries who abused the privilege of travel to acquire foreign luxuries unavailable to the av-

This research was funded in part by a grant from the Arts and Humanities Research Council.

1. Faik Mehanović, *Vodič kroz Italiju* (Belgrade, 1956).

2. Ljerka Damjanov-Pintar, *Putovanja i ogovaranja: Šest pasoša i jedna putovnica* (Zagreb, 1996).

3. Published at www.leksikon-yu-mitologije.net/ (last consulted 20 December 2005).

erage worker; the press also criticized such "state tourism."[4] But even the private tourist was open to criticism. When a magazine article asked in 1964 "why do we travel abroad?" the answer focused on illicit economic activity: the student trying to make his stipend last, the souvenir hunter intent on impressing friends, the petty speculator buying women's scarves in Italy.[5] On the other hand, the first guidebooks to western countries included explicit advice on where and how to shop. The 1956 *Guide to Italy* cited above observed that Trieste had few significant sights and therefore concentrated on the Triestine department stores, with notes on their prices (fixed, not open to haggling).[6] Yugoslav tourists shopped, and on coming home some of them published travel accounts, describing glittering window displays and advertisements as well as ancient monuments and picturesque villages.

Freedom to travel and a flourishing consumer culture have been singled out as epitomizing Yugoslavia's status as a peculiar hybrid, something between East and West, the result of Yugoslavia's separate road to communism. After Yugoslavia's expulsion from the Cominform in 1948 and a short-lived experiment with accelerated industrialization and collectivization, Tito's regime embarked in the early 1950s on a series of reforms, including moves away from central planning toward "market socialism" and a consumer orientation; decentralization under the label of "workers' self-management"; and openness to the West.[7] Yugoslavia came to seem very different from the other states of the Soviet bloc.

Still, travel restrictions in other socialist countries were gradually relaxed; and their citizens, too, tasted the pleasures of tourist consumption.[8] An issue of *Cultural Studies* edited by Anna Wessely put "shopping tourism"—leisure travel combined with purposive economic activity—at the center of research on the popular experience of east European socialism. The contributors argued that shopping tourism (and socialist consumerism in general) was not a matter of popular resistance but was tolerated and even encouraged by the state, describing the practice as contributing to a tacit social contract that maintained socialism in power, less through the use of terror than by trading consumer goods against popular political acquiescence.[9]

Was it different in Yugoslavia? There, open borders and access to material comforts were supposed to have conferred an unparalleled popular legitimacy on its socialist system. In her 1993 postmortem on Yugoslavia, *Balkan Ex-*

4. Milovan Djilas, *The New Class: An Analysis of the Communist System* (New York, 1957); "Državni turizam," *NIN*, 1 June 1952.

5. "Zašto putujemo u inostranstvo?" *NIN*, 9 May 1964.

6. Mehanović, *Vodič.*

7. Dennison Rusinow, *The Yugoslav Experiment, 1948–1974* (Berkeley, Calif., 1978); John R. Lampe, *Yugoslavia as History* (Cambridge, 1996).

8. See Gorsuch, in this volume.

9. Anna Wessely, "Travelling People, Travelling Objects," *Cultural Studies* 16, no. 1 (2002): 3–15.

press, Slavenka Drakulić saw Yugoslav passports and surplus income as something that set the country apart from the rest of the eastern bloc, contributing to a lively sense of Yugoslav superiority: "Millions and millions of people crossed the border every year just to savour the West and to buy something, perhaps as a mere gesture. But this freedom, a feeling that you are free to go if you want to, was very important to us." Still, the unspoken political contract she identifies is essentially the same: "We traded our freedom for a pair of Italian shoes."[10]

The Belgrade historian Predrag Marković, one of the first to discuss the interplay between Yugoslav politics and mass culture, has a rather different view. His pioneering study of Belgrade from 1948 to 1965 details the eager consumption of holidays abroad, foreign fashions, movies, and other consumer goods. He concludes that the ordinary citizen would always opt for "western" values, but only in culture and standard of living. The Yugoslav version of the good life meant that, paradoxically, Yugoslavia's citizens *resisted* any serious political or economic reforms, assuming they could have it all at no extra cost. Yugoslavia's synthesis of East and West thus combined a desire for western products with a lasting popular suspicion of market forces, risk, and social differentiation. Patrick Patterson's study of Yugoslav consumer culture through the prism of the advertising industry points out that the most consumer-oriented of the socialist states also saw the most lively critique of consumerism. The *Praxis* circle, for example, saw shopping trips to Trieste as evidence of the market reformers' choice of the comfortable life over the (socialist) good life.[11]

Yugoslav tourism cannot, of course, be reduced to the issue of consumerism. Varying experiences in different parts of the country, long-standing patterns of travel to neighboring states, changing political or economic circumstances, individual opportunities, backgrounds, needs, or fantasies—all these could contribute to very different expectations of travel abroad. But the contrasting assessments of Yugoslav shopping trips indicate that tourism was an important site for the discussion of socialist consumption. Travel writing was one place where this debate appeared. As well as describing the wonders of the world to the postwar generation, Yugoslav travel accounts of the 1950s and 1960s deal at length with issues of shopping tourism. They persistently pose the question of what is good tourism, and good consumption? What should be the relationship among needs, desires, and goods in a socialist Yugoslavia positioned between East and West?

It would be deceptive to claim that such travel writing can tell us in any straightforward way about the Yugoslav tourist's experience. Though access to

---

10. Slavenka Drakulić, *The Balkan Express: Fragments from the Other Side of War* (New York, 1993), 135–36.

11. Predrag J. Marković, *Beograd izmedju istoka i zapada 1948–1965* (Belgrade, 1996); Patrick Patterson, "The New Class: Consumer Culture under Socialism and the Unmaking of the Yugoslav Dream, 1945–1999," Ph.D. diss., University of Michigan, 2001.

the press widened dramatically over the second half of the twentieth century, in the 1950s and 1960s most Yugoslav travel accounts were published by journalists, professional writers, and academics. The authors varied in their relationship to party authority, but there is no doubt that they constituted a social and intellectual elite. While the Yugoslav press was more open than that of other socialist countries, there were limits to what could be published, even in travel writing. Even so, travel writing has much to say about the meanings attributed to tourism in the Yugoslavia of the 1950s–1960s and after.[12]

Yugoslav Tourism and Socialist Leisure

From the early 1950s, the official line promoted Yugoslav nonaligned, self-managing socialism as different from—and superior to—both western capitalism and Soviet-bloc socialism. Market-oriented socialism was meant to improve life for the individual Yugoslav citizen: "standard of living" was the last in the list of priorities in the 1948 five-year plan, but had moved up to the first rank in the 1964 plan.[13] Even before the reforms, Yugoslavia's leaders had stressed leisure as the state's reward for the worker's labor. The vacation, and in particular the holiday involving travel, was rapidly proletarianized after the war. The numbers of "domestic tourists" spending their vacations away from home, mostly through their union or place of work, nearly doubled between 1938 and 1948 (from 720,000 to 1,493,000), and rose by 1962 to around 4 million.[14] Such paid leisure was important in legitimating Yugoslav socialism: the worker was better off than under the old regime, and better off than in the capitalist West—where leisure was depicted as the prerogative of the idle rich. Domestic leisure travel within Yugoslavia also had a patriotic and ideological role, with holidays seen as contributing to "brotherhood and unity" by building personal ties between hosts and guests in different republics.[15]

Travel abroad was more problematic, as it invited the tourist to make comparisons. Official anxieties about unrestricted travel were initially reflected in a strictly controlled regime of passports, exit visas, and hard-currency al-

12. For approaches to tourism through literature, see James Buzard, *The Beaten Track: European Tourism, Literature and the Ways to Culture, 1800–1918* (Oxford, 1993); Patrick Holland and Graham Huggan, *Tourists with Typewriters: Critical Reflections on Contemporary Travel Writing* (Ann Arbor, Mich., 2000); Mary Baine Campbell, "Travel Writing and Its Theory," in *The Cambridge Companion to Travel Writing*, ed. Peter Hulme and Tim Youngs (Cambridge, 2002), 261–78. See also the special issue on Balkan travel writing edited by Wendy Bracewell and Alex Drace-Francis, *Journeys: The International Journal of Travel and Travel Writing* 6, no. 1 (2005).

13. Marković, *Beograd*, 291.

14. Miodrag Zečević, *Investicije i razvoj turizma u Jugoslaviji* (Belgrade, 1973), 149–55. On Croatian tourism, see Igor Duda, *U potrazi za blagostanjem: o povijesti dokolice i potrošackog društva u Hrvatskoj 1950-ih i 1960-ih* (Zagreb, 2005).

15. See, for example, Ljubo Babić, "Jugoslavija kao turistička zemlja, " *Turizam* 6, no. 1 (1954): 2–5. See also Vari and Moranda, in this volume, on "nation-building" travels.

lowances. Nonetheless, the political climate after 1953 included steps to open Yugoslavia's borders, first to tourism and later to economic migration.[16] From the late 1950s, travel abroad became easier for the average Yugoslav. Putnik, nationalized after the war as the state travel agency and responsible for domestic tourism, once again began to organize excursions abroad, available not just through the workplace but to private tourist groups and even individuals. The passport and visa regime for leisure travel was relaxed, and the numbers of those taking out a passport soared. The government's sense of confidence was manifested by abandoning overt surveillance of Yugoslav tourists abroad.

Yugoslav travelers repaid this confidence: they went abroad, and they came straight back home again. The possession of a Yugoslav passport offered unparalleled access to both East and West, since, by the early 1970s, Yugoslavs required no visa to travel in most European countries. Between 1959 and 1963, the number of those leaving Yugoslavia tripled, with most traveling in western Europe, fewer in the bloc countries or overseas.[17] These were not all holidaymakers: growing numbers of Yugoslavs traveled to work temporarily as laborers in western Europe. The numbers of border crossings also point to a flourishing cross-border traffic. Still, while some studies attempt to differentiate between travel for economic purposes and tourism proper, the distinction is difficult to maintain.[18] Economic migrants and small-scale speculators did not travel with their eyes closed: they brought back with them intangible impressions as well as suitcases full of soap powder or cigarette lighters. Conversely, Yugoslav tourists had to fund their trips abroad as well they might—often by selling or bartering what goods they could carry. While travel abroad had become an accepted way for Yugoslavs to spend their leisure by the early 1960s, spending their savings was made difficult by restrictions on the currency that could be taken out of the country and by customs regulations on their return.[19] Travelers predictably tried to evade these restrictions by smuggling extra funds out, and their purchases in. Alenka Švab labels this small-scale smuggling a "national sport" and notes the relative lenience of the authorities, but jokes over the ruses of returning tourists and the stupidity of customs officials also suggest frustration with spending limits.[20]

At the same time, however, spending was what foreign tourists were expected to do. From the early 1950s, Yugoslavia became a tourist destination

16. William Zimmerman, *Open Borders, Nonalignment, and the Political Evolution of Yugoslavia* (Princeton, N.J., 1987), 75–83.

17. Ibid., 80; Zečević, *Investicije*, 155.

18. Wessely, "Travelling People," 11–12.

19. In 1960 travelers could take $30 out of the country; "Više deviza za putovanja," *Ekonomska politika*, 27 February 1960: 213–14. The limits placed on imports were directly aimed at border traffic and shopping tourism and were justified by the need to protect domestic industry and limit "luxuries." See *Zbirka carinskih propisa* (Belgrade, 1964), vol. 2.

20. Alenka Švab, "Consuming Western Image of Well-Being: Shopping Tourism in Socialist Slovenia," *Cultural Studies* 16, no. 1 (2002): 63–79.

for westerners, compensating for the loss of Czech and Hungarian tourism after 1948. Initially this seems to have been a matter of chance rather than calculation, the unintended result of the devaluation of the dinar in 1952 (making Yugoslavia into an inexpensive holiday) and the simultaneous liberalization of the visa regime. Western tourists were courted both as a source of hard currency and because of the opportunity to cultivate Yugoslavia's image abroad. How to attract and cater for them became a theme in Yugoslav economic debate, with the need to entice such visitors to spend their money liberally constantly reiterated. Between 1950 and 1965, their numbers trebled.[21]

Tourists with Typewriters

At the same time as leisure travel became available to a much wider proportion of the population, travel writing in Yugoslavia burgeoned, taking on a new populist emphasis—though this is not necessarily directly correlated with the democratization of travel. The connections are slightly more complex.

"Literary" travels had been a relatively prestigious genre in interwar Yugoslav literature. Writers who had distinguished themselves in other forms also turned their hands to travel writing, to critical acclaim. Travel writing was a vehicle for cultural critique or the philosophical essay, as well as for the lyrical evocation of atmosphere. Such writings justified themselves through the authors' display of sensibility and style and were aimed at an educated reading public that shared the cultural horizons of the writers. Travel writing in this vein persisted, especially after the end of the brief hegemony of Yugoslav socialist realism in literature. But travel writing was also recruited into the project of building socialism. From the mid-1940s, there was a new emphasis on travel writing as socially engaged reportage. The immediate postwar focus was on Yugoslav domestic travel, with an entire subgenre depicting the creative leisure of youth groups or voluntary work groups building roads or railways, as well as the collective pleasures of vacations at the seaside or the mountain resort. These travels of the late 1940s and 1950s often followed a national "key," with a section devoted to each republic, following the spirit—if not necessarily the model—of Soviet travel guides.[22] Accounts of Soviet pilgrimages and "fraternal" travels were dedicated to the achievements of socialism (with Yugoslavia's distinctive contribution marked by descriptions of the universal acclamation for Tito). Travels in the capitalist West were initially limited to political journalism. But from the early 1950s, there is a growing focus on western Europe and the rest of the world in Yugoslav travel accounts.

21. John Allcock, "Yugoslavia," in *Tourism and Economic Development in Eastern Europe and the Soviet Union*, ed. Derek R. Hall (London, 1991), 239–40; Derek Hall, "Evolutionary Pattern of Tourism Development in Eastern Europe and the Soviet Union," in ibid., 92.

22. See, for example, Mihailo Lalić, *Usput zapisano* (Belgrade, 1952); and Ratimir Stefanović, *Zapisi iz naših planina* (Belgrade, 1951).

These works of travel reportage invited the reader into the world of politics, and particularly politics from the perspective of the "ordinary citizen." Fadil Hadžić's introduction to an anthology of Yugoslav travels, *Journey around the World*, sums up the premises of such writing: it is defined against the "false poetry" of literary travel writing, which cannot reveal "that which takes place behind the scenes of some pleasing foreign landscape or city panorama." Instead, the Yugoslav travel writer avoids "operatic snapshots of palms and cathedrals, descriptions of starry nights and the azure blue of far seas" for an analysis of "world events through the words and eyes of the ordinary people encountered in all the countries of all the continents—sharing the same wishes and the same cries for peace and the same protests: against those whose only perspective on the world is that of the war between the blocs."[23] The distinction was artificial: socially engaged journalists still indulged in the occasional starry sky, even in Hadžić's anthology, while "literary" travel accounts were by no means devoid of political comment. But as well as making nonalignment a principle of Yugoslav travel writing, Hadžić's remarks did indicate a new interest in the ordinary and everyday. Travel reportage sat easily alongside the commentary in daily newspapers such as *Politika* (Politics), as well as in the weekly magazines devoted to news and culture such as *NIN*, but these also began to carry more subjective and digressive accounts of travel and tourism.

These accounts were still usually written by professional writers and journalists in the 1950s and 1960s. As well as making the "ordinary man" an object of travel reportage, many of these authors also adopted the persona of the Yugoslav tourist. Writing as a tourist meant renouncing the claims to expertise of the well-traveled and well-connected correspondent (even if the writer was in fact under commission from a paper or traveled with the intention of working up travel notes for publication), but this stance conferred a different sort of authority, that of everyday experience. These travel accounts offered the writer an opportunity to explore—and to comment on—the experience of mass tourism that was increasingly available to Yugoslav citizens in reality, and not just through the vicarious pleasures of armchair travel.

Accounts of shopping and consumption play a notable part in these writings. What a tourist might want to acquire; how to shop—and how to pay; what you can and can't get, both abroad and at home; dealing with scarcity or abundance, choice or its absence; tipping; the attitudes of shop assistants; confronting Yugoslav customs on your return—all are subjects that are treated repeatedly, not to say obsessively. While a concern with consumption might be expected as an aspect of travels in the West, it was also an important focus of "socialist fraternal travels"; and it had a long afterlife in descriptions of travel to both East and West.

23. Fadil Hadžić, ed., *Put oko svijeta* (Zagreb, 1962), 6.

Tourist or Camel?

Representative examples of "tourist travels" can be found in the works of two Belgrade authors, Vasa Popović and Slobodan Petković, who present their adventures in tourism in a lighthearted manner, as something novel yet not completely unfamiliar to readers. Their position as professional writers and as men is typical. (The style employed by women travel writers such as Nada Marinković or Neda Erceg is more impersonal and their subject matter less populist, perhaps in reaction to stereotypes of women writers.) The Belgrade base gives these authors a shared frame of reference but there are pertinent differences between their accounts, due in large part to the changes that had taken place between the publication of Popović's first stories in the early 1950s and Petković's book in 1963.

Vasa Popović was a journalist for the newspaper *Politika* and the weekly *NIN*. His travel accounts were first published as periodical articles in the 1950s and then promptly collected in two volumes of travel sketches: *A Trickster's Travels* (1954) and *Hats Off to Travel* (1959). Their popularity is indicated by the fact that these sketches were then republished in a third collection in 1980: *Tales from the Wide World.*[24] The title of his first volume—the travels of a *šeret*, a trickster or joker—gives some idea of his authorial persona and approach. Popović writes in his author's note that he's always described as a humorist, but concludes: "you decide!"

Popović recounts his experiences in Vienna, Paris, Rome, and Prague as typical of "our circumstances," but at the same time, he makes it clear that he is traveling in order to write: he's a journalist first and a tourist second. He has a little fun with this in discussing his plans: "I'll have a nice excursion, it's good for the head and for the digestion, and I'll come back with some stories and, maybe, with some material (*štof*), since I'm one of our guys—a traveler abroad with average desires."[25] "Material" here is a pun: both material for stories and material as textiles, the stereotypical purchase of the Yugoslav tourist abroad. And his tales are full of such štof: tourism and shopping are all mixed up together.

> Maybe because of the Church of St. Stephen and Schönbrunn and the cigarette lighters and the nylon goods—I was excited about my trip. And why not? People talk about the Louvre, and about Sartre at first hand (they say the existentialist girls wear green makeup), about La Scala in Milan, and American architecture; and some come back wearing Mont-

24. Vasa Popović, *Šeretska putovanja: od Srema do Pariza* (Subotica, 1954; 2d ed. 1957); Vasa Popović, *Šešir dole—putovanju* (Belgrade, 1959); Vasa Popović, *Priče iz belog sveta* (Zagreb, 1980).

25. Popović, *Šeretska putovanja*, 140.

gomery jackets and striped socks and they give their friends ballpoint pens and combs and compact mirrors.[26]

His first excursion in search of material—a visit to Vienna on an organized excursion—turns out to be almost entirely about shopping or perhaps "something in our society that might once have been called petty-bourgeois snobbery."[27] He is one of forty travelers, of whom thirty-five are shoppers, two are engineers, two are "real tourists but only interested in sport," and one is a journalist who is ambivalent about his own motives: seeing the sights, gathering material or—doing some shopping himself. He describes the techniques of shopping-tourism: smuggling out "one whole kilometer of sausage casing, and bottles of rakija to be offered in the shops on the elegant Mariahilferstrasse— *Gut Morgen, srpska šljivovića kaufen . . . Ich bin Jugoslavija*":[28] the wildfire rumors among the tourists of things that are to be had better or cheaper than at home and the frenzies of shopping (to the point that one embarrassed excursionist is prompted to remark to the astonished Austrians, "we do have umbrellas too!");[29] the compulsion to spend "every schilling on a Viennese comb or a Viennese pocket mirror so my wife or some other *drugarica* can boast 'look what I have, excellent quality, we don't have these . . . It's from Vienna.' "[30] All this is described with a mixture of empathy and condemnation, and with such detail that it could be read as a primer in how to shop. The piece is called "Vienna Pocket Mirror"—a mirror that reflects Yugoslav social values as much as it does the face of Vienna.

The same themes continue through his travels to Paris, Brussels, and Switzerland. Consumer desire is constantly set in contrast to cultural enrichment in Popović's accounts. It intrudes even in the course of sightseeing and museumgoing, to comic effect. In Paris, Popović finds himself in the Louvre, in front of the Mona Lisa: "I stand and at first I just gaze, and then I wonder: is she smiling with her eyes or with her lips? And then I look at the dress she was wearing when she smiled that famous smile . . . and my eyes ask: is that taffeta synthetic, or is it real silk?"[31] Popović's humor has a caustic sting. It is directed at himself, but even more so at his compatriots and his society, exposing the gap between socialist principles (especially ones that are loudly proclaimed) and actual behavior.

Slobodan Petković was also a journalist, and author of a series of minor novels. In his travel book *Tourist or Camel?* Petković travels as a tourist, not in

26. Ibid., 149.
27. Ibid., 150.
28. Ibid., 149.
29. Ibid., 153.
30. Ibid., 152.
31. Ibid., 171.

order to write but—at least ostensibly—writing to fund his excursion to Italy.[32] His account is full of the details of Yugoslav tourism, treated as tongue-in-cheek epic: making up your mind to go; jousting with travel agents to acquire the tickets; the experience of travel on the train to Rome (what do you bring to eat?); dealing with hotels, with guides, with sore feet, with stingy companions. His tale is less critical of the materialism of Yugoslav tourists than are Popović's sketches, but he is equally concerned with tourist consumption, with chapters entitled "Acquisitions" and "Toboggan of Desires." He describes in exasperated detail his relatives' commissions (including a length of silk dress fabric "the precise color of the sea where the sandy shore gives way to deeper water, not green but not blue either") and elaborates on the desire to bring home a memento of the journey ("the covetous dream of autos, Vespas, typewriters, or radios; the more modest of textiles; the most modest are satisfied with leather goods, socks, pocket hankies, or lighters—but dreamers of such extreme modesty don't exist").[33] He is particularly vivid in recounting the frenzy that overtakes the tourists when they are let loose in their first Italian city—the "Comanche war cries with which our tourists fall onto the Italian shops"; the purchases of elaborately dressed Italian dolls in response to a rumor that these were amazingly cheap and could be resold at a profit in Belgrade commission shops; the mechanics of sales; and Italian street markets where everyone understands Serbian—especially the numbers.

Here, too, shopping is presented as the opposite of sightseeing. His female companions beg Petković to take them to the Coliseum, but their progress is endlessly delayed by the enticements of the shop windows, and culture is eventually abandoned for pink and yellow shantung silk. The women don't hide their preference for shopping, but Petković is equally susceptible. He pokes fun at the Yugoslav tourist by embodying all their foibles and appetites in his own person—his greedy desire demonstrated in the way he gobbles up, one after another, the cakes his neighbor has made for the train journey to Rome, concocting a new and more tenuous justification for each helping. Published nearly ten years after Popović's first book, and after a number of consumer-oriented reforms in Yugoslavia, *Tourist or Camel?* is still ambivalent about whether one should travel to consume culture or to consume goods, but presents the desires that overwhelm the Yugoslav tourist abroad as something normal and ordinary. The only limits the Yugoslav tourist recognizes are those of the pocketbook. Petković's critique is less about snobbery and social differentiation than frivolity and lack of self-restraint. The problem posed in the title is resolved by Petković's claim that a tourist is exactly like a camel: stubborn, enduring, and able to live off all that it has consumed and stored for the times of scarcity that might lie ahead.

32. Slobodan Petković, *Turist ili kamila?* (Subotica, 1963).
33. Ibid., 159.

Tourism and Shopping as a Problem of Representation

Why the preoccupation with these issues? The simple answer is that shopping is what Yugoslav tourists did. Postwar Yugoslavia was characterized by an economy of shortage and only slowly abandoned socialist asceticism and heavy industry for an orientation to the market and the production of consumer goods. Its citizens could not satisfy their requirements at home; and as soon as the government permitted travel, they used the excuse of tourism as a way of acquiring the things they wanted. Even with the reorientation of the economy, they still hungered for western goods. This travel writing reflects their experiences and attitudes. There's clearly some truth in such an explanation—but at the same time it's not enough. Why these particular preoccupations (with snobbery, with frivolous consumerism, with the gender of shopping, with the tension between shopping and sightseeing), treated in these specific ways? Travel writing, like other textual representations of the world, is not so straightforward.[34].

Another possibility is that these texts served the party line. Tibor Dessewffy has described the juxtaposition of the "tourist" and the "speculator" in the Hungarian press as an attempt by the Kádár regime to teach its citizens how to think and feel "properly" in foreign countries.[35] Humorous sketches criticizing social "deviations" were a standard form of moral-political education in Yugoslavia, and in some ways these travel accounts follow this format. But at the same time, it's hard to see them as written to order. Popović's jokes about snobbery constitute a critique of the economic reforms that encouraged such behavior, though his self-deprecating irony softens this. Criticism of the deficiencies of Yugoslav socialism wasn't impossible—but the fate of some of those who challenged the one-party monopoly of power (like Djilas) or attacked the precepts of self-management (like the *Praxis* Marxists) suggested a degree of caution, as did the absence of censorship prior to publication and the arbitrary nature of repression. The shopping adventures of Yugoslav tourists may have been intrinsically funny, but the writer's humor also served as a self-defensive strategy.

A different approach might consider the relations between social and political change and travel writing. Mass tourism abroad was a new phenomenon in Yugoslavia, and clearly a source of some anxiety—for those who wanted to travel as well as for officials worrying about the consequences. This is how the younger writer Momo Kapor remembered Vasa Popović's travel accounts at the beginning of the 1980s, analyzing their attraction:

34. Similarly, Patrick Patterson discusses the surprising *silence* about consumerism in Soviet-bloc travel accounts of Yugoslavia: "Dangerous Liaisons: Soviet-Bloc Tourists and the Temptations of the Yugoslav Good Life in the 1960s and 1970s," in *The Business of Tourism*, ed. Philip Scranton (Philadelphia, forthcoming).

35. Tibor Dessewffy, "Speculators and Travellers: The Political Construction of the Tourist in the Kádár Regime," *Cultural Studies* 16, no. 1 (2002): 44–62.

Why did readers of my generation await with such impatience the tales of this writer in the Saturday editions of *NIN*? A whole study could be written (probably one day it will be written) of a poor little country which had long been closed to the world, alone with its troubles and with the constant sense that everyone threatened it and no one liked it. Outside there was the Wide World, and at that time in the early 1950s only a few lucky people could travel and touch it with their own fingers. We were afraid of disappearing into it if by some miracle we ever had the chance of seeing it, and words like *metro, skyscraper, boulevard, aerodrome, calvados, existentialists* evoked a provincial confusion in our minds, so that we gathered around the first returnees from abroad and asked, how do they live out there? [. . .] We asked them how they had managed to get on there, how they kept themselves from getting lost in that foreign world, at foreign railway stations, how they got bread, or water, and was it expensive, and afterwards we went to bed with our heads full of exciting adventures, wondering how we would cope, and travel enticed us and a quiet yearning brought us close to tears. Our brave Srem *šeret*, Vasa Popović traveled in our stead then, and every Saturday he told us about his experiences, and told us that the Wide World was in fact the same as it was at home, that their language wasn't important if you could smile and point your finger at a bottle, a woman, a street, a house, a bed, or a slice of bread, that everywhere people suffer from toothache in the same painful way, that those foreign waiters of theirs aren't by any means gentlemen and that they'll accept a drink if a guest offers it to them—in a word, Vasa Popović dispelled our fears.[36]

But the didacticism of these travel accounts was not limited to practical matters. The authors are also writing, less reassuringly, about what socialist tourism ought to be (self-improvement through exposure to the world, relaxation as the worker's reward, building bridges among fellow travelers and between nations) and what the Yugoslav tourist's experience actually *is*.

In some ways the ironic claims by these two writers to be more shoppers than sightseers bear a resemblance to the traveler versus tourist dichotomy discussed by James Buzard in his analysis of British and American accounts of travel through the nineteenth century. He points to the "anti-tourist" strategy, the claim to social distinction through sensitivity to culture: "*I* am a traveler and an individual; *he* is a tourist and a passive member of the common herd"; and he locates this in the desire to reinforce social distinctions in the face of the democratization of leisure. These two writers also differentiate between the individual and the collective, but value them differently. Popović, in particular, is suspicious of the individualism displayed by tourist-shoppers, with their desire to distinguish themselves from their fellows through the material advan-

---

36. Introduction, Popović, *Priče iz belog sveta*, 6–7.

tage or social status attached to their purchases. The antithesis is between sightseeing as a cultural activity that contributes to the collective (good) and shopping as speculative consumerism aimed at distinguishing the individual (bad). This is reminiscent of the Soviet understanding of tourism as a collective social good.[37] But it is not the only possibility; older valuations also retained their weight. The Zagreb writer Milan Selaković, for example, is startled out of his musings on the aesthetic impact and cultural significance of the Palazzo Vecchio in Florence by hearing the sound of Croatian "from the brightly painted lips of two flabbergasted girls: Look, Milena, what's that then?" He has his revenge by telling them what he assumes they want to hear: "that is the biggest department store in Florence, like our Na-Ma in Zagreb!" "I kept quiet, maliciously, about the real, very popular Italian stores, Standa and Upim."[38] The sensitive, educated individual *traveler* could still claim a social and intellectual advantage in contrast to the uncultured or inexperienced *tourist* (however unsocialist such maneuverings may seem). And the traveler could make this distinction with reference to consumption, whether the faux pas of one's compatriots, the indiscriminate appetites of the American tourist, or the tasteless and hypocritical spending sprees of Soviet officials abroad.

When Milan Selaković noticed Croatian girls in Florence, he immediately thought "shopping." Popović and Petković also associate consumerism with women, and with the "feminine" vices of vanity, frivolity, and luxury. But both also make a point of showing men as in thrall to fashion and the world of things. Items such as cigarette lighters and Vespas feature prominently in their lists of western consumer desirables. Women may distract their male companions from the correct path in these tales (echoing Djilas's condemnation of the bourgeois wives of party officials) but the men follow along happily in their new Montgomery jackets. The moral is clear: how much more potent is western-style consumerism when it can seduce even our menfolk? One thing the socialist tourist cannot do, however, is be seduced by the sex on display in the West. Deliberately seeking out temptation in order to resist it—at least in writing—became a cliché of socialist travel writing, showing just where the line had to be drawn against capitalist consumerism. (As a result, frank accounts of western brothels, in deliberate contrast to these prudish morality tales, became a way of elaborating a rebellious, masculine identity for some Yugoslav writers of the 1980s.)[39]

These texts reflect and contribute to wider debates of the period: how to balance between satisfying basic needs and stimulating consumer desires; how

37. See Diane P. Koenker, "Travel to Work, Travel to Play: On Russian Tourism, Travel and Leisure," *Slavic Review* 62, no. 4 (2003): 657–65; and Anne E. Gorsuch, "'There's No Place Like Home': Soviet Tourism in Late Stalinism," ibid.: 760–85.

38. Milan Selaković, *Rodinova katedrala* (Zagreb, 1984), 75 (written 1959–1960).

39. See Wendy Bracewell, "New Men, Old Europe: Being a Man in Balkan Travel Writing," *Journeys* 6, no. 1 (2005): 115–46.

to choose between centralized planning and a consumer-driven market; how to nurture both the collective and the individual. Tourism to the capitalist West highlighted these questions. An article from 1961 in a pro-market journal, *Ekonomska politika* (Economic Policy), made some of the same points: "People ought to see the things they read about in their school textbooks: old basilicas, pigeons on ancient squares, masterpieces from the brushes and chisels of the world's old masters, and even the tumult of a foreign world in which a man can lose himself and then . . . long for home." But "our tourist wave hasn't gathered itself in order to break over historic monuments and the other relics of human creativity, but to peddle and barter, to buy and sell, to hawk abroad fresh meat, salami, butter and cigarettes, *rakija* and *gibanica* and similar folkloric products, and to bring back plastic raincoats, bouclé twin sets, and skirts made of Terylene." Tourism like this damaged society rather than contributing to it. It wasn't just the hard currency that was being wasted abroad on such frivolous purchases, the article argued; the Yugoslav image abroad should also be taken into consideration. *Ekonomska politika* thought that the problem should be solved by making bouclé twin sets at home and perhaps even importing luxury goods officially.[40]

But the journal ignored an issue that the authors of our travel accounts pinpointed. How could reforms reconcile individual consumer desires with a commitment to socialist collectivism and equality? How were limits to be placed on desire? The official position was that stimulating consumer demand was necessary and even desirable, as it was this that drove production and encouraged (at least in theory) disciplined work and productivity. Marxist critiques of self-managing socialism by the *Praxis* theorists pointed to the contradiction between universal ideals and the essentially private and selfish interests of the market principle. The predictable consequences of the principle of consumer sovereignty would be corruption, the accumulation of wealth, and social differentiation. Popović's vignette of the Viennese pocket mirror reflecting Yugoslav snobbery reinforced these arguments, suggesting that egalitarianism had little chance when set against consumer desire.

Petković's travel account explored the ways that desire could outrun need. Purchases like textiles "the precise color of the sea between the sandy shore and deeper water" were not just about warmth and decency: they were vehicles for fantasy, for caprice, prestige, sex, fun. The infinite transformations of the self that could be imagined through potential purchases were thoroughly described. Petković details a drawn-out negotiation over the exact Italian scooter that would be right for him. Even though he had only eight lire in his pocket, he could still quibble over whether a "super-luxury" or a "super-sport" model, a "Hercules" or a "Wings," would suit. And with impunity: the shopkeeper reacted to his discovery that Petković was wasting his time by slap-

---

40. "Tekstilni turizam," *Ekonomska politika*, 7 January 1961.

ping his assistant ("from this the reader can clearly see the high level of defer-
ence shown to the shopper in the capitalist countries").[41] Even window-
shopping had its satisfactions for the tourist who couldn't afford to bring
home the things he admired. Petković's descriptions of the tourist-speculators
nursing and baby-talking to the Italian dolls they planned to sell at a profit use
tourism to make a similar point. These tales hinted at the same contradictions
that other critics were to pursue: how far would the irrational, even frivolous
desires of the consumer be allowed to shape the priorities of a market-oriented
socialism?

Yugoslav Shopping Tourism between East and West

Consumption was not just a matter of debate within Yugoslav society; it was
also one of the distinctions between Yugoslavia and the capitalist West on the
one hand, and the Soviet bloc on the other. In describing their adventures in
shopping, Yugoslav travelers positioned their society with reference to East
and West. The capitalist world is the world of goods and of wealth (it hardly
needs saying). But, and again it hardly needs saying, western capitalism had its
social price. Vasa Popović in Vienna contrasted western abundance with Yugoslav scarcity, but he also qualified the contrast—abundance, yes, but these
were mostly unnecessary trifles or morally dubious goods: "Abroad, abroad.
Abroad there's everything: lighters and trinkets, compact mirrors, silk corsets,
refrigerators, half-naked women in the bars and half-clad women on the corners; colorful ties and coats made by foreign firms . . . and all cheaper."[42]

The association of capitalism and prostitution is constant: everything has its
price under capitalism. But so nicely offered: "On the Place Pigalle, a man
can't look at anything without it being offered to him immediately! Everything
is there, with a 'help yourself!' And when I turned away with a 'no, thanks,
miss!' she just pursed up her lips and said politely, 'you're welcome, sir!' Paris
is marvelous! But us, we're uncultured bumpkins, we'll never learn such nice
manners."[43] This is clearly ironic—but capitalism's politeness could be unnerv-
ing. Petković's story of tormenting a shopkeeper with no intention of actually
making a purchase is repeated endlessly, with variants, in the travel accounts
of the period. It is used as a device for self-criticism, with explicit comparisons
to the surliness of the Yugoslav waiter or shopkeeper. But Popović, in 1954,
linked service with servility and brought it all back home: the smile on the lips
of the Paris doorman is pleasant, but it's also "classical and exemplary, and
precisely because it is classical and exemplary, it reminds me from a distance
of the inhibited and unemancipated smile of our Gypsy *primaš* when he ap-

---

41. Petković, *Turist*, 196.
42. Popović, *Šeretska putovanja*, 149.
43. Ibid., 217.

proaches a tipsy guest with his violin."[44] But he also saw that the smile made the guest happier to pay, and to pay extra. This would be picked up and elaborated at length in other works: how was Yugoslavia to become a destination that could attract the western tourist and the tourist dollar—and at the same time retain its dignity? How could you sell yourself without selling out?

If the West was the world of goods, the eastern bloc was, equally predictably, the world of scarcity, shortage, queues. It was emphatically not a tourist destination for Yugoslav travelers. Aleksandar Tišma, in his 1963 account of a visit to Poland and Hungary, calls this "travel in the wrong direction," undertaken by accident rather than by tourist design.[45] Nonetheless, writers did produce accounts of bloc travels (often literary pilgrimages, or more overtly political tours). Even when the main point lies elsewhere, travel writers comment on consumption, since it was on this level that the difference between political claims and social realities could best be measured, whether the claims were of Yugoslav superiority or of Soviet achievement.[46] Travel accounts of the Soviet Union, especially, dwell on the cost, quality, and availability of consumer goods. Even when travelers describe relative abundance in the late 1950s and 1960s, this tends to be recounted against the background of earlier scarcity, as though this is the norm and any change is only temporary. Frane Barbieri's account of the Soviet Union, *Report from Red Square* (1964), is typical in its account of GUM as almost phantasmagorical in its array of consumer goods, which he describes Soviet citizens as buying as though they expect the whole array to vanish in a puff of smoke.[47] In 1959 Vasa Popović was already making fun of this stereotype of bloc deprivation and Yugoslav wealth when he describes travel as a chance to rid yourself of prejudices. For example,

> you assume that you will sell your suitcase in Prague for a good price, and that for the money you'll be able to pick up a tea service of that famous prewar Czech porcelain. But it's an obvious example of a prejudice! Because, when you stroll through Prague and look at the window displays, and judge for yourself, it turns out that what you'd *really* like is to buy a Czech suitcase.[48]

But he then undercuts this with descriptions of sordid private enterprise (being pressed to buy cheap porcelain—in his hero Švejk's tavern, to add to the insult) or by the difficulties of finding festive fare at Christmastime (the Czechs have bourgeois holidays but no geese).

44. Ibid., 202.

45. Aleksandar Tišma, *Drugde* (Belgrade, 1969), 51.

46. See, for example, Saša Vereš, *Moskovski dnevnik* (Zagreb, 1966); Zlatko Tomičić, *U zemlji Samovoj* (Zagreb, 1966); and Matko Peić, *Jesen u Poljskoj* (Zagreb, 1969).

47. Frane Barbieri, *Report sa Crvenog trga* (Zagreb, 1964); on GUM, see also Nada Marinković, *Smisao i ljubav* (Zagreb, 1956).

48. Popović, *Šešir dole—putovanju*, 6.

While Yugoslav travels to the West use shopping tourism as a means to evaluate both capitalism and the ambiguities of Yugoslav market socialism, socialist fraternal travel allows Yugoslav writers to see themselves as the West to the Soviet bloc's East. Political and economic cardinal points were relative, when it came to tourism. The poet Desanka Maksimović underlined the point in the middle of a volume of travels in both directions, when she described her desire to go to Paris: "the *real* West, not the sort of West that we represent in the eyes of those coming from Siberia, say, or Azerbaijan, or from Bulgaria."[49]

Shopping Tropes

After the economic reforms of 1965, fewer accounts focused on the problems of tourist shopping. Consumerism was becoming the norm for the average Yugoslav. True, the gap between western products and the things you could buy at home was never quite bridged. Yugoslavs shared an insatiable desire for things western with their relatively more deprived bloc cousins (hence the continuing attraction of destinations like Trieste). Still, Yugoslavia was different in being able to take its access to these consumer pleasures for granted. But it was different, too, in its citizens' active support for the political and ideological compromises entailed by "market socialism"—at least while the money held out.

In the atmosphere of economic and political crisis of the late 1980s, travel writing provided a way of reevaluating such attitudes. A 1987 account by the Novi Sad writer Milica Mićić-Dimovska, entitled *Austro-Hungarian Travel Prospectus*, illustrates the durability of shopping tropes.[50] She describes a bus journey from Novi Sad to Vienna, Bratislava, and Budapest, organized by secondary-school teachers intent on selling contraband Vegeta (Yugoslavia's legendary monosodium-glutamate-laced soup powder) and buying scarce goods. In many ways the excursion is a rewriting of Popović's 1955 trip to Vienna (the contrast between leisure tourism and black-market travel; the humiliations of being poor in the midst of plenty; the feverish search for bargains; the way that a whole foreign infrastructure exists to service the Yugoslav desire for cheap goods—carried out in Serbian), but all this is given added force by the way this inverts recent understandings of the normal: "Exactly ten years ago my husband and I were in Vienna as real tourists, we changed our dinars in a bank. Is it really possible, I think to myself, that then I could have been sitting in the Mozart-Café, eating Mozart-Kugel and drinking coffee with whipped cream?"[51]

The journey to Bratislava reverses the stereotypes of Yugoslav travel writing even more disturbingly. Mićić-Dimovska's shame (trying to flog her Vegeta to

49. Desanka Maksimović, *Praznici. Putovanja* (Belgrade, 1972).
50. Milica Mićić-Dimovska, *Putopisi* (Vranje, 1999).
51. Ibid., 15–16.

Czech housewives who avert their faces; squabbling over sheets and salamis that are better and cheaper than Yugoslav ones; the Czech customs officials' disdain) depends heavily on inverting stereotypes of Yugoslav consumer superiority in comparison to the socialist East. It's underlined by a scene in which she looks down on a Soviet pleasure craft on the Danube, and the tourists "look back at us, with our noise and clamor, loaded down with our packages and bundles. [...] Russians, I thought. Traveling without any hurry. They have a visitors program, a program that doesn't include black-market trafficking."[52] The Yugoslav world has turned upside down.

East/West polarities aren't the only things challenged here. So are new Yugoslav social values. Mićić-Dimovska begins her black-market tale with a confession: "Resilience and resourcefulness—lately these virtues have been exciting me, making me unhealthily enthusiastic, leading me into recklessness and loss of self-respect."[53] She struggles to reconcile the new imperatives of individual enterprise (or "hucksterism") with remembered dignity and collective pride—just as the excursionists insist on at least a little sightseeing, "on covering their customs evasion with a veneer of tourism."[54] For Mićić-Dimovska, the struggle for survival means that Yugoslavs now "care nothing for our reputations, nor for our country's reputation [...] we have so far lost faith in any common values, in our nation, in our homeland, that we look only to ourselves, think only of our own interests in the narrowest sense."[55]

A single text, however vivid, cannot tell us how far the freedom to travel and to shop legitimated Yugoslav socialism. Mićić-Dimovska's journal does suggest that the tourist account retained its utility in exploring the relations among travel, shopping, social values, and a specifically Yugoslav ideal of the "good life," while drawing on older patterns that had been established in postwar writing. Travel writings such as these engage with—and reveal—wider assumptions, expectations, and anxieties. As such, they can tell us perhaps more than they intended to, in this case about the halting, complicated development of ideas about tourism and socialist consumerism and about the ways at least some Yugoslavs used travel to position themselves and their society between East and West, the promises of socialism and the beguilements of western-style capitalism.

52. Ibid., 41.
53. Ibid., 7.
54. Ibid., 20.
55. Ibid., 32.

CHAPTER 13

East German Nature Tourism, 1945–1961

In Search of a Common Destination

Scott Moranda

"The hiking season has begun. In cities and villages, our youth are making plans for vacations and excursions. That is right and good. Our youth, who eagerly take part in the construction of socialism, have a right to enjoyable and eventful holidays."[1] In this speech from 1957, Walter Ulbricht, East Germany's first head of state, promised youth good times, but the ruling Socialist Unity Party (SED) had much higher expectations for tourism. In much the same way that planners in the Soviet Union fashioned "proletarian tourism" to make vacation activities more productive, the early German Democratic Republic (GDR) worked to transform tourism into a tool for "denazification."[2] To put it another way, the SED sought the transformation of suspect Germans into optimistic, modern, and activist "socialist personalities" ready to abandon their passive "authoritarian personalities" for the collective struggle against fascism and western imperialism. Ulbricht thus added, "I am certain that we [by building more youth hostels] will provide our youth many new possibilities to . . . increase their strength for the struggle [to defend] peace and socialism."[3] This GDR vision of purposeful travel built on a long-standing critique of "wasteful" tourism and preference for "productive" travel in communist youth groups and Soviet travel discourse (as well as National Socialist rhetoric).[4] Historically, though, German tourism had often been organized around short, leisurely excursions within a vacationer's local homeland, or *Heimat*.[5] The middle classes had also enjoyed more ambitious vacations organized with the help of Baedeker guidebooks or commercial travel agencies.[6] These private

---

1. Walter Ulbricht, "Schafft Wanderquartiere für unsere Jugend," 15 May 1957, Stiftung Archiv der Parteien und Massenorganisationen der DDR im Bundesarchiv (hereafter cited as SAPMO-Barch), DY34 1/266/4235.

2. See Koenker, Gorsuch, and Maurer, in this volume.

3. Ulbricht, "Schafft Wanderquartiere."

4. On National Socialist tourism, see Shelley Baranowski, *Strength through Joy: Consumerism and Mass Tourism in the Third Reich* (Cambridge, 2004).

5. *Heimat* is a virtually untranslatable word that means homeland, but also a place where one feels at home. For one introduction to the concept, see Celia Applegate, *Nation of Provincials: The German Idea of Heimat* (Berkeley, Calif., 1990).

6. Rudy Koshar, *German Travel Cultures* (Oxford, 2000).

tourist activities represented (for the SED regime) potential distractions from the creation of a true postfascist society. Tourists, of course, rarely passively consume destinations selected by authorities but actively produce "changing and historically specific social meanings."[7] Would Germans enjoy tourism that detracted from political reform and produced social meanings resistant to political coordination, or would they travel for enlightenment and physical improvement, thus forever leaving fascism behind?

In spite of its desire to cultivate collectivism and comradeship through *Touristik* (the German adaptation of the Russian term *turizm*), the GDR was constrained by its need to provide material living standards comparable to those found in West Germany. In fact, Germans had already begun to seek out relaxation and social interaction on par with prewar experiences in the 1940s.[8] East Germany, though, struggled mightily to prove that it could provide Germans with an advantageous alternative to both fascism and capitalist modernity—complete with a better quality of life, social equality, and economic stability. Seeking to balance popular legitimacy with social control was by no means a new problem, but expectations for a modern German state had only increased in the postwar period.[9] National Socialism, as the SED realized, had managed to provide many Germans with what they remembered as the best years of their lives, while other citizens weary of Nazi political indoctrination wanted pleasure without remorse.[10] Much to its disadvantage, German communism (due to both Soviet influences and tendencies within the German communist movement) downplayed consumer pleasures and celebrated proletarian asceticism, violent struggle, and sacrifice for the future.[11] Nonetheless, the GDR had at least to appear ready to offer its citizens the good life in a century often marked by mass death and suffering.[12]

7. On the formation of collective identities through tourism and leisure, see ibid.; and Rudy Koshar, "Seeing, Traveling, and Consuming: An Introduction," and "Germans at the Wheel: Cars and Leisure Travel in Interwar Germany," in *Histories of Leisure*, ed. Rudy Koshar (Oxford, 2002), 1–24, 215–30.

8. See, for instance, Ingeburg Wonneberger, "Breitensport: Studie zum Breitensport/Massensport in der Sowjetischen Besatzungszone Deutschlands und der DDR (1945–1960)," in *Der Sport in der SBZ und frühen DDR*, ed. Wolfgang Buss and Christian Becker (Schorndorf, 2001), 401.

9. For more on Germany's particular debates about consumerism, see Michael Geyer, "Germany, or the Twentieth Century as History," *South Atlantic Quarterly* 96, no. 4 (1997): 663–702; and Alon Confino and Rudy Koshar, "Regimes of Consumer Culture: New Narratives in Twentieth-Century German History," *German History* 19, no. 2 (2001): 135–61.

10. Michael Geyer and Konrad Jarausch, *Shattered Past: Reconstructing German Histories* (Princeton, N.J., 2003), 296.

11. Eric D. Weitz, *Creating German Communism, 1890–1990: From Popular Protests to Socialist State* (Princeton, N.J., 1997); Jonathan R. Zatlin, "The Vehicle of Desire: The Trabant, the Wartburg, and the End of the GDR," *German History* 15, no. 3 (1997): 358–80.

12. David F. Crew, "Consuming Germany in the Cold War: Consumption and National Identity in East and West Germany, 1949–1989. An Introduction," in *Consuming Germany in the Cold War*, ed. Crew (Oxford, 2004), 1–19. Recent literature on consumption in the German Democratic Republic is rich, and Crew's bibliography cites many of these texts.

The SED thus attempted to introduce the principles of proletarian tourism and forge a new GDR collective identity at a remarkably inopportune moment—exactly when Cold War regimes (including the Soviet Union) promised vacationers material pleasures. With a heavy hand, as this paper will show, the SED successfully eradicated independent leisure organizations and set up its own mass organizations for sport and leisure. Nonetheless, older identifications with a regional *Heimat* (experienced through tourism) survived after 1945 alongside the central state's assertion of political control.[13] The GDR promoted folk festivals to contrast East German authenticity with West German Americanization, despite its worries about romantic nostalgia for a pre-SED past.[14] At the same time, trade union representatives and others concerned about preventing worker unrest recommended more accommodation to popular consumer desires. Complaints about inadequate tourism opportunities grew louder in the 1960s and 1970s, but even in the GDR's early years, I argue, an alternative vision for the GDR emerged to challenge the regime's aversion to "less purposeful" vacation pleasures.

Reforming the Friends of Nature

To limit independent social activity and impose their own leisure regime, the SED established a central network of summer camps, tourist facilities, and leisure organizations. Inheriting the communist disdain for "mere" tourism and nature enthusiasm, the SED also moved to repress apparent allies such as the socialist Friends of Nature (Die Naturfreunde) hiking club. This crackdown on social organizations reflected a broader animosity between the German Communist Party and the Social Democratic Party beginning in the tumultuous years of the Weimar Republic; in 1946 the Socialist Unity Party merged the two left-wing parties, silenced reformist social democrats, and demanded adherence to a party line dictated by veterans of the Communist Party closely tied to Moscow.[15] Aggression against independent organizations, of course, also allowed the state to control limited resources in a period of economic scarcity and make its authority visible in a time of rapid change.

The new regime, however, did not find it easy to stamp out Germany's rich and varied travel cultures. By the late nineteenth century, the urban middle classes enjoyed jaunts to the countryside and encouraged working-class children to spend their summers at vacation colonies to improve their physical health.[16] *Wandervögel* youth hiking clubs before World War I escaped the

13. See Jan Palmowski, "Building an East German Nation: The Construction of a Socialist *Heimat*, 1945–1961," *Central European History* 37, no. 3 (2004): 365–99.

14. Ibid., 381–82.

15. For one introduction to divisions between Communists and Social Democrats, see Jeffrey Herf, *Divided Memory: The Nazi Past in the Two Germanys* (Cambridge, Mass., 1997).

16. Thilo Rauch, *Die Ferienkoloniebewegung: Zur Geschichte der privaten Fürsorge im Kaiserreich* (Wiesbaden, 1992), 58, 189. See also Thomas Lekan, *Imagining the Nation in Nature: Landscape Preservation and German Identity, 1885–1945* (Cambridge, Mass., 2003); and

stuffy confines of the classroom for jaunts in the countryside,[17] and National Socialism later provided "Strength through Joy" package tours and youth summer camps as examples of Nazism's "socialism of the deed."[18] The organizers of social democratic leisure culture, no less than their middle-class liberal and conservative counterparts, valued the nature excursion. Social democrats in Germany (much as in France and other neighboring countries) often blamed slum conditions and a lack of fresh air for the moral weakness of workers.[19] To improve the living conditions of workers, the Friends of Nature (founded by Viennese social democrats in 1895) offered organized hikes and access to over two hundred cabins throughout Germany. One of the founding members of the German Friends of Nature wrote in 1905 that tourists sought, "strength and health for the hard struggle for rights, freedom, and leisure time."[20] Friends of Nature organizers imagined a utopian future free of social and economic inequalities and hoped that socialist travel would avoid middle-class tourism's escape from economic realities. At the same time, however, actual hikes and festivals offered workers a refuge from the daily grind of urban life, and the Friends of Nature often appeared to participate in a travel culture remarkably similar to that of many middle-class tourist associations.[21] The left wing of Germany's Friends of Nature took note and attacked socialist nature tourism as a form of escapism. Dogmatic communists made political education their primary concern and developed war games, pageants, and marches to raise morale for the communist struggle.[22] The extremists also pushed for more confrontations with the middle classes rather than cooperation in the maintenance of trails. By the end of the Weimar era, in fact, the communists sponsored their own youth groups that practiced "proletarian tourism" as taught in the Soviet Union and learned fighting songs in preparation for military struggle with the fascists.[23]

William H. Rollins, *A Greener Vision of Home: Cultural Politics and Environmental Reform in the German Heimatschutz Movement, 1904–1918* (Ann Arbor, Mich., 1997).

17. On youth groups, see John Alexander Williams, "Steeling the Young Body: Official Attempts to Control Youth Hiking in Germany, 1913–1938," Occasional Papers in German Studies 12 (University of Alberta, June 1997); Elizabeth Heinemann, "Gender Identity in the Wandervögel Movement," *German Studies Review* 12, no. 2 (1989): 249–70; as well as older works such as Walter Laqueur, *Young Germany: A History of the German Youth Movement* (New York, 1962).

18. See Lekan, *Imagining the Nation in Nature*, as well as Thomas Zeller, *Strasse, Bahn, Panorama: Verkehrswege und Landschaftsveränderung in Deutschland von 1930 bis 1990* (Frankfurt am Main, 2000) for an introduction to this topic.

19. Laura Lee Downs, *Childhood in the Promised Land: Working-Class Movements and the Colonies de Vacances in France, 1880–1960* (Durham, N.C., 2002), 12.

20. Thomas Buchsteiner, "Arbeiter und Tourismus," Ph.D. diss., Eberhard-Karls-Universität Tübingen, 1984, 84.

21. This reference to middle-class tourist culture draws on Koshar, *German Travel Cultures*.

22. See Vari, in this volume, as well as Joachim Wolschke-Bulmahn, *Auf der Suche nach Arkadien* (Munich, 1990).

23. See John Alexander Williams, "Giving Nature a Higher Purpose: Back-to-Nature Movements in Weimar Germany, 1918–1933," Ph.D. diss., University of Michigan, 1996; Heinrich Steinbrinker, "Der Geist der Gemeinschaft: Wechselwirkungen zwischen Arbeiterjugendbewegung

While the SED continued this critique of moderate socialists, the fate of the Friends of Nature was not immediately clear in the 1940s. Even though the SED repeatedly dismissed "reactionary" German romanticism as an escape from pressing political tasks, excursions to the countryside assisted in taking youth off the streets and distancing them from anticommunist parents and capitalist influences. The countryside also offered an easily accessible and affordable space for education, especially since most gymnasiums and educational centers had suffered from Allied bombing. Free from "corrupt" urban spaces, the countryside remained for the SED a place for purification. Youth leaders, in particular, pushed young East Germans to "rough it" in natural spaces where bodies would be hardened by natural forces and fused into a collective, regaining a "natural" productivity that would protect them from "imperialist" corruption and pessimism.[24] Such language—often found in instructions for summer-camp organizers—remarkably resembled similar sentiments in the Hitler Youth and the Strength through Joy tourist organization in Nazi Germany; and given the prominence of a "Hitler Youth generation" among functionaries in the communist youth organization, these parallels were perhaps inevitable.[25] At the same time, the SED knew it faced challenges from competing narratives about nature. It feared German nature enthusiasm, which had glorified the countryside as a national space—home to a German *Volk* racially tied to the soil. In hopes of eradicating any allegiance to ethnic or local regional identities, GDR authorities shut down organizations such as the German Alpine Society and the Saxon Mountain Climbers League. On their own in the open spaces of the countryside, East Germans could not be trusted; nature tourists—especially youth—needed particularly strict guidance.

Veterans of the Friends of Nature and Heimat friends often chose to work with the regime despite its aggression against nature enthusiasts. Some individuals were being pragmatic; Soviet occupation appeared to be inevitable. Others were troubled by revelations about Nazi crimes and welcomed the SED's aggressive regime as the more radical and legitimate antifascist state in postwar, German-speaking Europe.[26] The German Communist Party had openly resisted the Nazi regime and seemed to offer the best possibility of a thorough

---

und 'bürgerlicher' Jugendbewegung bis 1933," in *Jahrbuch des Archivs der Deutschen Jugendbewegung 1978–1981* 13 (Burg Ludwigstein, 1981); and Eva Wächter, "'an der lauten Stadt vorüberziehen!' Naturfreundejugend 1918–1933, zwischen Jugendbewegung und Jugendpflege," in *Wir sind die grüne Garde: Geschichte der Naturfreundejugend*, ed. Heinz Hoffman and Jochen Zimmer (Essen, 1986), 13–62.

24. SAPMO-Barch, DY24 5928; SAPMO-Barch, DY24 3627; SAPMO-Barch, DY34 1/264/4234; Dr. Edelfried Buggel, *Die Touristik im Massensport* (Berlin, 1957, 1961); Freie Deutsche Gewerkschaftsbund, *Freude, Frohsinn, Ferienlager: Material für Helfer der Betriebsferienlager der Gewerkschaften* (Berlin, 1961).

25. Dorothee Wierling, "The Hitler Youth Generation in the GDR: Insecurities, Ambitions, and Dilemmas," in *Dictatorship as Experience: Towards a Socio-Cultural History of the GDR*, ed. Konrad Jarausch (New York, 1999), 307–24.

26. On this attraction to the GDR, see Wonneberger, "Breitensport."

rejuvenation of society through central planning and scientific expertise—a dream of many educators, social hygienists, and landscape architects critical of modern commercial culture.[27] The SED, moreover, promised to provide all East Germans (regardless of class background) with the "good life"—social equality, free health care, and leisure opportunities. Vacations in Nazi Germany enhanced the health of the Aryan citizens of a powerful racial empire, but the GDR promoted vacations as an entitlement to the working class and argued that central planning under scientific principles could provide more equitable vacation opportunities.[28] Even if Marxism-Leninism attributed little intrinsic value to nature, many nature-loving technocrats in new state planning agencies acted as if it did. They believed that nature revived the human spirit and that enlightenment owed much more to the healing powers of fresh air and strong sunlight than to *agitprop* and lessons in antifascist history.[29]

Given a certain level of sympathy for the regime's central planning, veterans of the Friends of Nature thus felt that they might actually find a home, possibly within the confines of the Free German Youth (Freie Deutsche Jugend [FDJ])—an organization established by the SED in March 1946 to organize the free time of the young. Like the Soviet Komsomol and the Hitler Youth, the FDJ served to prepare young citizens for leadership positions, introduce youth to military skills, and create loyalty to the regime. The FDJ also oversaw the short-lived Jugendheim GmbH, a company created in 1947 to confiscate intact hostels and cabins unscathed by Allied bombing and make them available for education and FDJ activities. In its early years, the FDJ even worked to attract new members with hikes, dances, and other purely social events.[30] While FDJ authorities often adopted uncompromising positions, the organization, like the Soviet Komsomol, initially negotiated with members to shape popular collective activities.[31] The FDJ, for instance, developed plans for a hiking organization that might have made room for the Friends of Nature. Early in 1948, the FDJ proposed the creation of Ferien und Wanderwerk (offices for recre-

27. Social hygienists were often doctors and scientists and advocated the state-led management and reform of lifestyles, health habits, and living conditions to ensure improved public health.

28. Baranowski, *Strength through Joy*, 234.

29. On debates over views of nature within left-wing leisure organizations, see, among others, Dagmar Günther, *Wandern und Sozialismus: Zur Geschichte des Touristenvereins 'Die Naturfreunde' im Kaiserreich und in der Weimarer Republik* (Hamburg, 2003).

30. For more on the FDJ attempts to provide entertainment, see Ulrich Mählert, *Blaue Hemden, Rote Fahnen: die Geschichte der Freien Deutschen Jugend* (Opladen, 1996); Helga Gotschlich, ed., *"Links und links und Schritt gehalten . . ." Die FDJ: Konzepte—Abläufe—Grenzen* (Berlin, 1994); Mark Fenemore, "The Limits of Repression and Reform: Youth Policy in the Early 1960s," in *The Workers' and Peasants' State: Communism and Society in East Germany under Ulbricht 1945–1971*, ed. Patrick Major and Jonathan Osmond (Manchester, 2002), 171–89; and Leonore Ansorg, *Kinder im Klassenkampf: Die Geschichte der Pionierorganisation von 1948 bis Ende der fünfziger Jahre* (Berlin, 1997).

31. Anne E. Gorsuch, *Youth in Revolutionary Russia: Enthusiasts, Bohemians, Delinquents* (Bloomington, Ind., 2000), 42.

ation and hiking) to provide tourist opportunities to young people.[32] Youth functionaries, after meeting with the Friends of Nature, then submitted a proposal to affiliate the hiking organization with the FDJ;[33] and in Dresden, former Friends of Nature embraced the new Wanderwerk.[34] They expressed relief at finally finding a home for their appreciation of natural landscapes and, more important, hoped to gain access to youth hostels and cabins confiscated by the Jugendheim GmbH.[35] The incompatibility of the FDJ and the Friends of Nature was thus not immediately obvious.

Soon, however, the Free German Youth turned against the Friends of Nature. In part, the FDJ worried about losing control over members if other organizations gained a foothold within the youth group. Youth leaders also worried that Friends of Nature tourists lacked ideological rigor and did not understand the need for constant vigilance against apoliticism. The Wanderwerk, as stated in new statutes from April 1949, needed to provide political education. The name of the youth hiking group changed from the "Young Friends of Nature" to the cumbersome "Free German Youth Interest Group for Hiking and Holidays." In explaining their action, the Free German Youth wrote, "In many cases there is the danger that the majority of the members in Friends of Nature groups . . . might even be enemies of the FDJ."[36] The Free German Youth then criticized the poor work done by the Ferien und Wanderwerk, dissolved the organization on 14 February 1951, and turned over responsibility for hiking to sport functionaries to ensure more purposeful tourist activities.[37] The youth organization would remain under the strict control of SED hardliners, and the Friends of Nature gave up on official recognition.

Constructing a Socialist Countryside

Eliminating rival leisure organizations was fairly straightforward; the regime banned and persecuted unapproved organizations and replaced them with ap-

32. "Richtlinien für das Erholungs und Wanderwerk in der sowjetischen Besatzungszone," 25 February 1948, SAPMO-Barch, DY30 IV 2/16/1.

33. Jugendheim GmbH, Letter to the Sekretariat of the FDJ, "Betrifft: Naturfreunde," 23 December 1948, SAPMO-Barch, DY24 3626.

34. Joachim Schindler, *Zur Entwicklung von Wandern und Bergsteigen in der Sächsischen Schweiz sowie zur Arbeit touristischer Organisationen Dresdens von 1945 bis 1953* (Dresden, 1999), 49.

35. "Protokoll der Sitzung der provisorischen Landes und Zonenleitung der Natur und Heimatfreunde," 6 July 1948, in Schindler, *Entwicklung*, 40; Erich Hobusch, "Naturfreunde auf dem Weg zum Kulturbund, 1945–1953," *Grüner Weg 31a: Zeitschrift des Studienarchivs Arbeiterkultur und Oekologie* 10 (January 1996): 68.

36. Central Council of the FDJ (hereafter ZR der FDJ), "Vorlage: Das Ferien und Wanderwerk der FDJ," 12 April 1949, 8a, SAPMO-Barch, DY24 3627.

37. ZR der FDJ, "Protokolle Nr. 132 der Sitzung des Sekretariats des ZR der FDJ am 14.2.1951," 14 February 1951, SAPMO-Barch, DY24 2406; Kurt Lemmer, "Schlussbericht über die Abwicklung der Arbeiten in der Jugendheim GmbH," 1 September 1951, SAPMO-Barch, DY24 3626.

proved "mass organizations." Of course, individuals continued to travel on their own, and small groups of disgruntled tourists and nature enthusiasts gathered in small clubs illegally, but such clubs remained isolated.[38] Transforming the meanings attached to physical landscapes proved more difficult, especially since nationalist praise for natural landscapes had explicitly juxtaposed a German culture rooted in the soil with "rootless" communist internationalism. Could the SED link the natural world to a new collective identity? To tackle this problem, the SED appropriated the idea of Heimat to promote the GDR as a new "socialist Heimat," but it also tried to reconfigure the countryside as a constructed socialist space that could be sensually experienced by tourists.[39] In the eyes of the SED and FDJ, the countryside had to be transformed from a realm of militaristic and capitalist values into a "legible" space incorporated into the modern socialist economy and easily monitored by the SED.[40] Part of the physical transformation involved the collectivization of farms, but leisure spaces also had to be collectivized. If successful, tourism would no longer evoke nationalist sentiments or regional pride.

In expanding its network of youth hostels, the SED regime hoped to appropriate private guesthouses for the new state, use them to instruct young tourists in socialist values, but also to rework the German countryside into a socialist space. As the geographer Barbara Bender has written: "Landscape is never inert; people engage with it, rework it, appropriate and contest it. It is part of the way in which identities are created and disputed, whether as individual, group, or nation-state."[41] Before 1945 in Germany, different states and social groups made competing claims over rural spaces and celebrated collective identities made physically tangible in the landscape. Regional Heimat clubs appropriated hills and valleys and marked them as their own with trails, monuments to local fallen soldiers, and cabins. Middle-class Heimat clubs destroyed the trail markers left behind by working-class hiking clubs, and communist hardliners unfurled red flags to claim a space as their own.[42] In Imperial Germany, as well as Nazi Germany, states exploited hostels to cultivate a national identity, and the SED hoped to do much the same thing after it began to acquire hostels through the Jugendheim GmbH. By 1956 East Germany had 330 youth hostels with 20,700 beds to serve tourists.

38. Schindler, *Entwicklung*.

39. See Palmowski, "Building an East German Nation."

40. See James C. Scott, *Seeing Like a State: How Certain Schemes to Improve the Human Condition Have Failed* (New Haven, 1998). For an example of how tourism helps reconfigure rural spaces, see Ellen Furlough and Rosemary Wakeman, "La Grande Motte: Regional Development, Tourism, and the State," in *Being Elsewhere: Tourism, Consumer Culture, and Identity in Modern Europe and North America*, ed. Shelley Baranowski and Ellen Furlough (Ann Arbor, Mich., 2001), 348–72.

41. Barbara Bender, "Introduction: Landscape—Meaning and Action," in *Landscape: Politics and Perspectives*, ed. Bender (Oxford, 1995), 3.

42. Jakob Schmitz, "Naturfreunde und Wegebezeichnung," *Rheinisches Land: Nachrichten des Gaues Rheinland in Touristin-Verein 'Die Naturfreunde'* 7 (1926), 152.

Youth hostels worked to make official historical narratives promoted by the SED visible in the countryside. Hostels that once might have been named after Nazi martyrs now were given the names of famous antifascists or other leading "socialist personalities." The largest youth hostel in East Germany took the name of Ernst Thälmann, the most prominent communist victim of Nazi concentration camps. The second largest hostel adopted the name Adolf Hennecke in honor of a coal miner who exceeded work quotas and was glorified by the state as a working-class hero (in the tradition of the Stakhanovites in the Soviet Union). By honoring the antifascist narrative that stood at the heart of GDR "national" identity, hostel educators suggested that the surrounding natural landscapes were not just places for romantic escape, but realms intertwined with the historical project of modernization that the GDR was undertaking.[43]

As with hostels, authorities planned for hiking trails to serve the SED project. Hiking paths, the new regime hoped, would lead tourists from youth hostels to sites of memory commemorating antifascist resistance and other historic achievements of the labor movement. The Kulturbund (the Culture League created as a mass organization for artists and Heimat enthusiasts) proposed a series of educational trails organized in a unified system of paths that would allow hikers systematically to explore and learn about the new socialist state.[44] SED loyalists in the Kulturbund even attempted to appropriate Heimat discourse and bend it toward support for the socialist project. In the new state, the Kulturbund's leaders suggested, affection for one's Heimat (local homeland) could be redirected away from racist nationalism and toward socialist values. They wrote, "Those who love their Heimat also love peace!"[45] A 1959 ordinance for marking hiking paths and a 1961 guide to the 4,000 kilometers of GDR hiking trails suggested that, by hiking, East Germans would learn to experience the new state as a real and permanent physical entity—as a new Heimat to be defended from threatening western imperialists.[46]

Like the Soviet Komsomol, FDJ organizers generally (but not always) believed that youth activities should work to discipline society, not to provide entertainment.[47] In other words, hiking had a purpose, and as one tourism plan-

43. Letter from Rat der Kriese (hereafter cited as RdK) Marienberg, Abteilung (hereafter Abt.) Jugendfragen, Körperkultur und Sport to Abt. Volksbildung, RdK Marienberg, "Betr: Bericht über die Tätigkeit der Jugendherberge im Sommer 1963," 16 January 1963, Kreisarchiv Marienberg-Zschopau: E1648.

44. Committee for Tourism and Hiking (hereafter KTW), "Sekretariatsvorlage über die Wegemarkierung in der DDR," 1958, SAPMO-Barch, DY12 4286.

45. "Protokoll zur Zusammenkunft der Lehrpfadgestalter des Bezirkes Leipzig," 26 March 1957, SAPMO-Barch, DY27 2805.

46. "Entwurf einer Anordnung über die Markierung der Wanderwege in der DDR," 1959, SAPMO-Barch, DY27 2810. See also Horst Berger, *4000 km Hauptwanderwege DDR* (Leipzig, 1960). For further reading on the concept of a "Socialist Heimat," see Palmowski, "Building an East German Nation," 377.

47. Gorsuch, *Youth in Revolutionary Russia*, 64–75.

ner wrote, "Our joy in hiking is altogether different from an escape into nature." Hikers, he argued, should listen to lectures on how workers and peasants contributed their labor power to shaping the East German landscape.[48] The FDJ asked guides to initiate conversations with local inhabitants; and hostel directors took youth to factories, immense hydroelectric dams, and sites of antifascist resistance to celebrate the GDR's achievements.[49] Educators, of course, were not being entirely innovative in this respect. Nazi "Strength through Joy" hikes took participants to Nazi monuments, and Weimar socialist youth groups had promoted "social hiking" to encourage working-class hikers to learn the social history of rural landscapes.[50] If purposely done, though, hiking could redefine former Nazi spaces as homelands within a workers' state.

Inevitably, FDJ pedagogy faced challenges both from older tourists and from young members of the FDJ seeking to claim the countryside for their own enjoyment. "Wild," unorganized vacationers, for instance, ignored the political education offered by youth hostels and took over facilities for private celebrations. These conflicts only worsened as planners pushed for an expansion of the lodging network to support education but invested much less money into addressing the leisure desires of the entire population. Promises of better living standards and the need for political education often stood at odds with each other. Educators wanted hostels to teach political lessons, but SED and FDJ leaders also recognized the appeal of outdoor activities as a source of pure pleasure.[51] The Soviet Union had already struggled with this problem in the 1920s, and pre-1945 German youth organizations had also walked a fine line between pedagogy and amusement.[52] As in the Hungarian tourist clubs described by Vari, political education and even the teaching of military skills took precedence in official FDJ planning. The East German situation, however, was unique; hypocritical propaganda campaigns against West German militarism tended to undermine the militaristic FDJ's legitimacy in public eyes. Without a doubt, popular aversion to the FDJ placed pressure on local gov-

48. Gerhard Wenzel, "Das entscheidende Jahr," *Unterwegs* 1 (1961): 1; FDJ, "Wanderfahrt: Durch unsere schöne DDR vom 5.8 bis 30.9.1956," 5 August 1956, 8, SAPMO-Barch, DY34 1/264/4234.

49. Ernst Schramm, "Kinder und Jugendarbeit in unserem Verband," *Der Tourist* 6 (1965): 4; Günter Lehm, *Die Ferienwanderung: Für den Ferienhelfer* (Berlin, 1965), 7–8; FDJ, "Betrifft: Einrichtung einer Sonderschule des Zentralrates zur Aus- und Weiterbildung von Funktionären der FDJ auf touristischem Gebiet," 31 August 1956, 1, SAPMO-Barch, DY24 6151.

50. Youth leaders in the FDJ and other leisure organizations often referred to Soviet models and attended conferences with counterparts from other Soviet-bloc countries. Specific examples include Dr. Edelfried Buggel, "Bedeutung der Touristik im Sozialismus," *Der Tourist* (June 1962); and "Letter from the State Committee for Physical Culture and Sport," *Unterwegs*, no. 1 (1957).

51. KTW, "Die Entwicklung der Touristik und des Wanderns in der DDR," 1956, SAPMO-Barch, DY34 1/264/4234; KTW, "Massnahmeplan zur Verbesserung des Unterkunftswesen in der DDR," 6 April 1957, SAPMO-Barch, DY34 1/264/4234.

52. Gorsuch, *Youth in Revolutionary Russia.*

ernments to respond to popular tourist desires rather than promote a youth hostel as an FDJ outpost.

Many East Germans continued to understand their local countryside as a space to enjoy with local friends and neighbors, and Heimat identities resisted political and cultural centralization. Local town leaders and Heimat clubs had traditionally maintained most trails, so the Kulturbund found it difficult to recruit locals to take part in maintaining statewide paths that did not immediately serve local leisure interests.[53] In the Harz Mountains, for instance, local Kulturbund activists could not convince villages to mark hiking trails for outsiders. Halle's Kulturbund leadership noted, "Completely different markings had been made in each locality." They added, "There still remains a tendency among a few local leaders to put up trail markings that direct [hikers] to an especially prominent excursion destination and then most often directly back to the trailhead."[54] It appeared that locals had little interest in transforming their region into an educational space for youth groups, and trail markings mostly served a town's own citizens.

Many locals also remembered that hostels had once been taverns or guesthouses enjoyed by families, Heimat clubs, or Nazi "Strength through Joy" tourists. Adult tourists thus argued that they deserved to use the facility as much as youth. Often, local state representatives willingly conceded to tourist desires and opened hostel doors to the public—justifying their choices by citing the regime's promises to provide better living standards. As in other locales throughout the Soviet bloc (such as the Black Sea), such unofficial, or "wild," tourist activities tolerated by local authorities challenged the central planning of youth leaders.[55] The SED state, in many ways, found itself in an even weaker position than the Soviet Union, given that many more Germans had experienced the pleasures of vacationing and tourism in their lifetime and could look back on perhaps better tourist experiences before 1945.

One such struggle between official youth education and "wild" tourists (or, put another way, between purpose and pleasure) took place at a popular Thuringian retreat in the late 1950s. In 1955 authorities from the central Institute for Youth Questions (affiliated with the education ministry) declared that the Krayenburg, a tourist destination and tavern popular with local residents before 1945, would be transformed into a youth hostel. Since 1945, the Krayenburg had housed a school and a Free German Youth clubhouse, even though local villages wanted to return Krayenburg to its original purpose.[56] A petition from authorities in the village of Merker noted that complaints about

53. Letter from Kulturbund, Zentralkommission Natur und Heimatfreunde, Dr. Liesel Noack to Members, 14 February 1957, SAPMO-Barch, DY27 2810.

54. Memo from Kulturbund, Kreissekretariat Quedlinburg (Bezirk Halle) to Zentralkommission Natur und Heimatfreunde, Dr. Liesel Noack,11 January 1958, SAPMO-Barch, DY27 2809.

55. See Gorsuch, Maurer, and Noack, in this volume.

56. Letter from Rat der Gemeinde Kieselbach to Rat des Bezirks (hereafter RdB) Suhl, Abt. Jugendfragen, "Betr: Krayenburg," 9 August 1955, Bundesarchiv (hereafter Barch), DR2 2814.

the Krayenburg hostel arose at numerous town meetings, and to highlight the monument's importance to community livelihood, local authorities emphasized that nearly five thousand locals flocked to the ruins for celebrations of nearby Kieselbach's eight-hundredth anniversary.[57] In this way, town leaders drew on a regional Heimat narrative as an alternative basis for communal identity. Often in the GDR's early years, such celebrations proliferated and took forms no different than before 1945.[58] In their complaint, however, town leaders never argued that local pride and the construction of socialism were incompatible; rather, they suggested that a truly responsive socialist state would accommodate the needs of local Heimat enthusiasts.

Union representatives for local miners also complained about the youth hostel and made a point of reminding youth leaders that workers had been promised a better standard of living in the new workers' state. While East German unions normally supported state objectives over worker desires, the union had an ear close to the ground and recognized issues that might lead to worker unrest. For example, youth hostels banned alcohol on their premises and thus interfered with the Krayenburg festivals organized for workers.[59] In this and other incidents, the trade union pressed to gain greater control over tourist facilities throughout the GDR. The union implied that the FDJ had an excessive amount of power over hostel management and tourism planning; it pointedly suggested that the Soviet Union did a better job responding to private vacation desires for tourist pleasures and that the SED should follow the lead of their big brother.[60]

The SED's attempt to reconfigure the East German countryside into a centralized "socialist space" thus collided with its need to live up to its promises of a better quality of life. Drawing on both Heimat identities and Soviet models, disgruntled East Germans challenged the FDJ—one of the main pillars of SED power—and district youth leaders in Suhl felt enough pressure from town councils and the union to question the necessity of a youth hostel at Krayenburg.[61] While the Institute for Youth Questions and the FDJ in Berlin made some minor concessions, they still defended their plans for a "socialist countryside" dominated by youth hostels. In their opinion, cultivating a cadre of SED loyalists and disciplining youth and teaching them to travel in a purposeful manner mattered more than the leisure needs of miners in Suhl.[62] Stories of

57. Letter from Rat der Gemeinde Merkers to RdB Suhl, Abt. Jugendfragen, "Betr: Krayenburg," 10 August 1955, Barch, DR2 2814.

58. Palmowski, "Building an East German Nation," 370, 373.

59. Letter from IG Bergbau Suhl Gera to RdB Suhl, 1956, Barch, DR2 2814.

60. Dr. Edelfried Buggel, "Bedeutung der Touristik im Sozialismus," Der Tourist (June 1962): 9; untitled report on a State Committee for Physical Culture and Sport research trip to the Soviet Union, 28, Ecoarchiv (Hofgeismar): DWBV Box 6.

61. Letter from RdB Suhl to Walter Ulbricht and Amt für Jugendfragen, 9 November 1956, Barch, DR2 2814.

62. Letter from Amt für Jugendfragen to RdB Suhl, 17 November 1956 and Letter from Amt für Jugendfragen to RdB Suhl, 28 November 1956, Barch, DR2 2814.

working-class decadence, moreover, appeared to be an effective weapon in blocking local access to a hostel. The FDJ, like Soviet Bolsheviks, saw most nonconformist behavior as threatening, demonized undisciplined activities, and believed that accommodation to popular behavior (as other GDR institutions were more likely to do) led to disaster.[63] Education officials in Suhl, for instance, complained of drunken workers supposedly threatening the safety of young girls at the hostel. Youth functionaries wrote, "Every day, the hostel director was disturbed multiple times [by the misbehavior of workers], and a few times he had to call on the police to prevent the disturbances created."[64] Such stories, no matter how little they were based on truth, were powerful, in part because they built on a discourse common to both the SED and National Socialist regimes. Animalistic, "wild" behavior (theoretically encouraged by the commercialization of leisure and unhealthy habits such as drinking or smoking) threatened normative social behavior and accepted gender relations.[65] The vehemence with which youth leaders dismissed popular tourist behavior suggested, however, that ideologues were incapable of fully controlling the public, which preferred coffee, beer, and carnivals to long marches and outdoor exercises.

While tales of moral indecency framed the FDJ attack on "ideologically suspect" tourist practices, the real confrontation appeared to be between the centralizing SED state seeking to commandeer tourist resources for political agendas and locals resistant to outside domination of local affairs. After all, the regime accepted Heimat traditions in other contexts to gain popular sympathies, but in this case youth officials needed to commandeer material resources for enhancing their own power. Ernst Schramm, from the Berlin offices of the Institute for Youth Questions, complained:

> The Kieselbach community and its mayor are attempting with all of their might to make the youth hostel at Krayenburg disappear. Funds for the hostel in the 1959 budget were eliminated, for example, even though there is an agreement that the hostel should be renovated in the coming years. Now the hostel is in poor condition."[66]

In another instance, youth officials wrote, "Often residents will direct unsuspecting hiking groups from Eisenach or other origins in the other direction [away from the hostel]."[67] Sources do not indicate that this was an ideological

63. Gorsuch, *Youth in Revolutionary Russia*, 2; Ansorg, *Kinder*; Mählert, *Blaue Hemden*.

64. Letter from RdB Suhl (Bezirksschulrat) to KTW, Schramm, "Betr: Beschwerde des DKB," 14 February 1959, Barch, DR2 2814.

65. See Uta Poiger, *Jazz, Rock, and Rebels: Cold War Politics and American Culture in a Divided Germany* (Berkeley, Calif., 2000). Reports of "animalistic" behavior by youth at youth hostels appeared in letters to the editor in *Skisport und Touristik*, January 1959: 11; and Ingrid Heinicke, "Jugendburg mit rock'n roll?" *Wandern und Bergsteigen*, May 1959, 2.

66. Letter from Amt für Jugendfragen to Erste Sekretär der FDJ Bezirksleitung in Suhl, "Betr: Jugendherbergswesen," 28 August 1960, Barch, DR2 2814.

67. Letter from KTW Suhl to Amt für Jugendfragen, "Betr: Angelegenheit der Jugendherberge Kreyenburg bei Kieselbach," 14 July 1960, Barch, DR2 2814.

conflict between communists and anticommunists, but rather, one among various interpretations of the responsibilities of a modern welfare state. Local tourists wanted pleasure and a better quality of life (defined by the enjoyment of Heimat landscapes or by the expansion of benefits for union members), while the FDJ and its allies insisted that better living standards could come only with greater control over education and everyday leisure.

State-owned hostels and resorts, in theory, could have been more responsive to tourist desires, but they refused to abandon their particular obligations within the SED system. Youth hostels primarily had to serve the FDJ, just as youth hostels under previous German regimes served state interests, but without private guesthouses opening to respond to popular demand, youth hostels created more popular resentment than they might have otherwise. To a certain degree, however, the state's attempted centralization of East German space failed, and loyalties to a local Heimat prevailed. Even if the FDJ insisted on purposeful tourist activities for youth and the end to "wild" tourism, other GDR institutions did recognize to some extent that popular tourist desires did not always fit into its vision of "proletarian tourism." With semiofficial approval, therefore, local workers tentatively appropriated the Krayenburg youth hostel for themselves, believing they were merely exercising their rights as citizens in a modern welfare state. Like Soviet citizens after 1945, they wanted to reap their rewards for the sacrifices of the recent past.

By the end of the 1950s, the limits of SED "nation building" were clear. While tourism can contribute to the formation of collective identities, a stable East German identity did not seem to emerge from GDR tourist culture—at least not in the early years of the Republic. Little evidence points to an embrace of the countryside as collective "East German space." To a certain degree, these Thuringian workers established their right to enjoy their local Heimat. At the same time, though, locals *never* pushed youth authorities out of the hostel and *never* secured an official stamp of approval for their festivities and leisurely day trips. Anxious about competing travel cultures linked to regional and national identities, authorities careened back and forth between antagonism and accommodation. The dispute between the trade union (accommodation) and the FDJ (antagonism) at the Krayenburg pointed to a larger schizophrenia in the GDR not unlike the tensions in 1920s Soviet Russia over social control and material pleasures during the New Economic Policy (NEP).[68] Tourism, like the countryside itself, ultimately became fractured, with private groups, youth, and employees enjoying vacations in isolated campgrounds, at FDJ-controlled youth hostels, and at insular employee resorts, but never sharing a sense that they had a common destination.

The issue was not, however, just that rural East Germans always actively resisted proletarian tourism and retreated into insular social niches after attempted centralization in the 1950s. Rather, some planners accommodated

68. Gorsuch, *Youth in Revolutionary Russia*, 7–8.

popular tourist desires, and many citizens believed their tourist desires com-
patible with the goals of the socialist welfare dictatorship. Critics of the FDJ
almost never questioned the state's role in planning leisure; vocal critics of the
regime fully expected the central state to play a key role in providing tourist
pleasures, as had previous German regimes. Revisionists within the Kulturbund or the trade union also shared with the SED an aversion to commercial
tourism. Whether tied to a Heimat, a conservative, or a social democratic tradition of leisure and nature enjoyment, a common critique of commercial
tourism—and thus the pitfalls of classical modernity—allowed for the imagination of a welfare state constructing a more equitable and more genuine future. As much as a holdover of regional and nationalist identities, local resistance to youth educators reflected a common belief that vacationing was a
human right guaranteed by a postfascist welfare state. Hence union representatives wrote, "We must without question recognize [miners'] requests for an
excursion destination."[69] Likewise, individual vacationers often voiced their
belief in the state's responsibility to provide tourist pleasures. One vacationer,
for instance, complained about the state's inability to protect recreation areas
from poorly planned development and wrote in a petition to a state ministry,
"Hiking paths [have been] blocked and the landscape's value for rejuvenation
[has been] appreciably reduced."[70] As expressed by individuals, leisure organizations, and local officials disgruntled with the Free German Youth, East Germans up until some point in the 1970s did seem to agree on one GDR national
mission (distinct from a West German one): providing strong central planning
to ensure a better, more equitable quality of life.

69. Letter from RdB Suhl to Walter Ulbricht and Amt für Jugendfragen, 9 November 1956,
Barch, DR2 2814.
70. Letter from K. K. of Bad Freienwalde to Ministry for Environmental Protection, 3 January
1974, Barch, DK5 4506. This is one example from the 1970s, but numerous such letters were sent
to local and central authorities.

CHAPTER 14

Coping with the Tourist

Planned and "Wild" Mass Tourism on the Soviet Black Sea Coast

Christian Noack

Soviet tourism became mass tourism during the Brezhnev period. Official figures and contemporary western reports agree that the number of Soviet domestic tourists more than doubled between 1965 and 1980, and that annual growth rates reached 10 percent in the late 1960s.[1] While in 1970 about seventeen million spent their holidays in Soviet recreational vacation facilities, statisticians counted about thirty million in 1975 and forty-five million in 1983. If one adds about seventeen million people who went on short trips and twenty-two to twenty-four million children and adolescents who spent the summer in youth camps (in 1980), about one-third of the Soviet population traveled during their holidays in the late Soviet Union.[2] Under the party's guidance, the state and the trade unions "for the first time in the world" sponsored an "all-embracing system of organized recreation and recovery for the toiling masses," as one official boasted in 1976.[3]

The expanding Soviet tourist infrastructure never even approximately met the growing demand, though. Soviet citizens learned to travel very quickly—and rather individually. In view of the chronic shortages of vouchers (*putevki*), and despite the persistent lack of transportation facilities and accommodation, every summer millions of Soviet citizens headed to the country's seashores independently. To be sure, nonorganized, individual tourism probably existed throughout the Soviet period, but it was precisely during the Brezhnev years that individual tourists started to outnumber those who traveled within the state-sponsored structures, at least during the summer season and to the most popular resorts. Official Soviet dislike for so much unwarranted initiative is hardly surprising and not very subtly connoted by the term "wild tourists" (*dikari* or *dikie turisty*), which was used interchangeably with "nonorganized" or "unplanned" tourists.

---

1. As throughout this volume, "tourism" is used in the broad western sense of the term.

2. Jörg Stadelbauer, "Der Fremdenverkehr in Sowjet-Kaukasien. Gesamtstaatliche Bedeutung, räumliche Strukturen und Entwicklungsprobleme," *Zeitschrift für Wirtschaftsgeographie* 30, no. 1 (1986): 5; Bernd Knabe, "Der Urlaub des Sowjetbürgers," *Osteuropa* 29, no. 4 (1979): 304.

3. Quoted from Knabe, "Urlaub des Sowjetbürgers," 300.

Somewhat delayed in comparison to the West, eastern Europe and the USSR faced their own postwar leisure boom. The present chapter focuses on social and cultural agendas connected with the emergence of Soviet domestic mass tourism. Following a discussion of changes in the tourist industry and in the official discourse about tourism, I analyze the complex interrelations between organized and wild tourism. Relying on contemporary social surveys and archival sources from the Krasnodar region and the Black Sea resort of Anapa, I then sketch the conditions under which both groups spent their vacations, examine the perception of individual tourism by the local authorities, and explore the willingness and ability of local Soviet agencies to cope with mass tourism, mentally and practically.[4]

The Beaten Track

Until 1960, the quantitative and qualitative level of Soviet recreational infrastructure remained underdeveloped and underfinanced. Due to its nature and the country's isolation, the regime had monopolized the discourse on tourism and had charged it ideologically. The population did not possess other than "socialist" travel habits when the regime started to pave the way for mass tourism. From 1961 on, however, the party and the trade unions displayed considerable interest in the development of recreational structures. This unprecedented concern was part of a new policy that tried to secure the Soviet citizens' loyalty to the regime by expanding consumption and by distributing far-reaching social benefits. Wages were raised, working time was reduced, and the regime refrained from harsh measures to secure social discipline. The state subsidized a better supply of food, housing, and, to a degree, consumption goods. The welfare and pension system was extended, with education and medical care furnished free of charge. State-sponsored social tourism was an integral part of the bonus system.[5]

Since the 1930s, when the trade unions had taken over responsibilities for the provision and planning of leisure and recreational facilities, health resorts

---

4. Some of the local material is presented in Christian Noack, "Von 'Wilde' und andere Touristen. Zur Geschichte des Massentourismus in der UdSSR," *Werkstatt Geschichte*, no. 36 (2004): 24–41.

5. An important argument was that in the early 1960s the share of workers enjoying organized vacations dropped below the quotas of 1940. See Gosudarstvennyi arkhiv Rossiiskoi Federatsii (hereafter GARF), f. 5451, op. 68, d. 360, ll. 141–43; d. 392, ll. 73–77; f. 9493, op. 8, d. 699, ll. 25–26; f. 9520, op. 1, d. 751, ll. 12–13; Gosudarstvennyi arkhiv Krasnodarskogo Kraia (hereafter GAKK), f. 1624, op. 1, d. 324, ll. 15–16; Stadelbauer, "Fremdenverkehr in Sowjet-Kaukasien," 3; Vladimir Anderle, *A Social History of Twentieth Century Russia* (New York, 1994), 246–75; and Stephan Merl, "Staat und Konsum in der Zentralverwaltungswirtschaft. Russland und die ostmitteleuropäischen Länder," in *Europäische Konsumgeschichte. Zur Gesellschafts- und Konsumgeschichte (18.-20. Jahrhundert)*, ed. Hannes Siegrist et al. (Frankfurt am Main, 1997), 205–41.

and tourism had been administered by different branches. These were reorganized in 1962 into Central Councils for Health Resorts and for Tourism (Tourism and Excursions in 1969), respectively. Each central council presided over subsidiary councils in republics, regions, and some major resorts. More important, the 1962 decrees dissolved the association of the Councils for Tourism with the Councils of Sport Societies and Organizations.[6] As a result, the councils emerged de jure as the chief coordinating bodies for tourism development in the country. Their responsibility stretched over a broad range of activities, such as the supply of accommodation and food, the provision of medical services, culture, and entertainment, the publication of information and literature and the training of personnel. The Councils for Tourism and Excursions were also to maintain a network of excursion bureaus, to organize and to explore tourist routes and to supervise "independent" (samodeiatel'nyi) tourism—that is, tourist activities organized by the tourist clubs and sections in Soviet enterprises and administrative or educational structures. But recreational development invariably had to be arranged in competition with many rival interests of industrial ministries or local and district administrations. Because of the strictly sectoral planning in the Soviet Union, coordinating bodies like the city or tourism councils could design and discuss development plans but had little means to implement them.[7] Spontaneity was hard to control in recreational development, and it was always doubtful whether other organizations operating vacation facilities would subordinate their interests. The councils' limited competitiveness became particularly evident at construction sites: contractors regularly withdrew labor power, machines, and other resources to complete other "more rewarding" objectives. Many recreation facilities stood only structurally completed for years. Recreational development, a complex affair all over the world, was particularly chaotic and ill balanced in the Soviet Union.[8]

Throughout the eighth and ninth five-year-plans (1965–1975), the councils received enormous state loans and subsidies from the social insurance funds to enlarge the country's vacation facilities. In addition, Soviet enterprises could retain a certain amount of their profits for social, cultural, and recreational

6. Monika Hennigsen, *Der Freizeit- und Fremdenverkehr in der ehemaligen Sowjetunion unter besonderer Berücksichtigung des Baltischen Raumes* (Frankfurt am Main, 1994), 35; "Polozhenie o tsentral'nom, respublikanskikh, kraevykh i oblastnykh sovetakh po turizmu," in *Fizicheskaia kul'tura, sport i turizm. Sbornik rukovodiashchikh materialov* (Moscow, 1963), 99–105.

7. GARF, f. 5451, op. 68, d. 454, ll. 1–4, 7–14, 68–72; d. 483, ll. 11–25; f. 9493, op. 8, d. 1342, l. 36; d. 1855, l. 3; d. 1981, ll. 54–55.

8. V. I. Azar, *Ekonomika i organizatsiia turizma. Metodologicheskie voprosy* (Moscow, 1972), 34–35; Knabe, "Urlaub des Sowjetbürgers," 301, 309, 375–76, 378; Denis J. B. Shaw, "Achievements and Problems in Soviet Recreational Planning," in *Home, School, and Leisure in the Soviet Union*, ed. Jenny Brine, Maureen Perrie, and Andrew Sutton (London, 1980), 198–202, 209–11.

services after the 1965 economic reforms.[9] Soviet tourism witnessed an overall increase in the numbers of tourist accommodations and beds, partly by construction and partly by measures that enabled a prolongation of seasons.[10] Moreover, the councils aimed at a more even distribution of facilities over the country's territory, albeit with limited success. A 1980 report stated that the Caucasus and the Black Sea coast (including the Sea of Azov) accounted for 12.3 percent of the Union's population but almost 40 percent of the beds in sanatoria, 35 percent of those in rest homes, 24 percent of beds in recreational camps, and close to 40 percent of all beds in tourism facilities. The Caucasian coast and Crimea remained the sole fully developed recreational zones in the country.[11]

Compared to the poor level around 1960, it was barely an exaggeration when Soviet sources spoke about a developing tourism industry.[12] This did not mean, though, that tourism became a top priority in Soviet politics or economics. On the contrary, many voices among officials and journalists in the 1970s and early 1980s opted for an upgrading and centralization of responsibilities in a ministry or at least a committee on the all-union level to enhance its performance. While for the West "a strange conglomerate called the tourist industry [. . .] often trying hard not to look like one" was characteristic, Soviet tourism business did not became a "real" industry, but was desperately trying to look like one.[13]

How far did these changes affect the nature of Soviet *turizm*?[14] There were only slight innovations in the provision of accommodations: in Soviet health resorts, sanatoria with medical treatment and rest homes or pensions without such treatment continued to offer full pension accommodation combined with a recuperative regime to their visitors. The standard of service was usually higher than in other facilities but at the same time more strictly regulated. It took a doctor's order (*spravka*) before one could to try to obtain a voucher for

9. GARF, f. 5451, op. 68, d. 392, ll. 73–81; f. 9520, op. 1, d. 1504, ll. 36–39, 43. In 1976 the trade unions alone spent about 300 million rubles, probably one-quarter of the total investment. Additionally, the trade unions received 2 billion rubles for the maintenance of vacation facilities and the distribution of free-of-charge or discounted vouchers (Knabe, "Urlaub des Sowjetbürgers," 377–78).

10. The capacities of the trade union's facilities alone grew fourfold between 1960 and 1980, from some 583,000 beds to 2,138,000 beds. See Denis J. B. Shaw, "The Soviet Union," in *Tourism and Economic Development in Eastern Europe and the Soviet Union*, ed. Derek R. Hall (London, 1991), 122; and Iu. A. Vedenin, "Sotsial'no-ekonomicheskie aspekty razvitiia TRS," in *Sotsial'no-ekonomicheskie i geograficheskie aspekty issledovaniia territorial'nykh rekreatsionnykh sistem* (Moscow, 1980), 16–30.

11. Shaw, "Soviet Union," 127; Knabe, "Urlaub des Sowjetbürgers," 307; Henningsen, *Freizeit- und Fremdenverkehr*, 85–87.

12. The personnel on the payrolls of the councils alone exceeded seven hundred thousand around 1980 (Shaw, "Soviet Union," 124–25).

13. Knabe, "Urlaub des Sowjetbürgers," 375; Orvar Löfgren, *On Holiday: A History of Vacationing* (Berkeley, Calif., 1999), 276.

14. A systematic overview is in Henningsen, *Freizeit- und Fremdenverkehr*, 56–72; and Shaw, "Soviet Union," 123–24.

three or four weeks' cure in sanatoria through the trade unions. Alternatively, vacationers could try to obtain an authorization (*kursovka*) at the point of destination that entitled them to medical treatment without accommodation. Vouchers for pensions without medical treatment or for rest homes could be bought without a medical prescription. Vouchers were heavily subsidized and sold for 30 percent of the nominal price.[15]

The recreation bases (*baza otdykha*) and camps (*lager' otdykha*) were customarily more down-to-earth facilities for stationary vacationing. Their conditions varied significantly: bases could comprise a group of solid multistory buildings, but up until the mid-1970s camps consisting of tents or wooden sheds prevailed. Since these facilities were much easier and cheaper to build, their number grew faster than that of sanatoria or pensions in the period under consideration. A still cheaper and very popular variant used by many enterprises and collective farms was to rent public buildings at the destinations (for example, schools) and improvise recreation bases within.[16]

In Soviet literature about tourism, tourist facilities are treated as a separate category from recreation bases and sanatoria. There were few tourist hotels, and most of the roaming tourists had to accept rather modest overnight accommodations. Most common were tourist bases, shelters, and refuges, and only one-third of these hosted tourists in solid buildings in 1965. A few motels and camping sites were opened for motorized travelers throughout the country.[17] Almost all these facilities were designed for group holidays. Even sanatoria seldom provided two- or four-bed rooms; usually a larger number of people was crammed together. This was probably as much due to economic necessity as to a latent disposition for social control and ideological indoctrination. Throughout the 1970s, existing structures were slowly but continuously upgraded. Qualitative changes, however, did not keep pace with the quantitative development.[18]

Who profited from the enlarged travel possibilities, then? This is difficult to say, and problems range from the dilemmas of Soviet statistics in general to the lack of adequate categories of social stratification within late Soviet society. The first apparent truth, however, is that supply always lagged behind demand. Despite growth rates that reached 10 percent in the best years, planned tourism could provide annual holidays for probably one-tenth of the population. This was no secret, although tourist officials did their best to obscure it by announcing fantastic figures of tourists served by their facilities.[19] Still,

15. Henningsen, *Freizeit- und Fremdenverkehr*, 55.

16. Arkhivnyi otdel administratsii goroda-kurorta Anapa (hereafter AOAGKA), f. 190, d. 131, l. 460; d. 132, ll. 14–15, 334–35; N. M. Stupina, "Izmeneniia v strukture rekreatsionnykh setei SSSR," in *Sotsial'no-ekonomicheskie i geograficheskie aspekty*, 30–40.

17. *Entsiklopediia turista* (Moscow, 1993), 11. For the Krasnodar region, see GAKK, f. 1624, op. 1, d. 322, l. 24.

18. Shaw, "Soviet Union," 122; Henningsen, *Freizeit- und Fremdenverkehr*, 53–54, 79.

19. The Central Council for Tourism and Excursions boasted that in 1988 some forty-two million guests were accommodated, and more than two hundred million went on excursions.

14.1. New building at the largest tourist base in the USSR, "Sokol," Sochi, on the Black Sea. Accommodating eight hundred travelers, rooms here were available only to tourists with vouchers. *Turist* 9 (1971): inside front cover.

there can be no doubt that the growth rates of unplanned tourism were constantly higher. Again, we have no reliable statistics, but Soviet media frankly admitted that wild tourists outnumbered the organized in the most popular destinations. In Sochi, the number of wild tourists was said to have exceeded the number of organized by two or three times. About seven times more wild tourists were counted in Anapa. Other estimates concerning the share of the wild vary between 50 and 85 percent of all annual vacationers in the Soviet Union.[20]

The second truth is that prices played no role in the accessibility of state-sponsored tourism. The trade unions distributed 10 percent of the vouchers free of charge, and about 80 percent at one-third of the nominal price. The

Entsiklopediia turista, 9. The first figure, however, represents overnight accommodations per bed per night and thus does not reflect the actual numbers of travelers. The second figure embraced virtually anybody who took part in any tour offered by one of the excursion bureaus.

20. L. Pavlov, "Otdykh v 'razreze,' " *Literaturnaia gazeta,* 3 December 1969, quoted from *Osteuropa Archiv* (1971), A 109–11; *Rabotnitsa,* no. 10 (1985): 22–23; Knabe, "Urlaub des Sowjetbürgers," 372; Stadelbauer, "Fremdenverkehr in Sowjet-Kaukasien," 8; Henningsen, *Freizeit- und Fremdenverkehr,* 85; N. E. Romanov, "Voprosy neorganizatsionnogo otdykha," in *Voprosy neorganizatsionnogo otdykha. Tezisy k pervoi mezhkurortnoi nauchno-prakticheskoi konferentsii g. Anapa, 1981 g.* (Anapa, 1981), 7.

problem, then, was the distribution of vouchers through the trade unions' local committees. Official sources differ on the criteria of allocation, and they say almost nothing about the usage in specific factories, educational institutions, or administrative bodies. The relevant instructions foresaw that "excellent workers, veterans, invalids, engineers, technicians, and blood donors" were to be preferred, while it excluded "hooligans, dawdlers, and alcoholics."[21] This may or may not reflect actual practices. However, the Central Councils for Health Resorts or Tourism and Excursions respectively distributed vouchers more or less proportionally to their territorial and local substructures. Particular needs or demands from below were virtually ignored. This is one of the reasons why the discursive separation of "recreation" and "tourism" had limited value in practice. People took what they could get, disregarding the particular indications of sanatorium cures or practical requirements on certain tourist routes.[22]

Many Soviet institutions built their own vacation facilities. Only the most influential ministries or industrial enterprises could afford permanently to maintain rest homes or tourist bases in well-known resorts. Others usually made use of simple homes or camps, often in nearby locations. Beyond this distinction between a small, politically promoted elite and the ordinary citizens, it is rather difficult to establish links between travel activities and social stratification. Soviet accounts and documents recorded the social background of vacationers, yet these classifications hardly ever reflected their actual status. In general, late Soviet wage policies had reduced differences in real income, and the introduction of the standard five-day working week (in 1968) and the prolongation of annual holidays increased the ordinary workers' and employees' abilities to participate in tourism.

More relevant was where a person lived, in which branches of the economy he or she was employed, the age group he or she belonged to, and, last but not least, the educational background he or she enjoyed. Urban dwellers, people from the administrative centers or the big industrial agglomerations, began to travel earlier than others, and they traveled more extensively. For the late 1960s a Soviet survey stated that up to 60 percent of the urban population traveled regularly, while figures for the total population ranged from 8 to 30 percent.[23] Among those who traveled, the younger and better-educated post-

21. "Instruktsiia o poriadke raspredeleniia i vydachi putevok po vsesoiuznym i mestnym turistskim marshrutam tsentral'nogo, respublikanskikh, kraevykh i oblastnykh sovetov po turizmu (5 fevralia 1965)," in *Fizicheskaia kul'tura, sport i turizm. Sbornik rukovodiashchikh materialov* (Moscow, 1971), 100–104; Knabe, "Urlaub des Sowjetbürgers," 305–6.

22. Henningsen, *Freizeit- und Fremdenverkehr*, 58; *Turist*, no. 2 (1967): 28; no. 12 (1973): 11; no. 6 (1974): 29; no. 1 (1974): 21; GAKK, f. 1624, op. 1, d. 164, l. 107; d. 322, l. 49; d. 323, l. 45.

23. Pavlov, "Otdykh v razreze," A 110; V. F. Bogatykh, "Organizatsiia obsluzhivaniia otdykhaiushchikh bez putevok," *Voprosy neorganizatsionnogo otdykha*, 18; Shaw, "Soviet Union," 124–26; Henningsen, *Freizeit- und Fremdenverkehr*, 89; Stefan Plaggenborg, "Lebensverhältnisse und Alltagsprobleme," *Handbuch der Geschichte Russlands*, vol. 5, part 2 (Stuttgart, 2003), 827.

war generation clearly dominated. The generation of the "sixties" (*shestides-iatniki*) continued to be over-represented in later polls, particularly among the nonorganized tourists.[24] As usual, the groups to benefit least were pensioners and collective-farm workers. But by this time even the collective farmers were better paid, enjoyed increasing holidays, and profited from the lifting of travel restrictions that had been particularly severe in resort areas.[25]

A New Theory of the Leisure Class?

What repercussions did the emergence of mass tourism have on Soviet discourse on tourism and recreation, which had long reflected ideological beliefs about free time and leisure? Tourism in the Russian sense of the term, active physical exertion and visual exploration, continued to be hailed for its physical and educational purposefulness. Tourism would strengthen the body and moral character of the Soviet tourist. It was said to enhance collectivism, courage, willpower, persistence, patience, and endurance, as well as help the individual to understand the political, historical, or cultural meanings ascribed to the landscapes, cities, or monuments the tourist was guided to visit.[26]

The extreme ideological loading of Soviet tourism dates back to the campaigns against the prerevolutionary tourist traditions and institutions in the late 1920s and early 1930s. The proletarian tourist toured the country to educate himself and others. The proletarian tourist was always expected to fulfill a multitude of roles, ranging from the geographer to the defender of the fa-

---

24. Azar, *Ekonomika*, 44–45. Pavlov, "Otdykh v razreze," stated that people in their thirties were the single largest group among the wild tourists. See L. I. Baklykov, "Nauchno-metodicheskie osnovy novoi sistemy ozdorovleniia neorganizovannykh otdykhaiushchikh na Chernomorskim poberezh'e Kavkaza" (Candidate's Dissertation, Sochi, 1983), 143–44, with data for the late 1970s. B. A. Grushin, *Chetyre zhizni Rossii v zerkale oprosov obshchestvennogo mneniia*, vol. 2, part 1 (Moscow, 2003), 140–41, cites a 1966 survey by *Komsomol'skaia pravda*. About 80 percent of the readers who commented on the state of affairs in Soviet tourism were under thirty-nine. About 90 percent had a secondary or higher education and were urban dwellers.

25. Mervyn Matthews, *The Passport Society: Controlling Movement in Russia and the USSR* (Boulder, Colo., 1993), esp. 31, 34. On villagers' tourism, see Shaw, "Achievements and Problems," 207–8; and GAKK, f. 1624, op. 1, d. 184, l. 15; d. 196, l. 3.

26. See Qualls, in this volume; Anne E. Gorsuch, "'There's No Place Like Home': Soviet Tourism in Late Stalinism," *Slavic Review* 62, no. 4 (2003): 771–75; and Evgeny Dobrenko, "The Art of Social Navigation," in *The Landscapes of Stalinism: The Art and Ideology of Soviet Space*, ed. Dobrenko and Eric Naiman (Seattle, 2003), 163–200. For late Soviet treatments, see V. F. Kasatkin, *Faktory razvitiia i obshchestvennoe znachenie turizma. Uchebnoe posobie* (Moscow, 1983), 54–82; V. I. Kvartal'nov and V. K. Fedorchenko, *Sotsial'noe znachenie turizma v SSSR* (Kiev, 1989), 6–15, 135–53, 178–93; and V. F. Omel'chenko, *Ekskursionnoe obshchenie. Poznanie, vospitanie, otdykh* (Moscow, 1991), 30–53.

therland. These proletarian virtues contrasted with the "idleness" and "waste-fulness" of bourgeois tourism.[27] While this ideological leitmotif was significantly toned down after Stalin's death, some basic prescriptions showed enduring persistence. For example, a 1989 account on Soviet social tourism echoed that tourism fulfilled important educational ends, "instructing people in ideological and political respects, morally, in respect to their work and their physical fitness. . . . The accomplishment of useful public work on their tours raises the social importance of self-organized tourism, renders it more interesting and purposeful, and positively influences the personality."[28] The authors emphasized that at least 67 percent of male tourists fulfilled household duties "no less than their wives," and thus did not show any resemblance to the rank-and-file Soviet husbands whose persistent domestic patriarchalism caused so many headaches to Soviet social science, at least theoretically.[29]

The rather passive character of "rest" and "recreation," on the contrary, had always required a more sophisticated treatment. A key to the Soviet understanding of these terms lies in the close interdependence of work and recreation—or work and leisure, more generally speaking. The prevailing approaches measure the pursuit of leisure time in strictly functional terms. Recreation should serve the individual's self-realization, but it was inconceivable without enriching the society in the sense of a restoration of psychic and physical energy (i.e., the work force) or participation in "socially useful" public activities.[30] The primary importance attributed to work (being per se satisfactory under the conditions of socialism) implied that leisure should no longer remain a simple distraction from work.

Leisure emerged as a broader social phenomenon and, subsequently, as a significant scientific issue only with Khrushchev's new social policy. In fact, sociological inquiries on the free-time practices of Soviet citizens flourished in the 1960s and provoked lengthy debates over ideological guidelines and scientific norms for a purposeful pursuit of leisure. In many of these deliberations the authors continued to show deep concern about the Soviet vacationers' passivity during their holidays. They constantly urged the managers of sanatoria, rest homes, and tourist and recreation bases to provide the prerequisites for a planned, rational, and possibly collective use of time: lectures, cultural circles, reading rooms, libraries, films, excursions, or physical exercise. These were opposed to the old but obviously very popular evils in holiday resorts like

27. This dichotomy is exposed classically in V. P. Antonov-Saratovskii, *Besedy o turizme. Azbuka sovetskogo (proletarskogo) turizma* (Moscow and Leningrad, 1930), 35. For a detailed analysis, see Koenker, in this volume.

28. V. I. Kvartal'nov and V. K. Fedorchenko, *Turizm sotsial'nyi: istoriia i sovremennost'. Uchebnoe posobie* (Kiev, 1989), 133.

29. Ibid., 130.

30. Paul Hollander, "Leisure: The Unity of Pleasure and Purpose," in *Prospects for Soviet Society*, ed. Allen Kassof (London, 1968), 425.

dancing, card playing, or drinking.[31] Discursively, Soviet travel thus remained what it had been under Stalin: "serious fun."[32] What had changed was that it ceased to be the prerogative of a small Stalinist "leisure class," since nonworking time and increasing income allowed broader strata of the population to travel—within or beyond state-sponsored social tourism.

If officials already doubted the planned tourists' competence to spend their holidays purposefully, they had to be even more anxious about their wild stepbrothers. Indeed, even sympathetic contemporary sketches reflect the dichotomy between wild tourism and kultur'nost' (cultured behavior), as in Sergei Mikhalkov's play Dikari. The play starts out with a lengthy description of the camp life of three young men. These wild tourists are very busy doing nothing and in that way try hard to pervert the sanctioned norms of Soviet behavior. But as soon as two girls show up, wild tourists themselves, one young man after the other starts to feel ashamed about his uncivilized behavior. Finally, a cultured shave helps to transform them back into respectable men and citizens.[33]

While official statistics continued to ignore unplanned travel, Soviet sociology started to explore everyday life and leisure pursuits of the population from the 1960s on. Time-budget specialists were quick to find out that the wild tourists allegedly had less leisure time than their organized counterparts. Given the large scale of subventions for organized tourism, the wild tourists not only had to spend more time but also more money for the purchase of necessities like accommodation and food. Consequently, tourism functionaries concluded, self-improvised individual holidays would be too strenuous to offer "psychologically sound" and "rational recreation."[34]

For Soviet media it was conventional wisdom that people who chose the inferior alternative of unorganized travel did so only because they had not been able to obtain vouchers. This thesis was hardly ever empirically based and contradicted sociological survey research, but it supplied the press with an effective tool to criticize the state-sponsored tourism sector, both in qualitative and quantitative respects (more on this below). It was argued, for example, that above all families traveled outside the state-sponsored structures, which were ill suited for family vacations. In fact, the distribution of vouchers through the enterprises rendered it difficult to obtain places for partners or children. Moreover, the architecture of Soviet holiday accommodations rarely provided family rooms or playgrounds for children, except for a few specially designed

31. Azar, Ekonomika, 22–27; Kvartal'nov and Fedorchenko, Sotsial'noe znachenie, 20–29; Romanov, "Nauchnye osnovy," 10.

32. Gorsuch, " 'There's No Place Like Home,' " 784. Gorsuch cites Robert Edelman, Serious Fun: A History of Spectator Sports in the USSR (New York, 1993).

33. Originally published in 1956, the play was reprinted in S. V. Mikhalkov, Teatr dlia vzroslykh (Moscow, 1979) and filmed as Tri plius dva. Kul'turnost', to be sure, is just one and not the most important issue that the play makes fun of.

34. Romanov, "Nauchnye osnovy," 6.

sanatoria and pensions. The standardized cultural, sporting, or socializing events, too, were exclusively staged for an adult collective.[35] Recreational planning and holiday routines thus reflected the inconsistencies that characterized the situation of families more generally; and indeed, many families traveled on their own.[36] Opinion polls testified that many citizens expected an extension of family-friendly vacation facilities. Wild tourism, though, has probably never been predominantly a family business in the Soviet Union.[37]

Wild tourists figured as negative examples where other inconsistencies of tourism development were concerned. The propaganda of new destinations, one focal point of the development policy, is a case in point. Sociological surveys attested again and again that people opted to travel during the summer season, and they were seeking sun, sand, and the sea.[38] During the 1970s, about half of the respondents constantly desired to spent their holidays either on the Black Sea or the Baltic Sea shores. According to Soviet specialists, however, these destinations were already developed to the limit and could accommodate only one-quarter of those who wished to spend their vacations there.[39] Sometimes drastically exaggerating the "hardships" the wild tourists were to encounter in overcrowded destinations, the press participated in the promotion of off-season holidays and hailed the rich culture and natural beauties of the Soviet hinterland.[40]

Additionally, Soviet journalists regularly treated the "problem" of wild tourism as a moral appeal to raise the effectiveness of organized tourism. As systemic reasons could not be made responsible for the anomalies of Soviet tourism, critics had to refer to concrete accomplishments or faults. Or they opted, more fundamentally, for a centralization and upgrading of tourism administration, pointing at possible rationalization effects. The idea of the total

35. GAKK, f. 1624, op. 1, d. 323, ll. 37, 47–49; d. 545, l. 77; d. 570, l. 12; d. 883, l. 7; AOAGKA, f. 300, d. 58, l. 93; d. 77, l. 47; Knabe, "Urlaub des Sowjetbürgers," 373–74; Henningsen, Freizeit- und Fremdenverkehr, 84–85; V. N. Avanesov, "Organizatsiia semeinogo otdykha trudiashchikhsia, pribyvshikh na kurort Anapa bez putevok," Voprosy neorganizatsionnogo otdykha, 24; L. I. Baklykov, "Rol' kurortnykh faktorov Anapy v ozdorovlenii neorganizovannykh otdykhaiushchikh," in Voprosy neorganizatsionnogo otdykha, 100.

36. Parents shared duties with state and society in the inculcation of behavioral norms. In return, the state upgraded the families' legal status and increased financial support. Yet anything that smacked of a retreat from the collective was regarded with suspicion. See Vladimir Shlapentokh, Public and Private Life of the Soviet People: Changing Values in Post-Stalin Russia (New York, 1989), 164–70.

37. N. A. Storozhenko, "Sovremennoe sostoianie i perspektivy razvitiia neorganizatsionnogo otdykha na kurortakh," in Voprosy neorganizatsionnogo otdykha, 12–18; Henningsen, Freizeit- und Fremdenverkehr, 86.

38. Eighty-five percent of the respondents deliberately chose to travel during the summer holidays in an opinion poll quoted by Pavlov, "Otdykh v razreze," 10.

39. Western observers described wild tourism as a "double escape"—from less favorite destinations to more popular ones, and from the collective habits of social tourism (Stadelbauer, "Fremdenverkehr in Sowjet-Kaukasien," 3).

40. Rabotnitsa, no. 10 (1985): 23.

14.2. "Wild" tourists at their roadside campsite. *Turist* 6 (1970): inside front cover.

resort, catering to all the needs of its visitors, never lost its grip on Soviet thinking. Not accidentally, large-scale development projects like *La Grande Motte* in southern France were prominently featured in Soviet journals.[41] But Soviet tourism continued to lack the administrative and financial resources to realize such grand projects.

Coping with the Tourist: The Case of Anapa

Discursively, wild tourism thus remained a tool to criticize the shortcomings of planned tourism. Still, the two travel styles were probably more complexly intertwined both in theory and practice than the discourse would allow. The development of tourism in Anapa, a large seaside resort on the western Caucasian Black Sea shore, is a good example. The local soviets' efforts to cope with an ever-growing seasonal influx of vacationers is exceptionally well doc-

41. Vedenin, "Sotsial'no-ekonomicheskie aspekty," 18–19. In the 1970s Krasnodar's Tourist Council consulted French specialists on the development of a ski resort at Krasnaia poliana (GAKK, f. 1624, op. 1, d. 867, ll. 7–8).

umented, since Anapa hosted one of the first ventures in the Soviet Union exclusively devoted to unplanned tourism.[42]

Anapa possessed some seventy years of history as a Black Sea resort when the Council of Ministers of the RSFSR chose to expand it significantly in 1960.[43] More important, in 1965 Anapa's Territorial Council for the Administration of the Trade Union Health Resorts (Territorial'nyi sovet po upravleniiu kurortami profsoiuzov) was directly subordinated to the central council in Moscow. This meant closer involvement in administrative decision making and better access to financial resources. The annual number of visitors doubled between 1965 and 1973, surpassing one million that year. In the same period, a network of cultural palaces, cinemas, and reading rooms sprang up.[44] Anapa, however, was connected to the Soviet railroad network only in 1978, a couple of years after a nearby army airfield had been opened for civil aviation.[45]

Anapa, now a town with some fifty thousand permanent inhabitants, developed as a typical Soviet health resort. Sanatoria and pensions lined the spacious avenues and parks in the city center, adjoined by restaurants, canteens, shops, or cultural and administrative buildings. To the west and the north, a sea promenade on steep cliff tops formed a natural boundary. To the south and east extended quarters with traditional, small one-story private dwellings, occasionally alternating with typical Soviet-style residential blocks, some of them built for service personnel. In these quarters, vacation facilities, shops, or restaurants were scarce. To the northeast of the city center the *pionerskii prospekt* stretched along the shore, and youth and pioneer camps lined up there one after the other. In this respect, Anapa was rather atypical, since hardly any other Soviet resort could boast that it accommodated two hundred thousand children and adolescents annually. The "Pioneers' Republic" became a trademark, and Anapa attracted more families during the vacation season than even the leading resorts like Yalta or Sochi.[46] Most of them traveled unplanned and occupied either improvised camping grounds in the outskirts and nearby villages, or rented rooms from the local population.[47] As typical for So-

42. *Voprosy neorganizatsionnogo otdykha.*

43. *Chernomorskoe poberezh'e i Kuban. Spravochnik po kurortam* (Moscow and Leningrad, 1925); L. I. Baklykov, *Istoriia kurorta Anapa* (Krasnodar, 1999); Baklykov, *Istoriia kurorta Anapa* (Krasnodar, 2002); V. N. Avanesov, *Kurort Anapa* (Krasnodar, 1998).

44. Avanesov, *Kurort Anapa*, 44–60; L. A. Frolov, "Kul'turno-massovaia rabota s neorganizatsionnymi otdykhaiushchimi na kurorte Anapa," in *Voprosy neorganizatsionnogo otdykha,* 74–78.

45. GAKK, f. 1472, op. 2, d. 420, l. 162; d. 485, l. 11; f. 1624, op. 1, d. 544, l. 11; AOAGKA, f. 190, d. 131, ll. 226–28, 374–75; d. 132, l. 71; d. 149, ll. 287–88; f. 300, d. 269, ll. 78–81, 88–89; Avanesov, *Kurort Anapa*, 44, 54, 59–60, 73–75, 78–88; *Sovetskoe chernomor'e*, 30 May 1978, 1.

46. As advertised on leaflets, envelopes, postcards, etc. On advertising, GAKK, f. 1624, op. 1, d. 737, ll. 1–10.

47. Avanesov, "Organizatsiia semeinogo otdykha," 24; Baklykov, "Rol' kurortnykh faktorov," 100. Yet adults accounted for more than 50 percent of the vacationers.

viet recreational development, the vacationers concentrated themselves in the immediate resort area. The underdevelopment of the urban periphery and the hinterland bound the tourist influx to the city centers, the only areas where catering facilities, shops, communication, and entertainment were available.[48]

When representatives from all levels of the Soviet tourism infrastructure met in Anapa in 1981, one of the major incentives was to exchange experiences with local and regional councils on problems caused by the immense influx of unorganized vacationers. The participants of the Anapa conference singled out four "problems" arising from unplanned tourism as the most pressing: (1) accommodation, (2) catering, (3) access to recreational resources, and (4) transportation. Why exactly were the officials worried about these issues, to what degree was their perception pragmatic, and how did they try to cope with these problems in practice?

Accommodation of tourists outside the planned infrastructure was certainly the most urgent problem. Annually about nine million tourists, many more than the existing structure could accommodate, traveled to the Krasnodar region, or, more exactly, to the developed coastal regions and mountain resorts. For Anapa, this meant that already in 1969 about four hundred thousand wild tourists added to some two hundred thousand planned visitors in sanatoria, rest homes, or youth camps. These wild tourists could either try to bribe employees to find accommodation in sanatoria or rest homes or look for private landlords who would rent out rooms. The majority of them, however, would camp somewhere in the vicinity of the resorts or sleep in their cars, to the discomfort of local Soviet officials and the militia.[49] The latter had a close eye on private landlords, too. Renting out rooms had probably been a common practice throughout the Soviet period, but it was always risky because Soviet law banned profits from nonproductive work. While the militia repeatedly claimed that vacationers and landlords ignored the registration rules, the local councils were more worried about the fact that private lodgers would not pay the health resort taxes.[50] Since the 1960s, though, local authorities displayed a remarkably pragmatic attitude toward the private accommodation market. They simply tried to regulate and control it. Some tourist councils even went as far as organizing tours with accommodation in private rooms, since it proved practically impossible to book tourists into hotels during the summer season.[51]

In Anapa, the city council had opened an office that rented out private rooms to visitors (*kvartirnoe biuro*) as early as 1966. Compared to western

48. AOAGKA, f. 300, d. 38, l. 2; d. 60, ll. 33–34; d. 80, ll. 72–73. See Stadelbauer, "Fremdenverkehr in Sowjet-Kaukasien," 12, on Sochi.

49. AOAGKA, f. 300, d. 187, ll. 10–11.

50. AOAGKA, f. 190, d. 165, l. 57; f. 300, d. 80, ll. 81–82, d. 405, ll. 4–5.

51. GAKK, f. 1624, op. 1, d. 883, l. 4; AOAGKA, f. 300, d. 145, ll. 20–22. One of the reasons why hotels were always crowded was that the local soviets used to accommodate medical or administrative personal there on a long-term basis (GAKK, f. 1472, op. 2, d. 831, l. 65; Grushin, *Chetyre zhizni*, 144).

standards, the minimal standards fixed by the city council were comparatively low: there had to be four to five square meters living space for each guest. Cellars, barns, or dark or humid rooms should not be rented out. The landlord was to change bed linen after ten days; he should provide fresh water and a place to store provisions. The rent for one bed was not to exceed 18 rubles per month, and no landlord was to accommodate more than seven lodgers. These rules remained virtually unchanged when in the mid-1970s the territorial council took over the office.[52] Against the background of steadily increasing demand, the limitations of the property owners' initiative proved counterproductive: local residents intercepted the incoming guests already at the railway or bus stations, long before the room office was in sight. The risk for the landlords was limited, since their guests could complain about high prices or inadequate lodging only anonymously, for they had violated the law, too.[53]

In addition, the level of expectations was comparatively low. Against the background of the generally sad housing conditions in the USSR, with two or more generations crammed into small apartments, people were obviously ready to accept what they were offered in order to spend their holidays with partners or, in the case of Anapa, with the nuclear family.[54] In fact, vacationers who had found accommodation that lived up to their expectations would try to make long-term arrangements with their hosts and thus minimize future risks. They passed on their knowledge to friends and relatives, with the result that the effectiveness of the official room office remained limited. In 1969, for example, the municipal rental office could arrange private rooms for about 115,000 guests, but another 274,000 seem to have relied on self-help.[55] The trade unions' takeover in the 1970s did not alter the situation much, for the office continued to serve between one hundred thousand and two hundred thousand vacationers annually. Monitoring unplanned tourists in Anapa and other resorts in 1979, Anapa's officials were to find out that only one-fifth of the wild tourists had relied on the territorial council's rental office. More than 50 percent had sought and found accommodation by themselves.[56]

Next came the problem of catering. Providing a sufficient seasonal supply of food and goods at the destinations regularly proved to be more than the Soviet planned economy could handle. Although Anapa and other bigger resorts

52. Landlords could claim additional payments if restrooms or kitchens were available (AOAGKA, f. 190, d. 131, ll. 61–62, 70–73; *Sovetskoe Chernomor'e*, 8 April 1978). See also Bogatykh, "Organizatsiia obsluzhivaniia," 21; Avanesov, "Organizatsiia semeinogo otdykha," 25–26.

53. Knabe, "Urlaub des Sowjetbürgers," 373; Henningsen, *Freizeit- und Fremdenverkehr*, 71–72; Stadelbauer, "Fremdenverkehr in Sowjet-Kaukasien," 4; *Rabotnitsa*, no. 10 (1985): 22–23; *Turist*, no. 1 (1967): 29. Occasional inspections documented that rooms were overcrowded and dirty or lacked basic sanitary conditions. Bed linen was filthy, torn, or absent. Guests occasionally had to wash their clothes and dishes right on the streets (AOGAKA, f. 300, d. 144, ll. 56–57).

54. Anderle, *Social History*, 264–65.

55. AOAGKA, f. 300, d. 80, l. 64.

56. Baklykov, "Nauchno-metodicheskie osnovy," 148.

received goods in greater quantity and of better quality than others, a broad variety of commodities regularly disappeared from shelves. It could be impossible for a couple of weeks to obtain cutlery, kitchen utensils or bathing accessories, fresh fruit and vegetables, fish, or dairy products.[57] The situation in Anapa was still bearable, since its geographic situation allowed the local trading organization, *kurorttorg*, to arrange short-term contracts with neighboring collective farms to overcome the most obvious deficits.[58] During the high season, however, when hundreds of thousands of visitors crowded the resort, the number of shops and stands turned out to be insufficient. Self-catering tourists could either line up for hours in front of the shops, or satisfy their needs at collective farm markets, where fruits and victuals were abundant but rather expensive. Since shopping in Soviet society was almost exclusively a female business, wild family holidays were presumably a heavily gendered experience.[59]

Those who would not bother with the preparation of meals had to line up at restaurants, cafés, and canteens. Most such eating establishments were operated by sanatoria, pensions, or rest homes. As a rule, their capacity was much lower than the numbers of beds in these structures, so that the residents had to be served in several shifts. Other structural problems added to the shortages. Due to the low level of wages in the Soviet service industry, hotels, restaurants, and canteens found it extremely difficult to recruit waiters and other trained personnel. Many of them employed temporaries, whose low qualifications and motivation further undermined the efficiency of service. Laments on queuing added to complaints that the food was usually lukewarm, conventional, and tasteless.[60] Since public catering (*obshchepit*) played a prominent role in Soviet everyday life, many vacationers nevertheless adhered to their custom of having lunch in canteens. No less than 80 percent of some five thousand wild tourists surveyed on the Caucasian coast during the 1978 summer season had lunch in canteens or restaurants and cafés. No less than one-third even chose to have breakfast or dinner there.[61] Little improvement was visible until the beginning of perestroika, when private cafés mushroomed all over the Soviet Union.

Millions of vacationers annually frequented the popular beaches of the Black and the Baltic Seas, and numerous complaints from nearby tourist bases or sanatoria attest that many "tourists" or "patients" came there simply to enjoy beach life. Doctors from the sanatoria observed that "long and uncon-

57. Rossiiskii gosudarstvennyi arkhiv ekonomiki, f. 195, op. 1, d. 15, l. 75.

58. AOAGKA, f. 300, d. 2, ll. 24–28; d. 60, ll. 14–15, 28–30; d. 61, ll. 49–50; d. 80, ll. 64, 69–70; d. 143, ll. 91–11; d. 197, l. 40.

59. *Osteuropa Archiv* 28 (1978): A 621–24; Knabe, "Urlaub des Sowjetbürgers," 371; Stadelbauer, "Fremdenverkehr in Sowjet-Kaukasien," 13; *Sovetskoe Chernomor'e*, 6 June 1978, 28 July 1978; *Rabotnitsa*, no. 10 (1985): 22–23.

60. AOAGKA, f. 300, d. 13, ll. 50–51; d. 80, ll. 81–82; d. 262, l. 145; d. 847, l. 160; Knabe, "Urlaub des Sowjetbürgers," 310.

61. Baklykov, "Nauchno-metodicheskie osnovy," 150–51.

14.3. An ice cream café in Sochi, one of the attractions of "beach life" for both planned and wild tourists. *Greater Sochi* (Moscow, 1968), 46.

trolled sunbathing" was the favorite pastime of most vacationers, "in order to boast among friends and colleagues afterward."[62]

Soviet ideological egalitarianism notwithstanding, access to natural resources was anything but easy. As to the beaches, the geographical setting was less favorable than the label "Soviet Riviera" attested. The Caucasian Black Sea coast was rocky, narrow, and steep in many places. The better parts were

62. Pavlov, "Otdykh v razreze," 10; Azar, *Ekonomika*, 26; L. A. Ulianova, "Mozhno li i kak ozdaravlivat' bol'nykh nervezom na kurortakh vne sanatorno-profilakticheskikh uchrezhdenii?" in *Voprosy neorganizovannogo otdykha*, 134; Baklykov, "Nauchno-metodicheskie osnovy," 153–54. As Löfgren put it, sun and sea "made you both beautiful and sexy" (*On Holiday*, 223–24). Sex was a major ingredient on the Soviet Riviera, too. A common topic in novels and films, sex is unfortunately completely underresearched to this day. For an exception, see Anna Rotkirch, "Travelling Maidens and Men with Parallel Lives—Journeys as Private Space during Late Socialism," in *Beyond the Limits: The Concept of Space in Russian Culture*, ed. Jeremy Smith (Helsinki, 1999), 131–49.

occupied by resorts reserved exclusively for the privileged. Only prestigious sanatoria and hotels commanded restricted beach areas reserved exclusively for their guests.[63] Anapa, with some 40 kilometers of sand beaches, was an exception to the rule. Large sections, however, were remote and barred by extensive coves, and only a few spots were accessible by road.[64] The beach areas closest to the city center were reserved for the bigger sanatoria and pensions. The resort association (*kurortnoe ob"edinenie*) managed adjacent strips, alternating with pioneer camps' beaches. These beaches stretched over 350,000 square meters and were frequented during the summer season by some three hundred thousand vacationers daily. Even the management admitted that the existing infrastructure "did not live up to medical or aesthetic standards."[65] The beach was jam-packed, the sand as dirty as the water polluted.[66]

Wild tourists had to make the best out of the situation, and could either appear on the beach as early as possible to reserve their place by rolling out their blankets and towels or try to invade the restricted areas. In the case of Anapa this was obviously not a difficult task. They could bribe one of the wardens or simply pass through the shallow water, since the fences extended just a few meters into the sea.[67] As the territorial council lacked the means and competence for more thorough solutions like the preparation of new beach areas, it opted for intensive rather than extensive development. Access should be controlled more strictly, and the beach management of the resort association was to offer paid services to the vacationers, such as renting out deck chairs, sunshades, and the like.[68]

While accommodation was a problem more or less confined to wild tourism, difficulties like catering and access to beaches affected both unplanned and planned tourism, if to different degrees. Transportation, the fourth dilemma singled out by the Anapa conference, certainly bothered organized and nonorganized travelers similarly. Vouchers never included transportation, except for children. Although the traffic infrastructure developed

63. Stadelbauer, "Fremdenverkehr in Sowjet-Kaukasien," 12; *Rabotnitsa*, no. 10 (1985): 23; AOAGKA, f. 300, d. 131, l. 274; *Sovetskoe Chernomor'e*, 8 September 1978.

64. Outside Anapa, the beach was accessible in the valley of Sukko and near the villages of Vitiazevo and Blagoveshchenskoe. During the 1960s and 1970s, different types of recreational structures sprang up there, too. In Blagoveshchenskoe, the Soviet operated a campground for motorized tourists.

65. L. I. Baklykov and S. V. Ol'khovskii, "Meditsinskoe obespechenie na pliazhakh Anapy neorganizovannykh otdykhaiushchikh," in *Voprosy neorganizovannogo otdykha*, 35–36. Some forty cabins, sixty showers, and fourteen toilets were at the disposal of three hundred thousand visitors, just one hundred thousand less than on the contemporary Los Angeles central beach! (Löfgren, *On Holiday*, 215).

66. On environmental problems, see AOAGKA, f. 190, d. 149, ll. 229–30; f. 300, d. 13, ll. 30–31; d. 269, ll. 82–87; d. 347, ll. 133–35.

67. AOAGKA, f. 300, d. 2, ll. 24–28; d. 36, ll. 8–9; d. 687, l. 270.

68. Avanesov, "Organizatsiia semeinogo otdykha," 26–27; Baklykov and Ol'khovskii, "Meditsinskoe obespechenie."

impressively in the late Soviet Union, any purchase of travel documents remained a precarious adventure.[69] Again, the problem was the bureaucratic system of distribution rather than the amount of money that had to be invested.

Soviet railways operated the comparatively long travel distances almost exclusively with sleeping cars. Passengers had to book bunks in advance. This restricted the number of available tickets. A centralized booking system was introduced only in the mid-1970s, and its introduction prompted little in the way of changes.[70] Booking in advance was possible, but it did not guarantee success. Vacationers were usually happy to obtain a one-way ticket to their holiday destinations. As a result, they had to waste considerable time there purchasing a ticket for the return trip or just try to bribe conductors right on the trains. Mutually obstructive rules for the booking of train and airplane tickets further complicated the situation. People had to book air tickets twenty days in advance but could not expect a decision until three or four days before the travel date. In the case of a refusal, this would be too late to switch to the railways. Logistically, the distribution of tickets was further complicated by massive double bookings.[71]

Tourism officials on the spot were therefore harassed regularly by thousands of vacationers stranded at their destinations, wild and planned alike. The Soviet practice of having guests vacate their "organized" facilities simultaneously further aggravated this problem.[72] Again, the local tourism councils lacked substantial means to solve it. They appealed to the responsible ministries to extend transportation capacities, but these capacities were already stretched to the limit: Soviet railways, for example, operated hundreds of additional trains during the summer. The only tangible result was the opening of new ticket offices. They could naturally not produce and sell more tickets, but they dispersed the crowd and made for shorter lines.[73]

The problem of an increasing number of individual motorized travelers pertained more exclusively to wild tourism.[74] Khrushchev's notorious disapproval of individual motorization and the low Soviet output of cars notwithstanding,

69. During the 1960s and 1970s, the railways remained the most import carrier for passengers, although domestic air travel expanded significantly. Its share in public passenger transport dropped from 69 percent (1960) to 38 percent (1980), while the share of air travel rose from 4.8 percent to 17.8 percent. Bus travel's share rose from 24 percent (1960) to 43.3 percent (1980). The total amount expanded almost fourfold during the same period. See Johannes Grützmacher, "Verkehr," in *Handbuch der Geschichte Russlands*, vol. 5, part 2, 1141.

70. *Turist*, no. 11 (1968): 24–25; *Osteuropa Archiv* (1979): A 500–510.

71. AOAGKA, f. 300, d. 60, ll. 31–32.

72. AOAGKA, f. 300, d. 399, l. 9.

73. AOAGKA, f. 300, d. 60, ll. 147–48; *Rabotnitsa*, no. 10 (1985): 22; Romanov, "Nauchnye osnovy," 10.

74. The central council launched a campaign for "organized" hitchhiking in the early 1960s. Hikers were provided with booklets and handed vouchers to drivers who took tourists along for a certain distance. Prizes were awarded to the "best" hikers and drivers. See GARF, f. 9520, op. 1, d. 462, ll. 44–45; and *Turist*, no. 5 (1966): 18.

motor tourism was a fairly common phenomenon already in the early 1960s. While the road network extended slowly, people who owned a car would nevertheless travel enthusiastically.[75] The long trip down to the south by car was certainly a challenging experience, and it required courage and a capacity for improvisation. There were but a few motels, camping sites, restaurants, filling stations or repair shops along the highways. Motor tourists had to rely on self-help and preferred to drive in a convoy with friends or colleagues and camp together en route.[76]

Arriving at their destinations, the drivers faced new obstacles: parking a car along the roadside was neither permitted nor advisable, for accessories might vanish instantly. Supervised parking sites were remote, if they existed at all, and their capacities and equipment insufficient.[77] Anapa, for example, offered only provisional parking lots that lacked basic sanitary necessities. The largest one at Blagoveshchenskoe faced the beach but was situated 40 kilometers away from the town. Nevertheless, in 1968 some sixty thousand motor tourists chose to camp out there.[78] Once more the tourism councils displayed limited concern. While the number of motorized vacationers multiplied, just a few new motels, hotels, or campsites were opened.[79] The same was true for Anapa, where the territorial council wavered between two strategies. On the one hand, it tried to get rid of the uninvited guests and close down improvised campsites; on the other it seemed inclined to include the motorized tourists in the category of commercial clients and make them pay for basic services rendered by the resort association.[80]

In sum, even the Anapa conference devoted to wild tourism reflected a limited understanding of the problems resulting from the rapid development of Soviet domestic tourism. Although the participants chose to speak about problems of wild tourism, it is rather obvious that Soviet tourism officials had to cope with the challenges of genuine mass tourism. In this sense, the Soviet citizens' unprecedented and unplanned travel activities just aggravated structural problems inherent to Soviet social tourism. In the end, the Anapa conference

75. Sections for motor tourism were created rather early under the aegis of the trade union tourist organizations (GARF, f. 9520, op. 1, d. 447, ll. 76–79). "The possibility of driving to their holiday destinations by car is the explanation given by the majority of those who buy one," as one contemporary Soviet expert observed (V. I. Azar, *Otdykh trudiashchikhsia v SSSR* [Moscow, 1972], 66). Indeed, Soviet drivers used private cars almost exclusively for leisure pursuits (Merl, "Staat und Konsum," 229).

76. GAKK, f. 1624, op. 1, d. 144, ll. 38–39; d. 323, l. 37, 46; *Turist*, no. 5 (1968): 18; no. 11 (1968): 17; no. 9 (1969): 23; no. 6 (1971): 2; no. 10 (1972): 26; *Osteuropa Archiv* (1974): A 653–56.

77. *Turist*, no. 8 (1969): 8–11; no. 11 (1972): 21.

78. AOAGKA, f. 190, d. 214, l. 168; GAKK f. 1624, op. 1, d. 164, ll. 111–12.

79. In the whole Krasnodar region only seven parking areas could accommodate some fifteen hundred cars simultaneously in 1975 (Bogatykh, "Organizatsiia," 23).

80. AOAGKA, f. 300, d. 12, l. 21; d. 38, l. 39; d. 60, ll. 31–32; d. 187, ll. 10–11; d. 271, ll. 40–41; Romanov, "Nauchnye osnovy," 11.

displayed at least limited willingness to face the difficulties brought about by the extension of individual tourism. The tourists were there, and they had to be dealt with. Many problems were certainly out of reach for the people locally in charge, and the example of the room offices most impressively illustrates both the potential and the limits of a pragmatic approach under late Soviet conditions. On the one hand, private enterprise was legalized and channeled rather effectively, regardless of the reservations of the local militia and fiscal administration. On the other hand, even the pragmatists felt uneasy with so much laissez faire. The already cited study of the vice-chairman of the Anapa Territorial Council, Baklykov, objected to the low efficiency of the rental office. Indeed, tourists sometimes had to wait up to three days to have their accommodation arranged. But this was not Baklykov's most urgent concern. On the contrary, he complained that vacationers wished to see the rooms before they rented them, which meant that the bureau's employees were permanently cruising through the city with their clients. Hence he proposed a solution reflecting both the traditions of Soviet social paternalism and the industrialization of leisure: the rental office should rent empty rooms, furnish them identically, and employ the landlords as a kind of room service, responsible for washing, cleaning, and other services.[81]

Les idiots de voyage?

As we have seen, the distinction between wild and planned tourism emerged largely as a discursive representation.[82] The dichotomy owed more to ideology and wishful thinking than to the experiences of both groups. Although the problem deserves further detailed research, it is evident that the two spheres were more complexly intertwined than official sources admit. On the one hand, many reports make it pretty clear that fun-seeking organized tourists eagerly dismissed the tutelage of Soviet tourism experts and sometimes behaved much more "wildly" than nonorganized tourists. Hundreds of complaints by functionaries and ideologically sound fellow travelers testify that late Soviet vacationers frequently managed to evade the trade unions' solicitude in sanatoria, rest homes, or tourist bases and simply did what they wanted to.[83] The wild ones, on the contrary, obviously internalized much of the discursive framework of official tourism and occasionally tended to reproduce, con-

81. Baklykov, "Nauchno-metodicheskie osnovy," 81–82. On the other hand, Baklykov feared, housing bureaus that worked too effectively might attract still more tourists to overcrowded resorts!

82. "[N]ew thousands of wild tourists, who, moreover, migrate from feature [fel'ton] to feature, starring as the main heroes" (Turist, no. 12 [1973]: 20).

83. AOAGKA, f. 190, d. 131, ll. 463–65, f. 300, d. 846, ll. 100–102; GAKK, f. 1624, op. 1, d. 176, l. 9; d. 209, l. 45; d. 547, ll. 117–18; d. 570, l. 13; d. 958, l. 43. On discos, see Turist, no. 4 (1985): 16–17.

sciously or subconsciously, some of the habits of the traditional Soviet social tourism. A case in point were "wild" motor tourists whose improvised camping sites along the coastal roads in 1963 looked very much like "organized" recreation camps—including signposts indicating where the "Commander" had put up his tent.[84]

Were the wild tourists' holidays less restful and relaxing than those of organized vacationers, then? The preceding discussion of holiday life in Anapa has already cast some doubt on the official narrative. Travel conditions for planned and unplanned diverged, but in many respects the obstacles encountered by both groups did not dramatically differ. Even if we accept Soviet standards and time budgets, differences appear modest rather than substantial. While the organized were probably served more rapidly in canteens, they were still served the same food. As for transport, they shared the pleasure of lining up for tickets with the wild. Qualitatively, restricted beach areas turned out to be only a relative advantage, too, with unauthorized vacationers penetrating them rather easily.

Even guaranteed housing, the most obvious advantage of planned tourism, might turn out to be a doubtful accomplishment. Certainly, in sanatoria, pensions, and many rest homes, conditions were quite acceptable, and statistically their guests enjoyed double the space stipulated by the regulations for private rooms.[85] But privacy was a very scarce resource in these facilities. Since guests were usually accommodated in large dormitories, furniture was simple and often worn out and shabby, and the regimen was rather strict. Accommodation with a private landlord was not necessarily the worse alternative. It was often inevitable for those who wished to spend family holidays, and it emerged as a real alternative for those who tried to evade the pleasures of organized sociability.

The most obvious difference was cost. The heavily subsidized vouchers were normally sold at 30 rubles, the amount of money a single wild tourist had to spend for accommodations alone, if he arranged it with the rental office. The prices on the black market were probably higher. If we take into account additional costs for food, excursions, or entertainment that were all-inclusive for planned tourists, wild tourism turns out to be substantially more expensive. Estimates vary between two or even four times the amount an individual had to spend for the trade unions' vouchers and a train ticket for a comparable kind of holiday.[86] But money was not scarce in late Soviet society. On the contrary, salaries were raised substantially, while prices were fixed. People more likely had problems spending their money for the consumption of goods.

How did the wild tourists themselves judge their experiences? How far did they feel deprived of the achievements and benefits the regime generously

84. GAKK, f. 1624, op. 1, d. 144, ll. 38–39.
85. Azar, *Ekonomika*, 126.
86. *Rabotnitsa*, no. 10 (1983): 23; Baklykov, "Nauchno-metodicheskie osnovy," 159–60.

promised to all citizens, but still distributed somewhat more exclusively? Certainly, answers to these questions have to remain tentative until we can utilize a greater quantity of subjective sources. These have entered Soviet media or Soviet archives very rarely, and there are but a few detailed studies based on oral history currently available.[87] Yet there is enough evidence to question some of the earlier-cited conventional Soviet wisdom on the wild tourist: sociological surveys recorded already for the mid-1960s that many Soviet travelers a priori regarded wild tourism as an attractive alternative to social tourism.[88] In 1966, when *Komsomol'skaia pravda* asked its readers whether planned or unplanned tourism should be developed more intensively in the years to come, nearly one-third (31.5 percent) of the respondents opted for "vacations without vouchers."[89] In 1969 a survey on contemporary vacation practices in *Literaturnaia gazeta* stated that about 40 percent of Soviet tourists favored individual and self-organized travel. It would thus be futile, the author concluded, to invest simply in the extension of the existing tourist infrastructure, since "demand outstrips the traditional forms of vacation that are offered."[90]

Moreover, sociological surveys regularly demonstrated that nonorganized travelers were on average more satisfied with their holidays than their organized counterparts. In 1969, 42 percent of wild tourists interviewed in Crimea considered their holidays as satisfactory, another 47 percent declared that they were "not entirely satisfied." Only 11 percent stated their dissatisfaction. The data collected the same year on the Caucasian coast did not differ much: 40 percent of the wild tourists were satisfied, 50 percent not entirely satisfied, and just 9 percent dissatisfied. In the mid-1970s the trade unions had to face the fact that planned tourism was judged more critically. While 60 percent of the respondents basically advocated "organized forms of vacation," no less than 50 percent were frustrated by their personal experiences to the degree that they did not wish to repeat them.[91]

The fact that many tourists preferred individual tourism was no secret to the hosts of the Anapa conference, too. The already mentioned Baklykov had surveyed some five thousand wild tourists in Anapa, Gelendzhik, and Sochi during the 1979 summer season. In 1981, however, he made rather selective use of the data at his disposal. While he admitted that the nonorganized

87. Daniel Bertaux, Paul Thompson, and Anna Rotkirch, eds., *On Living through Soviet Russia* (London, 2004).

88. The data appear to have been collected in a methodologically sound manner, and the highly selective use suggests their authenticity. Grushin, *Chetyre zhizni*, 136–76, is explicit on methods. Baklykov, "Nauchno-metodicheskie osnovy," 142–60, is an unpublished manuscript with rich and very useful tables. Many findings were at odds with the Anapa Soviet's approaches to wild tourism. Azar, *Ekonomika*, presents very interesting but highly selective figures.

89. Grushin, *Chetyre zhizni*, 154; 52.9 percent opted for "planned tourism," and 15 percent found it difficult to answer.

90. Pavlov, "Otdykh v razreze," A 110.

91. *Rabotnitsa*, no. 10 (1985): 22; Knabe, "Urlaub des Sowjetbürgers," 307; Bogatykh, "Organizatsiia obsluzhivaniia," 18.

tourists were generally pleased with their holiday conditions, he withheld information concerning the attitudes that wild tourists displayed toward the above-mentioned catalogue of problems.[92] About three-quarters of the respondents had rented rooms from private landlords, and between 75 percent (Anapa) and 88 percent (Sochi) were satisfied with their accommodations. Just 14 percent criticized the high rents, and 11 percent complained about bad housing or sanitary conditions. Eighty-six percent considered local catering and shopping facilities to be sufficient. More than 80 percent of the respondents felt "relaxed" after the first week of their vacation. Still more important, just a quarter of these wild tourists had tried to obtain a voucher before they decided to travel independently.[93]

All this suggests that the increasing accessibility of travel and tourism and the concurrent macro-sociological changes during the 1960s and 1970s made self-initiative and individual arrangements of travel experiences much easier than before. The population actively responded to the new opportunities. With other consumerist agendas tightly constrained by the meager output of Soviet light industry and restrictions on imported goods, it was (largely domestic) traveling and tourism that became the hallmark of a rising living standard under "developed socialism." Wild tourism emerged as a viable alternative to state-sponsored social tourism. To be sure, individual and maybe even hedonistic patterns of behavior were certainly not a privilege of wild tourism, even if some contemporary Soviet sources tried to make it appear this way. First, the expansion of tourism and travel could not but reduce the regime's ability to control the movement and the behavior of the individual. Second, changes in conduct and attitude were by no means confined to tourism, travel, or other leisure pursuits. Much to the regret of Soviet ideologues, consumerist and evasive agendas were on the march in late Soviet society as a whole. But tourism, in particular, turned out to be the ideal training ground for "the modern man in general."[94] If Soviet agencies had promoted space for the self-creating tourist even under the conditions of Stalinism, the new *contrat social* under Brezhnev could not but expand its scope significantly. The self-styled "good life" ceased to be a privilege of a small elite, at least as far as annual vacations were concerned.

92. Baklykov, "Rol' kurortnykh faktorov," 100–106.
93. Baklykov, "Nauchno-metodicheskie osnovy," 142, 148–54, 166.
94. Dean MacCannell, *The Tourist: A New Theory of the Leisure Class* (New York 1976), 1.

WENDY BRACEWELL is senior lecturer in history at the School of Slavonic and East European Studies, University College London. She is the author of *The Uskoks of Senj: Piracy, Banditry and Holy War in the Sixteenth-Century Adriatic* (1992) and director of an Arts and Humanities Research Council research project on East European travel writing.

ELEONORY GILBURD is a Ph.D. candidate in history at the University of California, Berkeley. She is completing a dissertation entitled " 'To See Paris and Die': Foreign Culture in the Soviet Union, 1955–68."

ANNE E. GORSUCH is associate professor of history at the University of British Columbia. She is the author of *Youth in Revolutionary Russia: Enthusiasts, Bohemians, Delinquents* (2000).

DIANE P. KOENKER is professor of history at the University of Illinois at Urbana-Champaign and from 1996 to 2006 served as editor of *Slavic Review*. She is author of several books, most recently *Republic of Labor: Russian Printers and Soviet Socialism, 1918–1930* (2005).

SUSAN LAYTON is honorary research fellow in the Department of Modern Languages at Strathclyde University (Glasgow) and an associate of the Centre d'études des mondes russe, caucasien et centre-européen (Paris). She is the author of *Russian Literature and Empire: Conquest of the Caucasus from Pushkin to Tolstoy* (1994; paper 2005).

EVA MAURER is a Ph.D. candidate at the University of Münster (Germany) and currently writing her dissertation on mountaineering, mountaineers, and landscape during the Stalin era.

LOUISE McREYNOLDS is professor of history at the University of North Carolina at Chapel Hill. She is the author of *Russia at Play: Leisure Activities at the End of the Tsarist Era* (2003) and *The News under Russia's Old Regime: The Development of a Mass-Circulation Press* (1991).

SCOTT MORANDA is assistant professor of history at the State University of New York at Cortland. He recently completed his dissertation, "The Dream of a Therapeutic Regime: Nature Tourism in the German Democratic Republic, 1945–1978," at the University of Wisconsin-Madison.

CHRISTIAN NOACK is wissenschaftlicher Assistent in the department for East European History at Bielefeld University (Germany). His publications include *Muslimischer Nationalismus. Nationsbildung und Nationalbewegung bei*

Tataren und Baschkiren, 1861–1917 (2000). He is currently working on a book on domestic tourism in the late Soviet Union.

ALDIS PURS is a research scholar affiliated with the University of Manchester (United Kingdom). He is the co-author of *Latvia: The Challenges of Change* (2001).

KARL D. QUALLS is assistant professor of history at Dickinson College and has published numerous articles in North America and Europe on Sevastopol, local politics, and urban reconstruction.

SHAWN SALMON is a Ph.D. candidate in history at the University of California, Berkeley. Her dissertation is titled "Showcasing Soviet Socialism: A History of Intourist, 1929–1991."

NOAH W. SOBE is assistant professor of cultural and educational policy studies at Loyola University Chicago. His work has appeared in *Paedagogica Historica* and *Educational Theory*.

ALEXANDER VARI is a postdoctoral fellow at the Center for the Arts in Society at Carnegie Mellon University. He is currently revising his dissertation manuscript on "Commercialized Modernities: City Marketing and Urban Tourism Promotion in Paris and Budapest, 1850s to the 1930s" and has a forthcoming article in *Journeys: The International Journal of Travel and Travel Writing*.

Page numbers in italics refer to illustrations.